A POLITICAL THEORY OF MUSLIM DEMOCRACY

Edinburgh Studies of the Globalised Muslim World

Series Editor: **Frédéric Volpi**, Director, Prince Alwaleed Bin Talal Centre for the Study of Contemporary Islam, University of Edinburgh

This innovative series investigates the dynamics of Muslim societies in a globalised world. It considers the boundaries of the contemporary Muslim world, their construction, their artificiality or durability. It sheds new light on what it means to be part of the Muslim world today, for both those individuals and communities who live in Muslim-majority countries and those who reside outside and are part of a globalised ummah. Its analysis encompasses the micro and the macro level, exploring the discourses and practices of individuals, communities, states and transnational actors who create these dynamics. It offers a multidisciplinary perspective on the salient contemporary issues and interactions that shape the internal and external relations of the Muslim world.

Published and forthcoming titles

A Political Theory of Muslim Democracy
Ravza Altuntaş-Çakır

Salafi Social and Political Movements: National and Transnational Contexts
Masooda Bano (ed.)

Islamic Modernities in World Society: The Rise, Spread and Fragmentation of a Hegemonic Idea
Dietrich Jung

Literary Neo-Orientalism and the Arab Uprisings: Tensions in English, French and German Language Fiction
Julia Wurr

edinburghuniversitypress.com/series/esgmw

A POLITICAL THEORY OF MUSLIM DEMOCRACY

Ravza Altuntaş-Çakır

EDINBURGH
University Press

To İnas Ala and Bensu Lal

Edinburgh University Press is one of the leading presses in the UK. We publish academic books and journals in our selected subject areas across the humanities and social sciences, combining cutting-edge scholarship with high editorial and productions values to produce academic works of lasting importance. For more information visit our website: edinburghuniversitypress.com

© Ravza Altuntaş-Çakır, 2022

Edinburgh University Press
The Tun – Holyrood Road
12 (2f) Jackson's Entry
Edinburgh EH8 8PJ

Typeset in 11/15pt Adobe Garamond Pro by Cheshire Typesetting

A CIP record is available from the British Library

ISBN 978 1 4744 7952 3 (hardback)
ISBN 978 1 4744 7954 7 (webready PDF)
ISBN 978 1 4744 7955 4 (epub)

The right of Ravza Altuntaş-Çakır to be identified as author of this work has been asserted in accordance with the Copyright, Designs and Patents Act 1988 and the Copyright and Related Rights Regulations 2003 (SI No. 2498).

CONTENTS

Acknowledgements — vii
Selected Glossary of Foreign Terms — ix
Series Editor's Foreword — xi

Introduction — 1

PART ONE   TYPOLOGIES OF MUSLIM AND MULTICULTURAL POLITICAL THOUGHT

1 Islamic Discourses on Governance and Pluralism — 31
2 Multiculturalist Discourses on Religion and Democratic Governance — 74
   General Conclusion to Part One: Typologies of Muslim and Multicultural Political Thought — 117

PART TWO   DECONSTRUCTING MUSLIM DISCOURSES ON DEMOCRACY

3 The Compatibility-based Arguments — 123

PART THREE CONCEPTUALISING MUSLIM DEMOCRACY

    General Introduction to Part Three   155
4 Pluralist Secularism   159
5 The Social Public Sphere   189
6 The Pluralising Constitution   217
    General Conclusion to Part Three: The Conceptualisation of
      Muslim Democracy   241

Conclusion   247

Bibliography   261
Index   301

ACKNOWLEDGEMENTS

I had the pleasure to work with the two wonderful advisors at Durham University, Maria Dimova-Cookson and James Piscatori. Maria has been a generous supervisor and mentor, and a true friend who has been there for me whenever I have needed help, academically or otherwise. James has been an unwavering source of intellectual inspiration and guidance both as a supervisor and as a person. For all their efforts, support and care, I am forever grateful.

I am also thankful to Frederick Volpi, who was the external examiner on my viva committee, and is the editor of the book series in which this book now appears. Without his faith in my thesis and his encouragement, this book could not have come into existence. I also thank Emma Rees, Louise Hutton and Eddie Clark – the editors at Edinburgh University Press – for seeing the book through to its eventual culmination.

I am indebted to my dear friends Holly Flynn-Piercy, Mohamed Moussa and Aya Sabri for reading through the entire manuscript. I am grateful to Durham University, SGIA and the IIIT, particularly Anas Al-Shaikh-Ali and Hatice Nuriler, for research funds they provided that aided the process of turning a Ph.D. into a book. I also thank Zehra Çekin for letting me use her art masterpiece, which now appears on the cover page.

I am deeply thankful to my friends and colleagues, Semra Akay, Mehmet Asutay, Nadia Eldemerdash, Hale Eroğlu, Jean Jacobi Heidcamp, Beth Kahn and Ömer Taşgetiren, who in various yet important ways helped in the writing of this book. Finally, I owe special thanks to my uncle İsmail Küçük, Nasr Arif, Thomas DeGeorges, İsmail Hakkı Genç, Arwa Hanif and Orubah Khan, who have contributed to my journey in achieving the Ph.D., hence producing this book.

I owe the greatest debt to my parents, Habibe and Halit Altuntaş, for their profound faith, sacrifices and love, and to my husband, Abdullah, for his unwavering support and understanding. Talha and Muhammet Ali, my brothers, have been a constant source of encouragement. I dedicate the book to my daughters, İnas Ala and Bensu Lal, not only for the time I had to take from them, but for being the inspiration behind my every idea and act.

SELECTED GLOSSARY OF FOREIGN TERMS

Al-amr bi al-maṣrūf wa al-nahy ʿan al-munkar	Commanding the right and forbidding the wrong.
ʿAdāla	Justice, fairness.
Ahl al-dhimma/ dhimmīs	Non-Muslims under the protection of Islam.
Amāna	Fidelity, trust.
ʿAmma	Laypeople.
Awlawiyyat al-Islam	The priorities of Islam.
Bayʿah	Allegiance.
Darura	Necessity.
Dīn wa dawla	Religion and state.
Fiqh	Jurisprudence (literally, deep comprehension).
Fiṭra	Innate intuition.
Jizya	Poll tax.
Fuqahāʾ	Religious legal scholars.
Hadīth	Prophetic traditions, sayings of the prophet.

Ḥākimiyya	Sovereignty.
Ḥākimiyyat Allah	Sovereignty of God.
İdāre-i maslahat	Political expediency.
İjtihād	Independent religious reasoning or juridical reasoning.
İftāʾ	Fatwa-giving.
Ijmaʿ	Consensus.
Jamāʿa	The group, the community.
Khāṣṣa	Elite.
Madhāhib	Schools of jurisprudence.
Maqāṣid	Underlying rationale, general goals.
Naṣīha	Morally corrective criticism.
Naṣṣ	Text (of the Qurʾan).
Qūḍā	Judges.
Shahāda	The confession of faith.
Sharīʿa	God's path; God's moral code.
Shirk	Idolatry, the opposite of *tawhīd*.
Shūrā	Deliberative consultation, collective deliberation.
Sunna	Tradition, exemplary conduct (of the prophet).
Tāʿat ulī al-amr	Obedience to executive leadership of a state.
Tāghūt	False idol or tyrannical ruler.
Tawhīd	Oneness of God, God's absolute unity.
ʿUlamāʾ	The class of scholars.
Ulī al-amr	Executive leadership of a state.
Ẓulm	Injustice.

SERIES EDITOR'S FOREWORD

Edinburgh Studies of the Globalised Muslim World is a series that focuses on the contemporary transformations of Muslim societies. Globalisation is meant, here, to say that although the Muslim world has always interacted with other societal, religious, imperial or national forces over the centuries, the evolution of these interconnections constantly re-shapes Muslim societies. The second half of the twentieth century has been characterised by the increasing number and diversity of exchanges on a global scale bringing people and societies 'closer', for better and for worse. The beginning of the twenty-first century confirmed the increasingly glocalised nature of these interactions and the challenges and opportunities that they bring to existing institutional, social and cultural orders.

This series is not a statement that everything is different in today's brave new world. Indeed, many 'old' ideas and practices still have much currency in the present, and undoubtedly will also have in the future. Rather, the series emphasises how our current globalised condition shapes and mediates how past world-views and modes of being are transmitted between people and institutions. The contemporary Muslim world is not merely a reflection of past histories, but is also a living process of creating a new order on the basis of what people want, desire, fear and hope. This creative endeavour can transform existing relations for the better, for example by reconsidering the relations between society and the environment. They can equally fan violence and hatred, as illustrated in the re-ignition of cycles of conflicts over sovereignties, ideologies or resources across the globe.

The series arrives at a challenging time for any inquiry into Muslim societies. The new millennium began inauspiciously with a noticeable spike in transnational and international violence framed in 'civilisational' terms. A decade of 'war on terror' contributed to entrenching negative mutual perceptions across the globe while reinforcing essentialist views. The ensuing decade hardly improved the situation, with political and territorial conflicts multiplying in different parts of the Muslim world, and some of the most violent groups laid claim to the idea of a global caliphate to justify themselves. Yet, a focus on trajectories of violence gives a distorted picture of the evolution of Muslim societies and their relations with the rest of the world. This series is very much about the 'what else' that is happening as we move further into the twenty-first century.

A Political Theory of Muslim Democracy is unmistakably a most timely contribution by Ravza Altuntaş-Çakır to the rethinking of the politics in the contemporary Muslim world. The notion of democracy in today's Muslim societies is a very debated current issue, both inside and outside the Muslim world. Rightly or wrongly, it is seen as the key to the future of the region, as well as the crucial factor shaping the relationship between Muslim and non-Muslim communities. While many controversies surround the question of what can or cannot constitute a true democratic order compatible with the Islamic tradition, far less is said about how the relevant democratic principles can be put into practice by citizens and institutions within a Muslim public sphere. Altuntaş-Çakır's book addresses this issue directly and creatively.

Refreshingly, the work approaches the notion of democracy from a pragmatic and operational perspective. It focuses on how to make a democratic system function in Muslim majority contexts by accounting for the religious issues that are relevant for the citizens who shape this social and political order. Altuntaş-Çakır brings together perspectives put forward by Muslim intellectual and Islamic thinkers, and those coming from the Western liberal tradition, to identify not only areas of overlaps and agreements but also the possibilities of combining their different approaches to the political. This analysis then paves the way for her own investigations and propositions regarding some of the most crucial components of a lived democratic order in Muslim societies.

Articulating perspectives grounded in the notions of pluralist secularism, social public sphere and pluralising constitutionalism, the book provides a fresh new take on seemingly intractable dilemmas. The central argument is about how a functioning, lived democratic practice could unfold more organically in contemporary societies of the Muslim world. Rather than trying to force a solution to never-ending conceptual disagreements, Altuntaş-Çakır suggests practical steps that could generate a momentum in favour of political implementation among citizens. The work outlines some promising avenues for thinking and acting democratically today in socio-political contexts where the Islamic referent remains very important. One can only hope more works will follow it its wake.

Frédéric Volpi
Chair in the Politics of the Muslim World
The University of Edinburgh

INTRODUCTION

I. The Emergence of 'Muslim Democracy'

The 'return of religion' refers to the greater reconsideration of the role of religion in contemporary political theory since the late 1990s, which has yielded new theorisations of democratic thought (Derrida, 2007: 78; McClure, 1997: 332; Juergensmeyer, 2017: 76). Shmuel Noah Eisenstadt's 'multiple modernities' thesis has opened up significant theoretical space for thinking about non-Western political forms of 'democracies' (Paley, 2002: 473).[1] In this vein of thought, 'the concept of democracy is entitled to be diffuse and multifaceted' (Sartori, 1987: 3). Notable political philosophers like Charles Taylor have suggested that democracy in Muslim countries will occur 'in a more inventive and imaginative way' than the Western mould (2008: xvii). Alfred Stepan has also envisaged that 'Islam can emulate or recreate, using some of their distinctive cultural resources, a form of democracy that would meet the minimal institutional conditions for democracy' (2000: 44).

These theoretical propositions for the rise of democracy in the Muslim world appear to have strong empirical support. A 2008 Gallup poll, which undertook 'the first ever data-based analysis of the points of view of more than 90% of the global Muslim community, spanning more than 35 nations', measured what Muslims want in a political system. As puzzling and paradoxical as it may sound to many, 'democracy' and '*sharī'a*' both ranked highest on the list (Gallup, 2008). Three important observations can be deduced from the general findings of this global survey. First, Muslim communities consider democracy, not theocracy, as the most legitimate and accountable practice of governance worldwide. Second, although most respondents were not able to clarify what *sharīʿa* meant in practice, it is important to understand it as a holistic concept denoting 'the much wider domain of rules' including *muʿamalat* (social and moral rules guiding all interactions and exchanges among people) and *ʿibadat* (ritual acts governing the relationship between a human being and God) (Berger, 2013: 8). Thus, *sharīʿa* in the broadest sense presents a normative basis for Islamic ways of life or Muslim expressions of Islam. Third, respondents see no inherent contradiction between democracy and their religion. Muslims' support for the norms of pluralism and human rights appears to be promising, although it may not yet be substantially established (Gallup, 2008).

Above all, the concurrent demands for democratic governance and a *sharīʿa*-observant life raise the following questions about their coexistence: (i) which model of politics can best respond to pro-democracy demands of political freedom, accountability and representation, as swept across the region during the 'Arab Springs' while incorporating the essential role of religion in society's different communities?; (ii) how can a significant normative commitment to democratic principles and complete recognition of universal human rights coexist with public Islamic claims?; and (iii) how can democracy for Muslims, or a Muslim democracy, be theoretically possible?

Such discussions on democracy are not new and emerged during the classical periods in Muslim history when the works of the ancient Greek philosophers were first translated. However, contemporary definitions of democracy entered the circles of Muslim intelligentsia with the advent of the Tanzimat and Nahda following the European Enlightenment (Browers, 2006: 34). Within contemporary Islamic discourses, the earliest written record of Islamic democracy can be found in the works of Rifa'ah al-Tahtawi (1801–73), Khayr al-Dīn al-Tūnisī (1810–99) and Muhammad 'Abduh (1849–1905), who identify a harmony between constitutional democracy and Islam. Although the political and philosophical debates on Islam and democracy date back to the early twentieth century, the idea of a 'Muslim democracy' is a more recent phenomenon. In 1970, Dankwart Rustow declared Turkey to be the only democracy with a Muslim-majority population (1970: 349). Bernard Lewis, more than two decades later, attributed Turkey's supposed exceptional democratic status to its secular establishment, experience of modernisation, economic growth and proximity to Europe (1994: 46). Yet it was only in 2005 that Vali Nasr coined the term in his 'The Rise of "Muslim Democracy"'. In this article, Nasr examined 'the emergence and unfolding of Muslim democracy as a "fact on the ground" over the last fifteen years' with particular reference to the Turkish political experience under the Justice and Development Party (JDP) as an embodiment of this particular form of democracy (2005: 11).

For Nasr, Muslim democracy 'rests on a practical synthesis ... in response to the opportunities and demands created by the ballot box', viewing 'political life with a pragmatic eye' (2005: 15, 13). He maintained that 'the answers [for democratisation] will not come from the realm of theory but from that of pragmatism' (2005: 25). The reference to pragmatism by Nasr is not indebted to the American pragmatist tradition of Dewey, Barber and Rorty. Rather, it means 'an approach to life that is purely opportunistic, guided simply by unprincipled exploitation of available opportunities without serious attention to values' (Baker, 2015: 226). One can argue that the pragmatist nature of the Turkish model stems from what can be described as an inattentiveness, rather than reflexive scepticism, or an inability to apply the norms and values of grand narratives to political practice. This tendency to disregard political theory in favour of empirical case studies and the concomitant positivist emphasis on rational actors has continued with more recent publications in Muslim democracy studies (Bokhari and Senzai, 2013; Karagiannis, 2018; Yavuz, 2009). The existing literature has focused on classifying Muslim movements' attitudes towards democracy, with partial theoretical conceptualisation. The procedural lens of this approach often assumes that policy changes and administrative reforms precede value change and democratic internalisation.

However, intellectuals like Anwar Ibrahim (2005, 2006) and Mohammad Talbi (1995a,b) acknowledge the importance of a conceptual and moral understanding of democracy. They have insisted that the core values of democracy – such as individual liberties, an independent judiciary, a free and independent media, moral pluralism, recognition of difference and tolerant civil society – can be conceptualised within contemporary Muslim discourses. Yet this task has not been adequately carried out. A systematic political theory of Muslim democracy at present is still lacking. Apart from a few notable examples such as works by Abdullahi An-Na'im (2006), Abdulkarim Soroush (2006), Nader Hashemi (2009) and Naser Ghobadzadeh (2014), the existing works on Muslim democracy are not normatively rigorous. Scholars have often studied Turkey in recent years as the concrete manifestation of this concept rather than attempting to theorise Muslim democracy.

Turkey's prominent position in studies of Muslim democracy has followed wider trends in international politics. In the period between 2003 and 2013, political turmoil in the Middle East and North Africa (MENA) has witnessed the emergence of a 'Turkish model' as 'a beacon of democracy in the region', with international hopes for it to offer a blueprint for the Muslim world's democratic transitioning (Aydın-Düzgit, 2016). Media pundits, academics and political actors (Atasoy, 2011: 86–100; *CNN* 2009; *CNSNews*, 2011; al-Ghannushi, 2011a; Harvey et al., 2011; Kalyvas, 2012: 189–98; Martin, 2017) during that decade promoted the Turkish model to the Muslim world 'under the brand of "Muslim democracy"' as an example of a positive interaction between the West and Islam (Gürsel, 2011: 94). Turkey was considered to be a 'real example' for the MENA, 'with its Muslim majority, a pluralist society and a vibrant multi-party democracy, with its own legacy of state-authoritarianism' (Benhabib, 2011). The Turkish model is credited with the ability to blend Islamic tradition with Western modernity, secular governance with a vibrant Muslim culture, democratic reforms with social unity and prosperity, with the expanding of social services and infrastructure. The JDP's policies of promoting civilian rule and greater ethnic and minority rights, expanding religious freedoms, outlawing the death penalty, repealing the headscarf ban and abolishing state security courts raised expectations for the consolidation of a genuine Muslim democracy (Cesari, 2014: 183).

However, the interest in the political experience of Turkey has not generated a normative and conceptual understanding of what a Muslim democracy is. Despite a decade of adulation in the secondary source literature, the Turkish experience appears unable to offer a way forward for issues such as state–religion relations, minority rights, individual freedoms, separation of powers, human rights and justice. Even the most ardent international advocates of the Turkish model have started to express doubts about Turkey's democratisation experience. Once a regional success story, the Turkish model after 2013 has been described as bringing about only 'a semi-democracy' with 'a long way to go', failing to inclusively institutionalise earlier democratic social and political policy changes (Somer, 2014: 1; Özbudun, 2016; Müftüler-Baç and Keyman, 2015: 3).

This book argues that current discourses on Muslim democracy suffer from theoretical under-development born from the lack of critical scrutiny of the Turkish example. The literature and current political environment have perceived Muslim democracy in an instrumentalist manner, reducing it simply to a mechanism of governance. What Aziz Al-Azmeh said almost two decades ago with regard to the Arab world still applies to the current state of democracy in the Muslim world:

> Instrumentalism is thus a primary feature of democratic advocacy in the Arab present. It is manifest both in short-term arguments for democracy with immediate political grounds and purposes. (1994: 113)

The departure point in this book is the commonly accepted assumption of democracy in political theory about its normative relevance in political practice. According to political theorists of democracy like Robert A. Dahl, for a political system to be qualified as a democracy it has to have 'free, fair and frequent elections', 'freedom of expression', 'alternative information (free media)' and 'associational autonomy', along with 'inclusive citizenship, rule of law, and good governance and accountability' (Dahl, 1998: 85; 2005: 188–9). Yet in addition to these institutional structures, Dahl has also emphasised that democracy 'would require extensive social indoctrination and habituation' and the development of civic 'virtue in citizenry', or what we could call normative dimensions (1956: 18, 133). Democracy is recognised here to be both political practice and normative ideal.

I propose a political theory approach to the question of Muslim democracy which can lead out of the impasse created by the dominance of strategic and functionalist motives, as shown below in my analysis of the Turkish case. The next section lays the ground for engaging with conceptual and thematic analyses to contribute to the development of a normative understanding of Muslim democracy. Contemporary Turkey is used as a foil to theorise

Muslim democracy, with attention given to political practices, norms and institutions and the presence or absence of what can be described as a normative anchor of democracy.

II. Rethinking the Once-acclaimed Turkish Model: A Theoretical Inquiry

The democratic transition in Turkey ostensibly experienced a 'downturn' and 'breaking point', usually dated to 2013, that affected the reputation of the Turkish regional model (Müftüler-Baç and Keyman, 2015: 2). However, holding Turkey up 'as a model of co-existence of Islam with democracy and pluralism' was for Sami Zubaida (2011) never fully accurate. One objection to the Turkish model is informed by the criticism that when Turkey

> became proficient in some democratic practices, and its constitutions established what resembled democratic institutions, but few of its leaders ever demonstrated a commitment to democratic norms. Without it, cynicism and authoritarianism flourished alongside, and even with the help of, democratic practices. (Cook, 2019)

Even during the late 2000s, considered the height of the Turkish democratisation process, Turkey was rated 'partly free' by Freedom House. Limits to freedoms of expression, religion, media and press, association and assembly, cultural and minority rights, gender equality and personal liberties were raised as Turkey's democratic quandaries (Freedom House, 2007, 2008, 2009, 2010). In this section, I will review the secondary source literature on the problematising of the Turkish model with the objective of offering a *principled*, *normative* approach to conceptualising Muslim democracy.

As Ghassan Salamé states, during the state-building processes, '[t]he abrupt introduction of that [whether Pahlavi, Kemalist or Arab] statist machine . . . might have favoured democracy more' (1994: 13). Aslı Ü. Bâli (2006) maintains, however, that Kemalism preferred a 'statist and authoritarian' model, which was tied to a homogenising national narrative and an undeveloped democratic ethos. This account suggests that the statist legacy remains a pressing challenge to the Turkish political system. Systematic tendencies of a strong state, under the influence of Kemalism, controlled political and social spaces. However, a moralising and hegemonic state has historical antecedents in the Middle East, according to Nazih Ayubi. Deeper causes for the state's absolute place in the pre-modern era can be explained by the following observation:

> The Sunnites tend to look at the state as the organizer of their religious affairs . . . Opposition to the state is therefore almost tantamount to abandoning the faith; it is not only to be condemned by society but is also to be prevented by the state. (Ayubi, 1992: 83)

Ayubi's insight into the state can be seen to apply to Turkish political culture. Nonetheless, Islamic orthodoxy cannot be faulted as the key factor for the continuity of the statist tradition in contemporary Turkish politics. Traditionally, the *bay'ah*-dominated political culture has often surpassed other Islamic ideals of *shūra* (consultation), *'adāla* (justice), *ijmā'* (consensus) and *amāna* (trust), in favour of legitimising and even sanctifying executive power both in monarchical and nation-state periods. Christopher Houston therefore explains that, except for short periods of pluralistic opening, the sacrosanct, paternalistic and 'periodically violent' state has been prevalent and tied to a state-regulated religion for its legitimacy (2013b: 332). State and religion have been 'brothers' of different kinds and had relations under different rules; yet they appear never to have been genuinely separated in Turkish politics.

Centralising, hegemonic and ideological tendencies of the statist framework, in some scholarly accounts, appear to have endured from 'Kemalist Turkey' to the 'new Turkey'. In Kemalist Turkey, the hegemony of the secular military, economic and political elites of the modern state was considered to be clothed with the legitimacy of nationalism and republicanism. According to this line of thought, swift democratisation in the 2000s apparently did not cause a change in the character of the state. The state in new Turkey, Ziya Öniş argues, still maintains paternalistic and homogenising state practices despite the rule of a 'civilian majority' and despite being legitimised through the notion of national will (2015: 5). Ergun Özbudun has observed that 'an authoritarian state tradition that seeks to impose an artificial homogeneity, even uniformity, on the society' has been the major hurdle to the process of democratic consolidation in Turkey (2012: 70). Other critics have found 'the persistence of patrimonial patterns', 'patronage relations' and 'dominant party' politics in both cases to have impeded the development of autonomous, meritocratic and neutral public institutions (Sözen, 2013: 238; Müftüler-Baç and Keyman, 2015: 4). The putative 'authoritarian aspects' of the statist establishment generated a system with highly fragile checks and balances, with a bureaucracy, legislature and judiciary highly prone to being politicised (Tezcür, 2010b: 84). These criticisms of the Turkish model share the assumption that it was prematurely celebrated in the region. They raise the question of whether a genuine change has occurred in the nature of the state, and its institutional design and rights discourse.

'Turkey's repressive definition of secularism' and homogeneous national identity, Bâli argues, were inherited from 'the founding republican ideology of Kemalism' (2016b: 801). Kemalist laicism, a state project 'from above', has been a variety of nationalism (Houston, 2013a: 255). The primacy of religion in the post-Ottoman nation was abolished in favour of the ideal of the nation state. However, Kemalism is understood to have obliquely justified the new identity of Turkishness on the grounds of cultural Hanafi Islam, where other Muslims (Alevis and Kurds) as well as non-Muslims were either assimilated or excluded from the definition of the genuine citizen (Göle 2015: 60). National solidarity seems to have had a paradoxical effect of appealing to different ethnic and social groups while integrating the citizens of the new Turkish Republic on the basis of a narrowly conceived identity. José Casanova notes that Turkish nationalism has been 'too secular for the Islamists, too Sunni for the Alevis and too Turkish for the Kurds' (2006: 6). In many instances, the Kemalist nation-state, like its peers in the region, has

> generally been constructed on a series of exclusions and ostracisms, the combined effect of which was to multiply the number of political orphans and orphans of politics, for politics henceforward was the state and nothing but the state. (Salamé, 1994: 14)

Houston argues that the 'Turkish-Islam synthesis immediately led to the closing down of space for democratic politics', which limited civil society's capacity to question and negotiate state–religion relations (2013a: 255).

Turkey's modern secular constitutional system was 'characterised by military tutelage, repressive secularism, limited individual rights, [and] discrimination against minorities' (Bâli, 2016a). Özbudun observed that some features of 'the "founding philosophy" of the Turkish Republic' are 'incompatible with the development of a true pluralistic political system' (2012: 61). The Kemalist version of secularism was clearly not concerned with the principle of neutrality and the institutional separation of religion and state but rather the state's intrusion in institutionally regulating and controlling religion (Barkey, 2012: 28). According to the Kemalist nation-building project, religion, too valuable a tool to leave to a burgeoning civil society, was necessary for the legitimisation of state power and the attainment of social consensus (Yavuz, 2003: 212). These arguments illustrate an account of the modern Turkish state's ideological capacity, namely moralising power, to shape not only political institutions but also cultural, normative and social patterns.

Ideas about modernisation from above had already gained a semblance of respectability in the Middle East when Kemalist reforms brought about the founding of the Turkish Republic. Modernisation was increasingly seen as the solution to the alleged backwardness of Muslim societies (Okyar, 1984: 49). However, very few Muslim countries have experienced such a secularist modernisation quest, which in turn, as Şerif Mardin argues, generated the state-dominated Kemalist centre and religiously conservative rural periphery (1973: 182). Conservative classes from a rural background 'had been largely marginalized through much of the republic's history' (Bâli, 2016a). Since 2001, these social groups have been the main support base of the JDP. Political and social tensions between these JDP-inclined social groups and Kemalist supporters have contributed to an existing climate of polarisation.

Resolving the tension created by the relationship between religion and the state has been a historical prerequisite for genuine democratisation. The Turkish state, like its peers in the Middle East, has often undermined 'opportunities for a public debate on the ethical underpinnings of the normative relationship between religion and government' and retained the authority to define this relationship (Hashemi, 2012: 21). During its first years in government, the JDP enjoyed a popular electoral mandate to revise statist secularism in favour of limited and tolerant governance. However, an observer identifies the continuation of the primacy of the state in defining the relationship between religion and government (Bâli, 2016a). Zubaida (2011) is also alert to the prospect of religious claims using absolute state power, and described the potential to generate a political system of 'moralistic conformity' or 'authoritarian moralism'.

The inference that the democratisation process in Turkey was futile cannot be made simply because it followed a more or less pragmatic path. Indeed, less emphasis on fixed ideological positions by an influential section of Islamic political forces in Turkey led to moderation by renouncing previously-held radical claims for state enactment of *sharīʿa*. As a result, the JDP has successfully moved into and integrated with the political centre. The new Turkish model has been associated with anti-Kemalist, anti-military, anti-elitist, pro-Western, civilian, welfarist and post-Islamist positions, all of which may accord with some moderate positions. However, a debate rages about to what extent the JDP has aligned these positions with a democratic and pluralist ethos and shaped the current outcome of democratisation. When the Turkish model was internationally praised, some observers were more cautious about the potential for democracy to be used as political capital on the domestic and international stage (Schwedler, 2011: 357). Critics have claimed the JDP has adopted strategies of 'political learning' to pursue its demands within democratic institutions by selectively using democratic rhetoric (Tezcür, 2010b: 84; Somer, 2011: 518).

For Güneş Murat Tezcür, the integration of Islamists in Turkish politics through political liberalisation and moderation 'is not necessarily conducive to democratization' (2010: 84). Such interpretations of the Turkish model do not link the renouncing of the pledge for an Islamic order with democracy. A theoretical differentiation of moderation from democratisation is required. While moderation mainly involves procedural and behavioural attitudes to change and does involve, but does not necessarily oblige, ideological or structural transformation, democratisation requires normative endorsement, social determination and institutional change. Unless norms and values take root in attitudes and institutions, they are prone to vary as interests and circumstances demand (Tezcür, 2010a: xi). This theoretical insight can explain why current examples of Muslim democracy, even in its 'most developed instance' (Nasr, 2005: 26), present only the promise of de facto moderation and partial and destabilising processes of democratic transition.

A free social environment maintained by legal safeguards is also essential if citizens are to engage in national dialogue and democratisation take place

(Connolly, 2005: 43). Most of the secondary sources surveyed above construct an account of the failure of the modern Turkish political climate to provide a safe, open and critical public sphere. Statist control is believed to have 'thwarted social agency' with the outcome of hampering the development of the common good, the shared values of civic society and a pluralistic ethos (Houston, 2013b: 333). In a country with deeply divided identities, the public sphere remains a field of bitter rivalry for power between groups with fundamentally different interests (Volpi, 2004: 1074). Secularists and Islamists compete to capture state power (Mahçupyan, 1998: 174). The state's hegemonic claims over the domination of the public sphere, the institutional maintenance of an official religion, the capacity to socially engineer the national identity and the extraction of wealth from the economy seem to preoccupy political actors. Democratic reforms initiated by the JDP have ostensibly not altered the state towards a power-sharing, inclusivist and pluralistic system (Sözen, 2013: 238). Civilian-authored constitution-making has not apparently resulted in the recognition of 'basic civil, political, social, economic, and cultural rights of individual citizens, while also granting rights its minorities' (Candaş Bilgen, 2008). More strident critics of the Turkish model argue that recent changes to the constitution have emboldened a populist executive at the expense of the legislature and judiciary, signalling a continuation of the hegemonic state tradition but in a different form (Ekim and Kirişci, 2017). This has raised concerns in the literature on the Turkish model that without a coherent, principled approach, democratisation processes can relapse into previous forms of political intolerance and repression.

Meltem Müftüler-Baç and Fuat Keyman attribute societal causes to 'a lack of tolerance for diversity' to explain its presence in Turkish politics (2015: 5). As mentioned earlier, Dahl (1976) highlights the importance of the normative formation of democratic consensus. Commitment to democratic values should occur during democratic consolidation and the development of social engagement (Linz and Stepan, 1996: 17). Democracy cannot be consolidated without the emergence of a pluralistic and vibrant civil society, and this civil society cannot emerge under the homogenising and moralising tendencies of statist control (Park, 2014). According to the prevailing orthodoxy, its consolidation cannot be attained within existing institutional and social structures in Turkey which have mutually reinforced each other in a vicious cycle for decades. In the current climate, one critic notes, a rhetoric of 'self-victimization' by the JDP invoking its earlier oppression under the Kemalist regime is used 'as an excuse not only for its unwillingness to deepen the democratization process but also for its authoritarian measures' (Taşkın, 2013: 299).

Turkish Islamism's tenuous moderation is assumed by Ruşen Çakır (2017) to be the cause of the putative lack of success of Turkish democracy. Zubaida (2011), on the other hand, suggests a different explanation for the apparent 'authoritarian developments' that are in part due to the ubiquitous global phenomenon of the search for electoral popularity. Despite the global phenomenon of authoritarian populism, specific attention to Islamism in Turkey can help us to understand how interests and realpolitik are legitimised and how they have gained widespread public support. Islamism's general feature of political expediency (*idâre-i maslahat*) has also manifested itself in its attempts to justify Islam and democracy on the grounds of *maṣlaḥa* (public interest). In other words, the engagement with democracy has not been grounded on norms, but was instead pursuant to the logic of necessity or instrumentality.

The JDP, which has rejected the Islamist label, signalled a rhetorical and organisational break from mainstream Islamist parties. Bassam Tibi's pessimism about Islamism is reflected in his verdict on the JDP that 'its goal is concealment, not a sincere shift to a truly post-Islamist politics' (2008: 45). A reluctance of the intellectual proponents and ideologues of the Turkish model of conservative democracy appears to be evident in the scarcity of theoretical approaches that adequately address normative issues of governance. Turkish political actors, especially those with Islamist roots, have reductively viewed democracy as a 'medium' via which to 'potentially reach a better condition' (Guida, 2010: 364). In this reading of the Turkish model, former Islamists now in the JDP participate in democratic institutions and employ democratic rhetoric when beneficial to them, despite the presumed philosophical discord with their doctrinal beliefs, rather than pressing for a reconfiguration of the normative relationship between Islam and democracy. Salamé's general observation that if 'the islamists [are] considered opportunist, reversible and insincere ... "secularist" forces certainly do not produce any more convincing professions of democratic faith' may also be applicable to the contemporary Turkish context (1994: 16). Democracy advocacy by Islamists, secularists and nationalists reveals their equally populist credentials in Turkey and, in many respects, elsewhere in the Muslim world.

Mehmet Gürses proposes to argue that the JDP's support for democracy has also been 'fragmented, provisional and driven by pragmatism more than a principled commitment to democratic norms and values' (2014: 464). The contemporary political context 'has not produced serious philosophical and theoretical debates among Muslim intellectuals' with the rise of political figures comparable to Soroush at the expense of Kissinger (Taşkın, 2013: 300). This observation finds that political philosophers are noticeably absent in the JDP, with political strategists and foreign policy experts at its helm. Such a pragmatic turn, according to Akif Emre, has led to an increasingly singular approach to Islamic political thought, often through 'the bureaucratisation of the intelligentsia', hampering its creativeness and reformist potential (Emre, 2012). This approach is not specific to Turkey, however, as John Waterbury notes that '[i]n many respects Middle East intelligentsias are state intelligentsias' (1994: 27).

Modern Turkish history between 2003 and 2013 witnessed a cluster of its most significant democratic reforms, such as greater ethnic, minority and linguistic rights, religious freedoms and economic development. However, these changes did not effect a transformation to pluralism and full democracy. Democratic changes were not institutionalised to modify the character of the state. The so-called Turkish model did not produce a new democratic social contract between state and society. Statist and authoritarian features of the political establishment, along with the pragmatic approach and 'reluctant reformism' of political actors, were ill-equipped to address the deeply entrenched problems which resulted in a political, social and institutional democratic crisis (Taşkın, 2013: 304). Democratisation in its unfinished process characterises Turkey's political experience, in which the functionalist convergence between democracy and Islam appears to have produced a 'semi-democracy'.

A systematic theory on Muslim democracy is currently absent. Lacking the constitutive values, institutions and attitudes of democracy, the current paradigm of *maṣlaḥa*-based pragmatist and populist approaches seems to be detrimental to Muslims' struggles for democracy. Very few proposals appear to adopt a political theory approach on the question of Muslim democracy addressing these normative imperatives. Departing from this approach of political analysis, I will argue in this book that only through theorising democracy and its normative commitments can we consider Muslim democracy in a more productive sense.

III. Approaches: A Comparative Turn

The preceding brief review of a selection of secondary sources on the Turkish model has attempted to illustrate the various explanations for the absence of a viable model of Muslim democracy. Muslim democracy, hitherto popularly espoused, is unlikely to emerge from 'political imperatives' to the neglect of 'theoretical suppositions' (Nasr, 2005: 15). A line of analysis that proposed democratisation without the presence of democrats has been disproved in light of the experiences of the Muslim world in general and Turkey in particular. Normative democratic commitments appear to be necessary for democracy to take root. I will argue that these normative commitments can be derived from a political theory approach to Muslim democracy.

Political theory approaches can be employed to formulate a conception of Muslim democracy so as to highlight its necessary values and institutions. I seek to combine Muslim perspectives on governance with multiculturalist discourses on pluralism in the formulation of a political theory of Muslim democracy. Loubna El Amine finds political theory unable to account for the mass appeal of and protests for democracy in the Muslim world, 'because it does not offer any language, tools, or approaches to deal with the convergence of normative claims across traditions' (2016: 102). I seek to engage with comparative political theory (CPT), or what is at times referred to as 'cross-cultural' political philosophy, 'as a subfield of political theory' (Dallmayr, 2004: 249). Unlike comparative politics, which concentrates 'on governmental structures and empirical political processes', comparative political theory focuses 'on ideas, perspectives, and theoretical frameworks as they have been formulated in the past, and continue to be articulated today' (Dallmayr, 2010: x). I will be deploying a CPT approach, to be discussed in greater detail in the following paragraphs, for my undertaking of a normative approach. I utilise two different traditions of political theorising, in a synthesis of mutually complementary elements, to effectively address the lack of political theory on Muslim democracy.

However, CPT is a contested sub-field. Josey Tom (2019) sees this burgeoning scholarly enterprise as a 'systematic effort to challenge the Western-centrism of political theory'. Roxanne Euben critiques the 'parochial mapping of Western answers to fixed questions posed by a pantheon of European American philosophers' (2010: 260). In addition, Tom proposes CPT in order to re-imagine 'existing categories and concepts and incorporating themes, thinkers, and cultural insights from non-Western societies'. Andrew March alerts us to the sub-field's embrace of 'religious doctrine and political thought', to expand the normative enterprise within political theory (2009: 552). The diversity of approaches within CPT also highlights tensions between different cultures. According to Sudipta Kaviraj, it is 'impossible' to understand modern political developments in the non-Western world both without Western political theory and 'entirely within the terms of that [Western] tradition' (2001: 287). Fred Dallmayr favours a 'dialogical' approach which can 'only arise from lateral interaction, negotiation, and contestation' of different traditions and canons of thought (2004: 249). On the relevance of other political traditions, Dallmayr concludes that 'the basic purpose of politics is to promote the "common good" or "good life"', as can be found in Aristotle as well as 'Alfarabi, Confucius, and the Indian shastras' (2008: 3). The post-Eurocentric brand of CPT, despite its varying expressions from author to author, provides instructive lessons for carrying out a political theory in a non-Western context. Common values and norms are acknowledged in 'the conclusion that cultures are morally and cognitively incommensurable' (Euben, 1999: 10). In this book, I study both Muslim and Western multiculturalist traditions of political thought for the purpose of systematic conceptualisation.

I examine Muslim political thought using the interpretative tools of political theory by engaging with the political arguments raised by prominent modern Muslim thinkers. This book investigates contemporary Muslim scholarship's responses to governance and pluralism and their similarities and differences vis-à-vis multicultural political theory. I aim to relate Muslim political thought to the multiculturalist political theorising of Muslim democracy. In doing so, I seek both to refute anti-democratic Islamic arguments and to develop latent and manifest democratic notions. While the strands of Muslim political thought are diverse, some generalisations can be deduced in order to formulate a typology. As Euben reminds us, categorisation and categories may 'essentialize and homogenize extraordinarily diverse areas'; however, 'they remain useful as a device that at once evokes familiar categories and provides an occasion to problematize them' (Euben, 1997: 234 as cited in Browers, 2006: 20). I re-evaluate these categories as heuristic devices to enhance their capacity to explore connections and overlaps with multiculturalism.

Here, it should be said that the selection and categorisation of thinkers examined in this book is based on the type of discourses to which they contribute. For instance, the Muslim thinkers chosen for examination in the first chapter have undertaken a direct engagement with Islamic texts, sources, terminologies and methodologies in their political thought. This frame of reference, however, is the explicit source of authority for these Muslim thinkers. They differ from other Muslim thinkers, mostly political scientists or international relations scholars, who do not make epistemologically distinct Islamic arguments. In this work, I make a distinction between scholars whose background identifier is 'Muslim' but who are not directly engaging with 'Islamic' traditions and scholarship and those Muslim thinkers whose work explicitly draws on and self-consciously appeals to shared markers of Islamic authority. While there is an abundance of Turkish scholarship on international relations, political economy and strategic studies on democracy, there is a dearth of political theory studies on Muslim democracy. Thus, I had a limited choice of Muslim thinkers within Turkey. By contrast, I was able to engage with the writings of Khaled Abou El Fadl and Abdullahi Ahmad An-Na'im, who engage with normative articulations on Islam and democracy, as well as less well-known scholars, such as Mohammad Talbi, who delve into the ethical terrain of diversity.

I made an initial interpretative decision to limit the scope of the typology of Muslim political thought to Sunni scholars so as to maintain a systematic and focused research analysis. The rationale for this was twofold. First, my scholarly background in Sunni thought, and second, the nature of the texts (especially *ḥadīth* literature) and the classical scholarship on which modern scholars base their theories, are historically different between Sunni and Shi'a branches of Islam. However, I decided to include Shi'a scholars like Abdolkarim Soroush, who have made great contributions towards addressing the weaknesses of the pro-democracy group in Muslim political thought as well as constructing a Muslim democracy framework. Their inclusion in the typologies in the first chapter was not necessary, as the selection of scholars in the progressive category sufficiently represented the democratic line of Muslim thought.

In the process of theorising, I acknowledge my different positionalities as a Turkish Muslim woman who has studied in the Arab world and the West. I have benefited from an intellectually enriching background and address the potential scholarly impediment this may also pose. My personal experience of the headscarf ban in schools in Turkey has made me think about the space for religion in so-called secular and public arenas. I have also contemplated the issues of difference, pluralism, and individual rights and freedoms. My reading of Islam was no longer provincial through my education at the American University of Sharjah. At Durham University, the study of political theory expanded my horizons to the global travel of ideas, democracy, multiculturalism and human rights. It seems that CPT offers a solution through the deliberate choices of engaging with Muslim and multiculturalist discourses. Furthermore, it provides an interpretative framework with which to bridge my different positionalities and serve as the basis of my scholarly engagement with Muslim democracy.

My book falls within the boundaries of CPT through the comparison of Muslim political thought with multicultural political theory. I seek to employ the ideas, concepts and claims of multicultural political thought to engage with non-Western political ideas, concepts and claims previously neglected by hegemonic modes of Western political theory (Tom, 2019). I intend to identify and address the problematic of the political protection of moral diversity and freedoms. Multiculturalists have argued that liberalism, despite its avowed commitment to the protection of diversity, has significant shortcomings in practice (Kymlicka, 2007: 107; Taylor, 1994: 62). Among other strands of Western political thought, multiculturalism represents a development of liberal democracy with more effective tools for accommodating pluralism. According to Chandran Kukathas, it is the 'most plausible response to the fact of moral, religious, and cultural diversity' today (1998: 690). In recent decades, the rise of multiculturalism in political theory has offered new interpretations of the relationship between pluralism and the state. It emerged as a constructive critique of Rawlsian liberalism's limitations, that recognised the significance of culture and religion in politics and the inadequacy of certain liberal principles in modern pluralistic societies. Saba Mahmood's critique of 'the hegemony of liberalism' contends that 'Islam bears the burden of proving its compatibility with liberal ideas, and the line of question is almost never reversed' in looking at 'the contradictions and problems' exhibited by certain liberal political principles (2004: 76, 74, 75). Multiculturalism, like Muslim political thought, problematises liberal democracy's relation to religion by addressing the hegemonic binary relationship between them.

In discussions about Muslim democracy, multiculturalism problematised certain ideas and assumptions of liberalism. Multicultural theorists have questioned the ability of liberal democracy to accommodate culture and religion, particularly religious adherents' private and public goods, rights and needs, in a plural society (Tully, 1995: 44). By doing so, multiculturalists acknowledge that orthodox liberal political theory's certain conceptual resources and normative paradigms are not nuanced enough to welcome a comprehensive religion such as Islam (Taylor, 1994: 62). Multiculturalism often offers more inter-disciplinary tools with which to address religion than liberal theory. It advances more pluralistic and inclusive conceptualisations of democratic institutions. Multiculturalist thinkers have viewed religion as a public frame of reference, rather than as solely a private matter, to be included in political theory. Religion is central to understanding public demands, institutional design of states and democratic consolidation; multiculturalism offers the theoretical capacity to rethink democracy on the basis of political theory in Muslim societies.

The individual contributions of Veit Bader, Gad Barzilai, Chandran Kukathas, Ayelet Shachar and Charles Taylor are distinguished in the typology below. They were divided according to their responses to three main issues of multicultural accommodation: (i) the type of legal–institutional mechanisms; (ii) the nature of institutional and normative change; and (iii) the role of religion in the public sphere. Multiculturalist insights on religion within political theory provide the opportunity to rethink the study of religion in the theorising of Muslim democracy. Yet these insights largely deal with the issues of cultural and religious rights within the context of established liberal democracies of the West. As such, the existence of a democratic government is taken for granted and is not subject to a critical analysis. The challenges faced by the developing democracies of the Muslim world are not typically addressed by multiculturalists. Liberalism can offer the necessary interpretative tools for an underlying background theory of democratic governance.

Although this work questions some of the dominant principles of liberalism, it utilises its theoretical depth and systematic maturity. In other words, liberal democracy is not treated as the ultimate end-point for a Muslim democracy. Yet any student of democracy should also be cognisant of the problems accompanying alternatives to liberalism. I recognise liberalism to be an advanced source of political wisdom and institutions which has been 'more effective than other political systems in restraining political power, preventing blatant corruption, and compelling elected officials to work for the well-being of the people and heed their opinions' (Chan, 2014: 192). However, I employ the insights of multiculturalist political thinkers in their rethinking of liberal democracy. Chapter 3's examination of 'compatibility-based arguments' acknowledges the need to incorporate liberalism to address the limitations of current articulations of Muslim democracy. The final part, on the framework of Muslim democracy, utilises Western political theories of liberalism, republicanism and constitutionalism in order to develop shared categories derived from the typologies developed in the earlier chapters. For these reasons, I rely on the two broad theoretical currents of multiculturalism and Muslim political thought along with supplementary intellectual currents.

My typology of various intellectual currents flowing to democracy informs this book's development of interpretative tools. Accordingly, I have systematically conceptualised key concepts towards the formulation of a normative democratic theory on Muslim democracy.

IV. Muslim Democracy versus Islamic Democracy: A Conceptual Clarification

This book reinterprets Muslim democracy from theological thought to political theory. A democratic alternative is offered to accommodate democracy, Islam and pluralism without majoritarian domination. I broadly define Muslim democracy as a constitutional democratic political regime that functions in predominantly Muslim societies, where religion is a significant marker of social, cultural and political identity for sizeable sections of the society. At the same time, Muslim democracy recognises the normative value of 'highly diverse' societies, where practising Muslims live alongside non-Muslims, the non-practising or the non-religious (Eickelman and Salvatore, 2003: 107). Muslim democracy in this book is formulated in a political theory accompanied by a normative quest for a democratic political system where religion can be voluntarily followed by Muslims. It insists on the fundamental human rights and democratic norms for all sections of society. Citizens with diverse political, religious, cultural or ideological affiliations, whether majority or minority, should enjoy their rights and freedoms through constitutional guarantees.

I propose to theorise democracy in Muslim-majority contexts in light of other factors in these contexts without invoking thick normative foundations. The more Islam is underscored as a foundationalist theory, the more problems of unjustified simplification arise (Mandaville, 2014: 23). Muslim democracy, by focusing on 'Muslimness' rather than Islam, argues that religion is attached to different meanings in different contexts on the basis of the situated needs, world-views and interests of people. Muslim democracy proposes theoretical tools derived from the debates within CPT, which allude to the role played by contexts in shaping ideas. While taking religion seriously, the theory of Muslim democracy as articulated in this book does not exclusively lie on epistemologically religious foundation.

The idea of Muslim democracy aims to negotiate the demands of politics, counter-hegemony and dialogue across cultures from the perspective of post-foundationalist norms. Post-foundationalism is adopted here to arrive at a position of being 'liberated from this dead-end debate' between foundationalism and anti-foundationalism when it comes to democracy (Gutmann, 1996: 347). It primarily consists of a rejection of a thick normativity, metaphysical truth, self-evident reason and fixed meanings. Norms, values and practices from different philosophical traditions are appropriated in an open epistemological framework. This pluralistic epistemology can better reflect democracy's 'inner pluralism and versatility' (Sadiki, 2004: 11).

Islamic democracy as 'a religious, political system' that is 'streaked by the culture and the vision of Islam and its worldview' is often mistakenly conflated with Muslim democracy (Candaş Bilge, 2008). However, I use Muslim democracy to deliberately distance my approach from the theologically or scripturally prescribed associations that 'Islamic democracy' might suggest. I think that the latter term is a mischaracterisation and a problematic concept, which carries perceptions such as the equating of Islam and democracy or the conflation of a theocratic democracy. For instance, the theories on Islamic democracy advocate the compatibility of Islam and democracy while also endorsing transcendental foundational principles for an Islamic state. Muslim democracy seeks to engage with democratic norms and principles as well as rights and liberties using political theory rather than the theological approaches present in the conception of Islamic democracy.

Muslim democracy in this book is conscious that democracy by definition is 'a condition of freedom from ideology' (Keane, 1993: 28). Democracy as an idea cherishes hybridity, transformation, controversy and compromise and is thus not tinged by any absolutist or moralising comprehensive view. Hence, I concur with the definition of democracy as 'freedom of religion as much as freedom from religion' in a political project that is pluralistic and inclusive enough to accommodate the different comprehensive views of citizens (Keane, 1993: 28). I do not discuss the different theories on democracy and other potential formulations of democracy using political theory in this book. I aim to identify the existing space for conceptualising Muslim democracy. I espouse the position that democracy is not a form of governance that can convey infinite differences. There are certain normative benchmarks such as universal human rights, separation of powers, the rule of law, judicial independence, established opposition, that any democratic governance has to implement (Dallmayr, 2011: 445). Muslim democracy is no exception.

This book acknowledges that democratic theorisation cannot be detached from the normative debates on the relationship between religion and politics. Attempting to draw the 'just', or rather proper, bounds of democracy and religion, Muslim democracy theory deals with the issue of religious accommodation more substantially than liberalism. The theoretical framework of Muslim democracy seeks to reconcile Muslim world-views with a constitutional democratic system in a more nuanced way than liberal democratic theories. Muslim democracy proposes to modify the collective understanding of certain democratic institutions to be adopted in a Muslim-majority context while safeguarding the characteristic attributes of democracy. My proposed framework searches for new forms of democracy and public religiosity under the modern state. It emphasises the importance of re-orienting politics to adopt democratic ideals, and collective religious beliefs towards pluralism, as well as the social habituation of democratic values.

On the other hand, internal and external dynamics, contexts and histories of individual Muslim societies differ from one another. I think these differences militate against a one-size-fits-all political model derived from CPT. This book recognises that 'there is no single mode for combining religion and democracy, nor is there a single model for defining the role of faith in the public sphere' (Benhabib, 2011). Therefore, this framework does not stipulate a particular legal, institutional and political system. Context-specific democratic pluralist models can emerge through each society's self-conscious, dynamic and active engagement with ethical and societal aspects of political governance. However, a normative and interpretative approach to a theory of Muslim democracy is essential to any meaningful discussion about practical application.

V. Prolegomenon to the Organisation of the Book

My theorising of Muslim democracy in this book follows three steps which correspond to six chapters, divided into three parts. The first part illustrates a typology of both Muslim and multiculturalist political thought. The second part, consisting of Chapter 3, critiques the stances of 'compatibility-based arguments' about Islam and democracy in contemporary discourses. The third part provides an alternative to orthodox liberal and compatibility-based arguments through the articulation of a political theory of Muslim democracy.

Part I presents typologies of Muslim and multiculturalist political thought in order to identify common ground between these two intellectual traditions. As mentioned earlier, the use of typologies aims to discover similar themes and normative conjunctions for the development of the key aspects of a political theory on Muslim democracy.

The first chapter's examination of Muslim political thought focuses on the relationship between Islam and democracy within contemporary debates. Muslim political thought provides concepts that are vital for studying Muslim democracy in terms of both opportunities and limitations. On the basis of their interpretations of *sharīʿa*, law, citizenship and statehood, the contemporary Muslim intellectuals examined in this book are placed in four categories: (i) statists; (ii) revivalists; (iii) modernists; and (iv) progressives. Statists advocate an ideological Islamic state. Doctrinaire Islamists who fall into this category put forward deeply entrenched doctrinal principles and concepts that block the development of democratic thinking. Revivalists are moderate Islamist intellectuals who, in most cases, are actively involved in political activism and enjoy popular public support. In their efforts to reform the legal and political systems of Muslim societies, revivalists emphasise the need for exercising *ijtihād* (independent reasoning) pursuant to the logic of necessity and pragmatism in line with today's world (Moussalli, 2001: 15). This methodology is also evident in their approach to democracy as a political instrument but not a philosophical or moral approach. Modernists advocate a critical, historical and contextual exegesis and rereading of Islamic moral precepts in an attempt to give birth to a 'new Islam' in modern times (Nettler, 2000: 50). Islam and liberal democracy are perceived to be complementary sources in forming a just and moral political order (Fadel, 2009a: 108). Finally, progressives support the project of secular liberal democracies in which the normative and practical separation of religion and state is carried out. Islam does not provide a theory for the establishment of a political community or a state. Religion is focused on individual morality and societal interactions. Progressives provide the most theoretically developed and coherent response to the idea of Muslim democracy. This typology helps identify different approaches to the task of incorporating Islamic moral precepts with democratic principles in Muslim political thought. Despite instances of intellectual engagements with the issues of political secularism, tolerance, equal citizenship and human rights, these efforts are not yet sufficient enough to engender a fully-fledged political theory on Muslim democracy. In fact, through this typology, I have identified normative issues that hinder the maturing of Muslim democratic theorisations. Chapter 3's critique of the notions of divine sovereignty and divine morality precedes the construction of a political theory of Muslim democracy in a systematic and elaborate manner.

The second chapter examines multiculturalist political thought in order to identify inclusive notions of democracy towards religion. I formulate a typology, similar to the effort of the first chapter, for classifying the various multiculturalist approaches. On the basis of their perspectives on secularism, the public sphere and institutional designs, multiculturalists are placed in four categories: (i) liberal pluralists; (ii) moral pluralists; (iii) legal pluralists; and (iv) institutional pluralists. Liberal pluralists highlight the dynamic and accommodative nature of liberal theory anchored in individual autonomy and liberty. Contemporary liberalism, exemplified by Rawls and Dworkin, is subject to significant revision. Within the context of cultural diversity, liberal pluralists have re-appropriated liberal values for expanding legal and political rights for cultural minorities. Moral pluralists believe that mainstream liberalism's overly abstract nature is disconnected from the realities of people with substantive moral visions. Normative recognition is believed to be the prerequisite for people's incorporation of diverse needs, choices and demands so as to fully actualise their individual agency and self-respect. Therefore, moral pluralists strongly emphasise the expansion of liberal political culture to include cultural and religious recognition (Boyd, 2004: 56). Legal pluralist multiculturalists acknowledge religion's moral importance for political theory in the areas of citizenship and jurisdictional autonomy (Barzilai, 2004: 6). Institutional pluralists advocate a radical transformation within politics that would serve as the catalyst for addressing the collective demands of religious minorities. This entails going from the unitary nature of the state that strictly controls public life to creating legal and administrative connections between the state and the groups. Unlike legal pluralist multiculturalists, institutional pluralists offer a framework within which the recognition of collective jurisdictional identity and constitutional scrutiny of the protection of individual citizenship rights are democratically integrated. These four approaches to multiculturalism help us understand liberal democracy's ability to accommodate religious and cultural claims and needs. They provide more pluralistic conceptualisations of the link between religion and liberal democracy through the rethinking of the state, secularism, law and the public sphere. Multiculturalist scholars have advocated for the inclusion of religion in political theory. Religion is not a private matter and should be moved to the foreground so as to engage with public demands, institutional design and democratic consolidation.

The third chapter, constituting Part II, addresses problematics such as divine versus popular sovereignty, *sharī'a* versus social legislation, and *shūra* versus public deliberation. This chapter critically analyses 'compatibility-based arguments' of mainstream Muslim democratic discourses in order to identify the intellectual and normative constraints that hinder the development of a political theory of Muslim democracy. Compatibility-based arguments have successfully refuted the claims of an inherent despotic essence in Islam that impedes democratisation. These arguments indicate how Islamic moral principles and democracy can be reconciled. However, the conclusion that there is not a structural incompatibility between Islam and democracy and that democracy can be justified in Islamic terms does not necessarily generate the theoretical clarity and methodological coherence needed for Muslim democracy. In some instances, revivalists, uncritical advocates of Muslim democracy, have shied away from investigating the challenges posed by genuine democratic transitions, such as the separation of religion and state, pluralism, and individual freedoms. A few advocates of compatibility-based arguments, in this book mainly modernists, have committedly addressed and investigated these challenges through their own intellectual and ideological frameworks or traditions of political thought. The result has been the formulation of elaborate normative and moral arguments on Islam and democracy. I depart from both genres of the compatibility argument and engage with these issues within political theory. On this matter, I join the progressive Muslim scholars' effort to articulate a non-theological, political theory on Muslim democracy in the next part.

In light of the weaknesses identified in Chapter 3, Part III theorises Muslim democratic theory in the attempt to go beyond the compatibility-based hybrids and the ad hoc theories examined thus far. Chapters 4, 5 and 6 formulate a theory of Muslim democracy drawing on Muslim and Western multiculturalist approaches to political thought. I utilise various insights from these intellectual frameworks to articulate a set of arguments and concepts for a conception of democracy in Muslim-majority contexts. Although this book does not undertake a study of the empirical cases of democratic consolidation in Muslim-majority states, I intend to develop normative imperatives that are amenable to such processes. My framing of a political theory of Muslim democracy is divided into three discussions contained in three corresponding chapters on pluralist secularism, a social public sphere and a pluralising constitution.

Chapter 4 begins with two main arguments on the link between secularism, religion and democracy, namely unsecular Muslim democracy and secular Muslim democracy. The former envisages an Islamically-informed notion of democracy distant from secularism. By contrast, the latter, while opposing philosophical or substantive interpretations of secularism, endorses political secularism as a fundamental condition for maintaining democracy. This chapter re-evaluates secularism within the framework of Muslim democracy. While it benefits from these existing models, it proposes a type of pluralist secularism. The chapter's discussion rejects the moralising state and constrains its powers for greater associational freedoms, recognising different accounts of public goods and ontologically-driven duties and obligations. I conceptualise pluralist secularism by developing four constitutive features: (1) a minimalist state; (2) public recognition of religion; (3) differentiation of the analytical categories of state and social public spheres; and finally (4), collective rights.

Chapter 5 elaborates two models of the public sphere derived from the typologies of Muslim and multiculturalist traditions of political thought. The idea of shared public institutions involves reforming state institutions so that they are, on the one hand, sufficiently accommodating of diverse and changing religious demands. The idea of plural public institutions, on the other hand, proposes formalising degrees of institutional and jurisdictional pluralism as the only adequate way of acknowledging comprehensive religious claims. The notions of the shared and the plural lead to the formation of the analytical category of a *social public sphere*. This category refers to a distinct political form where religious communal life is organised by civil society associations, as contrasted with a *state public sphere* in which the secular state controls the common institutional framework. The social public sphere is the location of a politics of difference, while the state public sphere facilitates the development of civic virtues, democratic toleration and the mediation of conflicting interests in the creation of shared goods. I develop four assumptions or norms of the social public sphere: (1) transformativeness; (2) social Islam; (3) democratic toleration; and (4) institutional pluralism.

Chapter 6 discusses two theories on constitutionalism, legal constitutionalism and political constitutionalism, followed by my own proposal of a pluralising constitutionalism. I aim to harmonise legally imposed minimal standards that guarantee individual autonomy and citizenship rights with democratic processes in collective and organisational aspects of religious and cultural life. I develop three key concepts regarding constitutions within the context of Muslim democracy, namely (a) incontestable legal norms, (b) democratic law-making and (c) jurisdictional pluralism.

In Part III, I attempt to wrestle with the disagreements around issues such as state–religion relations, minority rights, personal freedoms, human rights, religious jurisdiction and public morality. I propose a more nuanced narrative of the potential for the coexistence of public religiosity and the principles of democracy. The Turkish model appears to demonstrate that democratisation cannot happen without having developed a principled approach to democracy drawn from local social processes, institutionalised at the state level, protected by a constitution. The political theory of Muslim democracy articulated here focuses on the interlinked processes of institutions (pluralistic secularism), interactions (a social public sphere) and rights (constitutional provisions). This book utilises existing definitions of democracy in the formulation of a political theory that links value change and religious reform with the institutionalisation of political and constitutional reforms on the level of governance.

The framework of Muslim democracy developed in this book does not specifically put forward a particular political, institutional or legal blueprint for Muslim democracy. Rather, it theorises a set of political concepts, values and assumptions within a framework that can permit a principled reconciliation and coexistence between democratic governance and comprehensive public Islamic views.

In the conclusion, I provide a set of reflections on Muslim democracy as a simultaneously Muslim and democratic social construction, a relation shaped by the CPT approach. I argue that demystifying the normative principles explicit in liberal democratic institutions should be followed by their reconstruction through the insights derived from Muslim political and multiculturalist typologies. An alternative proposal for the functions of these institutions is advocated in contrast not only to existing pragmatist models of Muslim democracy, but also to orthodox liberal theory. I restate my original contribution to developing a political theory of Muslim democracy located in a dialogic interaction between Muslim and multicultural traditions of political thought.

Note

1. The 'multiple modernities' thesis asserts that institutional patterns that emerged in Europe are not universal but may have different paths of development within various cultural and religious traditions on the basis of their indigenous values (Eisenstadt, 2000: 3).

PART ONE
TYPOLOGIES OF MUSLIM AND MULTICULTURAL POLITICAL THOUGHT

1

ISLAMIC DISCOURSES ON GOVERNANCE AND PLURALISM

I. Introduction

The relationship between Islam and political systems constitutes an element of a wider political and legal crisis in the modern Muslim world. Debates rage about the need for the sovereignty of the people as a natural consequence of human vicegerency or divine sovereignty as the manifestation of the *tawhīd* (oneness of God). In addition, questions are posed as to whether democracy is the best possible existing political system or a system of *shirk* (idolatry). Controversy surrounds whether *sharīʿa* provides moral guidance or offers a legal code. Political and ideological positions range across a wide spectrum of opinions. This chapter will classify the ideas about the relationship between governance and religion according to a selection from prominent contemporary Muslim thinkers as part of my theorising of Muslim democracy. On the basis of their interpretations of the Qur'an, *sharīʿa* and the classical scholarship in addressing modern statehood, they are placed in four categories or schools of thought, namely statists, revivalists, modernists and progressives.

Statists are thinkers who espouse an absolutist, literalist and scripturalist position in understating the Qur'an and *hadīth*. They believe the *sharīʿa* to be an all-pervasive, fixed legal code that provides almost no room for multiple historical or contextual readings. The *sharīʿa* is immutable in the realms of state and authority (Afsaruddin, 2008: 24–5). Due to the insistence on the necessity of a particular model of an Islamic state, I describe these thinkers as statists. Statists argue that an Islamic state is the exclusive legitimate earthly manifestation of God's sovereignty (*ḥākimiyyat Allah*) for implementing the *sharī'a*. Most statists perceive democracy's claim of human sovereignty to be *shirk*.

Revivalists challenge the statists' reductionist and static understanding of *sharī'a* as a single, absolute law with detailed precepts and ready-made, divinely-inspired solutions to all situations. Although revivalists promote a flexible and continuous reinterpretation of *sharī'a*, they are still scripturalist in their approach to the texts. For them, the Qur'an, unlike for statists, is not a book of the law, but a book of moral and juristic principles for the construction of a political structure. Another area of difference between revivalists and statists is the revivalist contextualist approach to texts. Discovery of the normative premises of democracy in Islamic texts justifies democratic institutions in Islam on the grounds of *maṣlaḥa* (public interest).

Revivalists and modernists hold similar assumptions and norms regarding the compatibility of Islam and the exigencies of modern life. For instance, legal and political institutions of statehood are developed by revivalists and modernists that are compatible with both Islamic law and democratic political institutions. Yet the extent of reform and the place of *ijtihād* in their views significantly vary in their commitments to democracy.

Modernists seek to derive or discover the ethical values behind the apparent meanings of Qur'anic verses. Differentiation is made between the *maqāṣid* (objectives) or *ratio legis* and particular circumstances surrounding Islamic revelation (Afsaruddin, 2008: 25). For modernists, the *sharī'a*, a collection of values, is not unambiguously revealed by God, but rather requires 'the interpretive act of the human agent for its production and execution' (Abou El Fadl, 2004: 30). As such, the *sharī'a*, for modernists, 'is a work in progress', searching for the divine ideals through methodical efforts that are in a state of incompleteness by human agents in their efforts to comprehend the divine will (Abou El Fadl, 2004: 34). In order to adapt and accommodate to modern life, modernists advocate discerning *maqāṣid* of the *naṣṣ* (text). These theological assumptions are displayed in the modernists' attitude towards democracy. Modernists, unlike revivalists with their espousal of a functionalist approach to democracy, present a moral viewpoint that accepts the universal claims of human rights, democracy and pluralism.

Progressives support the separation of religion and state affairs. They reject the notion of an 'Islamic state'. For progressives, Islam promotes a moral community, not a political organisation, since it is a religion rather than a political ideology. Therefore, they claim that Islam neither legitimises nor imposes any particular form of government. The institutions of the state belong to the realm in which people exercise their prerogatives. The *sharī'a* is also understood to be a product of human interpretations rather than the revealed law of God. Progressives fiercely oppose the statist version of an Islamic state, for it is a utopian post-colonial invention doomed to failure or to be despotic (an-Na'im, 1999: 37). In addition, unlike revivalists and modernists, they express a philosophical shift away from the idea of divine sovereignty in politics. A secular state with equal citizenship rights is the most ideal polity, where Islam is a matter of personal conviction in people's lives.

This chapter will engage with the issues of governance, democracy and pluralism according to the different Islamic perspectives of these four schools.[1] I will now outline the formative features of the typology of Islamic political thought to explore their potential contributions, as well as their contestations and limitations, in conceptualising Muslim democracy. By exploring these Islamic approaches to politics, I aim to identify the most essential notions needed for democratic theorisation.

II. Muslim Political Thought on Governance

Asking how Muslim thinkers conceive of Islam and governance is more significant than asking the perennial question of what Islam says about a system of governance. By reframing the question, we can better understand how general interpretations of Islam have shaped particular interpretations of an ideal political system. In addition, such an approach can assist modern Muslims to reclaim the prerogative to develop political theories of government and democracy as an expression of social formation. In this process, developed and systematised theoretical propositions are formulated from modern political arguments, rather than classical or dogmatic conclusions, complemented by lived experiences and contemporary values and demands of Muslims. This section will identify the diversity within Muslim scholarship on democracy through examination of four different approaches towards the Qur'an, *sharīʿa*, law, authority and the state. The insights from the following discussion will help to stimulate new ways of theorising about democracy.

1. Statists: Abū al-Aʿlā Mawdūdī and Sayyid Qutb

Abū al-Aʿlā Mawdūdī, one of the leading Islamic ideologues of the twentieth century, is considered to be a representative of the statist school of Islamic political theory in this chapter. According to Mawdūdī, there are several characteristics of an Islamic state that can be derived from the Qur'an and *sunna*. In an Islamic state, absolute legal and political sovereignty belongs to Allah alone, and Muslims, His subjects, can only implement *sharīʿa* with limited authority in governance, without any amendments (Mawdūdī, 1960b: 18; Voll and Esposito, 1994).

To clarify these characteristics, it is crucial to understand how statists reinterpreted the political premises of *sharīʿa* in modern terms. *Sharīʿa*, as Mawdūdī defines it, is an all-embracing 'universal order' and 'an organic and integrated whole' that ordains laws for all dimensions of human conduct, political, economic and social alike (1978: 17–20). Sayyid Qutb, another principal thinker in this statist typology, also maintains that the untampered-*sharīʿa* suffices to create a written constitution through which divine law would be applied (1964: 8).[2] Accordingly, for statists, an Islamic moral order in today's world, where *sharīʿa* determines all human acts, would be impossible to realise without the agency of the modern state and its apparatuses (Adams, 1983: 112–13).

For statists, governance is a matter of faith and worship as they approach the issue within the realm of religious obligations. Mawdūdī writes that the cardinal principle of Islamic theology is the sovereignty and authority of God as a Lord (*Rabb*) over His creations. Injunctions are imposed in every sphere of human life from worship to governance. Mawdūdī maintains that the Islamic state is part of 'a broader integrated theology' that showed its essence from the very inception of Islam: Islam was both a political entity and a religion. Qutb also makes a similar claim that the establishment of an Islamic state embodies the cardinal principle of Islam, namely *tawḥīd* (the oneness of God) (2001: 120). For this reason, Qutb argues that the Islamic state is 'not a tool but a fundamental principle of creed. It . . . represented political and ideological obedience to God' (as cited in Moussalli, 2001: 14). As such, the statists' call for an Islamic state is based on their assertion that the immediate application of an Islamic state is obligatory upon Muslims (Adams, 1983: 113).

In general, Mawdūdī engages more with theological discussions about an Islamic state than with its practical aspects. Yet regardless of his neglect of procedural matters,

> Mawdūdī's application of deductive reasoning in his interpretation of the *sharī'ah*, and especially in his theory of the Islamic state, represents a triumph of scripturalist doctrine, both because of its logical coherence and because of its appeal to a new generation of the Muslim intelligentsia. (Binder, 1998: 171)

This theoretical dimension has enabled Mawdūdī to emerge as the most influential and coherent representative of the statist school. His ideas have inspired not only the development of Islamist philosophy, but also Islamic political economy and other contemporary projects of Islamisation throughout the Muslim world. However, Mawdūdī's attempt to implement a programme of the Islamic state in Pakistan has met with little success.

Qutb further developed the nature of the Islamic state that Mawdūdī initially outlined. He developed a political manifesto for its establishment. Two Qur'anic terms, *ḥākimiyya* and *ṭāghūt*, to which Qutb gave a modern interpretation, are crucial in his manifesto. *Ḥākimiyya* refers to the notion of divine sovereignty that precludes human sovereignty in governance as humans' lack of competence to legislate imposes only obedience to divine legislation. Any state that is not based on divine authority is *ṭāghūt* or tyrannical, illegitimate, unjust and against religion (Qutb, 2001: 123).

Qutb develops his conceptualisations of *ḥākimiyya* and *ṭāghūt* through a combination of theological and political reasoning. Qutb's anti-democratic stance can be better understood with reference to ontological notions. Within his overall view of the relationship between Allah and human beings, the idea of divine sovereignty is the foundation of a comprehensive system that endows all human institutions with value. Qutb suggests that 'only in the Islamic 'way' (*minhaj*) are all men liberated from subjection to others, in their subjection to God alone' (1988: 176). Human beings can only live in a free and just political order through their absolute submission to God's sovereignty. Emancipation of human beings from all forms of ideological or political servitude is accompanied by social justice and collective happiness.

It is 'high utopian Islamism', as Andrew March calls it, which unproblematically envisages a comprehensive moral doctrine encompassing moral, political and legal visions for both private and public life (2019: 75). There are two assumptions that guide Qutb's conception of a comprehensive Islam discussed above. The first assumption is centred upon the notion 'the Quran speaks for itself and directly to us, ignoring the chasm of language and context that separates us from seventh century Arabia' (Brown, 2014: 210). The second assumption emphasises the incapacity of moral discernment among humans which necessitates their submission to God's sovereignty.

A legitimate Muslim system of government for Qutb is unique and distinct from all other political regimes. Islamic governance cannot be adequately compared with non-Islamic political institutions, whether democracy or theocracy, regardless of 'any resemblance between Islam and manmade regimes'. For Qutb, the Islamic system is 'divine, complete and comprehensive, shaping society rather than being shaped by it' (Shavit, 2010: 351). This position best reflects the statist approach to democracy. For statists, democracy is essentialised as a Western product. Regardless of its perceived worldly success, democracy cannot be the desired form of governance (Shavid, 2010: 359).

Religion and politics for statists are inseparable and Islam was a state from its very inception. Mawdūdī and Qutb articulated modern theorisations on divine sovereignty and allowed the state to become central to Islamic discourse. In the case of Mawdūdī, the unprecedented reach of the modern state was evident in that it penetrated almost every realm of society. The state and its ideology became the overriding factor in the politics of the Indian subcontinent. In a context filled with ideological and political rivalries, Mawdūdī formulated a distinct model of an Islamic state (Ahmad, 2006: 13). By equating Islam with the ideology of the modern state, Qutb also aimed to pose counter-arguments against competing ideologies and their claims in the 1960s, such as Marxism, socialism, capitalism and Arab nationalism, which reached the Muslim masses (Haddad, 1995: 4).

In the writings of the statists, Asma Afsaruddin argues, Islam is conceived of as a system, polity or ideology rather than a faith (2008: 24). Qutb's arguments centre on the theological distinction between Islamic and non-Islamic systems (*ṭāghūt*). However, Qutb, unlike Mawdūdī, does not present a holistic conceptualisation of the Islamic form of governance because he had not arrived at Mawdūdī's phase of considering how to shape an Islamic state. Although Qutb discusses *ḥākimiyya Allah*, his elaboration, insufficiently, had 'no reference to structure or procedures for implementing or carrying out that regime' (Browers, 2006: 46). Theological terms are related to political notions within a self-enclosed ideological system. Particular answers about which agency will wield the final authority defining and implementing *ḥākimiyya Allah* in law-making in Qutb's writings remain ambiguous.

Mawdūdī and Qutb are not as contemporary as most of the other scholars examined in this work. Therefore, employing their positionality on governance and pluralism may raise concerns about the criteria for their presence in this typology. Yet there are two main reasons for selecting them as representatives of the statist school. First, dogmatic arguments of the statist school necessitate constancy and uniformity in thinking. Statist ideas thus have very limited scope for change and progress with regard to time and context. A period of a few decades does not pose a serious challenge in analysing this line of thinking. Second, the statist school has not to date produced other thinkers comparable to Mawdūdī and Qutb in terms of influence and ideas. Rather, the ideas of Mawdūdī and Qutb have influenced and are esteemed by different social movements and political organisations. These include Jamaat-i-Islami in South Asia, the Muslim Brotherhood in Egypt and elsewhere, Parti Islam se-Malaysia (PAS) and the Islamic Salvation Front (FIS) in Algeria. Abdul Hadi Awang in Malaysia, 'Abd al-Salam Yasin in Morocco and 'Ali Belhadj in Algeria have reflected the palpable effects of Mawdūdī and Qutb in their activism. Recent political thinkers have developed, questioned and reconstructed the ideas of Mawdūdī and Qutb in a contemporary context. Yusuf al-Qaradawi, Ali Bulaç and Rashid al-Ghannushi, the focus of the next category, are among the many Islamists who have been influenced in such a manner. The next section will also outline their differences, and on which grounds they have made a paradigm shift from statism to revivalism.

2. *Revivalists: Yusuf al-Qaradawi, Ali Bulaç, Hayrettin Karaman, Rashid al-Ghannushi*

Revivalists share some common features, such as the denial of the existence of a single model of an Islamic state. They offer alternative modern and pragmatic solutions to politics. Revivalists advocate revisionist understandings of *sharīʿa*. Islamic political principles and directives exist for the construction of political organisations (Afsaruddin, 2008: 25). On the basis of their positions on Islam and political discourses, revivalists are also categorised as Islamists. They represent a middle ground between statists and modernists. Most of the scholars who fall under this category of revivalists, Yusuf al-Qaradawi, Ali Bulaç, Rashid al-Ghannushi and Hayrettin Karaman, are often referred to as moderate Islamists.

Although revivalists do not claim that *sharīʿa* obliges Muslims to establish a certain version of Islamic statehood, they still support the idea that religion cannot be separated from government and political authority. For revivalists, there is a 'distinction', precluding 'unity, congruence, or blending' between religious and political authority, but it is not a 'separation or detachment' (Binder, 1998: 148). Rashid al-Ghannushi (2012) suggests that 'Islam, since its inception, has always combined religion with politics, religion and state'. Yet al-Ghannushi further explains that this does not mean religion and the state are the same. Throughout Muslim history, he notes, 'states remained Islamic not in the sense that their laws and procedures were divinely revealed religion' but in the sense that religion provided Muslims 'with a system of values and principles that would guide our thinking, behaviour, and the regulations of the state to which we aspire' within the context of a particular time and place (al-Ghannushi, 2012). Religious axioms and scriptures are supposed to guide responses to social and political problems. Islam is considered to be the ultimate source of political legitimacy in the Muslim world.

Revivalists do not subscribe to one model of the state. Human experience can shape specific forms of Muslim politics. Muslims themselves are able and should be able to construct political institutions based on a contemporary reading of Islam. Hayrettin Karaman, a renowned Turkish theologian and jurist, suggests that Islam neither defined the concept of a state nor offered a new concept of statehood. Rather, depending on a given set of circumstances, Islam approves, modifies and gives an Islamic quality or annuls existing political practices (Karaman, 2002: 203). Islam has only specified certain qualities as the supreme ideals of governance, such as *tawḥīd* (Oneness of God), *shūrā* (consultation), *al-amr bi al-maʿrūf wa al-nahy ʿan al-munkar* (commanding the right and forbidding the wrong), *jamāʿa* (the group or the community), *ʿadāla* (justice or fairness), *qiyāda* (leadership) and *amāna* (fidelity or trust). These fundamental values by themselves, Karaman argues, do not prescribe a fixed programme for an Islamic state (2003: 255).

Revivalists like Karaman have attempted to reformulate Islamic concepts in light of modern political ideals and practices. They, unlike statists, do not label all the systems coming from the West as un-Islamic. In fact, they display a willingness to accept and adopt democracy through Qur'anic moral guidance to give it an Islamic shading. Revivalists reinterpret concepts such as *shūrā* and *ijmāʿ* (consensus) and equate them with democratic representation and parliamentary system (el-Din, n.d.). *Shūrā* is 'Islam's and Muslims' democracy' in today's world in which the people elect their leaders, supervise them, and dismiss them if they fail to accomplish their public duties (Shavit, 2010: 353). Yusuf al-Qaradawi argues that democratic institutions in politics, such as political parties, free elections, public participation in governance, free legislation and a parliament, intended to support justice and challenge tyranny, best exemplify the principal goals of Islamic governance at present. Thus, he claims that the Muslim world must 'take the best elements of democracy' and implement them under the guidance of the ethical framework of Islam to ensure they do not clash with Islamic norms (as cited in Rutherford, 2006: 709–19).

This conditional support for democracy is also evident in Rashid al-Ghannushi's ideas. He remarks that 'the highest objective of all divine messages is to establish justice and realize people's interests, and this is done through the use of reason in light of the guidelines, objectives, values, and principles provided by religion' (al-Ghannushi, 2012). The Islamic form of democratic governance, according to al-Ghannushi, is guided by Islamic norms. However, al-Ghannushi states that if the establishment of Muslim governance is not possible, in order to promote the values of development, pluralism, an independent judiciary, freedom of expression and freedom of religion, Muslims should 'participate in the establishment of a secular democratic regime' to serve their best interests and well-being (Shavit, 2010: 356). As opposed to the statist's Islamic state, al-Ghannushi's account of Islamic democracy combines God's sovereignty with the *umma*'s (peoples') sovereignty 'by transforming the oligarchic instrumentalization of divine law into popular ownership of the sharia' (March, 2019: 225).

Karaman argues democracy can be endorsed by Muslim states' functional mechanism in a system of governance. He addresses the modern premises of human rights and democracy in Islamic texts and adopts Western political institutions in Islamic political thought. Yet Karaman offers greater adherence to the procedural aspects of democracy than to its normative aspects. In other words, he is committed to the democratic process, although not to the universal claims of liberal democratic norms. Karaman (2014c) points out that 'the greatest problem with democracy is . . . sovereignty'. In Islam, the final authority and last resort belong to Allah, while in a democracy they both belong to the public. An Islamic way of democracy, or a democracy that is Islamically valid, should promote 'an Islamically bounded authority, under Islamic reference, instead of the absolute sovereignty of people' (Karaman, 2014c).

Support for democracy, according to Karaman, is not only motivated by procedural factors but is also conditional, like al-Qaradawi's. He views democracy as the best man-made political system in the modern era, to be adopted without its liberal value system (Karaman, 2014a). If the establishment of 'a state whose main reference is Islam' is not possible, as a second-best solution, Karaman proposes, Muslims should participate in creating a new ideology of democracy of Islam. Islamic democracy would reflect Muslims' own 'particular program of modernity' under the guidance of revelation rather than copying a putative universal Western mould (Karaman, 2014b). In other words, '[t]he issue of democracy is then a matter of *darura* (necessity)' to obtain 'the best possible medium to improve society' and 'to potentially reach a better condition' (Guida, 2010: 364).

Ali Bulaç also shares similar views about democracy with other revivalist thinkers. For Bulaç (2012b), 'a form of government Muslims can accept without a *fait accompli* or without finding themselves in a crisis of legitimacy can be summed up as one which conforms to God's will and the will of the people'. God's will, Bulaç explains, is manifested in *shari'a*, which relates to every sphere of life, and '[f]or a Muslim, the desire to live according to the divine legal order never diminishes' (1998: 177). Muslims should develop a new model of democratic government based on Islamic beliefs. This government would be more morally adequate for Muslims and function better socially and politically in Muslim societies without the need to import a form from the West (Bulaç, 1998: 169). Many man-made regimes are present in the world and democracy appears to be the most successful. Furthermore, it is possible that in the future democracy will be replaced with a better political regime. However, Bulaç remarks that Islam takes its power from revelation that will continue to be relevant until *ķiyāma* (the end of time). Thus, the analysis of religion within a democratic framework leads to democracy becoming a principal criterion for discerning good and bad, right and wrong, and a guide for life. This would mean accepting democracy as a philosophy of life, as opposed to a political regime alone, which would involve intervention in the sphere of religion. Bulaç (2013) therefore warns that forcing Islam to be tested and to abide by democracy would, intentionally or unintentionally, make the latter an undesirable alternative form of religion.

In general, the revivalist support for democracy ranges from an entirely mechanistic and functionalist understanding to a pragmatic recognition of its contemporary relevance. Political compatibility between democratic processes and Islamic principles assumes that the normative foundations of society will influence democratic institutions. A democracy will emerge in harmony with Islamic morality from the dominant role played by religion. A general characteristic of Islamists is their conviction that the foundations of society and the popular will in predominantly Muslim societies naturally support Islamic values.

Revivalist support for democracy in the political sense is motivated by the recognition that it creates a fair, representative and free political environment similar to Islam's objectives. However, revivalists also raise some ontological and epistemological concerns regarding democracy vis-à-vis Islam. Blind imitation of the West is rejected in favour of restrictions on public sovereignty and personal freedoms when they contradict Islam (Karaman, 2014c; al-Qaradawi, 2002). Greater commitment to the procedural aspects of democracy is present among revivalists, but there is also a large distance from Western norms typically associated with these institutions.

An unconditional embrace of democracy is absent among revivalists. Selective, or rather reductionist, appropriations of democracy are evident in this category. Bruce Rutherford observes the ambivalence surrounding the definition of democracy, that can lead to the conclusion that revivalists are either in favour of or critical of 'full democracy', as a contrast between institutions and values respectively (2006: 730–1).[3] Revivalists adopting democracy have been accused of duplicity and tactical doublespeak (Dagi, 2012). Islamist functionalism, it should be noted, is not necessarily a manifestation of expediency for the acquisition of power. The ambivalence observed above is a product of an ontological and intellectual crisis, from which modern Islamic political thought suffers due to the absence of a political theory approach to Islamic moral and political reasoning among the scholars mentioned in this section.

The apparently instrumentalist approach of revivalists distinguishes them from modernists. Modernists' support for democratic principles and foundations is motivated by their conviction that the application of democracy and its premises are both universal and Islamic. The theoretical difference between revivalists and modernists is derived from their differing approaches to the Islamic sacred texts. While revivalists are more scripturalist, modernists employ historicist methods that at times challenge mainstream Muslim thought. The category of progressives in this chapter will contain further discussion about the resolution of the ontological and epistemological problems of Muslim thought with reference to democracy.

3. *Modernists: Fazlur Rahman, Khaled Abou El Fadl, Muhammad al-Jabri*

Muslim modernists seek a return to the essence of 'true' Islam. As a prominent pioneer of Islamic modernist thought, Fazlur Rahman writes that fundamentalists, traditionalists and modernists all want to 'return to the original and pristine Islam and perform *ijtihād* on that basis' (1982: 142). Yet their main difference, for Rahman, is that both traditionalists and fundamentalists are unable to go from 'historical Islam', consisting of time-bound customs and conventions, to the universal principles of Islam. Rahman and Khaled Abou El Fadl, another influential representative of the modernist school, both maintain that to take historical aspects of Islam, especially Islamic rulings, as universal and unchangeable, 'meant to be literally applied in all times and climes', is 'erroneous' and 'unfortunate' (Rahman, 1967: 216; Abou El Fadl, 2005: 11–12). Muslims should instead understand the background or 'occasions' of each verse and the principles derived from them to discover the true spirit and objectives of the revelation (Sonn, n.d.).

Sharīʿa is a principle-based mechanism for Rahman rather than a universalist, one-size-fits-all rule. In modernist thought, it consists of prescriptive or moral guidelines of revelation that are considered to be the sacred, permanent and unchanging message of Islam (Rahman, 1982: 141). Separating 'normative understandings of Islam from historical conceptions of Islamic orthodoxy' has enabled contextualised, dynamic and progressive interpretations of *sharīʿa* (Fadel, 2009a: 190). Modernists favour continuous reforms in different ages according to differing circumstances, which would, in turn, lead to the adoption of the necessary legal and political reformation in Muslim societies and their socio-economic and political advancement. The ostensible division between notions belonging to Islamic tradition and notions belonging to the Western heritage was overcome by modernists, with direct implications for their approach to democracy (Rahman, 1980: 451).

Moreover, Rahman challenges the statists' 'confusion over the concept of "the Sovereignty of God"' as meaning God is the sole legislator in state law (1967: 208). The statist account of *sharīʿa* suggests that 'the divine legislative will seeks to regulate all human interactions' as it is a 'complete' moral and legal code which offers prescriptions for every eventuality (Abou El Fadl, 2004: 9). Abou El Fadl argues that the issue of legislation being a divine sphere, not left to human beings, is 'a fatal fiction that is not defensible from the point of view of Islamic theology' (2003: 16). Similarly, *sharīʿa*, as Rahman proclaims, is the 'assembly of Divine imperatives' that carry primarily 'a moral character'. Thus, it is not 'an actual formal code of particular and specific enactments but is coterminous with the "good"' (Rahman, 1979: 115). The moral nature of the *sharīʿa*, Abou El Fadl maintains, derives from the premise that God 'does not seek to regulate all human affairs' (2004: 9). For Abou El Fadl, Allah values human intuition and reason as well as human freedom. His divine sovereignty over His creation as the Lord of the Universe does not imply direct rule over mundane life. Human beings, in the position of God's vicegerent, are granted substantial latitude to regulate their own matters with the guidance of His message. According to Abou El Fadl,

'God's sovereignty provides no escape from the burdens of human agency' (2004: 9) in

> pursuing justice through social cooperation and mutual assistance ... establishing a non-autocratic, consultative method of governance; and institutionalizing mercy and compassion in social interactions. (2004: 5)

While recognising *sharī'a* as 'the comprehensive principle of the total way of life', Rahman questions the possibilities of arriving at a perfect knowledge of its rulings and reaching and expressing the Divine will in its entirety, as the statists assume (1979: 101). Abou El Fadl also recognises that '*Shari'ah* as conceived by God is flawless, but as understood by human beings *Shari'ah* is imperfect and contingent' since divine perfection cannot be approximated by human effort (2004: 34) – for 'the Shari'ah, for the most part, is not explicitly dictated by God' as there is a 'vast array of possible subjective' interpretative determinations and applications of the divine law (Abou El Fadl, 2003: 64; 2004: 30). There could be different and equally valid legal responses to a single issue from the Islamic point of view, with none of these making the claim to solely represent the Divine.

Muhammad al-Jabri, a renowned Islamic modernist of the twentieth century, also maintains that Islamic law and jurisprudence, inattentive to contemporary events, still reflect the social, political and economic conditions under which the classical jurisprudential schools formed. Al-Jabri blames this unfortunate state of affairs on the preoccupation with theological arguments rather than practical ones. Contemporary Muslims need different discourses from those produced by the classical *mujtahidūn*, who should continue to inspire the project of reform (al-Jabri, 2009: 4). Similarly, Abou El Fadl argues that, in implementing Islamic law, contemporary Muslim scholars are overwhelmingly concerned with *sharī'a*-compliant legal codes and punishments and not with the moral intent of law, such as the dignity and freedom of human beings. Abou El Fadl emphasises that law in this account, neglecting the governed, serves to cherish what its protagonists mistakenly believe to be the Divine will. He advocates the pursuit of a just system of limited government and the rule of law in which people's welfare is fulfilled (Abou El Fadl, 2003: 25–9). Abou El Fadl also notes that '*awlawiyyat al-Islam*' (the priorities of Islam) within the legal and political realm ought to be how one establishes justice, not how to establish an Islamic government, regardless of its ability to support justice. (2002: 110)

Thus, modernists propose the necessity for 'the rebuilding of a conceptual methodology in *al-sharia*, based on new premises and contemporary [legal] "intent"' in order to overcome the dogma-centred understandings of religion that impede social and political development (al-Jabri, 2009: 81).

Modernists assert that there does not exist only one form of acceptable government, and the concept of state is not discussed in classical Islamic discourse. The first notion advances that in the Qur'an neither the form of government nor the relationship between religion, governance and legislation is addressed. There are only certain ideals and values prescribed by Islam, but they do not indicate a legal necessity for establishing a specific institution for believers to practise a moral life (Abou El Fadl, 2004: 5). The second assumption, for al-Jabri, is related to the classical Islamic concept of governance discussed within the Sunni theory of the caliphate. Yet the theory has not dealt with the state as an institution, but the person who will rule by *sharī'a* (al-Jabri, 2009: 35). Thus, al-Jabri argues that the statists' advocacy of an Islamic state is not only modern but also 'foreign to Islamic thought, with roots and terminology found in the European civilizational model' (2009: 31).

In addition, the statist account of an Islamic state insists God is the political and legal sovereign. According to this understanding, the authority of the people to legislate is, in democracy, equated with *shirk*. In its opposing narrative the modernist school presents two counter-arguments to this statist view. First, it challenges the notion of an Islamic state as the implementor of God's sovereignty and the embodiment of God's will (Rahman, 1967: 208). Abou El Fadl explains that state law can never be equated with *sharī'a* since 'the law relies on the subjective agency of the state for its articulation and enforcement'. Otherwise, the codification of *sharī'a* would imply a disclosure that 'the failure of the law of the state is, in fact, the failure of God's law' rather than a failure of human understanding (Abou El Fadl, 2010: 140). A code, even if inspired by *sharī'a*, is not *sharī'a* since 'all laws articulated and applied in a state are thoroughly human and should be treated as such' (Abou El Fadl, 2004: 36).

Second, modernists argue that the ideals and values prescribed by Islam do not indicate a legal necessity for establishing Islamic governance for believers to practise a moral life (Abou El Fadl, 2004: 5). However, for Rahman, 'the Muslim State is an organization set up by the Muslim society in order to implement the will of the society and no more', to promote where the Muslim people, guided by revelation, 'are the Sovereign and the law maker' (Rahman, 1967: 209). According to al-Jabri, the goal of the state 'is to find the best solution for the problem of the rule, by making or obliging the rulers to submit to the will of the ruled, through organisations and institutions freely elected by all mature members of the nation' (2009: 131). Al-Jabri further argues that there exist two contemporary political options in terms of political systems for Muslim peoples to live under: either democracy or dictatorship. There is 'no third alternative', and there is only one option to actualise justice, human rights, accountable government and the rule of law, and that is a democracy (al-Jabri, 2009: 156).

Abou El Fadl explicitly asserts that a democratic form of government best promotes the social and political values of Islam. The tradition of Islamic political thought contains 'both interpretive and practical possibilities that can be developed into a democratic system' (Abou El Fadl, 2004: 5). Democratic values do not contradict any of the values promoted by Islam. On the contrary, Abou El Fadl believes that although democracy and Islam might have 'separate moral ontologies, they share a common normative basis for practical commitments for just and representative governance' (2004: 4). Through democracy, Muslims can produce a discourse of rights and law that promotes Islamic moral principles. However, this discourse of rights and laws cannot claim to exhaust the perfection of divinity. Human attempts to understand and pursue divine guidance are evident in this process. Abou El Fadl maintains that democratic constitutionalism provides 'the greatest *potential* for promoting ethical imperatives and justice, exemplifying moral virtue and protecting human dignity, 'without making God responsible for human injustice or the infliction of degradation by human beings upon one another' (2000: 10). In an ideal democracy, 'no single person or group becomes the infallible representative of divinity' (Abou El Fadl, 2003: 10, 62).

Overall, modernists provide a normative commitment to democracy by justifying it on Islamic grounds as the best system for realising Islamic ethical aspirations. Modernist ideas about the moral compatibility between Islam and democratic governance need further theorisation with regard to the role of religion, state and law. Modernists believe that God grants people the prerogative to exercise political authority. Yet they leave the implications of an Islamic normative order for the organisation of communal life, law and public morality underdeveloped. The next section will examine progressives, who, in their advocacy of a democratic order, also support a normative separation between religion and political authority.

4. Progressives: Abdullahi An-Na'im, Asghar Ali Engineer, Mohammad Talbi

Progressive Muslim thinkers aim to reconcile Islam, secularism and democracy while differentiating between the sacred and the political. Abdullahi Ahmed An-Na'im is one of the most influential representatives of contemporary progressive Muslim thought, who challenges statists' arguments. An-Na'im believes that the concept of an Islamic state emerged from social, economic and historical contexts rather than being purely theological. Although the states that reigned over the Muslim world 'did seek Islamic legitimacy', the state in the history of Muslims was never 'Islamic' in the sense used by many present-day scholars (An-Na'im, 2008: 7). The concept of an Islamic state is a post-colonial construct based on a Western model of the state and an instrument of social engineering by the elite to subdue the people in their attempts to gain legitimacy. More importantly, An-Na'im points out that 'an Islamic state is conceptually impossible because, as a political institution, a state cannot be characterized as either Islamic or non-Islamic' (1999: 29, 40).

Similarly, Asghar Ali Engineer,[4] was an Indian intellectual, also argues that the statist claim of an Islamic state, a recent invention, is historically naive and theoretically misguided (1985: 7). He specifically focuses on secularism in his writings. Engineer asserts that 'there has never been any fixed or universally acceptable form of Islamic state' at any time in the history of the Muslim people (1985: 7). Even among the highest religious authorities, there has been no consensus on this matter. In essence, Engineer (2006b) contends that the values promoted in the Qur'an are indispensable to a Muslim society rather than to a definitive concept of an Islamic state. The Qur'an 'is concerned with morality rather than polity' in the establishment and maintenance of a just, egalitarian and virtuous society, with political matters left to human agency (Engineer, 1985: 199).

While Engineer questions the existence of an Islamic state, he acknowledges that a polity existed in the Prophet Muhammad's Madina. It was a primitive polity that was strongly influenced by Arab customs and local traditions and did not represent a new and purely Islamic of statehood (Engineer, 1985: 38). He also believes the institution of the caliphate that evolved over time is based on the consensus of the early and medieval *'ulamā'* and jurists who thought that religion could not be separated from politics. Thus, the principle of *dīn wa dawla* (religion and state) was 'a human construct' rather than inspired by 'a divine revelation' (Engineer, 2006a).

In this domain, Engineer concedes that religion is 'a culturally mediated phenomenon', which shapes Muslims' interpretations of *sharī'a* and even of Islam itself (2002: 32). Absence of a modern political culture upholding a secular and democratic government in the Muslim world cannot be attributed to the Islamic faith but must be attributed to Muslim cultures (Engineer, 2002: 33). Islam is distinguished from Islamic cultures by Engineer, for 'we cannot say secularism is essentially un-Islamic or anti-Islamic in any fundamental way' (2002: 30). Secularism here is used in a political sense, not in a philosophical sense, since political secularism creates social and political space for religious communities, but these communities need not support the philosophical notion of secularism (Engineer, 2006a).

Mohammad Talbi, similar to Engineer, conceives the Qur'an to be a book of moral guidelines and ethical principles rather than a constitution.[5] There exists neither a Qur'anic theory of a proper form of Islamic governance nor an Islamic political structure that 'has institutional or moral authority upon Muslims' (Nettler, 2000: 53–4). Talbi emphasises that Allah created human beings with *fiṭra* (innate intuition) so that they can implement Islamic ethical principles in their lives and times (Nettler, n.d.). He criticises both the blanket understanding of *sharī'a* based on classical schools and the approach of 'allying scripture to all sorts of modern political causes' without a historical reading of the Qur'an (al-Dakkak, 2011: 84).

An-Na'im puts forward a detailed conceptualisation of *sharī'a* as it relates to government. He understands *sharī'a* to be a 'historically conditioned interpretation of Islam', representing one among many alternatives, without being 'divinely predetermined' (An-Na'im, 2002b: 5; 1999: 33). Today, what we call *sharī'a* 'was, in fact, the product of a very slow, gradual and spontaneous process of interpretation of the Qur'an, and collection, verification and interpretation of Sunnah' during the first three centuries of Islamic history derived from the interpretations and methodologies of classical *fuqahā'* (An-Na'im, 1999: 33). Essentially, for An-Na'im, *sharī'a* is not Islam, but is rather 'effectively what Muslims make out of Islam', with the concomitant argument that there cannot be a body of individuals or an institution that exercises a monopoly over the *sharī'a* (2008: 10). It is for this reason that An-Na'im believes that

> Shari'a principles cannot be enacted or enforced as the positive law of any country without being subjected to selection among competing interpretations, which are all deemed to be legitimate by the traditional Shari'a doctrine. (2008: 10)

An Islamic authority that enforces an absolutist interpretation of *sharī'a* and enacts it as state law risks denying and eventually destroying the diversity in Islamic discourses, ultimately leading to tyranny (An-Na'im, 2005: 74). Like other progressive theorists, An-Na'im emphasises that *sharī'a*'s transformation into positive law or a set of rules is necessarily selective. However, Muslims adhere to *sharī'a* as the set of principles through which, and as the way via which, to understand and practise religion. The *sharī'a* has an undeniable importance in a believer's life as 'the source of a religiously sanctioned normative system' (An-Na'im, 1999: 29). Accordingly, laicism, which undermines the moral and social status of religions, is impossible within Muslim contexts, in which an agreement exists about living in line with 'private sharia of family law and devotional rites' (1987: 318).

An-Na'im criticises laicism for restricting religion to the private sphere. A liberal, secular democratic structure is praised for its ability to promote an environment for voluntary reflection and conviction through which to observe religion in private and public life. Liberal democracy, An-Na'im suggests, can overcome the weaknesses of laicism by providing a sufficient space for ethical Islamic commitments (2008: 203). On the other hand, he also emphatically rejects the exercise of coercive power by an Islamic political or legal authority (An-Na'im, 2008: 6). A liberal secular structure is the most ideal solution to managing the intricate relationship between the state and religion. One religious belief is not favoured by the state over others, and the state interacts equally with and responds to the demands of all religions and belief systems (An-Naʿim, 2000: 63). In Muslim contexts, liberal democracy can create a synergy between religion and secularism to promote Islam's existence in the public life of the community of believers, and politics (An-Naʿim, 2002b: 8).

In his article 'Arabs and Democracy: A Record of Failure', Talbi expresses his support for liberal democracy in the Arab world (2000: 59). He claims that 'Islam's universal human value . . . [is] in our historical epoch . . . most likely to be expressed in democracy' (Nettler, 2000: 55). When the Qur'anic text is read in accordance with a *maqāṣid*-based understanding, Talbi argues, we conclude that one cannot truly practise faith if the state eliminates freedom of choice. Religious ideals in a modern setting can best flourish in a democracy (al-Dakkak, 2011: 87). Unlike the revivalists attempting to reconcile democracy with *shūrā*, Talbi believes neither that democracy needs to be legitimised with reference to any Islamic tradition nor that there is any logical connection between these two concepts. He states that *shūrā* was a particular system in a particular time and place and that democracy is another system located in its own time. Thus, democracy is an achievement of our age and a system that best represents the voice of the people with the associated values of human rights and pluralism. Therefore, for Talbi, a progressive and critical reading of Islamic ideals in today's world leads to democracy, as opposed to *shūrā* or any other political structure (Nettler, 2000: 55).

Talbi opposes the dogmatic, absolutist and transcendent approach to political systems. A new system not confined to pre-modern models and classical scholarship would better exemplify universal Islamic ideals. Talbi criticises thinkers such as Khaled Abou El Fadl who argue for the compatibility of Islam and democracy. Talbi is against finding any equivalence between religious and political concepts, and religious and political institutions are found to be wanting. He notes that democracy is a modern concept that has existed neither in the Islamic tradition nor Western Judaeo-Christian history (al-Dakkak, 2011: 90–3). To equate religious ideals, which provide universal values for a just and virtuous society, with political systems, such as democracy, is mistaken. Islam does not impose and cannot be represented by a political system. Talbi strongly affirms that democracy is the best form of government at present. Muslims should give full support and endorsement to liberal democracy until a better system emerges (Nettler, 2000: 55). Collective decision-making can be used to choose the best political system rather than equating a political system with Islam and precluding all other possibilities. Democratisation should also be a democratic process (Talbi, 2005: 79 as cited in al-Dakkak, 2011: 100).

Progressives oppose the statist assertion that Muslims should not have different interpretations of religion. An informal understanding of religion is endorsed in a challenge to religious authorities as well as traditional scholarship on *sharīʿa*. For progressives, *sharīʿa* is a product of individual interpretations of the divine and is located in the sphere between God and human beings. By attenuating the relationship between Islam and state, progressives are able to focus solely on Islam's demand for an ethical society. Progressive support can be observed for the secular state to achieve the common good of this community.

To conclude this section on governance, competing formulations of political authority and democracy are derived from different interpretations of the relationship between God and human beings. Putative Islamic imperatives and claims of governance have been discussed. For statists, not only does an Islamic claim for a state exist, but its immediate application is also a sine qua non for Muslims. They propose a blueprint for the formation of an Islamic state where *sharīʿa* is the official law. The only possible way for Muslims to live a just and Islamic life is in a *sharīʿa* state. Statists consider governance to be a theological matter, for the Islamic state is the embodiment of *tawhīd* and other states not based on Islamic law epitomise *shirk*.

According to revivalists, although governance is still related to theology, they approach the issue more pragmatically than statists. Revivalists do not deny Western conceptions of governance, as demonstrated by their partial support for some concepts such as democracy. Revivalists also engage in mainly Islamic articulations of democracy. Context and time are important in the process of formulating Islamic political claims. For modernists, the idea of an Islamic state is 'foreign to Islamic thought, with roots and terminology found in the European civilizational model' and 'Shari'ah law, as a codified State-sponsored set of commands, is a serious break with tradition and a radical departure from the classical epistemology of Islamic law' (al-Jabri, 2009: 31; Abou El Fadl, 2003: 63). Modernists are against purist Islamic political solutions to contemporary conditions. Statists reject democracy, according to Abou El Fadl, due to their being 'far more anti-Western than they are pro-Islamic' (2003: 13). For modernists, implementation of liberal democracy best expresses Islam's moral values and aspirations in Muslim-majority countries.

Progressives share the view with modernists that the modern concept of an Islamic state suffers from rational, theological and historical incoherence. Yet unlike modernists, progressives make an appeal to a secular state in direct contrast to a divine foundation for governance. They also both propose plural readings and interpretations of the sacred texts of Islam. Hermeneutic arguments allow modernists to highlight the limitations of human interpretations of the divine. However, they insist that these limitations do not rule out agreement on certain norms and rules, which are open to constant adaptation, inspired as they are by Islamic texts in their social and political lives. Progressives espouse an individualist and private account of religion that modernists do not entirely share. Traditional scholarship is utilised by modernists to make a case for liberal democracy at odds with progressives, who do not consult tradition. Abou El Fadl writes as a jurist steeped in a jurisprudential tradition from which normative imperatives emerge through the symbolic construct of the *sharī'a*. Further, modernists tend to argue that the classical Islamic discourse has adequate resources for supporting a liberal democratic state. Progressives, however, do not rest their political positions in religious precepts from tradition or classical jurisprudence.

This chapter will now continue the preceding discussion with a section on pluralism where the ideas of the four schools of thought will be discussed. I aim to identify the relevant theoretical concepts for the later theorisation of Muslim democracy, as well as to reveal obstacles confronting the formation of a democratic opening in Muslim societies.

III. Muslim Political Thought on Pluralism

In modern Islamic thought, the debate about pluralism has centred on Islamic values concerning diversity, political toleration and accommodation of political and religious differences, the status of religious minorities and the status of women. This section will examine how statist, revivalist, modernist and progressive schools of modern Islamic political thought formulate principles on religious and political pluralism. The issue of pluralism in modern Islamic political thought has implications not only for followers of other religions but also for followers of different interpretations of Islam.

1. Statists

Statists often appropriate concepts of classical jurisprudence with modern emphases in the recognition of differences and tensions between values. One prominent example is the status of *ahl al-dhimma* awarded to non-Muslims living under an Islamic authority expounded in classical texts. According to Abū al-Aʿlā Mawdūdī, the modern Islamic state is an ideological state that envisages two kinds of citizens: Muslims philosophically committed to the principles of the state, and non-Muslim *dhimmī*s who 'have affirmed to remain loyal and obedient to the Islamic state' (1960a: 265). For Mawdūdī, non-Muslims citizens should enjoy security, dignity and rights in a modern Islamic framework (1960a: 263). Non-Muslims have rights for the 'preservation of the self and dignity, equality before the law, and maintenance of equal civil law – with the exception of allowing them to eat pork and drink wine and trade in them', preaching their faith, and participating in public arenas (Moussalli, 2001: 149).

The notion of the Islamic state as an ideological state implies two main policies for minorities. First, the state must be administered and run by Muslims. Additionally, high-ranking officials should not only be Muslim, but committed Muslims who live according to *sharīʿa*. In other words, for Mawdūdī, only *'true'* Muslims who endorse his version of Islamic ideology can effectively work to achieve the ideal Islamic society (Adams, 1983: 122). Mawdūdī insists *dhimmī*s cannot be appointed to senior political positions because they would not strive to implement Islamic principles or make sacrifices to defend Islamic beliefs when that is necessary. Thus, non-Muslims should not be given the authority to make general state policies that concern the entire population (Mawdūdī, 1960a: 264).

The second policy of the Islamic state as an ideological enterprise is manifested in its account of citizenship. *Dhimmī*s have their traditional guarantees of protection. However, these guarantees do not include full political expression as regards issues in governance. For instance, Mawdūdī claims that non-Muslims should not vote in general elections (Moussalli, 2001: 149). He justifies this stance by referring to the 'absence of even a single instance'

> where a *Zimmi* [*dhimmī*] may have been made a member of the Parliament, or the Governor of a province, or the Qadi, or the Director of any Government department, or the commander of the Army or a Minister of the Government or may have been ever allowed to participate in the elections of Caliphs. (Mawdūdī, 1960a: 264)

Mawdūdī also expresses a more pragmatist view on other issues. Minorities should be subject to the same taxation as Muslims so the secular state would not seem more favourable to them (Rahman, 1986: 20).

Sayyid Qutb holds a more rigid position than Mawdūdī on pluralism and civil society, in various respects. First, Qutb writes that religious minorities are free to keep and practise their faith in their own ways. However, in order to achieve and maintain a pious society, non-Islamic or anti-Islamic aspects should be restricted to the private realm. For instance, non-Muslim ideological groups and members of other faiths and irreligious groups should not be permitted to operate in the public sphere, such as in forming political parties (Moussalli, 2001: 113). This restriction is imposed on these groups because Qutb believes that ideological and religious conflicts within a society hinder its security, peace, solidarity and well-being (Moussalli, 1999: 99). In general, Qutb excludes the possibility of a genuine multi-religious civil society or multi-party system. Opposition from both non-Muslims and Muslims who hold 'unauthentic' views should be contained in Qutb's ideas. He suggests the death penalty both for non-Muslims who refuse to pay *jizya* (poll tax) and for Muslims who 'emulate the deviant ways of the People of the Book' (Haddad, 1995: 10).

Pluralist values remain under-developed within the statist school. The relevance of their ideas for the search for a pluralist democratic society, in which all citizens and groups gain recognition, is severely limited due to their theological understanding of an Islamic state. The particularities of the context in which statist scholars have produced their works has influenced them to concentrate on the establishment of an Islamic state. Furthermore, the strengthening of a rejectionist and exclusionist discourse against tolerance and pluralism can be traced back to the scholars' personal circumstances, evidenced by Qutb's experience of imprisonment and physical and mental torture (Moussalli, 1999: 97; 2001: 63).

2. Revivalists

Revivalists such as Rashid al-Ghannushi, Hayrettin Karaman, Yusuf al-Qaradawi and Ali Bulaç have written extensively on the issue of pluralism. Their critical reading of Islamic values in the modern context has led to a more tolerant approach to the subject.

Rashid al-Ghannushi lays the foundation for religious, cultural, political and ideological pluralism in Islam through retaining the *maqāṣid* of modernised traditional concepts. Minorities, al-Ghannushi argues, should enjoy equal citizenship rights for political representation and religious freedom (Yousif, 2000: 36). Non-Muslims can exercise their rights to vote, to run for elections, to be represented in parliament and government, and to form political parties that represent their interests (Moussalli, 1999: 95). He recognises the merits of multi-party and parliamentary systems in enabling all groups in society to have and express their religious, irreligious or anti-religious political orientations. In such a system, al-Ghannushi maintains, social justice and human rights can be realised (Haddad, 1995: 17). Al-Ghannushi also disagrees with the statist position of prohibiting non-Muslims from filling key posts for the general well-being of the faith and society. Political appointment should be based on a meritocratic criterion and non-Muslims can participate in any form of activity within the mandate and parameters of the law (Moussalli, 2001: 157).

However, al-Ghannushi still adheres to the traditional view that the head of state in a Muslim country should be a Muslim (Saeed, 2007: 317). Similarly, Yusuf al-Qaradawi also recognises that non-Muslims within an Islamic territory should enjoy all rights and share duties with their Muslim counterparts. Non-Muslims can be appointed to chief posts such as ministries and work in any high-ranking position in the bureaucracy, diplomatic service and army. However, non-Muslims cannot hold governmental positions that were traditionally occupied by the Prophet Muhammad or by the caliphs as a means of religious presentation (i.e. *imama* or the presidency) (Moussalli, 2001: 153).

In addition, al-Qaradawi argues that religious freedom is neither absolute nor without responsibility for both Muslims and non-Muslims, for minorities should respect the sanctity of Islam in the public sphere and be cautious that their actions should not undermine social harmony (Yousif, 2000: 37). On this issue, Karaman (2014c) also writes that under an Islamic authority, although the state cannot intrude into the private sphere and reveal people's personal matters, public acts that contradict Islamic law fall under the legal responsibility or mandate of the state. Karaman concedes that non-Muslims are not obligated to abide by Islamic law in public like their Muslim peers, with the one general exception that 'universal ugliness', acts that are universally prohibited by other monotheistic, Abrahamic religions, such as Judaism and Christianity, should be banned for Muslims and non-Muslims alike. He explains that Islam, in contradistinction to democracy, lacking a divine reference and making no claims to absolute truth, imposes specific normative boundaries on pluralism. Thus, under an Islamic system, the ability of non-Muslims to live 'quite freely' is not absolute and is restricted by certain 'universal ugliness' (Karaman, 2014c). In general, revivalists outline the fulfilment of conditions for individuals, groups, associations, political parties or forms of opposition to enjoy their freedoms in a Muslim-majority society. The scope of pluralism determined by the foundational principles of Islam is to be respected, and freedoms should be practised in a sensible way without endangering the interests and social well-being of the community.

In addition to religious and political pluralism, revivalist thinkers discuss pluralism among Muslims. Al-Qaradawi expresses his support for *ikhtilāf* (disagreement) in Islamic discourse and believes the plurality of views within the Muslim community and scholarship should be welcomed (Zaman, 2005: 65). Karaman also pursues an inclusive approach to relations among Muslims. For instance, Karaman adopts a historical approach to the development of the *madhāhib*. The *madhāhib* were a natural consequence of human interpretations of revelation in different cultures, times, heritages, needs and perspectives, which should not turn into a matter of conflict, separation and exclusion within the *umma* (Karaman, 2014c).

Al-Ghannushi revisits the apostasy debate through his reinterpretation of texts and history in the context of a discussion on internal pluralism. He supports freedom of belief and disbelief while rejecting the traditional ruling of capital punishment for erstwhile Muslims who abandon or renounce Islam. According to al-Ghannushi:

> The judgement on apostasy is in the hereafter. Abu Bakr, the trustworthy, when he fought the apostates, he fought them because of their political rebellion against Islam. It was not because of their position on creed.
> (Saeed, 2007: 316)

Revivalists are convinced Islam's historical success and current potential can create a pluralistic society. Al-Qaradawi contends that Islam gave birth to a more tolerant and pluralistic environment for internal disagreements and minorities than its Abrahamic peers, whose achievements can only be understood in evaluating its contemporaries in given times and places (Moussalli, 2001: 154). Renewed adherence to Islamic values and ideals, according to revivalists, can pave the way for Muslims to again develop new systems and institutions for accommodating diversity and difference.

The goal of revival has inspired such as Ali Bulaç and many intellectuals in the Muslim world. Bulaç's theorising of politics contains references to the Charter of Medina (*Mīthāq al-Madīna*). The Charter of Medina brought Muslims, Jews and pagan Arabs together in a single political community under the leadership of the Prophet Muhammad (Bulaç, 1998: 174). This document, believed by some to be the first written constitution in history, specified the rights and obligations of the groups that constituted the political community. The representatives of these groups 'agreed upon the basic principles constituting the foundations of a new "city-state" as stated in the Charter and differences among them were left to the autonomous sphere' (Bulaç, 1998: 170, 174). Muslims were granted the right of central governance in the city of Medina while ensuring the right of self-government of other groups. Bulaç argues that it was an agreement forming a political community reached as a result of participation and negotiations of interests between Muslims and of non-Muslim groups as opposed to the domination of one group over others (Kösebalaban, n.d.a). Everyone in such a society was entitled to live by the principle of 'you are what you are' (Bulaç, 2006: 190). The Charter sought to maintain the self-government of different groups in a multi-religious and multi-ethnic pluralist framework based on religious and legal autonomy (Bulaç, 2006: 190–3).

Hayrettin Karaman has made a similar contribution to existing scholarship on the Charter of Medina. Non-Muslims, mainly Jews, had their own legal courts and mechanisms through which to govern their lives. However, when Jews could not solve their issues by themselves, they often consulted a higher judicial authority in the person of the Prophet Muhammad. When he was approached to settle a dispute by non-Muslims, the Prophet Muhammad asked the contending parties to decide on their preferred legal system: the Torah, the Qur'an, universal ideals of justice, or Jewish customs. An earlier form of genuine legal pluralism appears to have existed in which Islamic law was binding only on Muslims (Karaman, 2008). In Bulaç's words, the prophet acted as an 'arbitrator', not as a judge, for the Medinan non-Muslim population (Bulaç, 2006: 190–3).

In contrast to the statist conflation of religious and political identity, al-Ghannushi also resorts to the historical example of the Charter of Medina. He suggests that the Charter recognises the difference between religious and political belonging by considering Jews and Muslims as members of different religious nations while also consisting of a common and distinct political nation (al-Ghannushi, 2012). The ideas contained in the Charter in al-Ghannushi's view can be a source for new political projects of mutual coexistence, respect and pluralism in a modern context.

Bulaç, inspired by the Charter's universal ideals, fulfils Ghannushi's desire for the formulation of constitutive principles in the modern theorising of a Muslim democracy. He elaborates on the principles of such a system as follows (Bulaç, 2012f):

1. People as individuals should have the freedom to choose a legal system and also accept its legal constraints without any pressure from their groups or the state authority.
2. All groups, as autonomous social units, have the right to define the legal principles that govern their socioeconomic and civil relationships in life.
3. There is a need for a social contract to arrange the public and administrative activities of these autonomous legal groups.
4. There should be assemblies at municipal and state levels so that each community can interact freely with other communities to prevent the alienation of groups from each other.

5. All social units, in order to render their civil services (religious, education, health, art, etc.), should pay a separate tax to their groups, and they should pay another to the state for government services (defence, infrastructure, transportation, etc.).
6. Disputes can in the last resort be brought to a higher authority and its independent ad hoc tribunals that are made up of representatives of all the different groups.

For Bulaç, cultural, religious and legal autonomy, defined by the principles of the Charter, can characterise a new system of legal pluralism in modern multicultural democratic systems (2006: 190–3).

A reformist approach to political pluralism has been developed by revivalists through the revision of traditional concepts. Commitment to pluralism appears to be selective in thought and practice. For instance, revivalists generally focus on religious pluralism and values such as justice and fairness rather than moral pluralism and equality. Justice is considered to be the most important Qur'anic principle in organising and governing a society. However, revivalists maintain that the principle of equality could at times impede justice since identical treatment of people with different beliefs, needs and demands might constitute an injustice (*ẓulm*) (Karaman, 2014c). These issues raise concerns in areas of universal human rights and gender equality that are not sufficiently examined by the revivalists. The following section will examine the deeper moral engagement by modernists, and, on the other hand, pluralism and human rights.

3. Modernists

Modernists often interpret classical sources using modern concepts through a *maqāṣid*-based reading. On pluralism, Fazlur Rahman criticises upholding the medieval categories, concepts and laws on minorities as the divine truth. Rahman contends that <u>*dhimmī*</u> is mentioned neither in the Qur'an nor in the *hadīth*. It is rather a historical concept developed in the context of the early expansion of the Muslim army. The medieval law for apostasy, still accepted by many, is not a Qur'anic order, since the Qur'an only says 'Those who repeatedly apostatised, there shall be God's curse' (Rahman, 1986: 16). The 'considerations of the solidarity of the community and the integrity of the state appear to have necessitated' this law in the early period of the war on *ridda* (Rahman, 1986: 17). Finally, Rahman argues that the Qur'anic term *jizya* was not a fixed practice and had shown a diversity of applications that did not necessarily imply second-class citizenship. For example, some non-Muslim tribes in Syria, who considered paying *jizya* as a mark of discrimination and humiliation, paid *zakat* like other Arab Muslim tribes (Rahman, 1986: 20). These traditional Islamic doctrines are not treated by Rahman as universal but as the results of particular contexts. Thus, these rulings and doctrines neither demand compulsory applications nor should they be relevant to any controversies in the present.

Islam, Rahman believes, brought values and principles for the vouchsafing of religious freedoms and their practice in an exemplary manner for centuries, and is capable of providing this moral guidance in the creation of a modern pluralist society. *Maqāṣid*-based readings of religious norms are necessary to achieve this objective (Rahman, 1986: 22). Khaled Abou El Fadl similarly states that the lack of pluralism in contemporary Muslim societies is due to Muslims' moral failings in their interpretations of religious texts rather than the claim that Islam is not a pluralist religion. The replacement of the pre-modern discourse with strict literalism, narrow readings of the text, intolerance of difference and indoctrination have led to the stagnation of Islamic thought. The following methodological reductionism is observed by Abou El Fadl:

> by emptying the Qur'an both of its historical and moral context, the puritan trend ends up transforming the text into a long list of morally noncommittal legal commands. (2002: 15)

This impoverishment of Islamic religious morality is also at odds with modern ethical requirements and irreconcilable with universal moral standards (Abou El Fadl, 2002: 106–7).[6]

Abou El Fadl points out that Islamic civilisation managed to produce a 'moral and humanistic tradition' via which to manage internal disputes among Muslims and inter-religious relations (2002: 22). The political, social and intellectual history of Islam has witnessed the development of doctrines on minority rights, legal pluralism and multicultural accommodation. Contemporary Muslims can make a parallel effort in the present to formulate a new interpretation in order to foster democratic politics and institutions, as well as human rights, in the contemporary world (Abou El Fadl, 2002: 23).

Human rights are an important concern for modernists. For instance, al-Jabri argues that justice and equality are Islamic values. No moral challenges are present in Islam to give full support to the universal human rights paradigm (al-Jabri, 2009: 240). Abou El Fadl insists that the human rights regime is necessary in order to achieve the justice today that Islam envisages. The 'commitment for human rights is a commitment in favour of God's creation and, ultimately, a commitment in favour of God' (Abou El Fadl, 2003: 56). Abou El Fadl addresses the claim of the philosophical incompatibility of Islam with a democratic human rights paradigm owing to the former's more collectivist ethos as opposed to the latter's individualist values. While the concept of individual human rights was not developed in the classical Islamic literature, this does not mean Islam is oblivious to individual rights. If the Islamic concept of rights happens not to be individualist, this is due to a cultural point of view when Muslim scholars of the day chose to conceptualise collectivist and duty-oriented norms. In fact, Abou El Fadl maintains that in Islamic theology, God holds human beings individually liable in the hereafter and asks them to have an individual relationship with Him. Any obstacles against human rights in the Muslim world emerge from reactionary, anti-Western sentiments in certain currents of thought that challenge these values due to their alleged Judaeo-Christian foundation (Abou El Fadl, 2003: 55).

Al-Jabri has also contributed to the human rights debate. He observes the 'mental tendency to generalize the oneness principle of God as a principle of human governance', although such 'a generalization [is] prohibited and prescribed by religion itself' (Al-Jabri, 2009: 131–2). This cognitive tendency prefigures Muslims' relationship to pluralism and their perception of human rights. Neither the universality nor the particularity of human rights arguments is sufficiently adequate in comprehending human rights' practical importance. A certain universality is identified by Al-Jabri in the theoretical basis of human rights with a universal account of human nature and needs within each particular culture, Western and Islamic alike. Freedom and equality, the normative origins of human rights, are not European or secular values. They derive from a common human history transcending cultures (al-Jabri, 2009: 177). Rights, according to modernists, should be universally awarded to everyone regardless of their fundamental beliefs and views, affirmed by the notion that what is good for humans and society is automatically Islamic.

Al-Jabri awards democracy an elevated normative position. For al-Jabri, '[d]emocracy, with its emphasis on the freedom of thought and expression, and the plurality of parties', is the best possible framework through which to allow sects, minorities and ethnic groups to coexist and share a public life (2009: 132). Modernists endorse a democratic system as the most effective mechanism for providing a political arrangement in which Muslims and non-Muslims can live by a universal set of rights.

Overall, modernists are neither rejectionists like statists nor do they propose Islamic concepts analogous to Western concepts like revivalists. The plurality of interpretations of Islam is instead adopted by modernists, with no one interpretation able to claim to be the sole truth. No hesitation can be found among modernists in their endorsement of liberal democracy and the conventional human rights paradigm based on religious grounds (Abou El Fadl: 2003: 55). Their writings are variously steeped in Islamic moral and legal tradition in a rationalist (Abou El Fadl), critical (al-Jabri) and contextualised (Rahman) manner. The defence of democracy variously emerges from the juristic tradition (Abou El Fadl), Islamic philosophy (al-Jabri) or Gadamerian hermeneutics (Rahman). Progressives, on the other hand, write within a 'pluralistic epistemology, which freely and openly draws from sources outside of Islamic tradition' such as liberalism and secular humanism (Safi, 2003: 48). This serves as a tool with which to articulate a conception of Muslim democracy with non-theological, political dimensions.

4. Progressives

For An-Na'im, monolithic accounts of Islamic law prevent a viable reading of Islam conforming with modern pluralistic values. He asserts that the traditional *sharī'a* concept of apostasy (*ridda*), a product of particular social and economic realities, was 'not the message Islam intended for humanity at large into the indefinite future' (An-Na'im, 2010). Different methodologies led to different accounts of the *sharī'a* depending on the period. Thus, contemporary interpretations of Islam should consider the current realities of our age. A progressive reading of the Qur'an prescribes 'the value of protecting the possibility of dissent and difference' since there is 'no value for any purpose in coerced religious belief or practice' (An-Na'im, 2010). Talbi is also critical of the death penalty for apostasy. This punishment is against the general normative framework of the Qur'an characterised by the notions of religious liberty and free will (Talbi, n.d.).

Traditional *sharī'a* was suitable for the particular political and social realities of the early Muslims from which it arose in the seventh century. An-Na'im claims that the current account of *sharī'a* 'is not the totality of the word of God' but is rather 'the understanding and interpretation of Islamic sources of the Qur'an and *sunna* by the early Muslims' (1987: 10). He critically examines the *sharī'a*'s classification of human beings into three groups: Muslims, 'People of the Book' and non-Muslims who do not follow scriptures. The third type, unlike the second, does not enjoy a permanent legal status. This classification of human beings could be understandable and even reflect the high standards of 'the historical context in which they evolved' (An-Na'im, 2009: 838–9). However, he insists it is not acceptable today in a context defined by universal human standards (An-Na'im, 1987: 12). He adds that 'modern notions [of equality for women and non-Muslims and freedom of religion] were not, and could not have been, dominant when sharī'a principles were developed in the seventh and ninth centuries' (An-Na'im, 2009: 838–9). Drastic changes in prevailing social and political norms in the world are acknowledged in this progressive reading. If Muslims continue to take 'historical' *sharī'a* as the word of God, the outcome will continue to be 'repression and discrimination at home and aggression aboard' (An-Na'im, 1987: 335). An-Na'im, therefore, concludes that the *sharī'a* should be derived from modern interpretations of holy texts, not from the replication of history.

Reinforcing this point, An-Na'im asserts that the contemporary application of *fuqahā*''s understanding of the holy texts to public issues would be disastrous for modern individuals. *Sharī'a* should be reinterpreted, in An-Na'im's preferred approach, by Muslims to construct a reformed modern Islamic law so as to eliminate all legal and political discrimination against Muslim and non-Muslim citizens. To achieve this end, a substantially revised *sharī'a* should adequately accommodate, if not also contribute to, universal norms of rights in order to respond to modern life (An-Na'im, 1987: 18). The reforming of the *sharī'a*, he concludes, can guarantee protections for religious minorities and avoid the irreconcilabilty of the status of non-Muslim minorities under *sharī'a* with universal human rights standards, as follows (An-Na'im, 1987: 17):

1. There should be reforms under the *sharī'a* that would both fulfil Islamic values and be 'consistent with universal human rights standards'.
2. All citizens must enjoy full and equal rights of citizenship, irrespective of any affiliations.

However, it should be noted that An-Na'im's position on pluralism in his later writings has evolved. He seems to place greater emphasis on the importance of the reconciliation and interdependence of religious norms and human rights discourse, rather than exclusively prioritising liberal values (An-Na'im, 2005).

Asghar Ali Engineer believes the Qur'an contains a divine vision of religious pluralism, justice, human dignity, tolerance, dialogue with others, respect and compassion. However, the interpretations of eminent theologians and popular religious practices have overwhelmed the ideals of Islamic revelation at the procedural level (Engineer, 2003). Moreover, Engineer's position on pluralism advises that

> [t]hose who are committed to [the] true spirit of religion should cultivate tolerance and respect for different religions and see to it that religious differences are solved through dialogue rather than through confrontation. (as cited in Esposito, n.d.)

His support for dialogue, peaceful coexistence and respect for difference derives from his recognition of the validity of all religions. The divine revelation of Islam accepts the existence of other religions, such as Christianity and Judaism, while classical theologians declared non-Muslims as *kāfirs* (non-believers) or enemies of Islam. Such interpretations are not based on the universal values of pluralism, equality, justice and the humanity of Islam revealed during the Meccan phase of the Prophetic era. They are politically motivated, contextual readings of the divine from times of conflict among the followers of different religions (Engineer, 2003). Progressives attenuate differences among religions to accept the salvific character of other faiths. For instance, Talbi's ideas also centre on theological diversity in his recognition of a 'plurality of the paths of salvation, both in and outside the Islamic tradition' (1995a: 63).

Muhammad Talbi writes extensively with a progressive ethos on religious pluralism and inter-religious relations. He defines religious liberty as a Qur'anic norm that entails the right to decide one's path freely and to follow a faith if one chooses to be a believer. On the basis of this definition of religious liberty, Talbi maintains, Islam is the most imbued with religious liberty, tolerance, human consciousness, voluntary acts and a pluralist ethos among all the revealed texts of the monotheistic religions, He believes that this Islamic ethos lays down the essentials for structuring a pluralist society to fulfil modern universal human values (Talbi, n.d.). For Talbi, the *maqāṣid* is reflected as follows:

> The goal of the *Sahifah* was to establish a single society with a diversity of religions and identities, on the basis of solidarity, justice, and equality. (Talbi, 1992: 177, as cited in al-Dakkak, 2011: 128)

The existence of diverse religious, cultural and ideological groups in a society makes mere toleration insufficient. Genuine dialogue is needed to achieve pluralism in order to foster a new era of co-operation and mutual respect. In other words, dialogue goes beyond the right to express and practise one's faith freely to include the right to be different. Human beings can 'live together with our consciously assumed difference' through finding a 'plateau' where 'mutual respect and full acknowledgement of difference are attained' (Talbi, 1995a: 62; Filali-Ansari, 2009: 2). The Tunisian philosopher maintains the practical and normative character of religious acceptance and pluralism. In this 'plateau', a shared space of ethical behaviour, the 'common denominator of a universal ethics' should prevail (Talbi, 1995b: 83). Engineer also envisions a pluralistic world where each religion or religious orientation gains recognition and respect in a harmonious and just society. For Engineer, such a society can only be ensured through secularism, the most desirable political framework of our times, in its equal treatment of all religious, cultural and ideological communities (2002: 30).

An-Naʿim also believes that liberal secularism encourages, safeguards and ensures pluralism in modern societies (2005: 58). Turkish and French versions of laicism are criticised by An-Naʿim for their violation of the principle of state neutrality towards religion and for infringing upon religious freedoms (2008: 203–4). Liberal secularism, he argues, overcomes the secular state's imposition of its comprehensive conception of the good, overtly hostile to religious ways of life, upon the citizenry by opening up democratic spaces for other comprehensive moral and political doctrines (An-Naʿim, 1999: 39). The key feature of the liberal secular state, An-Naʿim (2002) explains, is its ability to 'safeguard pluralism and difference by creating a political culture where all groups and competing entities are treated equally' in a pluralistic political community. As such, by preventing the imposition of a dominant religious group's values on others, liberal secularism recognises the plurality of moral and political values and voices in the public sphere.

An-Naʿim believes that liberal secularism can overcome laicism's forceful 'relegation' of religion into the private sphere to offer a new relationship between the state and Islam (2008: 9). Liberal secularism can provide a sufficient space for ethical Islamic commitments born out of individual conviction and voluntary compliance in both the private and public spheres (An-Naʿim, 2008: 3–4). A pluralistic space emerges through liberal secularism for diverse ways of life that are more effective than other political systems in affirming, nurturing and regulating the role of Islam in the public sphere (An-Naʿim, 2005: 63).

A criticism levelled against An-Naʿim and progressives is their espousal of constitutionalism and human rights as non-negotiable norms. Mohammad Fadel maintains that although progressives argue for the reinterpretation and re-appropriation of Islamic doctrines, they take liberal doctrines for granted and to be final. An-Naʿim is criticised for implying Islam can only play a political role so long as it is subject to and unilaterally accepted by liberalism (Fadel, 2009b: 106–8). Although Islamic reformation is an urgent concern for progressives, they probe the capacity of liberalism to respond to religious needs and claims. However, Saba Mahmood suggests these efforts may not effectively challenge the inevitably subordinate position Islam occupies in 'the hegemony of liberalism' (2004: 76). I will discuss the relationship between religion and liberalism in the next chapter on multiculturalism. The multiculturalism literature contains greater engagement with mutual transformation. Liberal and religious paradigms can be simultaneously reinterpreted in order for the former to accommodate diverse normative differences and not leave the burden of change to religion.

In conclusion, while revivalists offer selective support to democracy, Muslim modernists envisage liberal democracy with normative political significance in Islamic philosophy. However, the philosophical authority of liberal democracy is also contested. The source of morality, standards of justice and burden of justification for modernists are directly generated from religion. In addition, modernists argue that Islam is directly concerned with governance, political organisation and law. The *sharī'a* provides a set of normative principles and 'methodologies for the production of legal injunctions' in social life (Abou El Fadl, 2004: 30). Progressives, on the other hand, pursue a secular approach to politics and draw a line between the theological and the political. For progressives, Islam does not promote a certain political theory or theory of rights. A set of Islamic moral values is formulated that are consistent with universal good and human values. Islam as a moral system, rather than a legal one, leaving a wide space for human agency in understanding and interpreting revelation.

In other words, modernists restrict their interpretations within Islamic epistemology. Progressives, on the other hand, assert the importance of moral and epistemological pluralism in their political theorising. Universal ethics in political theory and Islam in personal piety are employed by progressives in an open epistemological framework. In democratic theory, the differentiation between the theological and the political can lead to a paradigm shift from Islamic democracy to a Muslim democracy in my theorising of the latter.

IV. Conclusion on Muslim Political Thought

I have attempted in this chapter to reach a systematic understanding of the themes of governance and pluralism within Muslim political thought. To this end, I formulated a typology of trends based on similarities and differences among the ideas of a wide range of Muslim thinkers. Except for statists, the intellectuals examined in this chapter discussed Islam's compatibility with democracy and often presented original ideas on the issues of secularism, law, pluralism and the public sphere. This conclusion aims to evaluate the degree of relevance and potential of these conceptualisations in developing a Muslim democracy framework.

Governance, in the writings of the thinkers examined above, is approached from a variety of positions, from classical theology to liberal humanism. One key conclusion from this examination of Muslim political thought is that very few thinkers actually reject democracy 'without any qualification or reservation' (Al-Effendi, 2006: 228). All the intellectuals studied here were influenced by the idea of democracy to some extent and have engaged with it at varying theoretical levels. Some key problematics in the debate on democracy were identified, such as: the impact of divine sovereignty on moral pluralism; *shūrā* as a fundamental political value of Islam; the core governing principle of justice; the relevance of *sharī'a* not only in individual but also in public issues; the challenge to Western ideas on secularism in favour of more nuanced formulations; and human rights as objects of serious ethical reasoning.

Secularism, sovereignty, human rights, *shūrā*, justice and *sharī'a* were equally contested concepts. *Shūrā* was the prominent Islamic political ideal referring to the consultative or participatory dimension of governance. It is contrasted with authoritarianism and promotes negotiation and dialogue in political decision-making. A debate persists among different schools of Muslim political thought about whether *shūrā* can be equated with public deliberation or democracy. However, *shūrā* can be seen as a legitimating principle enabling democratic debate to arrive at a set of common rules of coexistence among different groups.

This chapter has focused on political aspects and has not discussed the notion of social justice according to intellectuals such as Sayyid Qutb and Rashid al-Ghannushi. Nonetheless, the establishment of justice is a central theme in Muslim political thought. Among the thinkers in this chapter's typology, statists, adopting a theological approach, assert that justice, can only be implemented through governance directly connected to divine sovereignty. Modernists and progressives argue that any political system that realises justice among people is Islamically legitimate despite the professed ideology of the state (Abou El Fadl, 2002: 110; al-Jabri, 2009: 156). Revivalists do not agree with the latter point made by modernists and progressives, and emphasise that the moral values of governance should be taken solely from Islamic sources in order to establish a genuine form of justice (al-Qaradawi, 2002). A consensus exists that a just system consists of an independent judiciary, accountable governance, free elections, democratic institutions, civil society, state welfare and civil rights. The normative foundations of institutions and principles are the main focus of debate within Muslim political thought.

The debate on sovereignty has profound implications for justice and governance. Statists view democracy as essentially unjust in its disavowal of God's legal sovereignty, and by extension a disavowal of divine justice (Qutb, 2001: 120). Revivalists also, to a lesser extent, find popular sovereignty problematic. Within a democratic system, the general public, who may not possess Islamic moral reasoning, might go against the pillars of the Islamic faith. When revivalists support democratic procedures in the Muslim world, they assume the democratic outcome will be shaped by the Muslim majority's religious moral values. Thus, revivalists demonstrate a moral apprehension towards the notion of popular sovereignty (Karaman, 2014c). Modernists and progressives, on the other hand, espouse popular sovereignty and defend the establishment of liberal democratic institutions within Muslim countries. Their arguments for a democratic system are similar to the arguments of those urging multiculturalist expansion of the liberal democratic paradigm to accommodate the public role of religion.

The necessity of a public space for the *sharī'a* in order to allow Muslims to express Islamic identity is another point on which all schools of Muslim political thought seem to agree. Several key debates, however, occupy these schools concerning the conceptualisation of the *sharī'a*. First, disagreement exists about whether the *sharī'a* is immutable and revealed by God or is a collection of rulings determined by human interpretations. The statist thinkers favour the former belief, that the *sharī'a* is an integrated body of law that can be codified as a constitution and be systematically implemented by the state. Revivalists support the idea of the *sharī'a* being a source of the official law. Further, according to revivalists, differing from statists, the notion of the *sharī'a* is subject to changing interpretations through *maqāṣid* (objectives) and *maṣlaḥah* (common good). In addition, revivalists criticise liberal democracies for their failure to respond to public religious demands and accompanying legal needs. For instance, Bulaç's proposing of the Charter of Medina as a guide to political order has strong parallels with the legal pluralist critique of liberal democracy that will be examined in the next chapter (2006: 190).

The thinkers, modernists and progressives, who favour the latter viewpoint of an enlightened *sharī'a* also differ among themselves on its scope. Modernists do accept that some positive rules can be deduced from *sharī'a* principles (Rahman, 1967: 206). Progressives, on the other hand, emphasise the moral aspect of *sharī'a* as providing individual guidance rather than public law. *Sharī'a*, for progressives, is a religious philosophy, not a law for public matters, that influences social behaviour for a believer. Secular judiciary and legislative bodies are sufficient to co-ordinate the role of Islam in both the private and public realms (An-Na'im, 2002a: 20).

The schools examined in this chapter, with the exception of progressives, seek some form of religious authority for all or some aspects of Islamic law. Even modernists acknowledge that the collective aspect of the *sharī'a* may 'need to be applied by authority' (al-Jabri, 2009: 19). They believe that the secular state by definition does not deprive Islam of 'the "authoritative body", which must be entrusted with the execution of judgements' (al-Jabri, 2009: 33). What modernists appear to advocate is an office for a *muftī* (jurisconsult) or a council of Islamic religious specialists who will issue religious opinions on public matters that may or may not be formally binding depending on the situation and context. Religious authority is also addressed in the modernist argument for the compatibility of divine and popular sovereignty, with implications for public morality (al-Jabri, 2009: 18–19). This topic will be further examined in Chapter 3 on the compatibility-based arguments about Islam and democracy.

The arguments on the public role of the *sharī'a* are directly linked to the notion of secularism. There appears to be a hesitation within Muslim political thought towards the concept of secularism due to its negative connotations of authoritarianism and top-down modernisation in the Muslim world. Muslim thinkers in this chapter tend to distinguish between aggressive and passive forms of secularism. Nevertheless, the statist school entirely repudiates the concept of a secular state. It critiques the modern secular state's pervasive intrusion into people's lives. Replacement of the state with a religious state is a proposed solution to its totalitarian nature, to stop the subordination of religion (Mawdūdī, 1960b: 18). Quite the reverse: in this model, religion dictates governance and the struggle to implement divine justice in the world. This idea of an Islamic state is antithetical to the idea of a secular state and the separation of powers. Revivalists pragmatically engage in Islamist politics even under a secular system despite their reservations about its desirability. In this far from ideal situation, they ask for fundamental changes in the secular state to avoid clashes between religious and secular forces (al-Ghannushi, 2011a).

The modernists and progressives argue for different applications of secularism in Muslim contexts. Certain ideas from secularism are accepted, such as the separation of powers to contain authoritarianism, and impartial mediation between different religious groups including competing interpretations of Islam. Laicism's strict separation of religion and politics is repudiated by modernists and progressives while the latter group additionally emphasises separation should address religion and political authority, not religion and the public sphere. Progressives also acknowledge the virtues of a secular state with liberal democratic foundations in creating a pluralist environment to accommodate religious claims (An-Na'im, 2008: 203). Islamic morality can or should be part of civic deliberation and public reason within a democratic secular state for modernists and progressives. No authority, however, can be awarded to Islamic normativity in politics in the progressive account of democracy (An-Na'im, 2008: 3).

The concepts of human rights and citizenship rights have elicited different responses from Muslim intellectuals. Statist scholars adopt a rejectionist approach to human rights because of its alleged Western roots while revivalists emphasise a shared moral concern (Mawdūdī, 1960a: 263). Revivalists have developed a discourse on human rights, including recognition of religious beliefs and acts, with Islamic elements. Equal citizenship and minority rights are shown to offer valuable support for the human rights paradigm (Karaman, 2004: 13). Human rights are located within a framework of Islamic moral guidance that can lead to the creation of constraining mechanisms. For instance, the concept of 'universal ugliness' proposed by Karaman (2014c) is a regulatory public function for rights and liberties. In modernist and progressivist approaches, the concept of equal citizenship is located within the universal human rights paradigm. These schools maintain the moral universality of these concepts (An-Na'im, 1987: 17; Abou El Fadl, 2002: 23; al-Jabri, 2009: 156; Rahman, 1986: 20).

This chapter has illustrated the depth and diversity of Islamic views on the relationship between religion, the state, and pluralism surroundings debates/positions on Muslim democracy. The classification of contemporary Muslim thinkers in a typology in this chapter has aimed to uncover the potential of democratic thinking in concepts such as sovereignty, *shūrā*, public sphere, law and secularism. The final part, Chapters 4, 5 and 6, of this book will reinterpret and synthesise concepts deduced from this chapter in an attempt to conceptualise a theoretical framework on Muslim democracy. Through a critical treatment of Muslim political thinking, this chapter has arrived at the position that the theorising of Muslim democracy depends on the resolution of the tensions between divine versus popular sovereignty, *sharī'a* versus human legislation, *shūrā* versus public deliberation, and Islamic versus secular state. Further examination of these controversies is held to be a sine qua non in thinking about a Muslim democracy framework in Chapter 3.

In the next chapter, I will focus on various multiculturalist thinkers' critiques of secular and liberal politics in their attempts to expand an existing democratic paradigm. Common themes are discussed by both Muslim intellectuals and multiculturalists, themes such as the expansion of the secular paradigm, the restructuring of the public sphere, the devolving of more powers to civil society and, finally, just and participatory rule.

Notes

1. It should be noted at this point that one must distinguish between the ideas and the scholars in these groupings: the scholars' positions regarding the themes explored are analysed through their thought and their intellectual works, excluding their political behaviour or choices.
2. It should be noted that Mawdūdī accepts that there may be some cases where a particular religious prescription does not exist; however, he does not identify these, and apparently considers them to be trivial and unproblematic (Afsaruddin, 2011: 145). On the whole, statist thought offers little consideration of the historical context of legal practices and the application of specific rulings, and treats Islamic law as a uniform, monolithic set of rules that is beyond the mandate of human reason and adjudication.
3. To better elucidate: 'if democracy is a set of institutions that constrain the state, enforce law, and allow public participation in politics', and that provide an independent judiciary, an autonomous parliament and an executive accountable to the citizenry, then what revivalist, Islamist scholars promote is a full democracy (Rutherford, 2006: 731). 'However, if one views democracy as the adoption and

promotion of a set of values' such as individual liberty, gender equality, popular sovereignty and institutional separation of religion and the state, then we cannot equate what revivalists advocate with full democracy in this context (Rutherford, 2006: 730).

4. He comes from the Dawoodi-Bohra community, but he does not frame his position in terms of a restricted religious reference or any particular Islamic denomination or tradition (Engineer, 2009). Due to his consideration of himself a pluralist, humanist and secularist, I decided that including him in the progressive typology would be compatible with the overall typology created.

5. Talbi writes that 'more detailed time bound injunctions [were] meant by God only for the particular situations of the revelation', and thus their underlying ethical values are eternal and universal while the specific implementations are transitory and contextual (Nettler, 2000: 53).

6. Abou El Fadl writes that today's static, monolithic and sanctifying understanding of the text challenges classical Islamic scholarship, which 'was dynamic, diverse, complex, and constantly evolving' as '[t]raditionally, Islamic epistemology tolerated even celebrated divergent opinions and schools of thought' (2002: 106, 6). Yet, he insists, this tolerance of disagreement is an abandoned norm today.

2

MULTICULTURALIST DISCOURSES ON RELIGION AND DEMOCRATIC GOVERNANCE

I. Introduction

Peaceful coexistence and toleration among diverse cultures and religions in societies is not a new phenomenon. Multiculturalism, however, developed in the post-Second World War era as a response to intensified demands for cultural and religious recognition of new minority groups in Western democracies. Multiculturalist discourses emerged from an internal critique within contemporary liberalism seeking to modify its Rawlsian strand with more pluralistic and culturally appropriate tools. These discourses have now become a prominent trend of thought in political theory in their critique of a narrowly defined nationalism (Castles, 2005).

There are certain characteristics that broadly define multiculturalist thought. Multiculturalists tend to recognise the central role played by the community in constituting and shaping the individual self. Thus, they view the community as a primary source for the development and practice of autonomy, self-respect and dignity. Cultural or religious aspects of citizens' identities are politically relevant and a legitimate source of public demands. The current public sphere in orthodox liberal democracies is too limited to accommodate cultural and religious requirements in an even-handed manner (Kymlicka and Norman, 2000: 4). Multiculturalist intellectuals revise particular aspects of Rawlsian liberalism either to reform existing political frameworks or to create new frameworks for institutionalising pluralism.

Most of the multiculturalists examined in this chapter come from a liberal background – they live, operate and write within the context of liberal states. Therefore, many of them view liberalism as the most suitable framework for reconciling the principles of democracy with cultural diversity. Other thinkers, however, do not privilege current liberal models as the most effective frameworks of conciliation. Yet these thinkers still work within the liberal paradigm to develop more enhanced models. Several of these intellectuals are sceptical about contemporary liberal theory's ability to create a pluralist legal–political framework. Unlike the Muslim thinkers examined in the previous chapter, who have questioned the normative foundations of governance, the scholars in this chapter take democratic structures for granted. Considerable differences among multiculturalists reside in their theories on constitutional and institutional frameworks.

I illustrate the key arguments of the prominent multiculturalist scholars in this chapter through a classification of the various strands. The typology of multiculturalist discourses is based on their responses to the following three issues: (a) what kind of legal–institutional mechanisms should be endorsed and what role should the state and minority groups have within this new framework?; (b) to what extent should the mainstream political institutions and the cultural practices of minority groups undergo change to effectively maintain this framework?; and (c) what is the role of religion in public policy and law and what are the strengths and limitations of the proposed frameworks in dealing with religious claims in politics? Answers to these questions determine into which of the four categories multiculturalists are placed: liberal pluralists, moral pluralists, legal pluralists and institutionalist pluralists.

A proper understanding of multiculturalism's engagement with the challenge of cultural and religious diversity necessitates posing the three questions mentioned above. The first question addresses the accommodation of differences among ethnic, cultural and religious minority groups. In addition, it tackles the particular role of the state and minority groups in the process of establishing and operating a potential framework. The second question is derived from an existing tendency within multiculturalist thought towards transformation and value change. Recommended conversion typically targets either the liberal establishments or minority cultures, or both. The third question concerns the place of religion within multiculturalist discourse, especially as a normative basis for a new legal institutional design. Conceptual similarities and differences between religion and culture are critically discussed to ascertain whether the former concept can be used interchangeably with the latter or whether it is fundamentally different.

The answers to these three questions given by the thinkers examined in this chapter demonstrate shared and different emphases. These differences allow for the typological classification of four schools in multiculturalism. A brief introductory account, similar to that in the previous chapter, is given of each of the four multiculturalist schools, preceding their detailed examination in this chapter.

Liberal pluralist thought was born as a constructive critique of Rawlsian and Dworkian liberalism. A strong individualist moral ontology is present that rejects 'cultural goods' as normatively relevant to political theory (Kymlicka, 1989: 152). However, liberal pluralists maintain, following John Stuart Mill's classical liberal principles, that dealing with individuals, who are part of, shaped by and develop within cultural communities, does not only require dealing with the individuals themselves, but also with their organised communities. Liberalism's values and rights are dynamic and progressive, rather than static, when it deals with cultural claims. Liberal pluralists advocate a more profound and comprehensive account of goods in liberal rights, with cultural identity and membership considered to be a primary good. Despite the call for a revised understanding, liberal pluralists privilege liberalism above other theories as the universal form of a normative political order.

Moral pluralists challenge the liberal individualist view that human beings are 'self-sufficient' as individuals and can develop their full existence and potential independent from their social contexts (Taylor, 1985: 200). Individuals can only develop self-understandings and self-respect as members of a community (Tully, 1995: 190). In addition, moral pluralists criticise their liberal pluralist counterparts for undermining the validity of non-Western cultures while pursuing an agenda of transforming individuals to fit liberalism. Unlike liberal pluralists, moral pluralists' scope of accommodation, going beyond political or redistributive grounds, recognises the moral character of cultural and religious membership. In their arguments, moral pluralists advocate a pluralist public sphere where individuals with diverse normative systems are equally recognised by state institutions.

The law is not monolithic, legal pluralists argue, but rather plural, and not all 'phenomena related to law' in actual societies 'have their source in government' (Moore, 1986: 15). Rawls's theory of justice, on the other hand, is found to be based on standard rights, uniform treatment, secular rationality and monistic law, which leaves no room for the society's acknowledgement of 'the legitimacy of another group's claim to select its own principles of justice' (Woodman, 2009: 154). Legal pluralists interpret multiculturalism to acknowledge cultural and jurisdictional autonomy in the organisation of the collective lives of minorities. Followers of organised faiths – they single out in particular – should administer their own systems of law instead of mere accommodation.

Institutionalist pluralists tackle multicultural diversity generated between state and non-state authorities through a framework of institutionalised and legal co-operation. People's different versions of the good life involve diverse public needs that require different public services, for which the unitary institutions of the nation-state might fail to make adequate and impartial provision. Ayelet Shachar and Veit Bader propose complex political and legal models with which to adequately respond to the contemporary reality of cultural and religious pluralism. A proposed legal structure for the sharing of authority between national government and religious groups can resolve semi-public disputes, for example matters of marriage and divorce, among consenting adults, monitored by the democratic regulatory criteria of central government. In their models, institutionalist pluralists introduce democratic checks and balances to ensure the democratic character of the polity in practice (Shachar, 2009: 133).

This chapter will now further discuss the ideas of individual thinkers according to a typology of four schools of multiculturalist thought. I will conclude my discussion by considering the grounds on which this classification of multiculturalist political theory can provide relevant arguments and themes for my formulating of alternative ways of thinking about the relationship between religion and democratic organisation. Alternative interpretations of the public sphere, the role of the state and organised faith, and the relationship between religion and law, are present in the multiculturalist literature. These themes can provide advanced theoretical tools with which to study the politics of Muslims' needs and demands and those of liberal democratic institutions. Thus, examination of the depth and variety of traditions within Western political theory in the area of multiculturalism in this chapter furnishes the tools for developing a political theory on Muslim democracy in this book's final part.

II. Liberal Pluralists: Will Kymlicka, Chandran Kukathas

Liberal pluralists attempt to develop a coherent theory of cultural diversity by reinterpreting existing liberal principles. The choice of liberalism as their primary normative framework is based on the premise that liberal values should inform what Rawls would call 'the basic structure' of political society. This subsection will examine the multiculturalist arguments of Will Kymlicka and Chandran Kukathas as representatives of liberal pluralist thought. Their arguments on multiculturalism are divided into two main themes, namely their critique of orthodox liberalism and their positioning of multiculturalism as a liberal project.

1. *Critique of Orthodox Liberalism*

Kymlicka criticises contemporary liberal theorists for their limited conception of liberal principles in relation to minority rights (1997: 84). Post-war liberalism is guilty of rejecting 'the legitimacy of special measures for cultural minorities' by putting minority rights at odds with individual rights and liberal equality (Kymlicka, 1990: 209). Kymlicka maintains that the narrow definition of autonomy in Rawlsian liberalism has underdeveloped its ability to accommodate diversity in a denial of cultural rights for minority groups. For Rawlsian liberals, politics is shaped by autonomy based on individual liberty, with culture neither having normative power nor being a source for deliberation in politics (Kymlicka, 1992: 34).

Kymlicka argues that liberalism's attention to cultural claims is in line with the classical pre-war liberal tradition, since

> Mill, Green, Hobhouse, and Dewey . . . recognized the importance of our cultural membership to the proper functioning of a well-ordered and just society. (Kymlicka, 1989: 208)

Mill's comprehensive liberalism, rooted in the ideals of the Enlightenment, according to Kymlicka recognised autonomy as a general human interest. This account of autonomy applies to all human action in pursuing a conception of the good 'in both public and private contexts' (Kymlicka, 1992: 44). Culture falls into the category of a primary good, for the existence of common membership is a necessary means for pursuing the good life. Claims of cultural rights, according to Kymlicka, should be seen a precondition for the liberal commitment to individual autonomy (1997: 75).

The liberal pluralist defence of multicultural rights, derived from Immanuel Kant's autonomy of the individual, is individualistic in nature. Communities carry importance only in terms of the moral worth of the individual existence of members, rather than due to the validity of their cultures per se. Kymlicka argues that 'liberals should care about the viability of societal cultures' because of their contribution to an individual's sense of personal identity and capacity, as well as act as an 'anchor' for their inner sense of self-respect and self-identification (1995: 94). Chandran Kukathas is more concerned about the need for every individual member to receive equal treatment from the state (1992: 114). Public policy in this liberal context, both individualist and neutral, seeks to encourage people's freedoms and capacities for public action (Kukathas, 1998: 692). For Kukathas, there are no collective cultural rights in liberal multiculturalism, but simply the individual right to cultural practice. Liberalism is motivated by 'the politics of indifference', whereupon cultural recognition would constitute an intervention and disturbance to civil life and individual interests. Kukathas warns that recognition of cultures would generate tensions not only among different groups but also within particular groups. As a practical form of justification, he argues that different interests within a minority are borne out by the often dissimilar interests of the elite and the common masses. Recognition would thus hardly benefit individuals within groups (Kukathas, 1992: 114). In this context, liberalism intervenes neither to restrict nor to favour cultures. Groups or traditions should draw on their own internal means and resources in order to continue their existence (Kukathas, 1998: 698).

The definition of 'non-intervention' for Kukathas is influenced by his espousal of the liberal conception of the limited state. The state is not an entity that should aim to achieve consensus or social and political unity. Instead, a liberal state's primary tasks are to allow people to live in a morally diverse world and not intervene in philosophical matters or impose normative ideals on society (Kukathas, 2001: 89). Policies and arguments for reshaping cultures are 'surely unacceptable', for they clearly fail to 'respect minority cultures' and 'to take their cultures seriously' (Kukathas, 1992: 122–4). Regulation of interactions among citizens with different cultural backgrounds and ideological preferences is carried out by a liberal state that is both neutral and indifferent. Freedom in liberalism is concerned with the formation and development of any kind of individual identity or group membership. The state should maintain a sufficient space for the practice of individual autonomy by group members who have the right to be part of a community and to exit from this community (Kukathas, 2001: 95).

Kymlicka and Kukathas emphasise different arguments in their critiques of orthodox liberalism's inability to deal with the right to cultural diversity. Individualist norms unite both of these thinkers at the expense of a communitarian or recognitionist agenda. Their liberal projects claim to be a direct continuation of classical liberal values (Kymlicka, 2007: 107). However, claims for multiculturalism justified on liberal grounds are controversial among orthodox liberals.

2. The Liberal Nature of Multiculturalism

In response to Rawlsian critiques, Kymlicka argues that the multicultural reforms in the Western world after the 1970s 'is part of a larger process of social and political liberalisation' leading to 'a greater accommodation of ethno-cultural diversity' (1989: 97). There, reforms are a continuation of the universal human rights discourse and implementation of civil rights at a local level (Kymlicka, 2009: 37). Emerging consensus on human rights and democratisation has enabled 'multiple access points for safe political mobilization', which allowed non-dominant groups in the West increasingly to demand multicultural reforms and group-differentiated rights (Kymlicka, 2007: 133).

Kukathas also justifies multiculturalism on liberal grounds, with a greater focus on toleration. The fundamental idea of toleration is the basis for cultural, moral or political pluralism (Kukathas, 2003: 259). Toleration, through liberty of conscience, the right to difference and dissent, and moral diversity, assures freedom in practice (Kukathas, 1998: 5). Freedom, a constitutive principle in state–individual relations, has strong implications with regard to collective human activities. Minority groups as autonomous entities should enjoy 'a certain amount of independence and integrity' (Kukathas, 1992: 127). Neither the regulations of the state nor the pressures of mainstream society should interfere in in-group activities, even to correct illiberal actions, with the exception of extreme harm (Kukathas, 2003: 186). Kukathas's position is motivated by the concern that political powers, in the effort to reform cultural groups, will always pursue their own interests at the expense of the well-being of communities (Kukathas, 2001: 95).

Unlike Kukathas, Kymlicka pays more attention to liberal concerns over in-group violations of citizenship rights, gender equality and individual liberty. There is a need for 'external protection . . . that protect[s] a culture from the policies of the wider society' in order to ease minority groups' vulnerability to the economic and political power of the dominant population, and 'internal restriction' for 'group rights that limit the individual liberties of people within a culture' (Mookherjee, 2012: 198). Internal restrictions against vulnerable insiders, for Kymlicka, require favouring individual rights over cultural rights. The state should practise its 'right and responsibility' to intervene to correct discriminatory group acts (Kymlicka, 1995: 168). Dissent by individual members within minority groups can also be safeguarded through a multicultural framework by granting substantial civil rights (Kymlicka, 1995: 157). Autonomy, the key value in Kymlicka's theory, provides a justification both for promoting group-differentiated rights and for limiting them in favour individual interests (Kymlicka, 1989: 170).

Kukathas's idea of the limited state creates far-reaching perspectives for a Muslim democracy framework on the issue of religious freedoms and toleration as well as the handling of normative diversity. Kymlicka's focus on issues concerning the protection of individual human rights within the context of cultural accommodation has paramount importance as well. More pluralist forms of public organisation, in addition to personal and religious freedoms and human rights, can contribute to the theorising of Muslim democracy that is elaborated in the final part.

3. Concluding Remarks

Cultural accommodation is driven by a liberal multiculturalist rationale that is individualist. Normative appeals to the importance of national and ethnic culture are made in the light of their impact on individual progress. This cultural accommodation is an expansion of the liberal commitment to individual rights, not a substantiation of collective or group rights. However, liberal pluralist scholars also differ in their theories. Kukathas proposes to give cultural freedoms to individuals as citizens rather than as members of a particular community. For Kymlicka, by contrast, realisation of individual rights, bound up with minority and cultural rights, occurs in communities, which constitute an organic part of an individual's existence.

The second significant difference within this category centres on the desirability of state intervention. Kymlicka offers both positive and negative notions of state intervention in his multicultural citizenship model. First, granting of differentiated rights to support minority demands. Second, restricting minority practices to protect human rights. Kukathas, on the other hand, is against any form of state intervention either in support of or to correct minority group practices. The liberal state should merely tolerate citizens' choices and accord the freedom to live by these choices.

Another contrast relates to the issue of transformation of values. Kymlicka demonstrates a commitment to the liberal transformation of public institutions as well as the practices of minority groups. He envisages policies of multicultural accommodation as a catalyst for positive internal value change towards liberal norms. Kukathas's challenge to this position contends that the state should not expect or force cultural adjustment in line with liberal values, as people have the right to operate outside of its liberal framework.

Discussions of religiously-defined groups among liberal pluralists often lack detailed explanation. However, they include a religious element in their account of 'a culture which provides its members with meaningful ways of life across the full range of human activities, including social, educational, religious, recreational, and economic life, encompassing both public and private spheres' (Kymlicka, 1995: 76). Culture is accorded the highest level of importance for an individual. They undermine the fact that religions might need different, but equally important, accommodations in practice. Religion, however, for some groups, especially followers of organised faiths, is more central than culture to their communal character. In addition, people who have different cultures might share the same religion and view it as the most important part of their identities. In most of Europe, unlike Kymlicka's Canada and Kukathas's Australia, 'the issue of religious minorities within multiculturalism is greater than culture' (Modood, 1993: 99).

The normative relevance of cultural membership formulated by liberal pluralists is present in both liberal theory and the human rights paradigm. A general re-evaluation of liberalism, the increased importance of the community and group to the life of the individual, and liberal justification for cultural practice are the starting points of multiculturalist thought. Further opportunities to develop multiculturalist methods for accommodation are generated from considering cultural membership to be a primary good from which to make public claims. Although the role of religion in public policy is inadequately addressed by liberal pluralists, their arguments for the significance of communal identity inspire other frameworks of multiculturalism that award religion a more central place.

III. Moral Pluralists: Charles Taylor, James Tully and Monica Mookherjee

Moral pluralist multiculturalism differs from the liberal pluralist rethinking of liberalism on the question of liberalism's ability to respond to multicultural concerns. By placing greater weight on different forms of political rationality, moral pluralists seek to foster more commitment to diversity than liberal pluralists. This subsection will examine the arguments of Charles Taylor, James Tully and Monica Mookherjee as representative of moral pluralist thought. The two themes of the critique of orthodox liberalism and the formulation of pluralist models of accommodation will be examined in this section.

1. Critique of Orthodox Liberalism

Certain aspects of orthodox liberalism are criticised in Charles Taylor's search for a more pluralist and inclusivist democratic system. According to Taylor, although liberal democracy has a certain inclination that 'pushes towards exclusion' with regard to moral difference, it is the most inclusive political theory that humans have thus far achieved (1998: 143). Liberal democracies in the creation of a national political culture have occasionally ignored or subordinated cultural and religious aspects of their citizens' identities. A minority group that does not share the conventional definition of the good is not genuinely included in the national deliberative mechanisms (Taylor, 1997: 45).

This liberal tendency towards exclusion, Taylor argues, is generated by universalist conceptions of prinipcles such as fairness, equality, non-discrimination and freedom. When faced by the conditions of actual, often non-Western, societies, these universalist prinicples fail to materialise in practice. Orthodox liberalism is 'the political expression of one range of [Western] cultures, and quite incompatible with other ranges' and for this reason it cannot be 'a possible meeting ground for all cultures' (Taylor, 1994: 62).

James Tully launches a scathing critique of modern Western constitutionalist thought and its 'authoritative traditions' of liberalism, communitarianism and nationalism for their failure in responding to cultural diversity (1995: 44). According to Tully, European norms, through cultural and moral imperialism, were imposed both within Europe's national borders towards minorities and within colonies towards colonised peoples. Modern Western constitutionalism's failure to be 'culturally neutral' can be traced to the favoured position of Western culture at the expense of the will of minorities or colonised people in these two contexts. Justice is incapable of being rendered to the legitimate demands of indigenous peoples, minorities, immigrants and refugees struggling for various forms of public recognition (Tully, 2008a: 166).

Political rationality is faulted by Tully as a universalist position in liberal constitutionalism. The ideal of the universal impartiality of reason has determined the limits of inclusion in the public sphere, and more precisely the constitutional debate. Tully claims that the modern Western legal and institutional embrace of the abstract ideal of an impartial public reason has 'denied or suppressed, rather than affirmed' minorities' 'inclusion to the public reason' (Tully, 1995: 6, 5). A putative 'neutral liberal identity', imposing 'alien' and exclusionary forms of cultural, moral and philosophical uniformity, is incapable of creating 'a just form of constitution with the full mutual recognition of different cultures of its citizens' (Tully, 2008a: 166; 1995: 8).

Monica Mookherjee directs a similar criticism against the assumed universalism on liberal values such as autonomy, equality and freedom (2005: 40). Different cultural systems assign different meanings and multiple interpretations to these values which naturally give birth to their 'different practical usages' (Mookherjee, 2010: 98–9). People's capacities, freedoms and needs in most cases are interpreted and practised in 'culturally variable ways' (Mookherjee, 2009: 58). Mookherjee expands her discussion on value pluralism in consideration of autonomy. She proposes that autonomy should not be equated with 'a single meaning' or universal, 'reasonable' pattern, but instead it should be acknowledged that it 'can take significantly different cultural forms' (Mookherjee, 2008: 149). In contrast to the orthodox liberal account, Mookherjee believes a 'more concrete account of autonomy', integrating people's multifaceted lives as individuals and members of cultural associations, has to be conceptualised when re-assessing individual rights (2005: 34).

Moral pluralists reveal the inapplicability of orthodox liberalism in practice and its exclusionary impulses in democratic politics. To compensate for this weakness, Taylor pleads 'for a somewhat more complex and many-stranded version of liberalism', responding to the culturally diverse character of modern states, to revise secularism within Rawlsian liberalism (1998: 154). Taylor has sought to reconfigure secularism in contemporary societies through religious pluralism. Universal secularism is criticised for laying the exclusive foundation of the rational, scientific and irreligious modernity paradigm (Maclure and Taylor, 2011: 53; Taylor, 2007: 3). An 'ethnocentricity' is present in this understanding of secularism that assumes one single, universal secularism deriving its meaning from the relationship between Christianity and Western Enlightenment (Taylor, 2008: xi).

Secularisation theory is challenged by Taylor as regards its interpretation of the role of religion and secularism in other regions outside the West. Secularism, not independent of time, context or place, does not emanate from 'rational' human reason (Taylor, 2007: 26–9). Normative and functional features of secularism are not monolithic. Taylor further argues against the assumption that modern democracies have to be secular in the Western sense in their exclusion of religion from the public sphere. Islam, unlike Christianity and Judaism, is assumed to be secularisation-resistant with the conclusion that it is incompatible with democracy. Muslim societies did not experience the West's secularisation process, due to their colonial and state-building history, the particular characteristics of Islam, and religion's central place within these societies. Secularism and democracy in Muslim countries, Taylor underlines, would occur 'in a more inventive and imaginative way', in which religion can still play an important role in politics (2008: xvii).

Moral pluralists incorporate religion into the liberal democratic theory in many ways. First, they show the necessity for including religious reason as part of public discourse within Western democracies. Different and contextualised modes of secularism are proposed in order for liberal democratic governance to function within various religious environments. Moral pluralists, Taylor specifically, elaborate new modes of thinking about liberal democracy with alternative versions of secular governance within religious contexts.

2. Multiculturalist models of accommodation

The moral pluralist demand for a recognition of difference seeks to move 'from the negative meaning of non-interference to the positive sense of acceptance and recognition' (Galeotti, 2012: 139). Taylor argues that communal and cultural identities, which provide a distinctive moral value system, affect people's 'understanding of who they are, of their fundamental defining characteristics as a human being' (1994: 25). Political recognition of the moral character of communal cultures directly involves the normative recognition of the freedoms, choices and equal worth of individuals that satisfy a core and 'vital human need' (Taylor, 1992: 25). Marginalisation of minority group cultures can substantially diminish the quality of life and the capacity of political participation for their individual constituencies (Taylor, 1997: 64–8).

Taylor offers an alternative model of recognition via which to regulate moral and religious diversity. If secularism is conceptualised and implemented correctly, argues Taylor, it presents, at its core, a system of governance that has the greatest ability to guarantee moral equality and freedom of conscience among individuals with diverse cultural backgrounds (Maclure and Taylor, 2011: 41). A functional and political, not a moral or philosophical, theory of secularism emerges from Taylor's ideas. Liberal–pluralist secularism provides 'some kind of neutrality, or "principled distance"' from religion or religious institutions to ensure peaceful modes of coexistence among different communities (Taylor, 2008: xi). Neutrality towards religion here is designed 'to foster, not hinder, its expression' in public deliberation (Bouchard and Taylor, 2008: 46). Taylor's model of recognition compensates for modern political philosophy's lack of 'alternative models of how people can bond together in difference without abstracting from their differences' (1998: 153).

In Tully's theory of democratic constitutionalism, 'imperialistic', 'assimilationist' and 'uniformist' elements should be removed from within Western constitutions. Democratic constitutionalism, a 'post-imperial philosophy and practice of constitutionalism', envisages 'an endless series of contracts and agreements' within a constitution subject to constant revision, 'as opposed to a sacrosanct contract which ought to be amended solely in exceptional circumstances' (Tully, 1995: 26). Citizens can 'participate freely and with equal dignity in the governing of their society and to live their private lives in accord with their own choice and responsibility' driven by the contested nature of narratives (Tully, 1995: 183, 189). For Tully, the inability of people to participate with their own cultural identities in civic deliberation leads to unjust political institutions. In democracies, legal and political institutions should recognise and accommodate 'the cultures of all the citizens in an agreeable manner', as demonstrated by a 'culturally neutral' framework (Tully, 1995: 191). Although Tully can be placed in the moral pluralist category, free will, consent and social contract, acquired 'by being "free citizens"', are more important than culture for him (2008a: 160).

Mookherjee proposes an alternative model of recognition and rights, namely 'affective citizenship', which 'seek[s] to rethink the conditions under which . . . [the liberal goods of equal freedom and autonomy] can be comprehensively realised' (2005: 31–2). According to the affective citizenship framework, the importance of cultural and religious affiliations is 'based on equal respect and concern rather than uniformity and sameness' (Marshall, 2008: 651). Equal treatment of citizens, relative to their specific contexts, is to be realised through the principle of 'justice as provisionality'.

Diverse interpretations of religions and cultures are upheld by 'justice as provisionality' in the domain of rights. Impartial justice from this principle differs from the universalist liberal form of impartiality given the latter's neglect of the cultural contexts of citizens. Citizenship rights within the context of impartial justice, according to Mookherjee, can both empower people through their specific religious and cultural self-assertions and enable them to further pursue their socioeconomic interests in their societies (2005: 33–4). An important aspect of Mookherjee's argument is her harmonisation of multiculturalist forms of recognition with women's rights. She reconfigures 'women's rights as multicultural claims' so as to realise gender equality to satisfy women's own accounts of equality, justice and autonomy (Mookherjee, 2009: 156).

Orthodox liberalism's impartial reason in Mookherjee's account can be replaced with a 'plural public reasoning' composed of 'a more capacious, more generous account of "public reason"' (2001b: 21). Plurality of public reason, in the constant process of making, is determined by citizens' partial reasons derived from their diverse moral and philosophical views (Mookherjee, 2001: 69).

While acknowledging 'deep moral disagreement' among citizens, Mookherjee's position on impartial mediation by the state between opposing parties differs from Tully's advocacy of civic debate as the final authority (2001: 75). For Mookherjee, the post-imperial state has in some cases to undertake legal involvement 'in cases of extreme intra-community harm' to protect people's autonomy and basic human rights (2008: 148). In addition, people's 'capacity for reason itself requires institutional nurturing, protection and provision' (Mookherjee, 2001b: 15–16).

However, this state intervention is not a desirable method for Mookherjee, because it can harm people's meaningful choices, skills and life options. Instead, she suggests the empowering of group members' capacities within their social structures to promote their agency through non-legal methods (2005: 44). General arguments for the integration of cultural demands within democratic governance and a limited role granted to the state in Mookherjee's accommodationist model offer additional concepts for interpretation in this book's pluralist framework.

3. Concluding Remarks

According to moral pluralists, recognition is a universal human need that gives people the feeling of equal worth and self-respect, which facilitates the full actualisation of individual agency. Thus, the process of recognition must be primarily addressed within democratic politics. The commitment to cultural recognition strengthens the moral pluralist critique of Rawlsian liberalism and its homogeneous public sphere to substantially revise liberal theory.

Western liberal political systems in their current form, moral pluralists argue, cannot pursue the politics of recognition. One putative reason for this inability is philosophical secularism's predominance over political secularism. Moral pluralists emphasise that any democratic understanding of secularism must be in line with the philosophical neutrality of the state towards the competing narratives of goods and values. More inclusive trajectories are articulated by moral pluralists on secularism that enable the democratic recognition of religion.

Moral pluralist theories aim to revise the composition of democracies as well as to redefine democratic constitutionalism. A 'post-imperial' democratic theory consists of public and intercultural dialogue, a common language of citizens and negotiation within a diverse citizenry (Tully, 1995: 183; Mookherjee, 2001: 15). Due to their emphasis on public debate, social contract, negotiation and civic participation, moral pluralists insist on common public institutions, constitution and jurisdiction that are pluralistic, open to change and genuinely responsive to diversity. Conversely, legal pluralists, examined in the next section, lean towards alternative institutional mechanisms to those provided by the state.

The role of a democratic constitution is highlighted by Tully in the transformation of the dominant culture through a dynamic form of public dialogue. Mookherjee, like Tully, believes the existence of plural and impartial state institutions can satisfy the demands of people with different normative and moral backgrounds. Yet Mookherjee places greater focus on the modernisation of minorities to enable their effective participation, which for her carries a practical value that is not equal to value liberalisation. Taylor's approach to transformation has two dimensions, like Mookherjee's. He expects the state to be more pluralistically democratic, and religious and cultural groups to adapt to and become compatible with democratic governance.

Moral pluralist thinkers search for a more substantive diversity than that embraced by Kymlicka and other liberal pluralists. They also provide more complex theoretical tools with which to account for the presence of religion in politics. Their arguments about the place of religion in constitution-making are crucial not only for Western democracies, where Muslims are minorities, but also for Muslim-majority contexts. Different forms of public reason, derived from competing ontological and epistemological sources, are relevant in rethinking political institutional designs within the context of Muslim democracy. A different narrative of democracy and pluralist secularism is envisaged by moral pluralist arguments in order to conciliate comprehensive moral differences, with rich implications for theorising Muslim democracy in a cross-cultural context.

IV. Legal Pluralist Multiculturalists: Gad Barzilai, Ido Shahar

The legal pluralist argument 'starts from the principle that social life should be ordered [so] as to enable collectivities to practice their own cultures' (Woodman, 1996: 165). The thinkers classified in this category propose a multiculturalist theory where jurisdictional autonomy is the key component for organised cultures and religions which provide a normative order, juridical theory and societal legal system for their members. They demand a substantial revision of the official law in order to grant formal status to non-state legal authorities to mutually govern the realm of law.

Legal pluralist multiculturalists articulate a notion of the thin state with a decentralised legal system, in which law-making is not only restricted to the state. The modern nation-state has 'tried to centralize and uniformize' the legal system as a result of 'an imperial heritage' (Yılmaz, 2005: 11). Law-making in the nation-state is 'autonomous from the social context' and insensitive to the moral diversity within society (Yılmaz, 2005: 344). On the other hand, legal pluralism interprets the law, not an abstract system of principles, as 'a socio-cultural construct . . . rooted in society' (Yılmaz, 2005: 3). People cannot observe law, according to legal pluralists, without reference to the context provided by their moral frameworks.

Legal pluralist multiculturalists are value pluralists who recognise different moral accounts of justice and equality for people. Liberalism is conceived to be neither the ideal political theory nor a universal framework. For legal pluralist multiculturalists, multiculturalism does not necessarily entail a liberal project. Instead, the main aim of multiculturalism is to facilitate a pluralist legal–political framework for diverse normative orderings to function. This section examines the arguments of Gad Barzilai, Frédéric Mégret and Ido Shahar on orthodox liberalism and religious–legal accommodation.

1. Critique of Orthodox Liberalism

Orthodox liberalism is criticised by Gad Barzilai for its perceived failure to include religion in political theory and hence for denying religion as a source of political claims. Although a significant role for religion exists in democratic politics, such a development is not adequately reflected in liberal discourse. According to Barzilai, religions are

> unique in the sense that they have offered to their believers a structured and sacred text that has embedded detailed normative guidelines of alternative order in all spheres of life. (2004: 3)

Modern liberalism is incapable of understanding religion as a source of 'constituting, articulating, and generating identities' and empowerment in the lives of individuals (Barzilai, 2004: 24). Western constitutionalism and modern liberalism have incorrectly privatised religion by separating it from the state, law and politics. Religiously-based political and legal demands, as well as identities, goods, demands and needs derived from religious sources, have been neglected as a component of a democratic politics and modern legality (Barzilai, 2004b).

The exclusion of religion from the political debate, for Barzilai, is generated from certain premises that have shaped liberal constitutionalism. First, the 'irrational' character of religion makes it ineligible for inclusion in modern law-making. Second, secularism is assumed to provide a genuine equality among religious minorities and offer a free choice of religion and ideology. Third, the rights discourse has had an overtly individualist outlook (Barzilai, 2008: 302).

Barzilai challenges these three premises on democratic grounds. First, democracies should not impose a certain account of universal goods or universal rationality. Instead, they should be 'sensitive to the different expectations and needs of individuals and communities' and 'stress the virtues of non-ruling communities and communal rights' (Barzilai, 2008: 6). Second, the secularisation of law based on a perception of an 'imagined separation between state law and non-state legal orders' has been inadequate in addressing the role of religion in modern politics and legality (2008: 399). Third, the exclusively individualist set of rights within liberal theory has neglected the normative and practical importance of 'communities as collective entities' because it fails to acknowledge that 'some portion of our personalities is embedded in these collectivities' (Barzilai, 2008: 302). Liberal theory has not recognised that the participation of communities and their legal cultures need more formal recognition in politics (Barzilai, 2008: 1).

The liberal paradigm has been criticised for its inability to protect and accommodate non-ruling and religious collectivities. Barzilai's critique of contemporary liberal structures, based on secularist, individualist and universalist premises, highlights their inevitable failure to realise democratic ideals. Liberalism should not be seen 'as an absolute truth and the objective criterion for legal order' within the context of multiculturalism (Barzilai, 2008: 56). Barzilai particularly challenges liberal constitutionalism in favour of a legal pluralist judicial system. He argues that 'law should perceive liberalism with all its virtues and importance of democracy as a relative tradition by itself' in the search for more inclusive theories of justice in order to offer a multicultural policy (Barzilai, 2004: 6). Although this critique of liberalism's entrenched inequalities may be correct for the Rawlsian strand, Barzilai ignores other liberal approaches that aim to accommodate communities articulated by Kymlicka, Amartya Sen and Martha Nussbaum. However, modern liberal constitutionalism's association with Rawlsian ideas may somewhat justify Barzilai's critique.

2. Religious–Legal Accommodation

Barzilai argues that communities embody a collectivity with 'a common perception of the collective good', legal consciousness and 'distinct practices and organizations' (2003: 28). These 'communities, crucial pillars in the conjunction of law and politics', should be recognised as legitimate components in politics, and given autonomy to develop and restructure their communal lives (Barzilai, 2003: 2). Similarly, Frédéric Mégret identifies 'multiple sources and authorities of law for religiously diverse people' in pluralist societies, and the state alone is not the sole dispenser of law (2012: 13). Complexity and dynamism of the processual relationship are emphasised by Ido Shahar between different sources of law and bodies of legal doctrine. Law in modern multicultural societies is perceived and practised as a combination of official, customary and religious legal systems in different social issues. Thus, law can exist outside of the state and does not need to be enforced by its institutions to have an operational force on people (Shahar, 2008: 434–5).

Legal pluralist multiculturalists conceive Islam, like Judaism, as a religion with jurisdictional, legal and political dimensions and public claims, unlike the spiritual characteristics of Christianity. It provides a formal code of values. The social context of Muslim minorities is a focal point in understanding their jurisdictional needs and demands within Western democracies. As a particular justification for legal pluralism, for instance, British Muslims do in fact navigate across various types of law in arranging their lives. For instance, they prefer their own laws and customs, especially in relation to family issues, due to secular law's perceived misrecognition of their moral judgements and needs. While British Muslims adhere to secular English law on various issues, their experiences of legal pluralism are a 'direct result of the relationship between official law and society' primarily in family law (Yılmaz, 2005: 4–5).

Shahar's alternative conceptualisation of legality seeks to uphold this dual legal reality. He proposes a legal system where an individual is an 'active' agent who has the ability to engage in 'meaningful forum shopping' to choose among jurisdictions and appeal to the desired tribunal which they believe offers solutions to their issues (Shahar, 2008: 436). In Shahar's model, litigants, not bound to their ethnic, religious or cultural belongings, can access a range of pluralist legal remedies (2008: 124, 140). Legal pluralist theorists argue that the transformation from monistic positivist law to legal pluralism would lead to a democratic shift in the agency of citizens from 'law-abiding' to 'law-inventing' citizens, where new and practical solutions could emerge in tackling the issues of the complexities of social life (Kleinhans and Macdonald, 1997: 2).

In his legal pluralist framework, Barzilai addresses the issue of in-group oppression. He proposes two principles for protecting the basic rights of citizens who choose a religious jurisdiction: first, 'the right to exit', to leave the group under state protection; and second, the 'redemptive principle' requiring state intervention to correct certain deeds in order to protect the vulnerable insiders in a group without dissolving its 'internal normative order' (Barzilai, 2004: 14).

Legal pluralism is located by Mégret within democratic politics in full consideration of human rights. He articulates a 'human rights case for legal pluralism' to further democratise modern legal systems (Mégret, 2012: 3). Mégret suggests that 'the problem of legal pluralism is a human rights problem' among minorities requiring the recognition of democratic politics (2012: 7). Accordingly, legal pluralism has the potential to bring an innovative

> approach that translates abstract and broad human rights standards into the vernacular of everyday life, transplanting these norms into ordinary human relations where they can truly achieve their formative potential. (Provost and Sheppard, 2013: 1)

Inclusion of religion and community in democratic theory appears to be necessary in formulating a new approach to dealing with religion for accomplishing justice for religious people. Legal pluralist multiculturalists maintain that organised religions, which provide the moral rationale for action, impact the collective practices and societal needs of their followers. Islam, like Judaism, has a stronger case in making collective demands for formal legal pluralism. Legal pluralist multiculturalists criticise the legal monism making the state the exclusive power in the legal realm of legality that has annulled communities' traditional social structures of power. It should be noted, however, that this legal monism is not only characteristic of liberal states. The critique of legal monism can also be extended to the modern nation-state, and positivist and unitary law, in general. Modern liberal theory has founded the state's legal institutions on unequal power relations between the dominant secular ideology and minority religious normative systems.

Legal pluralism seeks to redefine the boundaries of secularism, 'positivist jurisprudence' and 'legal centrism' in favour of more plural and 'decentralised' concepts of law and power. Barzilai argues that legal pluralism should aim to alter not only the structures of legality but also the political regime itself. The correct focus of legal pluralism should be on the development of 'a theoretical concept of political power that takes legal decentralisation' seriously rather than on mere legal reforms (Barzilai, 2008: 395). For Barzilai, this change within the realm of rights and institutions is a shift from a universalist liberal democracy to 'the broader framework of a multicultural democracy' (2008: 279).

Like Barzilai, Mégret also argues that law has 'an inherently collective and even institutional character' that requires more than negative freedoms for its collective practices. Therefore, the recognition of minority cultures and religions necessitates 'a new division of power within the state' for 'an active institutional set-up designed to delineate the spheres of competence of minority law, arbitrate tensions, and so on' (Mégret, 2012: 25). Recognition of legal pluralism, contingent on the structural characteristics and political culture of a country, can take the route of 'allowing a separate form of jurisdiction' or constructing a legal system that accommodates a variety of normative orientations for arbitration (Mégret, 2012: 4).

3. Concluding Remarks

Shared legal and political institutions according to moral pluralists, examined in the previous section, can be responsive to cultural and religious ways of life in order to achieve equality. Yet unlike moral pluralists, legal pluralist multiculturalists, by taking the value pluralist argument into the legal sphere, diverge from the idea of common institutionalism. A multiculturalist theory is proposed where religion plays a central role in collective claims. The right of a 'juridical secession' from the mainstream system of law is defended by legal pluralist multiculturalists in alternative jurisdictional arrangements (Mégret, 2012: 4). Human beings have the right 'to be judged within the normative system pertaining to their culture' in a framework of a pluralism pursued 'through the prism of legal arrangements' (Boyd, 2012: 56, 4).

Religious accommodation, for legal pluralists, requires different theorisations. The state is inherently unable to practise impartial justice as well as respond to people with different moral and legal narratives. Thus, a degree of autonomy for religiously diverse communities is necessary. Religions like Islam and Judaism, possessing their own legal frameworks, have a particular need for a legal pluralism that is accompanied by a framework for accommodating religion-based collective demands.

Formalisation of religious legal systems advocated by legal pluralist multiculturalists, within a liberal framework, is often viewed as evidence of the limits of multiculturalism. Despite the sympathy of many multiculturalists for the efforts of theorising a pluralist notion of legal theory, a considerable number of them are not convinced about the capability and efficiency of existing legal pluralist theories to respond to the issues of democracy, peace and order. The relationship between the state, groups and individuals in a sustainable political model seems to lack a holistic theoretical dimension. For instance, legal pluralist theories are unclear about whether groups will accept developing self-understanding in a democratic manner and become active parts of democratic politics. Further ambiguity surrounds responses to the possible rejection by groups of the process of democratic public interaction. How can a pluralist democratic system be sustainable if communities of citizens do not endorse the ideals of democracy and pluralism? What are the necessary precautions for ensuring the sustaining of civic bonds, and the maintenance of social cohesion?

The legal pluralist criticism of legal centralism contributes to re-assessing the relationship between secular and religious legal systems. Yet legal pluralists do not provide, or to be precise do not necessarily aim to provide, a political theory on multiculturalism. However, I will examine institutionalist pluralists, another school in the multiculturalist literature, in the next section. These advocates of multiculturalism propose to develop and augment legal pluralist arguments and address social, political and legal debates concerning normative recognition in a more comprehensive manner.

V. Institutionalist Pluralist Multiculturalists: Ayelet Shachar, Veit Bader

Institutionalist pluralists recognise the complexity of the relationship between religion, culture, state, politics and law, as alternatives to absolutist and universalist approaches. They argue that minority groups, particularly religious groups, should be given an institutional voice and a level of autonomy in order to decide and preserve their distinctive lifestyles. Institutionalist pluralists provide effective theoretical tools with which to create practical frameworks for the institutionalisation of religious minorities. These frameworks aim to reform public institutional structures to facilitate effective public representation and satisfactory public services. Ayelet Shachar and Veit Bader, two leading theorists, propose representative institutionalist pluralist approaches as a means of integrating the democratic nature of governance and public religious presence. This section will analyse their critiques of secularism in liberal theory and joint governance models of accommodation.

1. Critique of Secularism in Liberal Theory

Religion is observed by institutionalist pluralists to be a crucial part of social reality that gives believers an existential meaning of belonging while morally motivating their actions. Modern identities of human beings are composed of multi-faceted political and religious memberships inseparably linked. Law, as Shachar argues, is the realm where this link especially shows itself in people's mutual affiliations with both the formal state and informal religious jurisdictional authorities. Yet institutionalist pluralist scholars believe existing democratic legal–political frameworks do not systematically address the complexity of these affiliations.

Shachar undertakes 'a significant revision of the secular' and its exclusivist treatment of religion to propose a democratic model of multiculturalism in the context of politics and law (2008: 606). Philosophical secularism, often referred to as laicism, sets clear boundaries between the spheres of 'public/private, official/unofficial, secular/religious, positive law/traditional practice' (Shachar, 2008: 578). This approach is not sophisticated enough to respond to the multiple affiliations of modern citizens. Absolutist secularist models, rigidly separating formal and informal jurisdictional authorities, constitute the most severe constraint for believers of organised religions with multiple communal authorities and who are subject to more than one legal system (Shachar, 1998: 81; 2001: 91). An alternative approach to the secularist state model is advocated by Shachar in 'joint governance'. Its concept of shared authority challenges 'modern assumptions about the exclusivity of jurisdictional authority', to be discussed in further detail in the next section (Shachar, 2008: 147).

Veit Bader makes a similar argument about the 'unfair', 'counterproductive' and 'morally arbitrary' provision of services to religious citizens when public institutions take no account of religion (2003a: 4). He observes that the political inclusion of religion, unlike culture, is neglected by multiculturalism studies. To respond to this gap in the extant literature, Bader's multicultural theory awards a foundational place to religion. In his theory, Bader seeks an 'Institutionalist turn' for the re-organisation of the public sphere through the allocation of administrative functions to minority religions (2003b: 134). Secularist ideology's influence on mainstream liberal theory has hindered the development of effective tools and concepts to enable such a turn.

Bader believes the influence of secularist interpretations on the liberal paradigm is the principal obstacle that prevents the creation of genuine pluralist public frameworks that are inclusive to religious minorities. His discussion of liberal political principles such as neutrality and public reason reveals how secularist ideology negatively impacts the interpretations of these principles. First, the secularist argument in favour of the complete separation of political, legal, administrative and constitutional realms from religions is a 'radical utopia' (Bader, 2001: 2). What this formal restriction entails in reality, Bader argues, is the removal of people who embrace religious identities from public deliberation and their loss of equal representation in the national public discourse (2007a: 49). Second, contemporary liberalism, predominantly influenced by the Rawlsian paradigm, conceptualises public reason as a product of secular morality and the consensus of 'reasonable' citizens that adhere to a secular ontology. Therefore, Rawlsian liberalism assumes the existence of homogeneous views on public reason that reflects a common public good shared by the community of 'reasonable' citizens and their shared account of political justice. Although public reason exemplifies a thin concept of the good in the Rawlsian paradigm, rather than a thick one, it still endorses the secularist notions of rationality, universality and neutrality, where religious argument is unwelcome (Bader, 1999: 610).

Bader questions liberalism's discarding of religious arguments and claims from political or constitutional debates and public deliberation mechanisms. Purported universal accounts of liberalism, although in actual fact particularistic, block and inhibit the realisation of a genuine democratic public structure. Consequently, Bader advocates for 'an explicitly wide . . . inclusively broadened and pluralized perspective' in public reason that would take into account or allow space for diverse moral, ideological and cultural viewpoints (2003b: 266). This transformation can facilitate mutual understanding and democratic decision-making for an institutional re-organisation that redresses structural inequalities and ensures justice for religious minorities (Bader, 2003a: 131–4).

In addition, Bader argues for the replacement of 'normative secularism by priority for moral minimalism and liberal democracy' as the basis of the political structure (2009b: 1). The idea of 'priority for moral minimalism and liberal democracy', in Bader's thinking, entails the recognition that no contested truth-claim of any kind, whether religious, philosophical, or scientific, is entitled to overrule democratic political deliberation and decision making. (1999: 602)

As a result, the liberal democratic state should be neutral towards all competing conceptions of the good, unlike normative secularism which excludes non-secular arguments from the public sphere. Conceptual resources available in liberal theory, influenced by normative secularism, 'are still not differentiated enough' to sufficiently explain and normatively assess the relationship between religion and politics. No 'institutional alternatives' exist that can satisfy and give adequate consideration to religious accommodation (Bader, 2003c: 15).

The institutionalist pluralist restatement of liberal democracy, bereft of the secularist outlook, aims to create a political structure that accommodates particularity and multiplicity of cultures, religions, or ideologies in public institutions. Institutionalisation of religious diversity can occur in proposed models based on joint governance.

2. Joint Governance

Interdependence of the public and the private as state law and non-state normative ordering respectively operate 'within the same social-legal space' (Sezgin, 2013: 23). This dual functioning of state and religious jurisdictions is most evident in family law. Religious people in secular states, especially Muslims and Jews, notes Shachar, marry both in secular and religious ceremonies. Although civil marriage makes the union legal, religious ceremony makes it legitimate in the eyes of the people concerned (Shachar, 2009: 137). While the same recognition applies to the case of divorce, more complications emerge in this area. For some Muslim and Jewish women, if they only obtain a civil divorce, without ending their marriage according to the religious precepts, they still consider themselves married but lacking any legal rights. This situation makes 'women prey to abuse by recalcitrant husbands who are well aware of the adverse effect this situation has on their wives, as they fall between the cracks of the civil and religious jurisdictions' (Shachar, 2009: 134). Religious dimensions of a divorce should be recognised so women are not left at the mercy of their husbands in family law issues (Shachar, 2009: 140).

Multiculturalist scholars in recent years have increasingly questioned the nation-state's uniform legal system, 'normative unification' and 'undivided domestic sovereignty'. Some aspects of internal affairs of religious groups should be outside of the state's intervention to enable 'differing levels and forms of decentralization and fragmentation by maintaining plural institutions and practices in various issue areas such as personal status or family law' (Sezgin, 2013: 22–3). In this area, the scholarship on joint governance has addressed the legal decentralisation of state power for religious accommodation. Religious and civic sources of authority that combine to regulate people's lives according to joint governance should formally and institutionally interact and co-operate on a frequent basis. Joint governance can reconcile the perceived oppositional dichotomy of citizenship and group membership, public and private justice, as well as individual and collective goods. This framework provides an alternative space for individual constituencies of groups to practise their multiple loyalties in in harmony. Institutional pluralism, which recognises these groups, can also help to generate transformativeness in their practices or reinforce the normative commitment to democracy (Shachar, 2001: 88; 2008: 575).

Shachar examines several existing models of joint governance while identifying their weaknesses. The first model is 'federal-style accommodation' that grants legal authority to local governments. It is a territory-based approach that includes only indigenous and minority peoples who have been historically located in a territory and have governed themselves by their traditional legal mechanisms. This model's weaknesses are similar to Kymlicka's model of accommodation as both are limited and fail to effectively deal with religious groups. The second model is 'temporal accommodation'. State and cultural groups possess their authorities for fixed periods of time and alternate their control when the allocated time is over. For instance, Amish children's education is under the authority of the state until the eighth grade, after which the Amish community's jurisdiction is in charge. For Shachar, the lack of plural options for public services and the inability to choose and negotiate do not fit her proposed interaction-based framework. The third model of 'consensual accommodation' involves the one-time choice of an individual in selecting a jurisdictional framework between the state and the groups. Selection of a particular jurisdiction does not allow further scope to change one's choice;

this mechanism, for Shachar, is not conducive to the protection of the democratic rights of individuals. Individual autonomy should be protected and the right to change jurisdictional authorities should be permanently accessible. The final model is 'contingent accommodation' in which the state allocates certain jurisdictional autonomy to groups under exclusively state-imposed regulations and rules. The moral character of the community, according to Shachar, is not adequately served by the state enjoying absolute authority in defining not only the terms of joint governance but also the nature of the jurisdictional regulations for the group (2001: 92–112).

Various proposals for joint governance seeking to create a framework that facilitates the co-functioning of state and non-state legal norms have left certain gaps in their efforts. They either have prioritised one aspect over the other or are bereft of effective democratic regulatory mechanisms. Shachar and Bader have revised the theory of joint governance to fill this gap in the literature to bring democratic formulations in line with contemporary multicultural societies. I will now examine, first, Shachar's transformative accommodation, followed by Bader's non-constitutional pluralism.

a. Transformative Accommodation
Transformative accommodation, in joint governance, seeks to institutionalise a 'permanent and comprehensive mechanism' between the state and 'religiously and culturally defined nomoi communities', with a common world-view and law, guided by democratic ideals (Shachar, 2001: 114). Religious sources of law contribute to the resolution of legal disputes, which in turn aid the progress of society by making use of religion to work for the advantage of democracy (Shachar, 2001: 120). Shachar argues that the legal recognition of groups would allow in-group jurisdictions to become subject to 'legal recourse', and subsequently allow the monitoring of democratic standards (2009: 144). Traditionally vulnerable groups such as women can find amelioration through transformative accommodation when informal, cultural discriminatory patterns are brought into the open for political scrutiny (Shachar, 2008: 579). Failure to achieve such an interaction between secular and religious jurisdictions, Shachar warns, can result in people unofficially living in isolated, underground and unregulated communities. In these situations, members' rights and freedoms would be violated by concealed

decisions, and state authorities' involvement often cannot provide remedy unless parties decide to inform them.

Transformative accommodation envisages 'a model of regulated interaction' of state law and group jurisdictions for an agreement-based voluntary accession mechanism to a legal authority (Shachar, 2009: 143). In doing so, it takes religious law to be neither a competitor nor an opposing system to the secular establishment but a complementary normative system. Re-alignment of religious and secular jurisdictions within Shachar's theory is restricted to the administration of semi-public law. Power and authority sharing is present in governing areas such as family disputes and education (Shachar 2008: 606).

In transformative accommodation's proposed legal system, the state creates 'predefined standard rules and procedures' of mutual checks and balances between communal and central authorities. Protection is extended to both citizenship rights for all and the collective goods of the members of the religious groups (Shachar, 2008: 148). State allocation of power to group jurisdictions should be followed by religious authorities making public their own rules, positions and jurisdictions in the designated social and legal arenas (Shachar, 2001: 128). Once this process has been completed, the constituencies can register in a preferred jurisdiction 'to which they are subject in different social arenas' (Shachar, 2001: 147). For instance, a person can register separately with the state jurisdiction in education and with the group jurisdiction in family law. The state becomes the 'original power-holder' in the educational authority and the communal authority becomes the 'original power-holder' in matrimonial issues (Shachar, 2001: 124).

Should constituents feel they have been offered a 'meaningful remedy' in a particular matter by the original power-holder, they can '"switch" their jurisdiction loyalty . . . to the rival-power holder' (Shachar, 2001: 123). Shachar calls this act 'reversal points', which ensures an individual's right to 'clearly delineated' and 'meaningful' options between jurisdictional authorities to protect her or his interests (2001: 118; 2008: 147). Through the provision of a meaningful legal and institutional choice, transformative accommodation intends to ensure 'vulnerable insiders' are no longer subordinated to either patriarchal group traditions or monistic state jurisdiction (Shachar, 2001: 122).

A jointly governed legal arena through legalising authority-sharing of official and unofficial legal systems promotes a 'non-exclusive' yet rewarding competition. Accommodation consists of interaction, negotiation, dialogue, and mutual learning between the state and groups in a mutual process of transformation (Shachar, 2008: 146–7). For Shachar, the state and religious groups are constantly racing 'for the loyalty of their shared constituents', and this provides individuals with potential influence over both state and groups (2001: 122). Despite discriminatory practices, people desire, most of the time, to remain part of their traditional structures while also often demanding to negotiate their positions in the group to improve their lives, for group constituencies' 'credible threats of exit' provide 'an important bargaining chip' and a 'realistic tool' to exercise 'in-group leverage' to achieve internal reforms (Shachar, 2008: 143, 149). The common good is served by transformative accommodation by creating incentives for the state and in-group leadership to provide better social and legal services, be more accountable, and constrain the leadership (Shachar, 2001: 107).

Shachar is aware of the potential discrimination generated by hierarchies and inequalities within minority groups that vulnerable individuals may experience at the hands of their leadership via supplementary group jurisdiction. Democratic standards provide the regulatory and reconciliatory framework for the coexistence of the liberal state and other non-liberal jurisdictions based on the priority of the protection of the human rights of these group insiders. She strongly emphasises that if any reason hinders in-group members from exercising their agency, the liberal state is obligated to intervene to ensure the realisation of 'state-defined' democratic standards for every citizen. The state should ensure the accessibility of state law and state institutions to all citizens without communal authorities preventing individuals from making appeals to them (Shachar, 2009: 148).

Similarly, Shachar acknowledges that the autonomous status gained by the groups could also generate a hardening of in-group leadership's attitudes. Communal authorities may well want dissident or unhappy elements to leave rather than undertake internal changes and reforms. Yet she believes that this would be the case in the short term. In the long run, the procedural safeguards of 'entrance', 'exit' and 're-entry' options put forward by the state, amid competing systems, make both democratisation of in-group structures and normative democratic change more likely (Shachar, 2001: 114). However, Shachar does not fully explore the issue of in-group transformation. Internal reform directly linked to normative and religious reform cannot be guaranteed. One solution might be the fostering of the reinterpretation by individuals of their traditional philosophies in social processes. Credible channels for internal change could arise from such a normative rethinking, which the framework of Muslim democracy will develop in the following chapters.

Another important feature of transformative accommodation is its context-sensitive application of its principles within a democratic setting. Individuals are afforded the opportunity to redefine their relations to communal and civic authorities within the framework of the already existing democratic model of a country (Shachar, 2009: 133–4). In other words, differentiation of institutional models should be expected in each country concerning how much power will be allocated to the internal affairs of the minority groups, or the boundaries between the state and the group. For instance, in countries with a secular absolutist model, 'this variant of joint governance requires the state to relinquish some of its legal powers and delegate them to nomoi groups operating within its borders' (Shachar, 2001: 147). Where institutional pluralism is already evident, the model will contain increased autonomy for groups in those countries.

Shachar presents novel arguments with implications for accommodating diversity in liberal thought. A more enhanced version of liberal democratic governance would be a product of a constructive dialogue between individuals who want to reconcile the multiple affiliations that might have jurisdictional claims with legitimacy for them. The idea of regulated, interactive and co-operating legal and institutional mechanisms 'appealing to, and integrating, the operations of two value systems' rather than separating their spheres of execution is central to Shachar's model (2001: 130). Shachar conciliates the aspirations of the multicultural and liberal commitments within a political community to open new horizons of thinking and action in multiculturalist thought. She shows how jurisdictional pluralism can create a public sphere that awards a status to religious private law, which is a central preoccupation of the Muslim democracy framework developed in this book, under a more pluralist and democratic version of secularism.

b. Non-Constitutional Pluralism

Non-constitutional pluralism, for Bader, generates a multiculturalist model of associative democracy (AD) (2003a: 271). This model proposes a morally thin state framework that restricts 'government to its core tasks' (Bader, 2007a: 189). The state is conceptualised as decentralised, 'multi-level governance', with many of its administrative and economic powers delegated to 'self-governing' civil society. A democratic superstructure provides associations which are based on the 'voluntary intermingling' of people based on institutional pluralism. As such, associative democracy enables citizens to 'build their own social worlds' where they enjoy 'greater control of their affairs . . . in welfare' (Hirst, 1997: 13, 25). Bader formulates his model of non-constitutional pluralist religious accommodation within the context of associative democracy theory.

The direct or indirect consequences of state policies cannot be completely impartial in pluralist or polarised societies when religion is cast aside in many other areas such as health, education and finance. Therefore, minorities should have the right to institutional representation through associations in organising and funding non-governmental welfare and quasi-public services. According to Bader, associational autonomy is necessary for empowering minorities, offsetting the discrimination they face and guaranteeing the state's even-handed approach in the public sphere (2001: 2). Non-constitutional pluralism, for Bader, can create

> opportunities for organised religions to provide a broad range of services like education, health care and care for [the] elderly, and it enables a wide variety of divergent service providers to participate in public, democratic standard setting and critically scrutinising service provision. (2003a: 287)

Like Shachar's model, Bader conceptualises a formalised interaction and dual legal authority-sharing mechanism supervised by the constitutional state in order to free religious people from the contrived choice 'between their right and their culture' (2009a: 67). Minority jurisdictional authority is also recognised in private and personal legal matters while maintaining legislation in the hands of the democratic constitutional state (Hirst, 1997: 18). Associative democracy provides 'no competence or jurisdiction [to religious groups] in matters of criminal law or law affecting the legal status' (Bader, 2009a: 51). Although functioning at a minimal moral and administrative level, associative democracy is still capable of guaranteeing the fundamental human rights of individuals and ensuring normative democratic benchmarks (Hirst and Bader, 2001: 190). A particular focus exists for the need to 'protect and guarantee the fundamental interest of vulnerable minorities, particularly children' (Bader, 2009a: 64).

Bader and Shacher are in common agreement about the formalisation of religious jurisdiction. It is preferable to informal methods of dispute resolution for the fulfilment of religious freedoms and human rights. Bader argues that religious practices are invisible to state scrutiny in the absence of their formal recognition. The state has almost no oversight over what is happening inside nomoi groups, and thereby cannot prevent human rights abuses of group members such as children and women by communal religious or cultural authorities (Bader, 2009a: 50–1). Non-constitutional pluralist models aim to protect the rights of individual members reinforced by the availability of real and meaningful exit options (Bader, 2003b: 154).

Bader is also aware of the challenges of national fraternity and unity. A non-constitutional pluralist model, in which religious minorities would have a considerable yet not separate autonomy, accommodates religious pluralism within a civic framework (Bader, 2003b: 286). A stronger sense of civic and national identity can be generated among minorities, overcoming feelings of otherness and isolation, accompanied by their recognition as equal participants in the public sphere within a democratically regulated framework (Bader, 2003a: 17). A non-constitutional pluralist model diverges from a strict institutional separation and unrestricted legal autonomy that can weaken the shared political membership among citizens, which in turn may cause the segregation of society.

Bader contends that the attempt to offer 'open', 'flexible' and 'context-specific' solutions should adhere to the 'non-establishment' principle of not constitutionalising religious recognition (2003b: 285). Constitutionalised recognition, 'prescribing definitive specified institutions', would create a '"rigid" and "inflexible"' system (Bader, 2003b: 285). Legalised recognition of groups can give unaccountable power to group leaderships that infringes on the rights of individual group members. A conflict between legal pluralism and non-constitutional pluralism surrounds the protection of individual freedoms and prospects for progress.

The normative principles of 'associationalist system' will now be examined and applied to the issue of education. Educational autonomy is a major component of Bader's theory of non-constitutional pluralism (1994: 176). Bader argues that 'if governmental schools cannot or do not live up to the requirements of legitimate or reasonable pluralism or cultural diversity of all sorts in the context and practice of teaching', then 'freedoms of education include the free establishment and running of religious schools and forbid enforcing a monopoly for governmental schools' (2007a: 278, 279). Individuals choose their associational administration in a non-constitutional pluralist framework so as to receive their education services through 'free', 'voluntary' and 'informed' consent. Guardians of pupils can register them in the schools that they think best serve their expectations and interests. Public regulation to ensure the voluntary membership of associations and the right to change associations involve 'appropriate but minimal content regulation' and minimal democratic standards of public scrutiny (Hirst, 1997: 18). For example, schools and hospitals founded by faith-based associations are free to hire their personnel but cannot control service-users such as students and patients respectively. Religious freedom outweighs the principle of non-discrimination in the former while in the latter the principle of non-discrimination takes precedence (Bader, 2007a: 143).

Direct or indirect public financing of religious schools is also a component of non-constitutionalist pluralism in which educational associations can 'obtain public funds [tax money] proportionate to membership for public purposes' (Hirst, 1997: 18). The funding, however, should be conditional. Bader explains that civil society associations 'are subject to public inspection and standard-setting' and 'must meet conditions of registration to receive public funds, among these would be compliance with public standards, acceptance of [annual] exit rights and recipient choice' (Hirst, 1997: 150; Hirst and Bader, 2001: 118). Competition among educational institutions for public funds and these institutions' effort to ensure the integrity and accountability of their rules to satisfy their members will most likely lead to an eventual internal reform and democratisation (Bader, 2001: 61). Educational autonomy provides religious freedoms and is an effective alternative to the unitary educational system in terms of its success. Cross-national data demonstrate the superiority of religious schools for better student achievement in academic subjects and values 'outside the traditional public school' (Bader, 2007a: 271–2).

A common weakness in both non-constitutional pluralism and transformative accommodation is the lack of a theoretical development on internal democratisation. Critics of multiculturalism often argue that such processes can lead to the opposite outcome: the segregation of the society and the radicalisation of youth. However, Bader proposes the tools of public regulation and the right to exit as a means of addressing these concerns. Yet religious reform and value change to internalise democratisation are also essential and may be facilitated through the expansion of religious freedoms. However, this cannot be maintained without the processes of internal religious transformation.

Bader's critique of liberal paradigms relates to their treatment of organised religions. Religion and morality possess political and legal relevance, and hence should be given public space. Certain forms of group rights need to be granted to religious groups that are at the same time compatible with the human rights paradigm as an embodiment of freedom of conscience, democratic representation and holistic autonomy (Bader, 2001: 10). A thick and morally pluralist diversity with a morally minimalist democratic regulatory mechanism is advocated by Bader to accommodate organised religions in a pluralist public sphere. This reformulation of multiculturalism represents a more advanced and sophisticated idea of political pluralism than orthodox liberalism.

3. Concluding Remarks

Institutionalist pluralists develop models of accommodation for 'nomoi communities'. In many contexts, it is religion, not culture, which has fundamental societal importance for citizens. A multiculturalist theory is proposed by institutionalist pluralists, inspired by multicultural principles, to award a more central place to religion in collective claims. Followers of organised religions, on account of their claims on the mechanisms of jurisprudence, inevitably have distinct societal needs. The concept of religious diversity for institutionalist pluralists requires different theorisations and policies to locate the concepts of law and legalism within multiculturalist accommodation.

Although both Shachar and Bader have similar views on the practical features of institutional pluralism, numerous significant differences exist between them on secularism and liberalism. Bader adopts a more critical posture towards liberalism and strongly challenges secularism. Secularism is a sphere of its own that is clearly differentiated from the democratic paradigm. Although Shachar is a liberal and Bader a moral pluralist, I have placed them in the same category because their models for a new institutional framework are more important to their overall theorisations than their positions regarding liberal theory.

Institutionalist pluralists propose a mechanism of legal and administrative interconnectivity to provide plural options within the public realm for citizens with diverse normative beliefs. For instance, in resolving lawsuit cases, litigants are offered a choice of dispute resolution mechanisms between either state or communal jurisdictions. When citizens access the service sector, they are offered a choice of public utilities between either communal or state organisations.

A crucial component of institutionalist pluralist thought is its profound emphasis on democratic standards to protect 'the minority within the minority'. Shachar argues that the duty to balance the rights and cultural membership in accommodationist models should not be left to the citizens themselves (2008: 575). The state has a duty to provide an institutional design that ensures this balance. In addition, the state should be in charge of political–legal accommodation, with public law in its hands, by expanding the public sphere for religions within a monitored sphere of influence.

Meanwhile, institutionalist pluralist multiculturalists aim for a transformation of a political culture so it can serve as the catalyst for an institutional turn, as well as the democratisation of the internal norms and practices of minorities. Accommodation is not a static process. Transformation and interaction characterise accommodation in the constant redrawing of the relationship between the state and groups as well as the relationships within each entity. Such a change entails going from the unitary nature of the state that strictly controls public life to a power-sharing state that minimally regulates the public sphere. Minority groups, through the experience of the interaction of different legal approaches and institutional paradigms, will gradually internalise democratic values out of their own volition. Citizens are likely to develop normative commitments to a democratic system, it is argued, where their comprehensive moral views are institutionally recognised. Both transformative accommodation and non-constitutionalist pluralism, through integration and co-operation between different legal systems, seek to achieve democratic value change within the state system and traditional structures. Bringing minority groups under a form of constitutional control, in a process of formalisation, is also believed to make it easier to regulate in-group interactions. Consequently, this would protect the rights of vulnerable insiders and empower them to demand the right to make claims within their groups. Institutional pluralist models seek to generate democratic deepening at various multi-faceted levels.

Conciliation of the key themes of the other three schools is undertaken by institutionalist pluralists in a single model. Institutionalist pluralists adopt a theoretical justification for multicultural accommodation from liberal pluralists and integrate this position with the normatively committed pluralist perspectives of the moral pluralists while also embracing the legal pluralists' support for jurisdictional autonomy. An institutionalist pluralist synthesis of the key elements of the three other multiculturalist schools has led to the formulation of models for the institutionalisation of diversity.

VI. Conclusion on Multiculturalist Political Thought

Multiculturalism seeks to conceptualise inclusive and accommodative ways within political theory to respond to cultural and religious diversity in Western societies. In its early formulation, culture, the main focus of the multiculturalist literature, seemed to provide the most essential basis for social context, group identity and community relations in an individual's life. Although multiculturalism has criticised liberalism's neglect of culture, it has never rejected liberalism in the quest to accommodate diversity. Rather, it was a theory that proposed the advancement of liberal pluralism motivated by the key liberal values of autonomy, toleration, equality of opportunity and freedom of association (Kymlicka, 1992: 44; Kukathas, 1992: 127; Mookherjee, 2009: 150). The balance sought between individual and cultural rights led multiculturalist thinkers to redefine the relationship between nation-state and cultural minorities through the adoption of political, institutional and legal changes.

After 9/11, however, the focus of religion was revived in debates within political theory. As a result, multiculturalists highlighted the component of religion in diversity. Debates in the West about the parameters of public rights of religious individuals and groups within a secular state emerged in the foreground. Multiculturalist intellectuals like Ayelet Shachar have argued that the non-recognition of Islamic norms among Muslims has generated the dilemma of being a member of a religious community and a citizen of a political community (2001: 122). Accordingly, models have been proposed to successfully resolve the ongoing disputes between secular statehood and demands arising from religious lifestyles. Through a critical evaluation of intellectual traditions, this book has first examined the different schools of socio-political and legal thought within the Western multiculturalist literature. This will be followed by an attempt to articulate more informed and pluralistic conceptualisations of secularism, law, state and public sphere within a Muslim democracy framework.

A democratic framework is often taken for granted within the multiculturalist literature. The thinkers examined in this chapter argue that justification of culturally or religiously derived rights presumes the existence of the political and legal requirements of a robust democracy. While affirming the necessity for a strong democratic constitutional order, most of the thinkers in this chapter's typology emphasise that democratic governance does not or should not require a strict separation of the secular and the religious. This position has led to calls for new forms of secularism through which collective rights could be introduced in democratic structures alongside established individual rights.

A common point within multiculturalist political theory is opposition to 'philosophical secularism' (Laborde, 2002: 167).[1] This notion of secularism envisages a separationist political model, exclusively limiting religion and culture to private life. It creates boundaries between progressive versus traditional on the one hand, and religious versus secular on the other, where politics is ultimately secular. In contrast, multiculturalist thinkers advocate a 'liberal-pluralist secularism' (Maclure and Taylor, 2011; Modood, 2010) which recognises the validity of culture and religion and supports the inclusion of comprehensive moral views in the public realm. In fact, a functional, rather than a philosophical or substantive, definition of secularism is also borne out through multiculturalist thinkers' more minimalist theorisations of the state (Mookherjee, 2001: 69; Shachar, 2001: 91; Tully, 2008a: 166). Their critique of universal, ideological secularism has given birth to alternative liberal conceptions. Pluralist secularism and its acknowledgement of religious diversity in the public sphere inform the discussion of the Muslim democracy framework in the final chapter of this book.

Liberal pluralists, such as Will Kymlicka, highlight the interdependence of the public and the private with reference to how culture penetrates these two spheres (1995: 94). No clear distinction exists between public and private identities as the pursuit of the conception of goods encompasses these two spaces. Liberal multiculturalists oppose privatising comprehensive philosophical views in their advocacy of cultural rights for minorities that go beyond the standard liberal protection. However, the normative arguments they make to validate this expansion are liberal in nature.[2] Moral pluralists take the agenda of the expansion of the secular paradigm even further. While supporting functional, rather than philosophical, secularism, they also assert that universal secularism does not have to be the only meta-narrative of a democratic system. Political philosophers like Charles Taylor recognise that the Islamic foundations for a democratic political system could result from a different contextualised narrative of secularity (2008: xvii).

More inclusive and democratic notions of the law have preoccupied multiculturalist thinkers. A pluralistic concept of a constitution, open to change, and a democratic balance of different demands and principles via civic deliberation can enable the state to provide justice and impartiality (Tully, 1995: 26). Unitary law and legal monism have been challenged by legal pluralists and institutionalist pluralists. States based on these foundations can neither provide equal distance to all philosophical world-views nor respond to the jurisdictional needs of different organised religions. Both legal and institutionalist positions present a multiculturalist challenge with different pluralist solutions to 'the legal modernity paradigm' and its universalist tendencies. Institutionalist pluralists support a pluralist yet common public system in which national government and religious groups share authority to resolve semi-public disputes. Marriage and divorce, among consenting adults, are monitored by the democratic regulatory criteria of the central government (Shachar, 2008: 575). Restricted juridical secession from the mainstream system of law is defended by legal pluralists to ensure collective rights and societal alternative jurisdictional measures for minorities (Mégret, 2012: 4).

Furthermore, a new agenda on law and alternative conceptions of the state emerge in the multiculturalist literature. The pursuit of a change in the relationship between the central authority and minority groups for multiculturalists also involves a change in the character of the modern state framework. Thus, multiculturalist intellectuals challenge the notions of universalist citizenship, homogenising state institutions and a uniform law. Greater limitations on the powers of the nation-state accompany the expansion of civil society's political sphere. Redistributive changes by the state are a liberal pluralist concern while moral pluralists have argued for a substantial change towards the normative recognition of difference that is also shared by legal and institutionalist pluralists (Kymlicka and Norman, 2000: 4; Taylor, 1994: 38).

Moral, legal and institutionalist strands of pluralist thought defy the philosophical theory of the state and the existence of a dominant ideology or religion within a state structure. The thinkers in these categories question the idea of a state that promotes a specific common culture, ideology, or comprehensive view. Philosophical matters should be left by the state to individuals and groups. Resolution of conflicts between the state and cultural and religious groups, as well as within the groups, is raised by political theory and multiculturalism.

The possibility of 'just bonds' between the state and religion has long been questioned due to the former's decision-making powers as the sovereign entity in matters of public and private, ethics and politics, and accepted public religiosity (Fish, 1997: 2274). Moral pluralists, institutionalist pluralists and legal pluralists challenge the idea of the nation-state having absolute sovereignty with the exclusive right of regulating and managing religion in its own hands. However, theorists working within a liberal nation-state framework cannot run away from 'an asymmetric relation of power' between state and religion, as 'the liberal democratic state enjoys sovereignty over all other groups and associations on their territory' (Berlinerblau 2017: 94; Laborde, 2018b: 162). Liberal democracy as a political ideology and system has developed within the context of nation-state. For Rogers Brubaker, the linked ideas, ideals, and organizational models of nation, state, citizenship, and democracy form a kind of package. This package has a certain common core, underlying the varying adaptations, appropriations, and transformations. (2015: 152)

In liberal democratic theory, criticism is present of the universalistic or hegemonic tendencies of the state. However, formulations of politics and civil society are restricted by a liberal normative paradigm and are unable to transcend the basic premises of the sovereign state. In other words, 'liberal-democratic theorists are more prepared to recommend relaxing state sovereignty than dismantling it' (Cunningham, 2002: 207).

Although the debate about the state is ongoing, liberal theory seems to favour the state in the domestic sphere as the final sovereign arbiter in deciding the boundary between right and good, public and private, and legal and moral (Lock, 2016: 156). The available conceptual tools and theoretical resources are not nuanced enough within liberal democratic theory to provide a 'just' relationship between religion and politics. Therefore, certain ambiguities and asymmetries are to be expected in theorising the relationship between the state and religion that multiculturalists cannot run away from. A 'just balance' between the state and religious groups in the public sphere is inconceivable despite the best efforts of multiculturalists to work out a fair balance in their theories and models. All schools of multiculturalism examined here manifest a clear commitment to the democratic resolution of state and group dealings and conflicts. The role of the state as the final arbiter does not preclude the process of negotiation with other groups and associations in their demands for more pluralistic state–religion relations.

Multiculturalist thinkers offer different mechanisms for state control and varying public powers to minorities. Yet they all see the state as the legitimate authority to preside over a pluralistic public sphere. Maintenance of pluralism makes state regulations unavoidable. However, these do not constitute an absolute exercise of state authority. For instance, moral and institutionalist pluralists declare the state does not have the mandate to impose a moral agenda of change. Intellectuals like Mookherjee emphasise that the state should facilitate a democratic environment so that challenges to undemocratic practices and the demand for change arises from within groups. The state's role is to persuade non-democratic minorities to be involved in democratic governance through good example, exchange of ideas and democratic communication (Mookherjee, 2005: 44). In addition, institutionalist pluralists like Shachar and Bader argue that the state remains in control of institutionalist pluralist accommodation through the establishment of minimalist standards of moral constraints. The redressing of human rights abuses within group arrangements falls under the responsibility of the state to protect the individual's rights and interests (Bader, 2001: 10; Shachar, 2008: 433; Shachar, 2009: 148).

All the thinkers examined in this chapter express the need for a reformed public sphere that recognises and reflects cultural and religious needs in an even-handed manner. They conceive of a more participatory, civic and heterogeneous public sphere, where more freedoms and recognition for minorities are realised. This notion of the public sphere can only be made possible through pluralistic accounts of secularism. Public norms and institutions for moral pluralists should be dynamic and open to change, not imposed, arising from the social context (Tully, 1995: 26). Legal and institutionalist pluralists advocate putting certain jurisdictional and public needs of different religious followers out of reach of the state. Civil society organisations should be given public authority in morally diverse societies. Regulated public autonomy in administrative matters, based on an institutionally pluralist public design, redefines the relationship between the state and the minorities in favour of a more democratic and pluralistic framework (Bader, 2001: 2; Shachar, 2008: 154–5).

Multiculturalist thinkers elaborate further the discussion of a pluralistic public sphere. In addition to marking out the spheres of autonomous governance, they also address the issue of shared governance. They discuss the necessity for normative consensus, and the degree of it necessary for a political organisation to be able to unify people with diverse comprehensive philosophical views as citizens. Multiculturalist theorists claim accommodation does not mean ghettoisation of minority groups and their members. Citizens participate in a process to agree on a notion of the common good in order to live alongside each other. Thus, moral and institutionalist pluralists emphasise the essential task of establishing civic unity. For instance, Bader states that a 'minimally required . . . [normative] commitment in the polity' is a must for institutional pluralism to work (2003: 144). Mookherjee (2001) emphasises the importance of constructing 'the common language of reasonableness' for pluralist public reasoning. In Mookherjee's account, pluralist public reasoning would involve the co-operation of diverse moral and philosophical views to formulate the shared rules of societal life. Tully's contribution to this debate centres on the significance he attributes to consensus-making: civic debate is the final authority of legal and political rules (2012: 124). Similarly, Taylor suggests that achieving an overlapping consensus, through public debate, 'peaceful coexistence' and public negotiations, constitutes the basis of a pluralist democratic system (1996: 20). Inclusive methods are offered by multiculturalists to rethink public life and its potential democratic reform.

Notes

1. Philosophical secularism is often referred to as republican secularism, and at times is defined as 'aggressive secularism' (Kuru, 2013) or 'militant secularism' (Soroush, 2007; Fuller, 2004; Ahmad, 2006).
2. Rawls's theory in its later version permits religious articulation of ideas of the shared good so long as they can be translated into rational language and argumentation. However, the pressure to translate could also be costly and could hinder people with different onto-ethics. In the final chapter, the public inclusion of comprehensive moral doctrines will be addressed in a more focused framework within which a certain level of translation can take place in a more inclusivist manner under the analytical category of the social public sphere.

GENERAL CONCLUSION TO PART ONE: TYPOLOGIES OF MUSLIM AND MULTICULTURAL POLITICAL THOUGHT

Muslim and multiculturalist thought contains debates on the relationship between Islam, law, public sphere and institutional design. Multiculturalist and Islamic thinkers have discussed similar topics and highlighted common notions. For instance, Muslim scholars have examined whether Islam is compatible with secularism, democracy and liberalism, while multiculturalists have reversed the line of questioning to address whether democracy, liberalism and secularism can accommodate Muslims' public roles and demands. Multiculturalism has embarked on revisions of liberalism and secularism to explore how these ideologies could accommodate Muslim public lifestyles. Some thinkers, such as Taylor, formulate theories in which Islam is capable of laying moral foundations for democracy, which echoes the arguments of al-Jabri, of the Islamic modernist school.

Muslim and multiculturalist political thinkers share a scepticism towards the powers of the secular state and its relation to religion. They both advocate the re-organisation of the political sphere to reflect and respect religious identity. The choice between common political–legal institutions shaped by their contexts and separate, autonomous institutions, co-functioning with the state, has dominated scholarly debates. Multiculturalist thinkers like Shachar and Barzilai have discussed whether Islamic legal norms should or can have some form of legitimacy in the modern state (Shachar, 2009: 133). Other thinkers, such as Bader, have examined the options for administrative, jurisdictional and institutional autonomy resonating with Bulaç's arguments (Bader, 2003b: 134; Bulaç, 2006: 190). However, multiculturalist thinkers have gone beyond their Islamic counterparts in proposing practical models and mapping out the formalisation of religious law and institutions and the modalities of state regulation. These alternative formulations of the link between religion and politics entail reconceptualising the state, secularism, the public sphere and the constitution. A theory of Muslim democracy can productively utilise these revised concepts.

While the multiculturalism literature has addressed the norms of democracy to envisage more pluralistic democratic models, Muslim political thought has mostly focused on the functional aspects of democracy. The debates among Muslim political thinkers, with the prime exception of progressives, have either not broached the contentious areas of the principles of democracy or have engaged with them in a reductionist or eclectic manner. Muslim political thought has struggled with the debate on popular versus divine sovereignty, with the outcome of de facto theories to overcome contradictions. The issues of the socio-political status of non-Muslim citizens, the application of Islamic law, and rights and liberties continue to elude a meaningful resolution. Theories proposing political models present in the multiculturalism literature can enhance the arguments raised by various Muslim thinkers. I concur with the argument that multiculturalism can provide 'a more appropriate discourse than the more traditional notions of religious pluralism and tolerance for understanding Muslim civic claims-making' within democratic settings (Modood and Ahmad, 2007: 196). The examination of two intellectual traditions has provided new perspectives for redefining the relationship between the state, religion, minorities and politics and hence has offered more adequate tools for a theory of Muslim democracy.

The purpose of this book is the theorising of Muslim democracy through establishing normative conjunctions between Muslim and multiculturalist approaches to political thought. To pursue this aim, the next chapter will examine Muslim thought's compatibility-based arguments on democracy in order to identify their weaknesses and ambiguities. This step will contribute to the formulation of a theory on Muslim democracy, which is the focus of the third part of this book. The fourth, fifth and sixth chapters in Part III will bring together the themes that emerged from the examination of Muslim political and multiculturalist thinkers in Chapters 1 and 2. Part III will also reinterpret and contextualise these themes with arguments from liberal and republican theories in order to construct a theory of Muslim democracy.

PART TWO

DECONSTRUCTING MUSLIM DISCOURSES ON DEMOCRACY

3

THE COMPATIBILITY-BASED ARGUMENTS

I. Introduction

The chapters in Part I surveyed Muslim political thought and multiculturalist political thought. The former was examined in order to identify contemporary Muslim formulations of governance and pluralism. The latter was studied to locate a pluralist critique of liberalism in the context of more inclusive and normatively accommodating notions of democracy. Building on the presented debates and typologies in these chapters, this next part of the book will explore the possibilities for their synergy, with the aim of developing a theoretical understanding of Muslim democracy. However, before moving onto this theoretical enquiry, in this chapter, I will engage in a thematic, in-depth study of certain concepts of democracy within Muslim political thought. In light of the previous discussion on multiculturalism, Muslim political thought appears, in contrast to Western political thought, to lack a tradition of political theory on democratic governance. Compatibility-based arguments on the relationship between Islam and democracy have been formulated by Muslim thinkers within Islamic traditions of political thought. However, their usage of political terminology is often conflated with jurisprudence and theology, which I argue has resulted in the tenuous usage of democratic concepts. I aim to deconstruct these concepts and arguments to aid the process of constructing a political theory on Muslim democracy in the following part of this book. In addition, this chapter makes a novel contribution through the category of compatibility-based arguments. The formulation of an original framework will help in identifying the problems within Muslim discourses on democracy, providing a substantive critique of these discourses and contributing to a paradigm shift from a *theological* discourse to a *political* theory of democracy within Muslim contexts.

In recent decades, many Muslim thinkers, some of whom were examined in Chapter 1, have proposed democracy as a means of creating a just, accountable and representative political order. Two trends have emerged to illustrate the legitimacy of the compatibility of Islam and democracy. The first trend, of revivalism, highlighted functionalist purposes for a more just political system through elections, often with the aim of gaining political power in competition with authoritarian regimes and military rule. The second trend, of Islamic modernism, reinterpreted the moral imperatives of Islam, such as *ḥākimiyya*, *sharīʿa* and *shūrā*, to provide theological support for democracy. While revivalism advocates a functional compatibility between Islamic politics and democratic development, Islamic modernism contends that theological imperatives in the Islamic tradition enjoin democracy as a form of governance. Within Muslim scholarship, these two strands of the pro-democratic stance, oriented around compatibility-based arguments, derive their arguments from Islam's supposed theological compatibility with democratic processes.

Muslim thinkers align themselves with modernity's moral and political requirements in compatibility-based arguments. These arguments assert that there is no structural incompatibility between Islam and democracy given the 'repurpose [of] classical Islamic legal concepts for a modern structural and institutional context' (March, 2019: 221). Although complex moral arguments have developed on Islam and democracy, these have not developed into a systematic, coherent, well-developed political theory. Present hurdles to the advancement of Muslim democratic political thought are not necessarily created by anti-democratic camps. Hybrid, ad hoc and unsystematic scholarship, in mainstream Muslim political thinking, poses the greatest challenge to a conception of Muslim democracy in political theory.

II. The Compatibility-based Arguments

Recent attempts to produce a vision of 'democracy for Islam' were accompanied by the acceptance of democracy by Muslim mainstream publics as 'the only morally defensible political order' (Bahlul, 2004: 99). Anti-democratic lines of Muslim thought, grouped under the statist school in Chapter 1, have been losing traction in the process. This rejectionist attitude has been abandoned by most Islamist groups as democracy, the only legitimate alternative to authoritarianism, has become popularly associated with just and representative political governance. As Bokhari and Senzai argue, only a tiny minority among Islamists, represented by groups such as al-Qaeda, denounce democracy. Mainstream revivalist Islamists have discarded statist ideologies in favour of a democratic political structure that responds to the demands of Muslim populations (Bokhari and Senzai, 2013: 44). Revivalist support for democracy is based on the assumption of the functional compatibility of Islam and democracy. Although a philosophical disagreement between Islam and democracy is highlighted by revivalists, they have accepted and participated in democratic political channels. Unlike revivalists, Islamic modernists, such as Abou El Fadl and al-Jabri, have championed a substantive endorsement of democracy. Islam and democracy are believed to be philosophically compatible. Modernists recognise democracy does not only 'establish a basis for pursuing justice' but it also fulfils 'a fundamental responsibility assigned by God to each of us' (Abou El Fadl, 2003).

The typology of Muslim political thought in Chapter 1 highlighted the common argument of Islam's compatibility with democracy in different instrumental (revivalist) and moral (modernist) justifications, with very few exceptions, for democracy. Pro-democratic Muslim thinkers, belonging to revivalist and modernist strands, have engaged in efforts either to demonstrate the compatibility of Islam and democracy in a conciliatory manner, attenuating their possible conflicts, or to envisage their ultimate concurrence through a series of analogies between Islam and democracy. The revivalist thinkers, in the first category, do not express a serious normative engagement with democracy but employ a selective, reductionist conceptualisation of democracy that shows limited knowledge of political theory. Modernists, falling into the second category, have explored principles and ideas within

Islamic moral and legal traditions in an attempt to demonstrate their compatibility with the values of liberal democracy. In their justification of democracy against concerns over Islamic authenticity, modernists reinterpret Islamic imperatives through a rationalist prism. A moral recognition and legal justification of democracy is made beyond the pragmatism of *maṣlaḥa* (public interest). Islamic principles do not preclude the possibility of democracy, as both are now seen as fully compatible. However, this verdict of compatibility requires problematisation in the context of democratic political theory.

This chapter will highlight the main challenges confronting Muslim democratic thinking. It will address the arguments for the compatibility of Islamic political, moral and legal values with that of democracy. Critical issues have been raised in terms of (i) divine sovereignty versus popular sovereignty, (ii) the consensus of the *'ulamā'* versus public deliberation and (iii) divine law versus human legislation. In this section, the ideas of Mawdūdī and Qutb, representatives of the anti-democratic Muslim camp, and of al-Ghannushi, Bulaç, Karaman, Rahman and Abou El Fadl, prominent thinkers within the compatibility-based arguments, will be discussed. Muslim thinkers opposed to democracy are examined to establish to what degree the compatibility-based arguments have effectively confronted anti-democratic thinking and whether or not this confrontation can be considered part of a systematic democratic theory. A third camp, composed of progressive intellectuals like An-Na'im and Talbi, is brought into the discussion to illustrate the theoretical weaknesses of compatibility-based arguments. Progressive methodological arguments are characterised by a philosophical transformation from compatibility-based arguments, with an awareness of their potential undemocratic facets, to a Muslim democracy paradigm.[1] This chapter will undertake a thematic deconstruction of compatibility-based arguments, which is vital in order to lay the ground for reconstructing a political theory of Muslim democracy in the next part of the book.

1. Sovereignty

God's sovereignty holds a vital place in Islamic political discourse. The theme of sovereignty encompasses competing ideas about the source of political authority as well as its nature and scope. Debates emerge about the legal and political implications of 'whether God's omnipotence and immutability can be equated with the political concept of sovereignty (*ḥakimiyya*)' (Abou El Fadl, 2014: 330). Moreover, controversy centres on 'disagreements about the degree of right, liberty, and popular rule' (El Amine, 2016: 106). This section will interpret the ideas of various schools of Muslim political thought on sovereignty and their positions within Muslim democratic thinking.

For the statist school of Muslim political thought, sovereignty is primarily a tenet of faith rather than a political concept. Qutb claims that belief in God's sovereignty subsumes believing in the Islamic faith, His power, His *sharī'a* and His creation (2001: 120). Divine sovereignty is the foundation of political legitimacy and the ultimate source of political authority. In the statist school, the idea of divine sovereignty manifests itself most clearly in the sphere of law, where God is exclusive supreme legislator (Qutb, 2001: 123). Muslims have to renounce sovereignty in favour of 'what God has prescribed', which 'is not contingent on the whims of fallible human beings' (Qutb, 1964: 8). Although Mawdūdī is a prominent statist, he is a transitional figure to the revivalist school on this matter. For instance, like revivalists, Mawdūdī also argues that 'mankind is not the ruling authority himself but is the deputy of the original sovereignty' (1978: 20). Unlike revivalists, however, Mawdūdī does not engage in compatibility-based arguments in explicating the relationship between divine sovereignty and democracy.

Revivalist thinking is oriented around an attempt to 'reconcile visions of divine and popular sovereignty precisely through the doctrine of the universal covenant of vicegerency', maintaining that both God and the people are sovereign within their own separate realms (March, 2015: 19). Al-Ghannushi explains that political authority is executed by the *umma*, who act in the role of deputy to God's ultimate sovereignty, and that legislative authority is shared by the divine (i.e. sacred) texts and popular sovereignty (i.e. *shūrā*). Religious orthodoxy and constraints on the exercise of the popular will of the *umma* are not anti-democratic for revivalists, who argue that Muslims 'voluntarily and freely' accept God's authority in their vicegerency (March, 2015: 19). In revivalist thought, God bestows His original sovereignty on the people and makes the *umma* his deputy under His guidance. However, the *umma*'s role in the sovereignty of God here is somehow ambiguous. While it possesses political authority as the representative of God there is no consensus about who in the *umma* should exercise this power: 'the People who Loose and Bind', the entire Muslim community, or monotheists in general encompassing all Abrahamic religions (Piscatori and Saikal, 2020: 40).

Revivalists like Karaman (2014c) suggest that 'the greatest problem with democracy is about sovereignty'. With similar reservations, Bulaç argues that Islam is accepted as the higher moral authority for Muslims. While political sovereignty belongs to the ruled, or the people, 'moral' (*değerler*) sovereignty is based on the Qur'anic injunction, the 'decree belongs to Allah', that political legitimacy comes from God and its application is left to the people (Bulaç, 1998: 189–90). This model 'will happily bring together God's desire and the will of the people' (Bulaç, 2012b). Revivalists, unlike statists, do not take the issue of sovereignty as a mere matter of theology but approach it more functionally. Transcendental and popular sovereignty are to be made harmonious, or at least modified to be procedurally compatible in their political justification of an Islamic democratic system. For instance, al-Ghannushi (2011a) ties political legitimacy to religious and associational freedoms such as multi-party politics, civil society organisations, and executive, judicial and legislative accountability.

The revivalist conception of Islamic democracy focuses on organisational freedoms. Michaelle Browers finds 'civil society is . . . prioritized over democracy' in revivalist thinking, with associational freedoms accorded greater importance than the normative principles of democracy (2006: 157). A free and pluralistic civil society's implications for the complex socio-political and normative issues, especially the need for democratic norms and institutions, which face Muslim societies are not tacked in revivalism. Toleration of moral disagreement derived from entrenched ethical and political divides as a challenge for an Islamic political authority is downplayed. However conciliatory, tolerable or accommodationist it may be discursively, revivalist Islamic democracy assumes a political model, where God's sovereignty dictates political and legislative sovereignty. Revivalists have a utopian approach to politics, underscoring individual agency and reason, in the search for a consensus about the ethical purposes of human life (March, 2019: 223).

The concept of divine sovereignty adopted by modernists, however, provides greater agency to popular authority. In addition, unlike revivalists, modernists do not directly link God's sovereignty to legislative authority. Modernists argue that *sharī'a* in the classical period, created and applied by non-state actors such as the *'ulamā'* and *qūḍā*, was considered to 'be a doctrine and a method rather than a code' (Schacht, 1960: 108). For Fazlur Rahman, divine sovereignty sets the standards of justice rather than specifies the details of law. Nevertheless, moral guidance and political legitimacy do come from God, with Islam vested in the moral character of the state (Rahman, 1967: 213). Democracy, according to Rahman, is 'a tricky business' as its outcome, decided by the will of the people, is unclear and difficult to predict. Islam can inform the moral background of a democratic political system in order to offset the volatility of democracy and to maintain the ideal of justice in Muslim democracies (Rahman, 1987: 206).[2]

Abou El Fadl also maintains that 'God is the authority that delegated to human beings the task of achieving justice on earth by fulfilling the virtues that approximate divinity' (2004: 33). Reciprocal relations between 'divine authority and human authority are needed' because 'pure reason standing alone' cannot create or define 'what is good and moral' (Abou El Fadl, 2004: 114). In this vein of thought:

> A case for democracy within Islam must accept the idea of God's sovereignty: it cannot substitute popular sovereignty for divine sovereignty but must instead show how popular sovereignty expresses God's authority, properly understood. Similarly, it cannot reject the idea that God's law is given prior to human action but must show how democratic lawmaking respects that priority. (Abou El Fadl, 2004: 30)

Modernists in general suggest the exercise of political power in 'this delegation [by God] serves as a moral check on the power of those who exercise it, as they must acknowledge its divine source' (Kalanges, 2014: 279). Divine morality, derived from the idea of God's sovereignty, provides the incontestable moral background for the state. However, Abou El Fadl adds the caveat that God's sovereignty cannot be represented and enforced by an authority as no human authority can be 'the perfect executors of the divine will without inserting their own human judgements and inclinations in the process' (2004: 9). Political sovereignty, completely distinct from God's sovereignty, is possessed by citizens in the nation-state (Abou El Fadl, 2014: 365). God's sovereignty, in Abou El Fadl's account, is more of a principal moral notion than a set of legal rules (2003: 42).

Closer philosophical correspondences about the link between the foundation of political legitimacy and the source of morality between the statists, revivalists and modernists appear than initially assumed. Statists believe the idea of divine sovereignty is antithetical to the notion of popular rule and democracy. In contrast, both revivalists and modernists identify the 'dual authority' of divine and popular authority, albeit in different ways and understandings. Revivalists maintain that 'despite appearances to the contrary, popular sovereignty and divine sovereignty are not mutually exclusive' (Bahlul, 2003: 57). Modernists, on the other hand, suggest popular sovereignty can reside in the idea of divine sovereignty through the division of different spheres of sovereignty, as opposed to the monolithic conception of sovereignty endorsed by the statists.

In their attempt to prove the compatibility of democracy with Islam, in opposition to anti-democratic statist arguments, modernists display certain theoretical weaknesses in the use of the concept of sovereignty. First, Rahman, despite his critique of statists for misunderstanding divine sovereignty, confuses various aspects of sovereignty in his arguments. Rahman explains that the term 'sovereignty' 'is of a relatively recent coinage and denotes that definite and defined factor (or factors) in society to which rightfully belongs *coercive force* to obtain obedience to its will' (1967: 208–9). Divine sovereignty is not coercive. God is not sovereign in a political and legal sense, although He bears the moral authority in these realms. However, in contrast to the modernist perception of statists, the latter in fact do not reject the proposition that coercive political force belongs to humans. Qutb notes that God's sovereignty is not concerned with who practises coercive power but with whose authority legitimises this power. He observed:

> Many people, including Muslim scholars, tend to confuse the exercises of power and the source of power. Even the aggregate of humanity does not have the right to sovereignty, which God alone possesses. People only [have the right to] implement what God has laid down with His authority. (Qutb, 2001: 40)

Coercive political power to exercise authority belongs to the people, but God is the only source of sovereignty.

Modernist thought mischaracterises sovereignty as the entity that possesses and exercises coercive political power. In political theory, sovereignty is outlined as a matter of authority that involves 'the right to command and correlatively the right to be obeyed' (Wolff, 1990: 20). In other words, sovereignty refers to the moral origins of political power: what informs, and whose name and right give legitimacy to, political authority. Therefore, 'sovereignty is not only a matter of who decides when the law is suspended in the name of law, but also of who decides on the boundary between ethics and politics' (March, 2015: 23). The anti-democratic camp here shows a more methodical understating of the notion and presents a coherent antithesis to it, while compatibility-based arguments fail to theorise a fully-fledged conception of democracy.

In fact, modernists do not systematically explore how 'a dual authority' is simultaneously generated by the popular will and obtains its legitimacy and moral guidance from a transcendental 'supra-democratic source' (Tezcür, 2007: 482). The idea of divine sovereignty has implications that may lead to certain difficulties in a democracy which are not addressed by modernists. Modernists argue that the connection between morality and politics ensures Islam is not left in the hands of the state. In their theories, pluralism within Muslim-majority societies is recognised and non-Islamic diversity accommodated. However, modernists seem to be unaware of the idea of divine morality's inherent ethical monism, where moral certainty is likely to be transformed into political policy. Their idea of divine morality not only dictates individual ethical orientation, but also exerts influence on the limits of the public life. These limits in turn can create political structures and norms that resist deliberation despite the claim that religious texts are open to interpretation, as modernists repeatedly emphasise. Modernist endorsement of political and moral pluralism may lead to ambiguities in the legal, political and religious spheres. For instance, public reason and the public good are liable to be defined within the parameters of religion in modernist thought.

Modernists appear also not to be aware of the likely barrier posed by Islamic morality, upheld by the majority, to the development of democratic institutions and to groups that do not conform to it. The modernist defence for the compatibility of divine and popular sovereignty does not achieve a sound resolution of certain obstacles. In modernists' writings, it is unclear how the tension between the norms of the majority and the rights of the minorities would be resolved in the public sphere. Modernists do not discuss the non-negotiable implications of the idea of God's moral sovereignty in a Muslim democracy. No significant tensions are assumed to exist in compatibility-based arguments between the acceptance of the divine nature of morality and the implementation of democratic political arrangements. Persistent questions plague compatibility-based arguments, even in their most developed versions, regarding their potential to develop institutions that support political pluralism and the rights to difference within Muslim-majority contexts. Despite their defence of internal Islamic pluralism and minority rights, compatibility-based arguments overlook the intermingling of political power and moral righteousness. The potential for a dominant religious discourse to engender oppressive political power is largely neglected in the assumed harmony between the popular will and the sovereignty of God.

Compatibility-based arguments seem to articulate conceptually hybrid theories on sovereignty in an attempt to reconcile Islam and democracy. Qutb's and An-Na'im's criticisms of eclecticism point to the limitations of such approaches. It is vital to recognise that the 'logical coherence' (Binder, 1998: 171) within the statist theories of Mawdūdī and Qutb is absent in the alternative positions of the compatibility-based arguments on the idea of sovereignty. In other words, the statist conception of divine sovereignty treats an Islamic state as 'the agent for creating and maintaining morality, both individually and collectively' (Moussalli, 2001: 63). A lack of systematic and coherent, democratic thinking by compatibility-based arguments undermines their responses to the place of the state as a moral agent.

Modernists represent the most democratically developed version of compatibility-based arguments. They, however, do not explain how a Muslim democracy could resolve the the tensions between the majority and the minority. There is also silence on what institutional and legal features in this conception of democracy could ensure democratic checks and balances. Even a leading advocate of democracy in Islamic discourses, Abou El Fadl, who asserts the right of Muslims to create democratic models, operates within a jurisprudential theory. This jurisprudential theory endows his 'Islamic democracy' paradigm with normative values; however, it also restricts his move from an Islamic democracy paradigm to a Muslim democracy paradigm (Abou El Fadl, 2003: 276–7).

In developing a democratic line of thinking, progressive scholars advocate abandoning the notion of divine sovereignty in favour of popular sovereignty. This entails replacing divine morality in politics with self-conscious social constructions of moral authority. Abdolkarim Soroush provides an alternative basis for social morality rooted in the premise that

> there is no higher morality than the existing morality. By 'existing morality,' I mean our familiar exception-bound moral rules. Following these moral values is the best guarantee of justice and desired moderation in society. The history of human vice is replete with moral violations and deceptions perpetrated in the name of a higher morality and justice. (2000: 116)

Soroush argues that the objective of the popular will in democracies is to balance the power of the state sovereignty to fight authoritarianism and totalitarianism. He proposes that 'the discussion surrounding governance should revolve around the principles of justice and human rights, not theological justification necessary to popular sovereignty or democracy' (Soroush, 2000: 131–3). The foundation of political legitimacy and authority should be disassociated from religious knowledge. A comprehensive moral doctrine, for Soroush, does not have the potential to produce a political outcome amid a diversity of moral sources. He argues that the original intention of religion is a transcendental connection between human being and God. This transcendentalism is of a strictly spiritual nature without any political implications. Accordingly, Soroush replaces the religious basis of Muslim political thought and practice with mundane reason, experience and consent. In other words, for Soroush, political and legal spheres within a democratic state derive from 'a rational conception of morality' that is 'firmly ensconced in experience which does not invoke revelation' (Moussa, 2014: 7). Two domains of morality are distinguished, motivated by a

> humble vision of morality apropos of fallible human beings who are far from being Gods. It is not the human morality but the divine morality and justice that adjusts itself to all societies. It behoves us, fallible creatures, to act as fallible creatures not as infallible gods. One should leave God's work,

God's morality, and God's affairs to God. This is the meaning of reliance on God (*tavakkol*). (Soroush, 2000: 121)

Democracy is construed to be 'a method of governance aiming to "reduce management error" based on the principle of "popular sovereignty"' and achieved through civic reasoning (Soroush, 2010 as cited in Ghobadzadeh, 2014: 60), Naser Ghobadzadeh, building on Soroush's work, has engaged with a political theory on Muslim democracy. He claims that until the philosophical disaccord on secularism and popular sovereignty is resolved in Muslim political thought, democratisation will be wishful thinking. Like Soroush, Ghobadzadeh also aims to develop a 'non-jurisprudential' and non-theological idea of Muslim democracy.

The emergence of '"divine sovereignty" as the key principle of Muslim political thought was less an inevitable consequence of Islam's radical monotheism and theological voluntarism than a modern discovery' (March, 2019: 78). Ghobadzadeh argues that the idea of divine sovereignty, implying human access to 'eternal, sacred, and error-free knowledge' of the divine, has led to a totalitarian understanding of the state (2014: 60). On the other hand, for Ghobadzadeh, the principle of popular sovereignty 'deprives the state of any claim to a sacred foundation and legitimacy through religious symbolism' and 'removes holiness and divinity from politics' (2013: 33). Popular sovereignty also creates the 'conducive environment' for the consolidation of Muslim democracy, where Muslims can, with individual volition, interpret their divine texts and practise their religion (Ghobadzadeh, 2014: 66).

Progressive thinkers go beyond a compatibility-based conception of Islamic democracy based on religious morality, in their formulation of the idea of Muslim democracy. Governance, a non-religious sphere, is sufficiently pluralistic to accommodate comprehensive Muslim doctrines as well as non-Muslim ones. As will shortly be seen, An-Na'im, as well as other thinkers, has greatly contributed to the next chapter's conceptual analysis of Muslim democracy complemented by the inclusion of multiculturalist insights on politics. This chapter will continue to critically examine compatibility-based arguments and the sources of their impediments to democratic thinking.

2. *Shūrā*

Shūrā as a concept emerges from the Qur'anic verse 'consult with them in matters'. Although *shūrā* had been a pre-Islamic Arabian custom, it became a key Islamic principle in political authority and decision-making. Its nature, function and scope have been contested: whether the Qur'an, through the Prophet Muhammad, commands Muslims to consult with other Muslims only or all members of a society; whether it is the elite (*'ulamā'* and *khāṣṣa*) or the lay people (*'amma*) that constitutes the people of consultation (*ahl al-shūrā*); and whether 'the result of the consultative process was binding (*shūrā mulzima*) [compulsory] or non-binding (*ghayr mulzima*) [advisory]' on the ruler (March, 2015: 17). The leading modern debate regarding *shūrā* revolves around its equivalence to democracy, and whether it is indicative of emerging democracy in the Muslim world. Modern interpretations of *shūrā* raise the issues of consultation, participation, consent and public deliberation in political discussions. This section will revisit the diversity of perspectives in Muslim political thought on the relationship between *shūrā* and democracy in compatibility-based arguments.

Different interpretations of consent, popular will and decision-making can be discerned in the relationship between Islam and democracy. The statist school, representatives of the anti-democratic line, argues that the source of political authority and legitimacy comes from the divine, not from the Muslim community, elections, institutions, or *shūrā*. Qutb maintains that the practice of *shūrā* within the boundaries of *sharī'a* ensures that the popular will functions according to divine sovereignty. He did not specify the forms or mechanisms that *shūrā* should take. Instead, Qutb referred to the time of the Prophet Muhammad as one of the ideal application of *shūrā* but left it to Muslims, inspired by the Prophet's example, to agree on its concrete form and the later political applications of his teachings. Ambiguity characterises Qutb's understanding of *shūrā* with its perfectionist and utopian facets. Within the statist school, Mawdūdī contends that the *umma* inherited the vicegerency of God, with limited political power to implement *sharī'a*. In Mawdūdī's theory, *shūrā* is exercised by the entire *umma* wherein

> [t]he theocracy built up by Islam is not ruled by any particular religious class but by the whole community of Muslims including the rank and file

> ... If I were permitted to coin a new term, I would describe this system of government as a 'theo-democracy,' that is to say a divine democratic government because under it the Muslims have been given a limited popular sovereignty under the suzerainty of God. (1999: 230)

Mawdūdī does not totally reject democracy like Qutb. However, his idea of an Islamic state enacts inequalities between Muslim and non-Muslim citizens. Moreover, strict limitations on public debate, freedom of speech and dissent based on traditional *sharī'a* in this 'theo-democracy' directly contradict the principles of democracy.

Challenges to such statist ideas by modernists highlight *shūrā*'s consultative function and the necessity of consent, a source of legitimacy for political authority. *Shūrā* as a form of collective deliberation and consent from the entire community are underlined by Rahman to fulfil the moral duty of creating a just political order (2009: 28). Rahman's interpretation of *shūrā* exhibits a democratic nature where open channels and criticism are incorporated to determine political decisions. To this end, an inclusive and participatory *shūrā* in politics is not merely restricted to an elite such as the *'ulamā'* or *khāṣṣa* (Rahman, 1967: 206; 1984: 3; 1987: 216). The Muslim community will employ 'the various media of mass-communication and when a general public opinion, i.e. *ijma'*, has crystallised, this will be embodied in the form of law by the representatives of the people' (Rahman, 1967: 206). Through this process, the *fuqahā'* (religious legal scholars) could function as experts who issue guidance in the making of propositions rather than legislation. Although *shūrā* could have been transformed into 'an effective and permanent organization' to be an 'instrument of participatory and accountable government' (1965: 94; 1987: 210), Rahman concedes that the *'ulamā'* have used *shūrā* to ensure obedience to rulers (1994: 94). Thus, the democratic potential of *shūrā* was never realised and was often sacrificed for the ruler's *maṣlaḥa*. Yet he maintains that in *shūrā* where 'the public participate with responsibility in the affairs of the state, the state must be some form of democracy' (Rahman, 1966: 240). A Muslim democracy is to be developed in Rahman's interpretation of *shūrā* as an ideal Islamic model. Inequity and ambiguity characterise *shūrā*'s ability to develop democratic institutions in its historical record. While the words Rahman uses may be classical, the concepts he develops are modern, with few or no parallels with past scholarship. However, Rahman's fixation on a religious lexicon in politics, instead of him focusing on developing a modern political terminology, can be seen as a barrier to him developing a political theory of Muslim democracy.

For statists, *shūrā* is not compulsory, but functions as 'an expertocracy headed by the Just Ruler', who is considered to be the final authority who can accept or reject this advisory opinion (Kramer, 1993: 7). *Shūrā* is binding for revivalists, as the Islamic system they advocate contains majority rule and free elections. Unlike for statists, there exists in the revivalist interpretation of *shūrā* a place for non-Muslim social and political forces. Revivalists support the protection of minorities, and equal fundamental citizenship rights for Muslims and non-Muslims, as well as the coexistence of secular and religious political parties. They do not, however, espouse a philosophical commitment to moral pluralism. The revivalist position on *shūrā* appears to be democracy run by the will of a majority Muslim population that seeks to eventually create institutions shaped by Islamic teaching. As the examination of the ideas of Karaman and al-Ghannushi in Chapter 1 demonstrates, Islam's role is 'to provide the system with moral values' where *shūrā* constitutes a strategic place in its expression and realisation (Wright, 1996: 73). The legitimacy of decisions through the process of *shūrā* depends on the opinion in question being 'supported by evidence from the *Qur'an*, Sunna or other valid sources' (Sinanovic, 2004: 252). Contestatory and participatory processes in this account of *shūrā* are clearly regulated by values and concepts from religious knowledge. Therefore, contrary to their claims for the conciliation of theology and politics, it is not evident how modern interpretations of *shūrā* in revivalist thought are the equivalent of democratic public deliberation and contestation.

Rahman and Abou El Fadl interpret *shūrā* as a compulsory and binding principle. Modernists emphasise the necessity 'to accept the principle of a majority decision and to see it as a formal process and an institution' (Kramer, 1993: 7). Institutional expressions of *shūrā* include the creation of a legislative assembly elected through fair elections, reflecting the will of the people and the guarantee of free speech. Rahman suggests that *shūrā* can take the form of an elected national legislature with which the head of the executive co-operates in the decision-making and is bound by its final decisions

(Rahman, 1967: 213). Thus, this institution is a parliament that consists of democratic consultation among conflicting opinions and interests.

Modernists argue that consultation is an important democratic channel. In addition, *shūrā* can be reformulated to develop its potential for representation, accountability and consultation for democratic governance. However, the accentuation of religious–political concepts like *shūrā* is insufficient for a theory of democratic public deliberation. Democratic deliberation as an ideal aims to ensure that citizens are given both the right and the ability to defend their rights and interests irrespective of their political and moral convictions. On the other hand, the modernist interpretation of *shūrā* fails to address the implications of a free political discourse and public debate in which unorthodox public reasons are offered that may diverge from the majority's viewpoints.

There exist limitations within revivalist and modernist schools on their democratic conceptions. The usage of *shūrā* within the perimeters of religious normative value in a theological framework, which precedes and informs political practices, falls short of the requirements of a normative democratic system. Its theological origins in a religious moral framework restrict *shūrā* from achieving an ethos of genuine moral pluralism. Revivalists and modernists cannot completely envisage 'consultation and participation as a genuinely political process involving interest representation, competition and contestation' (Kramer, 1993: 7). Their interpretation of *shūrā*, to a certain degree, 'reflects the continued prevalence of a moral rather than a political discourse … provided they remain within the confines of the faith and common decency' (Kramer, 1993: 7). This observation can be extended to the example of Karaman's idea of 'universal ugliness' wherein certain 'moral wrongs' cannot be tolerated in the public sphere.

In revivalist thought, there is strong disapproval of allowing unrestricted freedom of speech and association for dissenting world-views. Modernists appear to be more tolerant than revivalists in their approach to sceptics, atheists and 'heretics'. For instance, within Muslim-majority societies, modernists move away from universalist and absolutist understandings in their understanding of the public sphere. However, modernists seem to overlook the fact that pluralism and democracy may be in jeopardy if the complete separation of religion and governance in the state realm is not in place. When the state is influenced by the comprehensive moral views of the majority, lacking the internalisation of rights and freedoms among the people, democratisation can inadvertently turn into a new form of political intolerance and repression. On this matter, it is essential to see the risks that the compatibility-based democratic transitions are carrying.

Muslim revivalist and modernist thinkers, in contrast to the anti-democratic statists, have put forward ideas on *shūrā* with democratic themes. However, they are unable to reinterpret *shūrā* as an institution capable of facilitating free, democratic and public contestation as an equivalent of public deliberation. Compatibility-based arguments fail to clearly explain the role of religious justifications in public debates and their implications for civil and individual rights and freedoms. These efforts have not culminated into a political theory on Muslim democracy.

On the hand, progressives seek a paradigm shift from compatibility-based arguments to Muslim democracy. Progressives aim to separate governance from religious morality in their attempt to overcome the dilemma modernist face. They claim there is no need to legitimise political good with religious terminology. For instance, Mohammad Talbi is against establishing an equivalence between religious and political concepts and institutions. He criticises modernist thinkers such as Abou El Fadl who propose religious justifications for the compatibility of Islam and liberal democracy (2011: 90–1). Talbi believes democracy does not need legitimacy through its supposed compatibility with religious concepts such as *shūrā*. Democracy and *shūrā* are different systems located in their own particular times and contexts. For Talbi, democracy is a modern phenomenon, an achievement of our age and a system which best represents the voice of the people with the associated values of human rights and pluralism. Thus, it does not need to be treated as a modern model of *shūrā*: a progressive and critical reading of Islamic ideals in today's world favours democracy, not *shūrā* or any other political structure (Nettler, 2000: 55). The decision to choose the best political system, for Talbi, should be left to the reasoned thinking, experience and collective decision of people. According to Talbi, the development of democracy should be left to the agency and rationality of individuals and not be dictated by theology or jurisprudence (2011: 100).

Legitimising a political good through theological justifications should be abandoned, according to progressives. The development of a non-theological, non-jurisprudential political theory is more appropriate for Muslim democracy. Although theological rationale should not dictate the structure of the state, progressives maintain it should continue to guide individuals' private and public actions. In other words, the critical reinterpretation of Islamic ideals can lead to the separation of political and theological reasoning. Normative commitments to democracy on the individual level can emerge from theology and its arguments; however, a democratic political system should not derive from political theology. I will draw on these insights in the development of a political theory of Muslim democracy in the next part. The following section continues the scrutiny of compatibility-based arguments in relation to law within the context of Muslim democracy.

3. Law

Absolutist state sovereignty does not only claim on the monopoly of legitimate violence. It also determines what constitutes lawful and unlawful forms of behaviour by dictating the legitimate limits on political forms, rights and legality. Thus, 'sovereignty has in common with monotheism a host of attributes', which makes the modern nation-state act like an 'omnipotent' and 'godlike Law-giver per excellence', by intervening and shaping citizens' ethical and moral life (Hallaq, 2014: 27). For Muslims who take their moral guidance from the *sharīʿa*, however interpreted, its moral authority was derogated by the modern state.

In contemporary Islamic discourses, debates on sovereignty revolve around competing conceptions of the source of law and ethics. These debates, proposing readings of the relationship between the divine and the human, shape the ethical positions towards Muslim democracy. Muslims, statists claim, must exercise 'the right to create values, to legislate rules of collective behaviour and to choose a way of life [which] rests with what God has prescribed' (Qutb, 1964: 8). Legal sovereignty, belonging to God, assumes that divine justice cannot a priori be shaped by context (Mawdūdī, 1978: 17). Human beings exercise authority within limited boundaries. Revivalists also espouse the principle of God's legal sovereignty. However, they do interpret its practical implications in the form of an Islamic democracy. The democratic outcome in Muslim societies, where the majority endorses the idea of God's law, will be consistent with Islamic principles. Thus, democracy would eventually function as a way to Islamise law and politics as a result of the electoral process. Revivalists expect democracy in the Muslim world to overwhelmingly benefit Islam and be in line with divine morality.

For modernists, on the other hand, divine law can be adapted in specific social, political, economic and cultural contexts. Abou El Fadl illustrates a relationship between God and human agency or vicegerency that diverges from the statist unequivocal and mechanical reading in which Muslims simply implement God's commands. He is aware of the pitfalls of claims made by political and legal institutions to represent the divine law. Tyranny is a foreseeable outcome where the attempt to usurp and monopolise divine sovereignty is accompanied by the attempt to 'possess the mercy of the divine and portion it out for self-serving purposes', and 'yields an intoxicating but also corrupting sense of power' (Abou El Fadl, 2014: 198).

Similarly, Rahman notes that 'the spirit of the Qur'anic legislation exhibits an obvious direction towards the progressive embodiment of the fundamental human values of freedom and responsibility in fresh legislation' (1966: 39). Human intellect and experience are prioritised by Muslim modernists in the interpretation of divine law. More importantly, no human being can claim the mantle of infallibility for their interpretations to the exclusion of other interpretations.

Although modernists conceive law and rights in the human sphere, they uphold the divine source of morality for legislation (Rahman, 1984: 14). *Ijtihād*, Rahman asserts, cannot be separated from legalisation in which 'a systematic attempt must be made to elaborate an ethics by the Qur'an' (1966: 256). Recognition of the dual authority of divine morality and human autonomy leads Abou El Fadl to state:

> I do not believe that pure reason standing alone creates or defines what is good and moral or that the law of God should be subordinated to human autonomy. I wholeheartedly agree . . . that justice, as philosophically formulated, informs, but does not ground, the interpretation and application of the revealed law. Most of all . . . divine authority and human authority are needed in a system that achieves justice through the revealed law while avoiding the distortions of oligarchies, whether clerical or secular. (2004: 114)

Contemporary Muslim thinkers' arguments on law and ethics also revolve around the nature and role of *sharī'a*. Common disagreements arise about whether *sharī'a* is a system of moral reasoning or a system of positive law. Different positions on these issues lead to competing views of democracy. I will now briefly revisit the particular relationship between democracy and Islamic law within the context of moral authority and pluralism. This examination proceeds with reference to the typology developed earlier in this book with the aim of understanding compatibility-based arguments.

Statists perceive *sharī'a*, an alternative to the secular positivist account of law, to be equivalent to a constitution. Revivalists acknowledge *sharī'a* as one source, among others, of the constitution, pointing out that religion inevitably influences law, politics and society. The *sharī'a*, for modernists, is an ethical system that encompasses public and private morality, which is 'coterminous with the "good"', yet it does not dictate 'an actual formal code of particular and specific enactments' (Rahman, 1979: 115). Unlike statists, who equate religion with governance, modernists 'situate religion around an ethical axis', which 'means paying special attention to Islam's overarching ethical goal and message to humanity above and beyond any specific ruling(s) on any particular issue' (Rahman, 1979: 256). In modernist thinking, while the moral framework of politics, and its burden of proof, are still derived from religion, the interpretations and executions of moral ideals are dynamic, relative and contextual.

The primacy of the *sharī'a*'s divine morality in modernist thought seeks to prevent the 'manipulation and whims of a positivist entity', not simply religion's subjugation of politics (Hallaq, 2012: 157). However, the process of translating God's moral laws into legal or political norms even in a dynamic and contextual manner may prove to be problematic. Divine sovereignty has to authorise a select few who speak in the name of Islam for the exercise of power. Thus, morality in this context will tend to reflect the commonly-held values of a particular group, society and generation, as human agency in this process of interpretation is unavoidable, which inevitably renders all of its results, ironically, 'positivist' in nature.

On this matter, progressives make a clear distinction between religion and the state, while still preserving an interaction between religion and the public sphere. An-Na'im asserts law 'should not be founded on sharia' because 'like all aspects of the legal system . . . [it] is an articulation of the political will of the state, and not on the will of God' (2002a: 20). However, he maintains that the state should ensure all rights and freedoms for Muslims who voluntarily want to follow Islamic legal dictums, without a religious public authority to enforce them.

Legislation is another contested issue in the debate about the compatibility between Islam and democracy. Statists do not differentiate between state law and religious law and leave the entire legal sphere to the Islamic state. Revivalists also link religious law to state authority. Modernists, however, draw a line between these two spheres. Yet *Ijtihād* is not fully separate from legalisation in 'a systematic attempt' to benefit from divine law (Rahman, 1966: 256). In this pursuit, modernists disagree with statists and revivalists about the role of public authority in Islamic law. The *sharī'a* should not be in the sphere of the state, but should be left to non-state actors, either *'ulamā'*, such as is the case for *iftā'* (fatwa-giving) institutions, elected officials, or the entire Muslim community (Alam, 2007: 1262). Rahman recommends *ijtihād* be practised by individuals as opposed to remaining in the *'ulamā'*'s monopoly on jurisdiction and legislation. In Abou El Fadl's account, the separation between Islamic law and the state allows him to argue that the latter is not a divine prescription. However, unlike Rahman, Abou El Fadl allocates the sphere of Islamic law and the practice of *ijtihād* to the *'ulamā'*, who are 'authoritatively' religiously trained in law (2003: 36). This category of scholars is qualified for the following reason:

> The role of the faqih, or of the Shari'ah expert, is critical – as the Qur'an describes it the role of those who study the divine law is to act as teachers and reminders to people of the call of conscience and the indicators (*adilla*) that point to God's will. (Abou El Fadl, 2014: 365)

Abou El Fadl notes that, with the rise of Islamism, technocrats, primarily self-taught and with a superficial knowledge of Islamic law, have positioned themselves as religious authorities. Breaking the traditional structures by replacing the authoritative voice of the *'ulamā'* with lay-educated Muslims has caused a deterioration in the Islamic intellectual tradition, accompanied by radicalisation (Abou El Fadl, 2003: 47). Rahman disagrees with Abou El Fadl's position on the role of the *'ulamā'*. He claims that 'the Qur'an is not such a mysterious or complicated work that one needs technically trained people to interpret its imperatives' (Rahman, 1979: 261). Thus, he suggests that the educational role of the *'ulamā'* should be restricted to help people to understand religion better, but ordinary Muslims should be able to interpret divine imperatives. In fact, Rahman's and Abou El Fadl's principal difference rests on their approaches to tradition. Abou El Fadl, having had a traditional Islamic training, is an advocate of a robust methodology in Islamic thought. Yet Rahman is a modernist within Abduh's salafiyya, a school of thought that does not restrict Islamic law to the authoritative opinions.

Overall, some difficulties emerging within modernist thought cannot be entirely bypassed. For instance, the main reason 'epistemologically, democracy is thought to be the best decision-making method, on the grounds that 'it is generally more reliable in helping participants to discover the right decisions' (Christiano, 2012: 82). In democracies, many reasons, religious and otherwise, are included in autonomous and critical assessment of law and policies, 'to think in terms of the common good and justice' (Christiano, 2012: 83). Informed and deliberative debates need to be protected from any force that may restrict or undermine democratic mechanisms and processes. A criticism is directed by Muqtedar Khan at Abou El Fadl for his account of the role of the *'ulamā'* in politics. Although Abou El Fadl does not stipulate an institutional role for *'ulamā'* that gives the state a monopoly on *sharī'a*, Khan argues that 'as long as the commanding authority of jurists remains in place and the jurists retain a monopoly on interpretation (Ijtihād), there can be no Islamic democracy' (2004: 64). Hakan Yavuz also warns about the dangers of the public influence of religious authorities in democracies. His objections are worth quoting at length:

> The intervention of religious authority in the public decision-making process restricts national sovereignty, and therefore hinders democracy in two ways. The first restriction imposed by religion on popular sovereignty may be that decision-making regarding certain public issues is monopolized by religion; in this manner, those issues are moved away from the realm of public deliberation and turned into 'non-issues' or 'forbidden issues.' The second type of restriction may be that, though there may not be any particular issues monopolized by religion, it is still required that the decisions

of the lay institutions (parliaments, courts, and others) conform to the letter and spirit of religious principles. (Yavuz, 2007: 487)

Progressives find flaws in the compatibility-based arguments. An-Na'im identifies a universal distinction between politics and religion. Human reason should be exercised without any hindrances in politics. An-Na'im further argues that the state in democracies is the realm of political power, reason and compromises, lacking a comprehensive moral authority. The state, a sphere for all citizens, should not be shaped or dominated by a philosophical or metaphysical doctrine. Its policies should be the outcome of public deliberation and universal, eternal commitments to justice, dignity and human rights. Politics can only result through citizens' negotiation, undetermined by comprehensive views that should have a right or legitimacy in the making of the political (An-Na'im, 2008: 14). These arguments by An-Na'im appear to be influenced by Rawlsian liberalism. However, An-Na'im, like many multiculturalists, seeks to expand the liberal paradigm to accommodate the role of the *sharī'a*, through the personal conviction of individuals, in the public sphere.

In essence, divine justice is a principal notion for statists in a legal system. Modernists focus on the importance of human agency, consent and deliberation. Revivalists take a middle way between statists and modernists while progressives separate religious and political authority. A common point in compatibility arguments is that they do not provide a clear distinction between political–legal and religious–legal activity based on the conviction that *sharī'a* is an indivisible entity in the lives of Muslims. In their propositions, secular and religious, legal and political authorities are still connected and conflated. The fact that the political and divine are intermingled, however, raises the question of the utility of compatibility-based arguments about political and moral pluralism, and the rights and liberties of non-Muslims and dissenting Muslims. In fact, the public role of *sharī'a*, which is a crucial point in the conceptualisations of Muslim democracy, has been more effectively addressed by multiculturalist thinkers like Bader and Shachar. These multiculturalist arguments go beyond the ambiguities and ideological obscurities that currently persist in compatibility arguments, which the next part will build on.

III. Conclusion on Chapter 3: Deconstructing Muslim Discourses on Democracy

This chapter has critically examined three Islamic concepts that have been central to discussions on Muslim democracy: sovereignty, *shūrā* and *sharī'a*. Statists have expressed an anti-democratic position while progressives have defended democracy, beyond existing compatibility-based arguments, in their support of pluralism, secularism, human rights and religious freedoms. Revivalists and modernists have tended to formulate compatibility-based arguments through different frameworks. In their attempts to show the compatibility of democracy and Islam, revivalists often ignore Western political theory and combine democratic and Islamic political ideals in an eclectic synthesis. They seem to attenuate the doctrinal challenges to the idea of Muslim democracy. Their justification of democracy lacks theoretical precision and remains somehow tactical in response to certain political realities. Modernists, on the other hand, raise the revivalists' political commitment to democracy to a more substantial normative level providing 'Islamic doctrinal justification and reconciliation' for democracy (Abou El Fadl, 2004: 112). In their moral justification of democracy, modernists, like Rahman and Abou El Fadl, draw parallels in demonstrating that 'democracy and Islam share certain fundamental moral tenets' (Fadel, 2006: 81). Islam's moral capacity to cultivate democracy here is not only pursued as a process for developing individual or collective political commitments for democracy. A religious justification is found in Islam for the existence of a democratic political system in the Muslim world.

To reiterate a previous point, compatibility-based arguments maintain that the dual authority of God's sovereignty and popular sovereignty is a distinctive feature of Islamic democracy. In this simultaneity of divine and popular sovereignty, the political sphere belongs to the field of human's agency and consent is the basis of political authority while the source of morality and justice comes from God. The people in this model decide the contents of law, but divine sources retain the authority to delineate the relationship between ethics and politics. A number of pressing questions are unanswered and sidestepped by the idea of dual sovereignty. It does not address the issues of public debate, political participation, civil and human rights, minority, and conciliation of two competing notions of sovereignty in a single constitution.

Democracy has some intrinsic universal attributes, such as authority being vested in the people and government being accountable to citizens. The idea of dual sovereignty fits awkwardly into this definition. A notion of divine sovereignty, under the positivist enterprise of the modern state, precludes the participation of citizens in public deliberations or in reconciling conflicting comprehensive moral claims. There would be an inordinate risk that democracy will be undermined under the influence of a single religious or moral community. An unequal power balance could emerge between different communities in their access to political and legal decision-making. A political system based on dual sovereignty may foster the criminalisation of political and moral differences (Yavuz, 2007: 487). Modernists are against such a totalitarian notion of a religious state or institution. However, their formulations of sovereignty in an Islamic democracy still can lead to its development, albeit inadvertently.

Consequently, the idea of Muslim democracy, in compatibility-based arguments, inevitably faces challenges from the tenuous relationship between the primacy of Islamic morality and the necessity for democratic politics. As Tezcür cautions, majority rule, within Muslim contexts, can easily 'decay into the tyranny of the majority', unless measures are effectively taken to protect individual and minority rights 'against the abuses of stronger members and majorities' to uphold a certain comprehensive moral doctrine (2007: 496). Prevalent notions of Islamic democracy, present in compatibility-based arguments, 'offer little novelty in institutional and constitutional design' (Tezcür, 2007: 496).

In compatibility-based arguments, democracy is justified by religious motives which indirectly influence the obligations and limits of political action. However, democracy 'fears and resists the absolutism of the pure, the Grand ideology' that may block 'public spaces for citizens to challenge and to reject' sacrosanct norms (Keane, 1993: 29). Democracy is in fact 'the unique realization of public equality in collective decision-making about this common world' (Christiano, 2012: 76). A condition of 'freedom from ideology' characterises democracy, which is depreciated by moralising comprehensive views in compatibility-based arguments (Keane,

1993: 28). Transcendental authority in a democratic system should neither define executive and legislative authority nor legitimise it. Rational deliberation disappears and dissent is criminalised when a religious morality makes public debate illicit. These democratic concerns are addressed by progressives in their opposition to the link between religious morality and political legitimacy.

Thus, I argue that it is essential for conceptualisations on Muslim democracy to differentiate the philosophical source of governance from 'private' ethical sources of individual political action. Democracy is a non-religious political system that can create pluralistic spaces so as to enable Muslims to think, act, deliberate, reflect and uphold Islamic comprehensive views in their lives. Progressive and multiculturalist formulations of democracy do not necessarily require religious morality to be separated from political action. However, both of these two trends insist on the separation of claims of divine authority from state and political authority. In other words, religious morality can only play a role in the public debate through the participation of the members of religious communities as individual citizens. Unlike progressive justifications for democracy, compatibility-based arguments do not engage these relevant issues within a political theory approach.

These contentions of compatibility-based arguments are neither unique for Islamic thought nor dissimilar to those experienced in Western democratic theory. Theological arguments on divine sovereignty resemble foundationalist arguments about democracy within liberalism. The constitutional underpinning of who is sovereign in the liberal theory is no less abstract than compatibility-based arguments' definition of authority in Islamic doctrines. Sovereignty is located in a discrete entity often described as 'the nation' or 'the people'. In liberal democracy, this issue resides between anti-foundationalist and foundationalist moral theories. Resolution of the ontological issue of sovereignty may not be necessary or even possible in the development of a normative theory of Muslim democracy. A 'post-sovereignist' turn in Muslim political thought, proposed by Andrew March, is the most preferred course for developing a political theory of Muslim democracy in which Islamic jurisprudential arguments do not dictate formulations of democracy (March, 2019: 227). I argue that reasoning on sovereignty should be moved from metaphysical to political grounds. Carl Schmitt follows the genealogy of popular sovereignty back to the Judaeo-Christian notion of divine sovereignty with absolutist, essentialist and transcendental tendencies (2005: 36). The 'people' in popular sovereignty is 'like a metaphysical entity' with theological connotations (Ahmad, 2015). Irfan Ahmad and John Keane argue that democracy can easily alter into populism and even authoritarianism, with the former's norms and ideals obscured in the name of popular sovereignty (Ahmad, 2015). I therefore argue that sovereignty should be studied with reference to the principles of democracy rather than minimising their normative implications.

The search for compatibility-based democratic arguments during the eras of Tanzimat (1839–76) and Nahda (1870–1950), when democracy in its modern sense first entered the intellectual Muslim discourses, may have been necessary. The intellectual project of compatibility-oriented theories was

> aimed at the elevation of our [Islamic] heritage and civilization to the level of the present age . . . [it] was an act of self-affirmation and self-defence. (al-Jabri, 1994: 42)

Earlier Muslim advocates of democracy aimed to incorporate democratic concepts while retaining the position of Islamic authenticity against the accusations of westernisation and heresy. For instance, *shūrā* was a key principle for promoting participatory modes of governance and the Medina model was for the pluralistic notion of a civil society and tolerance. Thus, in the nineteenth century, the compatibility-based thinking had a beneficial function in providing a basis for democratic thinking in Muslim intellectual discourses. However, these efforts did not culminate in a coherent political theory on democracy.

Muslim discourses on democracy have demonstrated that Islam provides a wide space for reinterpretations. Islam's multi-vocality gives rise to doctrines that are supportive of or adverse to democratic ideals. Thus, current academic discussions 'exaggerate the benefits to be gained by establishing the compatibility of Islam' with democracy today (March, 2011: 4). Current debates on the compatibility of Islam and democracy can contribute to a certain reconciliation of Muslim thought with democracy. However, because the benefits were overstated in these debates, they have often ended with the conclusion that Islam and democracy are compatible. A critical discourse or well-developed political theory on Muslim democracy has not emerged through compatibility-based arguments and their positions.

This chapter has examined the shortcomings of compatibility-based arguments about Muslim democracy. It has found that these arguments gloss over significant tensions between political and theological forms of reasoning. Compatibility-based arguments have formulated an understanding of democracy which consists of divinely-inspired political sovereignty, transcendental public morality, public deliberation confined to a certain moral space, and a lack of commitment to pluralism. A further limitation of compatibility-based arguments is the restriction of intellectual reasoning to the realm of Islamic jurisprudence. It cannot produce a non-theological idea of democracy. Compatibility-based arguments among Muslim thinkers convey 'signs of *ambiguities* and *ambivalences* inherent to political theology that proclaims both monism and pluralism, both divine and popular sovereignty' (March, 2013: 2). Most of these arguments shy away from confronting issues such as secularism, constitutional safeguards, institutional checks and balances, the public sphere, individual rights and freedoms and dissent. Blasphemy, ethnic and cultural rights, gender equality, freedom of expression and press, and sexuality fall outside of the scope of a meaningful resolution in these pro-democratic compatibility-based arguments. All these issues constitute barriers to the idea of a Muslim democracy that the following chapters aim to overcome.

Innovative and coherent notions are not offered by compatibility-based arguments to address the relationship between religion and the state, majority and minorities, and rights and liberties. Even the democratic ideas advanced by the modernist school have not given birth to a coherent Muslim democratic theory. This chapter has revealed the areas of internal incongruity in compatibility-based arguments in order to pave the way towards a political theory of Muslim democracy that departs from political theology. Accordingly, a novel framework will be theorised in the next part through a normative synthesis of the concepts and values of Muslim political and multiculturalist arguments. I will also address and resolve the ambiguities, gaps and fallacies present in compatibility-based arguments as well as orthodox liberal and secularist paradigms.

Notes

1. Thus not all, but only some, Muslim thinkers examined in the first chapter are classified here under the compatibility-based arguments.
2. Wael Hallaq, although not a modernist like Rahman, takes a similar idealist approach in which he argues that '[b]efore being transcendental and theological, divine sovereignty was moral. An expression of this sovereign will, the Shariʿa came to articulate the moral principles through a morally constructed law' (2012: 49). Hallaq argues that divine morality sets the incontestable standards of norms, truth, justice and rule of law that can curb the whims and tyrannies of the modern positivist state (2012: 157).

PART THREE
CONCEPTUALISING MUSLIM DEMOCRACY

GENERAL INTRODUCTION TO PART THREE

Religion has always been a major moral reference in social and political matters in the Muslim world. Those calling for secularism, in the Western, orthodox sense of the term, have been in the minority among contemporary Muslims. This tendency points to the likelihood that political developments will take dissimilar paths in contexts that have different religious, cultural and social characteristics from those of Western societies. Thus, different forms of democratic politics in these contexts may develop (Beller, 2014: 20). Contemporary debates about different models of democracy, in relation to different normative and religious traditions, have included Confucians and Jewish scholars (Chan, 2014: 22).

In the previous chapters, both multiculturalist and Muslim thinkers argued that democracy does not necessarily need to be determined by mainstream Western theories. The multiculturalist school has proposed new ways of thinking about democracies through the possibility of more inclusive forms of secularism, public sphere and law in relation to substantial cultural and religious claims. While multiculturalists consider the prospect of different democratic models, they demonstrate a conceptual rigour in maintaining ideals that underpin democracy.

The search for 'new models of democratic polities', derived from Islamic foundations, has occupied the works of Muslim revivalists and modernists (al-Effendi, 2006: 229). Revivalists, and to some extent modernists, think the particular political history and culture of Muslim societies can engender distinctive democratic systems (Ibrahim, 2006: 12). Muslims' 'own immense ontological resources' are believed to be capable of providing sufficient moral and political resources for building a Muslim democracy (Yenigün, 2013: 396). However, my examination of the various strands of Muslim political thought, in the previous chapters, has led to the conclusion that most of the works on Islamic democracy incorporate compatibility-based arguments. The failure of these arguments to develop certain democratic benchmarks at the level of a political theory may reinforce autocratic structures. They have evaded the following problematics:

1. The difficulty of curbing the political power engendered by the predominance of comprehensive moral discourses, where divine morality and political authority are fused.
2. The incompatibility of the beliefs and norms of a majority in society with fundamental democratic values, with particular respect to tolerance and civility in the public sphere.
3. The absence of the theorising of legal and institutional safeguards to protect individual freedoms and human rights.

The advocates of compatibility-based arguments have not adequately addressed these limitations for Muslim-majority contexts, where neither institutional nor normative democratic change is consolidated.

A systematic discussion about secularism, pluralism, the public sphere, freedom of expression and individual rights is mostly absent from Muslim political thought. The explorations of these normative issues often do not extend beyond compatibility-based arguments, neglecting to develop a conception of Muslim democracy with theoretical articulations. This part of the book seeks to address the inability of compatibility-based arguments to produce a political theory on Muslim democracy. Such a theoretical approach can better address the challenges plaguing contemporary Muslim societies.

Normative inquiries into Muslim democracy require a balance between a type of democracy that accommodates Muslims' faith-based conceptions and practising of a good life and the maintenance of democratic pluralistic norms and institutions. Although it is also essential to recognise that differentials may exist here for a variety of democratic regimes, 'such differentiation cannot be limitless if regimes are to qualify as "democratic"' regardless of the context, culture and demographics they work within (Dallmayr, 2011: 445). Basic democratic qualifications for pluralism combined with tolerant, inclusivist and egalitarian norms are the sine qua non of any democratic theorisation.

I will discuss in this part the core benchmarks of a democratic political system and their relevance to the needs and claims of Muslims. My discussion of a democratic framework will illustrate a dialogical interaction between human rights, democratic tolerance, political secularity and public religiosity within predominantly Muslim contexts. Conciliation of a comprehensive Islamic world-view with the values of democracy motivates many of the proposed arguments. This line of inquiry aims, through a set of interpretative tools, to contribute to existing democratic political theories.

This part maps out three interrelated concepts most relevant to the democratic theorising of Muslim democracy: (i) secularism, (ii) the public sphere and (iii) constitutional conditions. For the purpose of formulating a theory of Muslim democracy, arguments and insights from Muslim and multiculturalist political thought are utilised. Both multiculturalist and progressive Muslim thinkers have discussed dissociating democratic state institutions from thick philosophical backgrounds espoused by individuals and communities to enable these institutions to adapt to pluralist contexts. They have also highlighted the importance, in fostering democratic institutions, of value change, the development of civic virtues and a pluralistic political culture. Accordingly, through three interrelated chapters, this part of the book will engage with debates on support for the pluralist expansion of the secular paradigm, devolution of more powers to civil society through restructuring the public sphere, institutionalisation of pluralism, legal protection of diversity, and internalisation of democratic tolerance and human rights accompanied by religious reforms. Successful resolution of these issues can potentially contribute to creating the required normative commitments of Muslim democracy.

By offering specific theoretical responses to these debates, this part attempts to reconcile the tensions around issues such as popular sovereignty, minority rights, civil liberties, religious jurisdiction, secularism and public morality. Two primary lines of argumentation will be presented in each of the following chapters: Chapters 4 (secularism), 5 (public sphere) and 6 (constitution). Each chapter concludes by highlighting the impact of an alternative conceptualisation of pluralist secularism, the social public sphere and pluralising constitutionalism on the debate on Muslim democracy in political theory.

4

PLURALIST SECULARISM

I. Introduction

The attempt to define the relation between the modern state and religion has generated various types of secularism. Republican secularism, also described as 'philosophical secularism' (Laborde, 2018a: 167), 'ideological secularism' (Modood, 2010: 5), 'ethical secularism' (Bhargava, 1999: 492), 'nationalist secularism' (Asad, 2003: 199), 'aggressive secularism' (Kuru, 2007: 576) or 'militant secularism' (Soroush, 2007), has been the most common model of secularism experienced by, and often coercively imposed on, Muslim societies. It has claimed 'a monopoly over the meaning of secularism by rejecting the possibility of its diverse interpretations' (Kuru, 2008: 8). According to republican secularism, in order to maintain neutrality and equality among citizens religion has to be removed from the public sphere and limited to the private realm (Maclure and Taylor, 2011: 14). Republican secularism and its moralising attitude cannot properly mediate the relation between religion and politics in a political system. A quasi-secular equivalent of religion has emerged, with a 'moral and social philosophy, a complex set of ideas and commitments' that 'has too many dogmatic aspects' (Laborde, 2008: 8; Kuru, 2008: 8).

During recent decades, previously assumed universal definitions of secularism have been criticised for their inability to guarantee religious freedoms and minority rights in increasingly multicultural Western societies, and to account for the public nature of religion in non-Western societies (Asad, 2003: 200; Bhargava, 1999: 492; Maclure and Taylor, 2011: 13). Revision of secularism for the development of contemporary democratic societies, especially in the case of morally diverse communities, has preoccupied political theorists like Taylor, An-Na'im and Shachar. In the debates on secularism, some Muslim intellectuals, such as al-Qaradawi, al-Ghannushi and Bulaç, express their conviction that democracy can be conceived without it. They argue that a state founded on Islamic principles can ensure justice and pluralism better than secularism. An-Na'im and Nader Hashemi, disagreeing with the preceding argument, insist that democracy demands a form of secularism. At this point, they join multiculturalists in their call for moving away from current forms of assertive secularism. These thinkers re-evaluate secularism in order for it to become more tolerant of religion, neither rejecting nor privatising faith, in the public sphere.

In Muslim-majority countries, a large number of people hold the conviction that religion is the basis of legitimacy of governance and the main source of law and social structure (Nieuwenhuis, 2012: 154). At the same time, a considerable number of people who endorse secular ontology want a separation of religion and state power as well as the restriction of religion in public affairs (Hashemi, 2012: 21). In addition, even among the segments of society espousing a moral system based on religious sources, there is an intractable dispute about the nature of the relation between religious morality and politics. As Abdelwahab El-Affendi rightly observes, the tension between religion, secularism and democracy 'remains the dominant feature of Muslim politics to this day' (2004: 172).

This chapter examines secularism by engaging with the question of whether democracy without secularism is possible and whether it can uphold political pluralism, or whether secularism is an indispensable element of democracy. It will study the two conflicting sides of the argument on the link between secularism, religion and democracy, namely 'unsecular Muslim democracy' and secular Muslim democracy. A secular model, pluralist secularism, is proposed through the theorising of a Muslim democracy. I will develop pluralist secularism in more detail by exploring four constitutive features of this normative category.

II. Unsecular Muslim Democracy

Prevalent attitudes in Muslim societies towards secularism perceive it to be a philosophical belief particular to the Western tradition that cannot be reconciled with Islamic religion. As Hashemi observes, '[a]t the moment, reliable polling suggests most Arabs oppose the idea that democracy requires a Western-style form of secularism and large majorities support the idea that Sharia law should be "a" source (albeit not "the" source) of legislation' (2012: 21). This tendency is also valid for the Muslim counties in general where '[t]he cultural and political expectations about religion and politics' are not in favour of secularism, at least not its dominant version (Cesari, 2014: 118).

Frequent opposition to secularism among Muslims tends to be motivated by disagreement over the issue of sovereignty. While ruling dynasties exercised sovereignty, in the position of 'the successor of God on earth and his shadow over his servants', through legitimacy derived from divine writ, the people are the source of legitimacy in secular states (Abd al-Raziq, 1982: 30). Thus, secularism in the Muslim world has implanted a foreign notion of sovereignty in politics and society. On the other hand, the recognition of the nation, possessing sovereignty, did not necessarily guarantee the introduction of democratic government. In fact, secularisation has been an elitist process and often benefited a small segment of 'westernised' elites. Hakan Yavuz observes that secularisation initially led to authoritarian republics, rather than liberal democracies, where the populace, kept at a far distance from public decision-making, was not allowed to exercise popular sovereignty. For ordinary Muslims, secularisation brought new secular legal, political and civic institutions, perceived as alien and 'heretical from Islam's point of view', that oppressed, controlled and excluded religious lifestyles (Yavuz, 2007: 482). Therefore, secularism did not function as a neutral mediator in regulating political life but as an ideological force defining and managing religion.

Secularisation, against the expectations of its exponents, did not lead to the decline of religion as a political and social force in Muslim societies. On the contrary, religious communities have sought, even under secular authoritarianism, a formal presence in education, health and social services in spaces allowed by political authorities (Bekaroğlu, 2016). Moreover, the adoption of the Western secular institutions in the public sphere produced a different relationship between Islam and politics in which Islam was redefined as a political ideology in direct opposition to secularism (Cesari, 2014: 7). Secularism, by virtue of the experience of secular authoritarianism in the Muslim world, was not perceived as a desirable relationship between religion and governance but rather an antithesis, rival, or even a substitute for religion itself (Yavuz, 2007: 482).

Although republican secularism in the Muslim world has endorsed a strict separation of religion from the public sphere, it still controlled the power to define and regulate a national religion for citizens to follow in the private realm (Mahmood and Danchin, 2014: 5; Turner, 2007: 124). However, all the Muslim thinkers, including progressive voices, discussed in Chapter 1 have found republican secularism wanting and insist that a strict separation of Islam from public life is not possible. Yusuf al-Qaradawi (2002), a revivalist supporter of Islamic democracy, asserts that Islam cannot accept the division between the divine and everyday life, and secularism's demands are 'downright apostasy'. A non-secular idea of a 'civil state' (*al-dawla al-madaniyya*) is proposed in Rashid al-Ghannushi's account. Al-Ghannushi (2011b) argues that secularism is not required in order to either establish a democratic regime or achieve equal citizenship, minority and women's rights, and separation of powers. These values can be realised under a Muslim democracy without secularism.

Ali Bulaç makes a similar argument that Western democracies sought to accommodate diversity through secularism to ensure no single religion dominates politics. Such an arrangement, where religion is no longer a moral authority, can work to ensure pluralism. However, secularism does not necessarily facilitate diversity in societies where religion exerts a strong moral influence in the social and political spheres (Bulaç, 2012f). According to Bulaç, secular political authorities have either asked religious people not to bring religion into the public domain or pressured them to endorse the ideals of modernity in public life. Liberty in the truest sense cannot be witnessed when the concepts of rights and freedom of religion in the secular paradigm are dictated by the state. Islam offers a more capable alternative approach, compared to secularism, of accommodation and pluralism, through institutional and legal pluralism, for non-Muslim minorities to pursue their own way of living (Bulaç, 2013).

Modernists, similar to revivalists, also strongly emphasise the role of religion in politics. Unlike progressives, who locate secularism and the secular state at the core of their theories, modernists contend that secularism is a colonial construct, hostile to religion, and an instrument of authoritarianism. They aim to demote the dominant status of secularism in their discourses. Instead, a modified language, based on rights, is offered,

> as 'democracy' means protecting the rights of individuals and groups, while 'rationality' means exercising politics according to reason and its logical and moral criteria [behind the *sharī'a* rulings mentioned in the Qur'an and *sunna*], and not in accordance with whims, fanaticism and capricious moods. (al-Jabri, 2009: 56)

Revivalist and modernist thinkers have argued that democracy, through compatibility-based arguments, can be viable and divorced from secularism, one of the 'ideological' 'value-elements' 'historically associated with it in the West' (Bahlul, 2004: 106, 112). None of democracy's core principles such as majority rule, political equality and representative government appears to require secularism.

This line of thinking also finds support among Western thinkers. For instance, Michael W. McConnell (1992, 2000) and Graham Walker (2000) mount a critique of secular democracy in preference of an all-inclusive religious pluralism. Jocelyn Cesari also makes a point of arguing for a non-secular form of democracy in Muslim societies, which questions the importance of secularism for a democracy. The acceptance of democracy does not mean the unconditional acceptance of secularism and all civic liberties. She argues that 'all democracies differ in the ways institutional, social, and individual levels of secularization interact' (Cesari, 2014: 269). Unsecular democracies 'arise in which there are free and fair elections', and the rule of law can limit or selectively implement individual freedom 'on religious grounds' (Cesari, 2014: 204). This form of democracy exercises reasonable pluralism, where not all liberties, especially the ones 'that are seen as a threat to the national community', are guaranteed, but the most fundamental rights are given a constitutional guarantee (Cesari, 2014: 204). In other words, whereas economic and most political and civil rights, to political association, affiliation and opinion, as well as selective freedoms of the press, would be recognised, 'the rights granted to the person, from sexual freedom to the right to exit or criticize Islam' would not. These limitations, Cesari insists, 'concern the third level of secularity (that of the individual), but do not necessarily affect the institutional or social level of secularity' (2014: 241).

There is support for the idea of unsecular democracy among certain Western thinkers who argue that secularism has lost its claim of 'neutrality' and 'is no longer a viable political solution' in our pluralist age (van der Zweerde, 2014: xx). Veit Bader, of the institutionalist pluralist school, presents a conception of democracy that upholds the idea of active co-operation between the state and all religions. He argues that 'we are better able to economize our moral disagreements or to resolve the substantive constitutional, legal, jurisprudential and institutional issues and controversies' by 'drop[ping] secularism as a "fuzzy", chameleonic, highly misleading or "cacophonous" concept' from democracy (Bader, 2010: 1, 9). The secular strategy of neutrality, which might be suitable in a hypothetical world, exhibits the state's partiality through universalising 'the particular' in the service of 'the resourceful and powerful' (Bader, 1999: 600–8). Bader's opposition to the doctrine of secularism comes from his conviction no philosophy or ideology should supersede a democratic governance that reflects widely shared political principles among the population. Secularism, by its very nature, cannot provide a political superstructure that is based on common political values, through impartial democratic political deliberation of the citizens, where citizens with secular and religious philosophical outlooks would be equally represented (Bader, 1999: 602; 2009b: 1). Democratic theory can maintain the differentiation between state and religion, disassociating itself from a secularist ideology, due its ability to appropriate all the necessary political principles that secularism can potentially offer (Bader, 2007a: 47).

Certain restrictions in an unsecular democracy, for the well-being of the community, imposed on some personal freedoms do not threaten its democratic integrity as long as the state maintains its neutrality towards every citizen. Nonetheless, concerns arise about the democratic nature of an unsecular democracy, defined by a dominant religious culture, and its ability to ensure 'equality of all religions in public spaces and political neutrality of the state vis-à-vis all religions' (Cesari, 2014: 264). The lack of feasible alternatives to political and legal instruments is borne out by the fact that 'minorities are often the foremost supporters of secularism' (Greenberg and Steinmetz-Jenkins, 2016).

In a Muslim democracy, the limits of freedoms may vary from those imposed in a Western setting, but, as I will argue in Chapter 4, section 3, this by no means implies that personal freedoms and human rights can be left to the will of the majority and its account of morality. The idea of an unsecular democracy, similar to compatibility-based arguments, is unable to take into consideration the deleterious impact of a public morality, espoused by the majority, on democratic processes. Present concerns exist about the models of democracy without secularism for a Muslim-majority context. Weak democratic institutionalisation of democracy, the separation of powers, the rule of law, an independent and impartial judiciary, commitments to fundamental human rights and the ethos of pluralism is an urgent area requiring amelioration for secular Muslim democracy advocates.

III. Secular Muslim Democracy

This section seeks to answer the question as to whether secularism or the processes of secularisation which some Muslim societies underwent has given the concept its ill repute in Muslim political thought. Universalist efforts to define 'the shape of secularism throughout the world' based on a separationist republican model appear to have failed to take root in the Muslim world, where the role of religion is paramount in organising social life (Jakobsen and Pellegrini, 2008: 2). The origin of a universalising and moralising secularism was the emergence of a sharp demarcation between the religious and the secular in post-Reformation Europe. In this context, the secular was considered to be rational and emancipatory, while religion was a hostile and divisive force within the public sphere. The separation of religion from the public sphere in the West may have been caused by the modern spiritual 'Protestant understanding of religion with belief and faith at the conceptual center' (Jakobsen and Pellegrini, 2008: 8). Problems surround the expectation that Islam and Muslims will conform to 'the generic model' of secularism as a process of modernisation involving Protestantism (Jakobsen and Pellegrini, 2008: 8).

Taylor and An-Na'im both single out Turkey's experience of secularism. According to Taylor, secularisation in the country as a form of authoritarian laicism 'came about at the cost of a bitter struggle against a dominant religion' (2011: 14). A similar observation is made by An-Naʻim that the Turkish state was motivated by 'strictly limiting – as well as controlling – the role of religion and religious institutions' (2008: 182). Bader points out that Muslim societies never publicly debated the role of religion and politics and never developed their models of secularism of their own volition. Authoritarian regimes undertook a top-down project of secularism, and they solely defined, controlled and imposed the normative relationship between religion and government (Bader, 2007a: 111). As a result of the alienating legacy of secularism in the Muslim world, the term carries a lot of negative connotations, generates mistrust and 'is a conversation stopper' (Hashemi, 2009: x). Disagreement has emerged about the explanatory usefulness of the term 'secularism' in referring to laicism. Taha Parla and Andrew Davison have suggested:

> Kemalist laicism is most often described throughout the literature as 'secularism,' leaving the impressions that Kemalist laicism achieves everything from a radical separation between state and tradition to the privatization or elimination of religion in the conscience. As we argue, Kemalist laicism is at odds with these ideas in both concept and practice. (2004: 14)

Defenders of secular Muslim democracy such as An-Naʻim and Hashemi note that the secularisation process in the Muslim world has pushed democracy in the wrong direction. The notion that religion should be practised in the private sphere and should not exert any influence on the public sphere is challenged simultaneously by Islamic political and multicultural critiques of secularism. Muslim and multiculturalist political thinkers have underlined the inseparability of comprehensive moral doctrines and politics, particularly Islam, and have put pressure on the liberal paradigm to expand to accommodate this situation. Thinkers from these two separate traditions, Muslim political thought and multiculturalism, have offered various alternatives involving the conciliation of secularism, democracy and religion.

First, Muslim thinkers have engaged in reconceptualising secularism in a way that would be in harmony with Muslims' social, cultural and political experiences. Progressive Muslim scholars, such as An-Naʻim, contend that secularism in the Muslim world must be more responsive to *sharīʻa*-driven public religious claims of individual Muslims. An-Naʻim promotes an

'Islamic argument for a secular state' in order 'to reconcile Muslim commitment to Islamic law with the achievement of the benefits of secularism within a religious framework' (2008: vii). While he is alert to 'the dangerous illusion that Islam can or should be kept out of the public life of the community of believers', there persists the need to disentangle Islam from state institutions (An-Na'im, 2008: 6).

From an Islamic point of view, for An-Na'im, the legitimacy of the state does not come from the claim to enforce 'divine law' or morality. It is derived from protecting religious freedoms and human rights, which enables religious participation in a democracy and recognition of the public role of *sharī'a*. Unlike the discourses on Islamic democracy, according to which a religion with universal normative claims strives to shape political rules regulating common life, liberal secularism exhibits a unifying factor ensuring political and moral pluralism among diverse religious communities (An-Na'im, 2005: 63). Liberal secularism, which recognises the plurality of competing moral and political voices in the public sphere, can provide sufficient space for ethical Islamic commitments to be fulfilled through personal conviction (An-Na'im, 2008: 203).

Second, multiculturalists have demonstrated that Rawls's political liberalism does not recognise the importance of religious beliefs. Multiculturalism has advanced the idea that the orthodox liberal goal of keeping religion outside public institutions is misguided. Although multiculturalist thinkers like Veit Bader and Gad Barzilai are critical of the conventional idea of secularism, multiculturalists overall are emphatic that 'of all available alternatives, secularism remains our best bet to help us deal with ever deepening religious diversity and the problems endemic to it' (Bhargava, 2014: 39). One emerging explicit agenda in multiculturalist thought is that secularism must be re-evaluated within Muslim contexts, in which culture and religion are intertwined in public life. Thus, multiculturalists have pleaded for a more complex notion of secularism that accommodates religious demands in the public sphere (Taylor, 1998: 154). New non-Christian and Islamic formulations of secularism can overcome the religion–secularism binary present within the dominant discourse of secularism (Black, 2014: 13).

Maclure and Taylor (2011), in their book *Secularism and Freedom of Conscience*, re-articulate secularism as a central plank of a liberal democratic theory for modern states containing religious diversity. They endorse a functional, rather than a philosophical or substantive, interpretation of secularism to give it a more inclusive framework with which to engage with organised religions and religious freedoms. Moreover, Taylor's liberal pluralist secularism is based on a separation of religion and governance at the state level without the elimination or suppression of religion (2008: xi). He suggests that secularism, if correctly understood, is essential to any liberal democracy in which citizens adhere to different or competing comprehensive philosophical views (Bouchard and Taylor, 2008: 46; Taylor, 1998: 154).

The idea of a secular Muslim democracy rests on the assumption that 'reconciling Islamic political thought with secularism is a critical precondition for the construction of a liberal-democratic theory for Muslim societies' (Hashemi, 2009: 22). Taylor and An-Na'im, among other intellectuals, have opened up new ways of thinking about democracy through alternative narratives of secular governance. They have formulated different flexible models of secularism that incorporate democracy and pluralism. In addition, the insights of Taylor and An-Na'im demonstrate that neither secularism nor religion has been static, unchanging and ahistorical. An evolving secularism is evident relative to changing conditions.

The creation of new forms of secular democracy is feasible on the basis of secularism's historicity. Differing from the outright rejection of religion in the secularisation thesis, a shift from religion will lead 'eventually to governance by reasoned debate and ultimately to democracy and peace', the idea of a secular Muslim democracy, with the potential for more religion-friendly formulations of secularism to fulfil democratic values (Jakobsen and Pellegrini, 2008: 4). Critiques of ideological republican secularism have engendered alternative formulations to incorporate the claims of individuals and groups with non-secular ideological dispositions. The next section will show how a more pluralist form of secularism can be conceptualised as part of the Muslim democracy idea and how this secularism, which I call 'pluralist secularism', can advance the idea of Muslim democracy.

IV. Pluralist Secularism within the Muslim Democracy Framework

I will now address the persisting challenges and unanswered questions on difference and diversity in compatibility-based arguments. Non-secular democracy and the ambiguity surrounding this idea will also be examined in this section. Recent arguments for secular Muslim democracy have expressly shown that Islam and political secularism do not stand in direct opposition. A fair state–religion equilibrium is possible through different manifestations of secular democratic forms such as the 'liberal-pluralist secularism' of Taylor (Maclure and Taylor, 2011: 19) and the 'liberal secularism' of An-Na'im (2008: 203).

I propose to argue that a democracy, in my conceptualisation of pluralist secularism, requires a form of political secularism that in some sense separates religion and governance to establish mechanisms for ensuring pluralism, equality and religious freedoms. My formulation of pluralist secularism extends the modernist and progressive Muslim intellectuals' critique of the ideological Islamic state. It demonstrates the possibility of an alternative inclusive and religiously-friendly secularism accommodating Muslim ways of social and public life.

Pluralist secularism draws on multiculturalism's criticism, also shared by the Muslim political objection, of republican secularism as an ideological project that 'has morphed into a religion of its own' (Ibrahim, 2006: 8), with the character of a sacred moral ideology (Connolly, 2005: 43). The pluralist secular state in my theoretical formulation neither takes a stance about what ought to be a good life nor engages in the moral process of shaping individual identities on the basis of a philosophical ideology. In this book, pluralist secularism affirms that transcendental foundations should not single-handedly dictate public discourses, be they in the form of secularism or a religious doctrine.

I will now demonstrate how a shift from universalist, philosophical secularism to a pluralist secularism can create new ways of thinking about the relationship between religion and the state. This reformulation will also elaborate the ability of pluralist secularism, accompanied by a critical understanding of the complex role that Islam plays in Muslim politics, to address the issues of diversity, equality and difference. Therefore, this discussion can contribute to resolving the interrelated challenges of religious accommodation and individual right and freedoms. This section will illustrate four main features of pluralist secularism: a minimalist state, the public recognition of religion, the differentiation of state and social public spheres, and collective rights.

1. A Morally Thin and Minimalist State

The first feature of pluralist secularism to be elaborated here is the notion of a morally thin and minimalist state framework.[1] In a democratic system, establishing the proper limits of the state authority is necessary in order to regulate its relation to social and religious affairs. The modern nation-state's 'capacity to penetrate society institutionally and thereby create the conditions for the effective control over, and governance of, society' is critically probed by the multiculturalist and Muslim thinkers (Gill, 2007: 32). An alternative approach to this issue, in the case of the morally minimalist state, aims to facilitate moral pluralism and a cultural diversity. The notion of a minimalist state in this book is rests on the examination, in previous chapters, of the theories of Bader, Kukathas, An-Naʿim, Bulaç and Taylor.

A morally minimalist state can be broadly defined as the institutional realm of compromise and consensus that is impartial about citizens' normative beliefs and practices. The morally minimalist state does not establish, control or impose a 'contested truth-claim of any kind, whether religious, philosophical, or scientific' (Bader, 1999: 602). It refrains from refashioning society in line with a particular version of the good. Kukathas awards to the liberal state the responsibility for enabling the successful coexistence of people from diverse moral backgrounds without intervening in philosophical matters or imposing normative ideals (2001: 89). This account of the minimalist state reflects the classical liberal distrust of state authority and its ostensible tendency to infringe on civic freedoms in the name of a dominant ideology, public morality, or national security.

Thus, the idea of a minimalist state grants primacy to the rights of individuals over the power of the state (Kukathas, 1998: 692–3). In a moral minimalist framework, the state is more of a 'night watchman', composed of the police, army, justice system, armed forces, infrastructure, communication services and the stable economy, and leaves a large space of liberty to individuals and groups (Rand, 1963: 111). In other words, 'the role of government is not to govern but to facilitate self-governance' (Khan, 2019: 243). Muqtedar Khan argues that a minimalist state, in an Islamic repertoire, is 'a device that enables the sovereign human to act on earth as witness to her Lord (when she is a believer) and as witness against herself when she is a disbeliever' (2019: 214).

Kukathas's notion of the state echoes Muslim revivalist references to the Charter of Madina. Bulaç notes that the Charter laid down a pluralist project based on the multi-religious legal sovereignty of self-governing groups. Education, legislation and health fell under the legal and administrative autonomy of religious groups while the defence, organisation and judiciary of the community were the responsibility of the central political authority led by the Prophet Muhammd (Bulaç, 2006: 190–3). For al-Ghannushi (2012), the articles in the Charter, in which religious freedoms were given paramount importance, made a distinction between religious and political belonging.

Essentially, the Madina model of Muslim revivalist thinkers, centred on institutional pluralism and religious diversity, contains the underpinnings of an Islamic democracy. However, Dahl notes:

> To say, then, that independent organizations help to prevent domination and bring about mutual control is not to say that they guarantee justice, equality, or democracy. A political system can be pluralist and yet lack democratic institutions. (2001: 136)

He differentiates between institutional pluralism and democratic institutionalism. Although ahistorical interpretations of the Madina model may not provide a reliable foundation for theorising about democracy, their normative ideas can be readily incorporated in discussions on pluralism and its forms.

Exponents of compatibility-based arguments and unsecular democracy suggest that the core of public life, influenced by dominant comprehensive views, may change from one social context to another. Unsecular democracy theorists argue that the boundaries of the public representation of private acts may vary. The scope of freedoms differ as restrictions on certain personal matters are brought in line with established public values. Advocates of compatibility-based arguments and unsecular democracy emphasise that political institutions will inevitably be influenced by the demands, inputs and concerns of citizens as the will of the majority. This approach has a certain democratic value. However, when the majority decides the public rules of conduct and morality, a deeply problematic situation arises from a democratic point of view for reasons that will be explained below.

In a predominantly Muslim context, a majority of the people may hypothetically agree, through participatory and contestatory processes, on the rules of a religiously inspired code of conduct and social values. However, a democratic state should not yield to the morality of the majority in a majoritarian manner. A simultaneously secular and democratic state stands at an equal distance from all religious, ethnic, cultural or identity groups. Democracies do not only guarantee political rights for voting and participation, but also protect the rights of the most unpopular against the intrusions of ruling and dominant groups. In principle, comparable importance is granted to the norms and beliefs of both minorities and majorities in democratic regimes. An automatic privileging of majority norms is unacceptable according to democratic criteria. Pluralist secularism affirms that a political culture should accept difference and recognise the equal value of minority ways of life, rather than requiring minorities to conform to the standards of the majority (Mookherjee, 2001: 15; Tully, 1995: 183).

In addition, conflating the moral standards of the mainstream with public morality is also objected to by Muslim thinkers, on various grounds. For modernists and progressives, morality is a personal responsibility before God and sins fall within this realm, where God provides the chance for repentance. Moral life is not supposed to be controlled by a coercive institution, but can only be espoused by conscience and free will. Modernists and progressives recognise no Islamic imperatives sanctifying a moralising state. They argue that statists advocate a modern ideological construct, a comprehensive Islamic state enforcing a religiously-defined good, which is not derived from a genuine tenet of the Islamic faith (Ibrahim, 2006: 11).

Moreover, intellectuals such as Bulaç, An-Na'im, Talbi and Abou El Fadl have all engaged with similar lines of argumentation in defending a minimalist state, similar to multiculturalists. Bulaç has argued that 'the state [should have] . . . much less intervention capacity – with minimum shared institutions and procedures – and is based on a thinner yet truly neutral normative ground' (Denli, 2006: 98). Abou El Fadl's advocacy of democracy seeks to deprive the state 'of any pretence of divinity by locating ultimate authority in the hands of the people' (2001: 36). In his conception of religious secularity, so Ghobadzadeh finds:

Under a secular democratic political structure believers are offered with a more conducive environment to cultivate their faith. By contrast, the authoritarian secular and Islamic states in the Muslim World have compromised religion. Due to these experiences with state power, religious secularity insists on the need to uncouple religion from the state to capture the true spirit of religiosity. (2013: 33)

Eickelman and Salvatore argue that the state's enforcement of morality is problematic for normative and sociological reasons (2003: 107). Modern Muslim societies are more morally diverse, complex and heterogeneous than often assumed. Not only does there exist a fundamental 'gap between secular and religious catalogues of virtues', but also competing religious orientations differ from dominant understandings of Islam (Mangini, 2016: 257). Thus, the assumption of a collective basis for a thick moral consensus in a political order appears unrealistic in Muslim societies, similar to in other modern societies. It is unlikely that any political regime, not just Muslim democracy, will finally resolve the moral questions of the entire citizenry. No political system can respond to every conception of the human good present in a single context. Nevertheless, democracy, among all of its alternatives, offers the best possibility of maintaining open channels for discussing these differences in policy-making. It can uphold mechanisms to safeguard citizens' right as equals. Influential groups in society would be prevented from imposing their own conception of the good by virtue of their class, status groups, wealth and control of the media.

In order to ensure impartiality regarding all philosophical and moral positions and leave the choice of right and wrong to individuals, a minimalist state does not take a moral stance on public matters. I treat the state as the sphere of political consensus, eschewing a philosophical theory of the state, defined by the 'priority for moral minimalism' and a thin idea of the common good (Bader, 1999: 602). In a Muslim democracy framework, the morally minimalist state, based on pluralist secularism, does not possess religious authority. It neither endorses an absolute account of universal goods or universal rationality nor 'impose[s] moralistic controls on family, sexuality and personal conduct' (Zubaida, 2011). Instead, the state is 'sensitive to the different expectations and needs of individuals and communities' (Zubaida, 2008: 6).

In the proposed theory of Muslim democracy, the objective of overcoming normative differences in politics is qualified by the establishment of a political space that respects difference (Stuvland, 2012: 713). The key feature in this political theory is a secular state with a minimalist normative content that is able to 'safeguard pluralism and difference by creating a political culture where all groups and competing entities are treated equally' (An-Naʻim, 2002b: 8). Impartiality towards all comprehensive views, in the context of a secularism with morally minimalist character, ensures pluralism, with sufficient space for participation, by preventing the rule of one group and the imposition of its values on others (An-Naʻim, 2005: 63). Muslims and peoples with other religious and non-religious beliefs, in a liberal democracy with a secular political structure, can develop their ethical selves with access to reason, agency and individual freedoms (An-Naʻim, 2008: 3).

The morally minimalist state is grounded on a thin, non-transcendental morality bereft of substantive moral foundations. Even a morally minimalist state enterprise is, however, unlikely to be value-free for the purposes of functionality. Certain coercive instruments are needed to guarantee democratic benchmarks, grounded in as thin a morality as possible, to maintain effective levels of neutrality. States derive their authority from different sources such as rule of law, social contract, common good and morality. In a Nozickean minimal state, power and legitimacy are derived from a morality centred on the political ideas of individual rights and liberties (Nozick, 2001: 29).

There is an undeniably strong connection between democracy and a conception of human rights. The conception of the state and its minimally shared normative background in this book draws on the discourse of human rights. I argue that human rights are the best 'idealizations' we can with work in democratic politics, because they are human-centred and curb the power of governments, religious institutions and corporate economic powers. Therefore, human rights are the essential basis for ensuring the freedoms of people in a democratic state.

I propose that treating human rights as a non-negotiable component of a political system is not incompatible with the idea of moral minimalism. Pluralist secularism's position of 'the basic human rights of the common moral minimalism' is not based on a comprehensive political justification of norms (Riley, 2012: 110). Human rights emerge from a rational and political consensus rather than philosophical and metaphysical reasoning. A deontological theory of morality is present in this account of human rights, which relies principally on political participation and deliberation. Deontologists argue that 'we can discover certain moral rules by reasoning or intuiting which constitute the overriding duties that are correlative with human rights' (Campbell, 2012: 180). This is a major difference between pluralist secularism and orthodox secularism, which is based on duty-based ethics that neglects the unjust consequences of acts considered to be ethical. Unlike orthodox secularism's account of a comprehensive ideological doctrine and dominant deontological bias, pluralist secularism, with its morally minimalist character, can welcome a plurality of moral and political claims in the public sphere.

There is a difficulty in the idea of minimal morality, in however minimalist and neutral a way it is conceptualised, in a secular political framework. A deontological understanding of morality eases this difficulty. Despite the ambiguities in moral minimalism, a scheme of basic human rights within this conception appears to be the most feasible path towards a pluralist democracy. In this model, there is no one dominant comprehensive ideology. Various ideological and normative systems, at the hands of individuals or as members of communities in an interactive plural framework, enjoy a level of public freedom.

Finally, moral minimalism requires the central political authority to define minimal democratic and legal standards, to both maintain moral and political equality among citizens and safeguard impartial access to public life. These democratic standards include 'right to life, liberty, bodily integrity, protection against violence, rights to basic subsistence, basic education, basic health-care; minimal due process rights; minimal respect; collective and individual toleration [the right to privacy and freedom of conscience]' (Shachar, 2000: 53). Moreover, these standards are to be awarded to people 'regardless of nationality, sex, national or ethnic origin, race, religion, language, or other status' (DePoy and Gilson, 2010: 206). The issue of normative thinness premised on a minimalist understanding of human rights will be further revisited in Chapter 6. Now, the chapter will examine the second feature of pluralist secularism with a view to contributing to a resolution of the relationship between religion and politics within predominantly Muslim polities.

2. Religion as an Element of Politics, Not of the State

Compatibility-based and unsecular democracy arguments threaten to bring public life in line with a majoritarian democracy that appears to contradict the notion of a morally minimalist state. I propose a morally thin state, to address the shortcomings these arguments engender, which has a pluralist and inclusive approach to moral sources of social norms rather than imposing the morality of the majority. Meanwhile, I articulate that religion cannot be privatised, in order to tackle the flaws of philosophical laicist positions, through dissociating it from the collective dimension in politics. Pluralist secularism finds that the strict separation of public and private, excluding religion from the public sphere, is neither feasible nor democratic. Accordingly, the second main feature of pluralist secularism consists of the recognition of the public character of religion.

The question of whether religion can become part of the public sphere, that allows and facilitates moral debate among different perspectives, has produced diverse responses. In the public sphere, Rawls expected that rational citizens, defined as people who are not directed in their thinking by traditional or religious impulses, would deliberate issues and exchange ideas in the process of reaching an overlapping consensus. The Rawlsian model upholds a robust rigid separation between the private and public spheres, where political debate is restricted to the public domain and religious arguments are to be confined to the realm of the private (Shachar, 1998b: 85).

On the other hand, multiculturalist political theorists like Kymlicka have shown that human relations in actual situations do not follow a clear division or rigid boundaries between the private and public spheres. Kymlicka demonstrates the interdependence of public and private through the ability of cultures to simultaneously penetrate the private and public spheres. His liberal reading of autonomy, 'the view that we have a fundamental interest in our moral power of forming and revising a plan of life', not only revolves around individualism but also encompasses collective organisations (Kymlicka, 1992: 140). Thus, he maintains that making cultural associations and infrastructures publicly available for individuals is necessary for the attainment of individual autonomy, which a strict neutrality fails to recognise (Kymlicka, 1989: 197).

Shachar has developed Kymlicka's liberal multiculturalism by including religion. The restriction of religion to the private sphere serves to exclude religion-based arguments and collective demands from the political realm and does a disservice to the needs of religious people and communities (Shachar, 1998: 81). Gad Barzilai also brings religion into political theory by highlighting the importance in the daily life of religious believers (2008: 302). He has defended the necessity of integrating religious ways of life into the public sphere through 'cultural and institutional tolerance' (Barzilai, 2004: 6). Bader has also criticised liberal and republican theories for assuming that neutrality, unification and stability can be achieved by removing the allegedly divisive force of religion from politics. However, a 'strict' or 'formal' secular neutrality displays structural biases against people who do not accede to the dominant ideology and discriminates against religious lifestyles (Bader, 2007a: 49).[2]

Similar to the multiculturalist critique of philosophical secularism, Muslim political theorists, such as al-Ghannushi, Abou El Fadl and An-Na'im, argue that the public–private distinction, that assumes religion is irrelevant to law and politics, does not work in Muslim contexts. Islamic modernists like Mohammad Fadel redefine secularism to accommodate religion and grant greater space for it contribute to public issues. For the majority of Muslims, Fadel asserts, the secular neutrality of the state or the secularity of state institutions do not constitute a legitimacy problem as long as the state recognises 'a Muslim's right to live according to an Islamic vision of the good life' (2007: 4). Competing comprehensive theories of the good, including those of committed Muslims, can be retained yet kept separate from clearly demarcated 'political institutions' (Fadel, 2008: 8). The endorsement of religion being 'politically relevant' leads Fadel to state:

> What this [normative independence] implies, then is that in lieu of a separationist paradigm, the law should adopt a paradigm of principled reconciliation in which legal values and religious values are in a state of continual dialogue with the potential that each may inform and shape the other. Only through this process of constant dialogue can there emerge legal principles that all 'reasonable doctrines' can accept for the 'right reason'. (2013b: 1260)

Common criticisms, from both multiculturalist and Muslim political thought, of philosophical secularism are utilised by pluralist secularism. An account of political secularity, at the level of the state, is articulated to accommodate Islamic conceptions of a good life. Pluralist secularism's idea of neutrality and impartiality implies emancipating the state from religion and equally 'emancipating religion' from the state for religion's own sake (Stepan, 2000: 35, Ghobadzadeh, 2014: 8). While the mutual emancipation between religion and the state is pursued, politics and religion do not function in distinct spheres, as one 'continually informs and affects the other' (An-Na'im 2005: 71).

Bader and An-Na'im, among other thinkers, have repeatedly underlined that religion and morality are relevant within the sphere of politics, but not to state power (Bader, 2001: 10). An-Na'im advances the idea that the state under liberal secularism is 'as neutral as humanly possible' (2008: 5). However, 'the connectedness of Islam and politics' still remains intact (An-Na'im, 2008: 4). An-Na'im's acceptance of the interdependence between religion and secularism seeks to promote Islam's existence in the public life of the community of believers and politics (2002b: 8). In a Muslim democracy framework, the replacement of comprehensive philosophical doctrines, whether laicism or Islamism, with the 'priority for moral minimalism' allows neutrality in the state realm while accommodating thick moralities within the public sphere (Bader, 2009b: 1).

Religion as a source of 'thick moralities' for Aaron Stuvland can still be 'a part of normatively "thin politics"' in which religious arguments, based on moral guidance from a religious tradition, enter public deliberation (2012: 711). Through pluralist secularism, I argue that religion, as a personal or a communal issue, can play a social and political role in democracies. In other words, religion becomes part of public debate and organisation by virtue of the individual followers who are members of religious communities. As such, the religious experiences of human agents as political articulations, as well as reasons rooted in religious concerns, are constituent components of politics. Religious authorities, on the other hand, are precluded from determining how group members participate in public life and contribute to the decision-making process of politics.[3] Moreover, I join Stuvland in making the argument that thick moralities 'must communicate a thin normativity for the continued, internal coherence of liberal democratic politics' (2012: 711). This idea will be further developed in the next section on the public sphere under the theme of democratic toleration.

When the state's secularist ideology was normatively thick in restricting public functions for religion, echoing An-Na'im's point, Islam re-emerged, in the form of a political ideology, as a defensive and reactive political struggle 'on the periphery' (Yavuz, 2007: 484). A lack of channels for effective political participation or restricted public services for Islamic visions of a good life drove 'Islamists underground', stiffening their political ideology, or 'helping to radicalize them', all of which could have been substantially lessened with more pluralistic applications of secularism (Kurzman and Naqvi, 2010: 35). For this reason, pluralist secularism with a thin normativity of the state allows the mutual flourishing of competing thicknesses, where religion is an important marker of social identity (Gregg, 2003: 6).

Public accommodation of religion does not necessarily mean de-secularisation. Pluralist secularism embarks on a simultaneous process of secularising the state and democratising the public sphere. In a Muslim democracy framework, the moral minimalism of the state implies that no religious doctrine or organisation, be it a majority or minority, has constitutional or institutional privilege. Impartiality in pluralist secularism is exhibited towards all philosophical and religious positions. Moral choices are left to the individual, as the state's relation to all religions is informed by a non-denominational and neutral ethos. For instance, pluralist secularism would eliminate the establishment of majority religions that exists even in Western democracies in the form of state subsidy of faith schools of majority religions, 'religious ceremonies at the state level' and 'exemptions granted to certain religious groups' (Bekaroglu, 2016). In addition, the separation of religious marriages from civil unions would no longer allow the state to 'define the parameters of marriage or to specify mandatory rules other than those necessary to preserve the minimum values of a liberal state' (Crane, 2005: 1250).

To summarise this subsection, state institutions, which form the shared basis of living in a Muslim democracy framework, are not legitimised with reference to a comprehensive moral doctrine. This does not mean that secular state institutions would prevent or oppose the demands made by Muslims to organise their lives according to their religious beliefs and practices. Rather, pluralist secularism guarantees the public role of religion while safeguarding the autonomy and liberty of individuals to pursue their preferred moral lifestyle for the religious or non-religious alike. The following subsection will discuss the role of religion in political life against the background of the separation of the state and politics in a Muslim democracy framework.

3. The Differentiation between the State Public Sphere and the Social Public Sphere

A constructivist turn in the study of states reveals they 'are not the sort of abstract, formal objects which readily lend themselves to clear-cut, unambiguous definition' (Jessop, 1990: 340). Ido Shahar has argued that 'the boundaries between the state and the society are blurred, constantly reshaped by actors, and by no means well-defined' (2008: 420). For legal pluralist theorists like Shahar, state–society relations are socially constructed, processual and open to change. This subsection does not aim to examine the entirety of contested debates on the state. It more narrowly aims to construct a more inclusive idea of secularism by highlighting certain facets of these debates. This 'valuable new [constructivist] direction for theorizing the state and state–society relations' can generate, beyond universalist secularism, new understandings of state–civil society relations (Shahar, 2008: 432).

In political theory, the study of the boundaries between the state and the public sphere, often neglected, is important. The general debate on the 'public' has ambiguous implications for the relationship between state and civil society. For instance, on the one hand, the public sphere could directly refer to the domain of government (e.g. 'public schools' refers to a government school in the North American context), and on the other, it could refer to non-governmental institutions (e.g. British 'public schools' are 'privately' run). The next section, on the public sphere, will attempt to address its ambiguities within the context of Muslim democracy. I differentiate two components in the public sphere, the state public sphere and the social public sphere, as the third constitutive foundation of pluralist secularism. The idea of a social public sphere, to be further theorised in the next chapter on the public sphere, is introduced here under the discussion on secularism. Differentiation of the categories of the state public sphere and the social public sphere is an important interpretative tool in the conceptualisation of pluralist secularism in this chapter.

In republican and liberal models, the state and the public sphere are integrated and are treated as belonging to the realm of the political. In these models, decoupling the state and the public sphere from religion is presumed to maintain political neutrality (Habermas, 1989: 3). Identities, goods, demands and needs deriving from religious sources are often overlooked as components of politics (Barzilai, 2004: 13). The form of secularism which sets clear boundaries between the spheres of 'public/private, official/unofficial, secular/religious, positive law/traditional practice' is not broad enough to respond to the multiple affiliations of modern citizens (Shachar, 2008: 578). Secular Muslim democracy theorists have offered multiple institutional alternatives, derived from political secularism, to better reflect the complex relationship between comprehensive moral doctrines and liberal democracies.

An alternative interpretative approach to differentiated public spheres is offered by pluralist secularism for Muslim-majority contexts. Functionally differentiated public spheres can arise, where individuals as part of active and free civil society are able to, as Amyn B. Sajoo puts it, 'freely associate with others outside the control of the state' (2002: 215). Democracy does not only need the institutional separation of the state from the religious and other comprehensive moral views, but also 'requires the institutional division between a certain form of state and civil society' (Keane, 1993: 28). Sajoo also emphasises 'the need to separate the institutions of the state, religion and society, as a shared modern democratic and ethical imperative' (2004: 226). On this matter, An-Na'im advocates the necessity for 'the distinction between the state and politics' (2000: 3). He argues that 'the organs and institutions of the state' and the 'dynamic process of making choices' for 'organized political and social actors' holding 'competing visions of the public good' are to be differentiated from one another (An-Na'im, 2000: 5). In addition, for An-Na'im, even in morally minimalist states, 'complete independence is not possible because of the political nature of the state' (2000: 3). Thus, 'a degree of separation of the state from politics' is necessary for the state to show equal respect and neutral treatment to all groups. This degree of division becomes vital in guaranteeing the state's impartiality to 'mediate and adjudicate among the competing visions and policy proposals' (An-Na'im, 2000: 3). An-Na'im strongly believes that the failure to observe this distinction 'tends to severely undermine the peace, stability and healthy development of the whole society' (2000: 4).

The distinction, within politics, between the government and the public sphere is essential in Muslim politics, where social and political claims are frequently made about Islam. Individual Muslims often perceive the realisation of these claims to be mandatory in their pursuit of their definitions of a good life. Popular convictions about the inseparability of religion and politics motivate arguments for an ideological Islamic state as opposed to a secular political order. I will now respond to the objections engendered by anti-democratic thinking. The following discussion identifies an assertive civil society, distinct from the morally minimalist state, for creating and maintaining spaces for Muslim ways of life in public.

Neutrality within the state realm, by separating religion and state power, is a core secular pluralist principle. At the same time, pluralist secularism recognises civil society's rights of religious practice. Political processes should be in place to satisfy substantive moral needs, demands and interests. The formulation of the idea of the morally minimalist state in this book endorses the position that people with different accounts of the good require different public services. In order to provide these services, outside of the classical functions of the state, greater scope to form public institutions should be left to civil society forces. Pluralist secularism differentiates between the state public sphere and a civil society public sphere to achieve this objective, with the latter reframed in this book as the social public sphere.

The social public sphere is 'an extensive interpretation of associational freedoms' wherein '[m]any of the positive effects that states can bring about can also be obtained . . . through voluntary mechanisms' (Bader, 2007a: 53; Vallentyne and van der Vossen, 2014). It offers an alternative view of civil society organisations, as 'governing powers', that can regulate, organise and administer religious as well as collective affairs, as categorically separate from the public power of the state (Hirst, 1994: 13). A 'democratically negotiated freedom of religion from state interference' would 'allow religious groups freedom not only to worship privately but to organize groups in civil society and political society' (Stepan, 2000: 42). This amounts to a democratic decentralisation of state power, allocating a degree of decision-making to organised religions and identity groups, through administrative and political autonomy of voluntary minority associations (Bader, 2003b: 132). Dynamic and multi-layered understandings of the relationship between state, civil society and public sphere enable the social public sphere to provide resources and opportunities for formalisation of the public functions of civil society (Hirst and Bader, 2001: 6–7).

Here, the public 'focus of [religions] is no longer the state but, rather, civil society' (Casanova, 1994: 63). In this understanding, Islam has 'an autonomous life in the hands of social actors' and not in the hands of hierarchical and formal religious authorities (Yavuz, 2007: 489). In this way, 'public policy can benefit from the moral guidance of religion, and pluralistic societies can enjoy peace and stability by regulating the relationship between religion and the state through secularism' (An-Na'im, 2002b: 8). The arguments examined so far may raise concerns about the issue of the creation of a collective morality imposed by organised groups on their individual members. They will be addressed in the discussions on the social public sphere in Chapter 5 as well as those on the pluralist constitutional provisions in Chapter 6. I will demonstrate the democratic coexistence between voluntary associational freedoms and inalienable human rights.

Moral diversity and pluralism appear to be key components of the social public sphere that are crucial for theorising Muslim democracy. Comprehensive moralities are treated as legitimate forces, allowing public space for the diversity of lifestyles, whether professed by majority or minority groups, to be practised out of volition. In addition, the separation of religion and governance can maintain the state public sphere as morally minimalist and impartial towards all citizens. Therefore, the social public sphere provides a pluralistic space, beyond the state practices and moral discourses, for the accommodation of dominant and non-dominant outlooks and their legitimate public rights. The topic of collective rights for civil society organisations will now be discussed in the theoretical elaboration of pluralist secularism. I will attempt to illustrate an account that avoids the tendencies of compatibility-based arguments to undermine the importance of impartial state institutions, and of laicism to reject the importance of public religious claims.

4. Collective Rights

The discussion on the social public sphere examines the fourth characteristic of pluralist secularism: the acceptance of collective rights. Collective rights will be further developed as part of the examination of institutional pluralism and jurisdictional pluralism in the following chapters. The principles of pluralist secularism may take different practical forms, in pursuit of the recognition of cultural and religious differences, with different arrangements of collective rights in particular contexts. This section will not expound a specific and detailed blueprint, but will instead formulate a notion of collective rights within the political theory of Muslim democracy.

Orthodox liberalism has created an individualist liberal set of rights ruling out the community as 'a locus of normativity' (Provost and Sheppard, 2013: 2). Thinkers such as Kymlicka, Kukathas, Mookherjee and Taylor have maintained that the classical liberal ideal of personal autonomy, individual freedom of association and toleration are rooted within a collective good and cultural membership. Freedom for individuals is conditional on the accessibility and maintenance of in-groups. Rights discourse, within orthodox liberalism, demonstrates an inability to understand the significance of the normative order shaped by culture and religion in the everyday life of individuals and is thus unable to respond to political demands couched in their terms (Barzilai, 2004: 24). Multiculturalists find an individualist set of rights to be sufficient for bringing justice 'neither in matters . . . of "race" and "ethnicity" nor in matters of religion' to citizens with diverse accounts of norms, goods and needs (Bader, 2001: 12).

In order to ensure the moral autonomy of individuals as well as to protect their capacity to act, pluralist secularism is 'sensitive to the different expectations and needs of individuals and communities' (Barzilai, 2008: 6). Rather than ignoring existing complex social realities and moral disagreements, the pluralist secularist rights discourse seeks to accommodate them. Followers of organised religions, including Islam, raise public demands for education, health or social services, generated by their collective nature, that are beyond the reach of accommodation by the modern state and its difference-blind institutions (Shachar, 2009: 133). This project of pluralist secularism draws on liberal notions. Freedom of conscience, democratic representation and holistic autonomy, as well as the call for control of minority cultures and religious lifestyles to be eased from both the domination of the state and the wider society, inform the need for some form of collective rights (Bader, 2001: 10).[4]

Specific demands made within Muslim societies, going beyond both the Rawlsian liberal paradigm and compatibility-based arguments, are to be accommodated by the pluralist secularist feature of collective rights. Pluralist secularism endorses the multiculturalist principle that rights and freedoms can only be realised both individually and collectively. Ostensibly opposing dichotomies of citizenship and group membership, public and private justice, and individual and collective rights are realigned in a working synthesis (Shachar, 2008: 575). Religious, cultural and ethnic communities in the Muslim democracy framework can receive collective rights in the political and jurisdictional realm, such as in private law, education and health, as long as their internal organisations are compatible with freedom of conscience and do not violate moral equality among individuals. While collective rights would be generated through public consultation and deliberation, citizens' equal moral worth, dignity, and capacities to follow their conceptions of a good life are under the constitutional protections (Shachar, 2000: 67). Collective rights to groups and 'the minimalist but sturdy standards of basic rights, the moral constraints of toleration and accommodation' simultaneously exist in the Muslim democracy framework (Bader, 2007a: 291).

Conflation of collective rights with minority rights often occurs in the multiculturalist literature. In this theory of Muslim democracy, collective rights are awarded to religious groups, even if they may be part of the majority population. Collective rights can prevent the state or other established sources of authority from disproportionally dictating public policy in society. Allocation of collective rights to groups, in order to meet Islamic comprehensive claims, is not only a requirement of a pluralist democracy, but is also necessary to maintain the existence of a democratic system. As I have argued in Chapter 3, section 3, should these societal demands and needs not receive public acceptance, religious actors may strive to capture the state apparatus driven by the assumption that it is the only way to realise their moral worldviews. In other words, collective rights are indispensable for an inclusive and pluralistic democratic theorisation to stave off radicalisation of religious actors.

An institutional separation between religion, symbolised by religious authorities, and the state apparatus is needed for democracy. In societies where religion is a strong political force, prevention of domination by any religious denomination is necessary. In responding to these two issues, pluralist secularism, conceptualised here in this chapter, aims to mediate the relationship between Islam and democracy by reconciling, through political theory, the potentially conflicting concepts of secular statehood and public religious presence. Religious-based collective demands require a response, at the level of the state, while safeguarding the institutional separation of religion, moral diversity and civil liberties. In essence, pluralist secularism aims to ensure the separation of religion and governance. Minority groups and majority Islamic religious groups are given collective rights in this framework. Comprehensive philosophical claims are removed from the state realm. The combination of collective rights and institutional and jurisdictional pluralism is essential for more inclusive religious and associational freedoms in a pluralist democracy and for preventing a top-down Islamisation of the state.

V. Conclusion: Pluralist Secularism

This chapter has critiqued republican secularism for its failure to offer a viable foundation for pluralistic forms of democracy. It has suggested an alternative form of secularism, pluralist secularism, to more effectively accommodate religion. A morally minimalist state is a primary feature of this conception of pluralist secularism. Devolution of moral and spiritual authorities from the state to the institutions and practices of the social public sphere is advocated. The state is not endowed with moralising, paternalistic powers and capacities. Political compromises, not invested in ideology or religiosity, in the realm of the state are a commonplace practice. Pluralist secularism does not impose a substantial ideological stance or comprehensive normative position, but respects, accommodates and guarantees differences between different accounts of a good life.

Republican secularism demands that religion be privatised and banned from public space. Pluralist secularism, by contrast, recognises the normative and practical importance of individual as well as collective religious needs as a legitimate source for political rights. Various measures of public accommodation are elaborated for collective religious practice, a prerequisite for peaceful coexistence, which are not antithetical to state neutrality. A revised secularism within the context of Muslim democracy serves as the impartial mediator and adjudicator among competing political, cultural and religious actors. The collective rights of these actors to a defined realm of authority allow the public expression of their comprehensive views. The state enterprise has also a normative component, on the basis of universal human rights standards, in order to safeguard democratic governance.

A change is required by pluralism secularism in the character of the unitary nation-state. Legislative, executive and judicial structures should change from existing monistic structural power relations towards pluralist ones. The differentiation between politics and the state enables greater consideration of the various ways in which secularism and inclusive religious freedoms can go hand in hand. Muslim democracy, by moving the locus of religion from the state to civil society actors, provides sufficient spaces to protect the liberty of conscience and autonomy, the right to difference and dissent, toleration, freedom of association and moral diversity. This pronounced emphasis on pluralism in this book's political theory of democracy differentiates it from compatibility-based arguments. The discussion on the devolution of power is not only conducive to the institutionalisation of pluralism, but also prevents the rise of a religious state legitimised through Islam. A delicate balance between universal human rights and public religious demands is offered by pluralism secularism under the Muslim democracy framework. The next chapter continues the elaboration of the Muslim democracy framework with reference to the social public sphere.

Notes

1. The minimally moral state is part of a broad literature on the 'minimal state' as discussed by classical liberal and libertarian thinkers. In both these schools of thought, a state is given a 'restricted mandate' to protect individual rights of life, liberty and property, and a contract to uphold its main goal of letting individuals flourish (Scalet and Schmidtz, 2002: 27).
2. Multiculturalist arguments are more relevant than ever if we interpret the modern public sphere as more sophisticated, with electronic technologies transforming the nature of the 'public', 'blur[ring] the dividing line between private and public behaviours' (Meyrowitz, 1986: 93).
3. It is essential to recognise that religious authority has been transformed from traditional and localised forms to more deterritorialised expressions due to globalising forces. Religious orthodoxy or religious norms can neither be genuinely controlled nor democratically represented by an authority 'at a time of global communication and expedited circulation of ideas' (Cesari, 2014: 115).

4. Although multiculturalism's main focus had initially been on culture and ethnicity, it later expanded to include religion. Today, the idea of multicultural recognition further includes other minority people such as 'women, LGBT people, and people with disabilities' (Song, 2014). Accordingly, the concept of collective minority rights is advocated for different kinds of minorities within different models. Due to its main focus, this project has focused in particular on those relating to religion. However, the Muslim democracy framework recognises that all identity groups and minorities, regardless of religion, ethnicity or culture, should qualify for collective rights under democratic systems. This issue will be further addressed in the coming chapter on constitutional provisions.

5

THE SOCIAL PUBLIC SPHERE

I. Introduction

A central postulate in democratic thinking is that 'the development of a public sphere and a civil society constitutes a critical condition for the formation and continuity of constitutional and democratic regimes' (Eisenstadt, 2002: 140). Democracy presupposes a critical political space, which 'constantly generates alternatives' to state power and contests the monopoly of the state in deciding the shared good (Stephen, 2000: 39). As such, the development of a public sphere independent from the state is necessary to sustain democracy (Eickelman and Salvatore, 2003: 99; Habermas, 1964: 52–3).

Rethinking the public sphere is a central component in the theorising of Muslim democracy. Multiculturalist and Muslim political thinkers have agreed that the existing republican and liberal theories of the public sphere are not normatively sufficient for Muslim-majority contexts. To transplant theories on the public sphere that have emerged and developed within Western contexts, without critical appropriation, to Muslim societies where 'the boundary between public and private is often more blurred than in Western societies and rarely fixed' is highly problematic (Eickelman, 2002: 7). Taylor, Bader and An-Na'im have provided the impetus for the development of alternative conceptions of the public sphere in favour of new divisions for state authority and political–institutional organisation.

Two prominent models of the public sphere emerge from the examination of Muslim and multiculturalist political thought: (i) shared public institutions, where the state institutions are reformed so as to be sufficiently pluralistic, dynamic and accommodating of difference, and (ii) plural public institutions, where degrees of institutional and/or jurisdictional pluralism are formalised. The debate over autonomous public institutions or common yet context-sensitive state institutions has dominated both Muslim and multiculturalist arguments. In this section, I examine the proposal for a shared public sphere, developed by Mookherjee, Taylor and Tully, that includes majority and minority cultural and ethical reasons. The public vision of the common good is based on a reconciliation of diverse ethical and communal values, which leads to shared and inclusive state institutions. On the other hand, I also examine the arguments for plural public institutions, according to Bader, Barzilai, Bulaç and Shachar. When the public sphere is dominated by the moral doctrine of the majority, pluralism can be best facilitated through giving autonomy to groups with different normative systems.

This chapter will re-evaluate the public sphere within the framework of Muslim democracy benefiting from these existing models. To do so, these two conceptions of the public sphere will be briefly presented in order to highlight their strengths and weaknesses. In this account, I formulate a new concept of the 'social public sphere', already discussed in Chapter 4, section 3, but which will be discussed in more detail here. This chapter will develop a conceptualisation of a social public sphere, as distinct from a state public sphere. The social public sphere aims to recognise a greater role for the communal character of religion than liberal models. It also aims to uphold individual rights and safeguard the prospect of political and ideological freedoms and dissent as successfully as liberal models. The final section will develop four further concepts under the category of a social public sphere – transformativeness, social Islam, democratic tolerance and institutional pluralism – through which the norms and values of Muslim democracy can be fulfilled by the public sphere.

II. Shared Public Sphere and State Institutions Framework

The argument for a shared public sphere and state institutions aims to propose a normatively inclusive public sphere. State institutions result from public deliberation and consensus, and are sufficient for the accommodation of cultural and religious diversity. Unlike institutional pluralism, the shared public sphere framework relies on the pluralistic and accommodating values of state institutions guiding public life. Tully and Mookherjee, categorised as the moral pluralists in the chapter on multiculturalism, are discussed here as key exponents of the shared public sphere model. They propose two fundamental conceptions to illustrate the distinct features of the shared public sphere notion: overlapping consensus and political stability.

A deliberative consensus is proposed for citizens to have the ability to engage and broadly agree on the common good (Mookherjee, 2005: 42). A consensus is achieved through the political process, where there is public dialogue among equal participants with diverse comprehensive philosophies. No authority, legal, religious or governmental, has a monopoly on the construction of a shared normative culture. The process of arriving at the common good should be all-inclusive, for the liberal paradigm should ensure the '"accessibility" of cultural and religious reasons to develop a necessary "overlapping consensus" in a democratic society' (Sachedina, 2009: 177).

The absence of cultural and religious recognition, for the advocates of the shared public sphere, undermines individual and collective autonomy, and leads to unfair treatment and unequal representation. They envisage state institutions as a product of plural reasoning in an ongoing project driven by democratic communication, inter-cultural dialogue and a common language of citizens. Mookherjee (2001) suggests 'the common language of reasonableness' is required for the construction and functioning of such a public sphere. Public reason is plural, 'provisional' and 'incomplete' in a constant process of making by people through the co-operation of plural moral and philosophical views (Mookherjee 2001: 69; 2005: 40).

Mookherjee argues that '*plural* public reasoning' is 'a more capacious, more generous account of "public reason"' that allows minorities to argue in their 'traditional languages' in public deliberation (2001: 92). A public sphere should be a shared political space that harbours a diverse range of moral and political perspectives, where no perspective is persecuted or criminalised. Whose ideas should exert more influence on the state institutions is decided through the active and critical participation of civil society forces 'both within and outside the essentially unstable and contested boundaries of the political sphere' (Mookherjee, 2001: 92, 93). A shared public sphere is based on democratic politics and democratic deliberation in which everything, except basic human rights, is decided through their processes (Tully, 2008a: 160).

The second crucial aspect of a shared public sphere is the existence of essential common institutions as a stable basis for social unity and democratic regime. Common institutions, characterised by a civic spirit and democratic ethos, can prevent excessive social and economic inequalities and ensure minimal standards for everyone. A shared public sphere problematises the alternative model of institutional pluralism on the grounds that it may lead to the unintended outcome of divided public spheres. This model risks intensifying the differentiation of religious identities, jeopardising social unity and cohesion, and damaging a conception of a common good. In addition, Mookherjee highlights the transformative power of the shared public sphere. Dialogue and participation within the political sphere orients liberal state structures towards more inclusive ends and leads to the democratisation of the groups with an anti-pluralistic ethos (Mookherjee, 2005: 44).

The argument for a shared public sphere contends that pluralist yet common state institutions for citizens are both democratically desirable and practically viable to accommodate collective demands of organised religions and cultures. However, not all multiculturalists believe that it is the most effective and resourceful means of accommodation. The advocates of plural public institutions question the ability of a shared public sphere to incorporate citizens' diverse cultural needs and choices in an inclusive form. Unequal power relations and structural exclusion of normative difference may persist in the politics of the everyday. These limits of the shared framework are further explicated in the next section on a plural public institution in terms of the relationship between religion and public life.

III. Plural Public Institution Framework

In Western contexts, the argument for plural public institutions questions the rigid differentiation of the private and public spheres that excludes comprehensive views from the latter. Liberalism and republicanism are perceived to be unable to account for the essential role of comprehensive doctrines in providing moral motivation for action, shaping collective lives and inspiring consensus (Barzilai, 2004: 24). Among secular states in the Muslim world, religion is split from its societal foundations and the public sphere is left to secular powers alone (Bulaç, 1994: 5; 2012f).

Critics of republican secularism such as Bader and Shachar highlight the existence of a shared state ideology that unduly dominates the public sphere. Only a narrow scope exists for republican secularism to accommodate other comprehensive views. Discrimination against organised religions and minority belief systems will be an inevitable occurrence. Recent exponents of a plural public sphere also emphasise that people with diverse normative systems are unlikely to agree on common terms of living in every aspect as envisaged by a thick state morality, even if it is of a liberal nature (Bader, 2003b: 134; Shachar, 2009: 133). On the other hand, comprehensive views have their own conception of values, with significant implications for how social life and legal institutions ought to be structured. Communities with distinct views of the good can legitimately contribute to the public sphere with certain political and institutional mandates.

I examined in a previous chapter how Muslim thinkers such as Bulaç use the historical case of Prophetic Madina to formulate a political model. Although its political authority possessed an Islamic nature in this model, Islamic personal law was only enforced on Muslims in their own public framework while non-Muslims were allowed to have their own public structures in educational, legal, religious and economic affairs. The Madina Charter promoted a conception of a polity that went 'beyond an apparatus controlling every aspect of life' (Bulaç, 1998: 178). For Bulaç, devolving certain executive and judicial powers to civil society can enable individuals and groups 'to define their own identities' and choose their institutional services and legal systems (2006: 190). This account of pluralism, couched in Islamic terms, does not imply acknowledging the equal value of other moral views in debates about the common good. It instead grants institutional autonomy to groups with different moral conceptions.

In a plural public sphere framework, the state and its institutions are often dominated by a doctrine, whether it is Islam in Bulaç's thought or liberalism in Shachar's. Liberal sceptics such as Bader and Barzilai also defend the plural public sphere model. Religious groups should be delegated power instead of the state alone unilaterally and impartially allocating what it assumes to be the right place for public religious demands (Bader, 2001: 2; Barzilai, 2008: 399). In a plural public sphere, the state discharges the key functions of judiciary as well as infrastructure and defence and culturally and religiously defined communities are granted public autonomy 'in religious life, juridical system, education, trade, culture, art, science and in daily affairs' (Bulaç, 1993: 41). In-group dealings are recognised according to their respective cultural and jurisdictional norms on the basis of some generally agreed-on regulatory arrangements by the state and social actors (Bulaç, 1992: 109).

Multiculturalist thinkers propose different models to institutionalise the plural public sphere framework for the accommodation of religious and cultural diversity. The viewpoints of Shachar and Bader are concerned with accommodating diversity in stable and well-functioning democratic systems. Institutional pluralist thought is anchored in 'the idea of permitting a degree of regulated interaction between religious and secular sources of law, so long as the baseline of citizenship guaranteed rights remains firmly in place' (Shachar, 2009: 133). Shachar's (2001) 'joint governance' and Bader's (2003) 'non-constitutional pluralism' emphasise the connection between morality and law while leaving democratic safeguards intact. They differentiate between public law and semi-public/private jurisdiction and formalise the latter only in the form of civil dispute resolutions rather than permitting the existence of a parallel legal system (Shachar, 2008: 575).

These multiculturalists suggest that a degree of administrative or jurisprudential autonomy is to be given to religious groups. In addition, democratic structures with minimal but robust regulatory mechanisms are essential to ensure that the exercise of collective rights does not violate the human rights of group members. The state's role as the guarantor of the protection of fundamental constitutional rights and freedoms leads it to intervene in in-group organisations. The need for connections and co-operation between the state and public institutions, to provide not only comprehensive and effective religious freedoms but also to prevent any infringement of group members' basic human rights, was discussed in the chapter on multiculturalism. While multiculturalist models support plural public institutions for the inclusion of minority groups, they do not advocate multiple public spheres as do models such as the *millet* system (Bader, 2007a: 147).

Institutional pluralist models are based on plural public institutions and their regulatory mechanisms for established Western democracies. Thus, the conceptualising of institutional pluralism within the context of Muslim societies requires a different approach. Neither the framework of the shared public sphere nor that of the plural public institution is fully able to account for the public sphere in a Muslim democracy. The former lacks the autonomous mechanisms to accommodate diverse expressions of comprehensive normative views while the latter requires normative and political qualifications to allow it to effectively operate in Muslim contexts. The next section will explicate the relevant notions from the frameworks of the shared public sphere (intercultural dialogue, overlapping consensus and plural reasoning) and plural public institution (associative freedoms and institutional pluralism). A novel concept of the social public sphere will be developed to provide the grounds for a theory of Muslim democracy.

IV. The Conceptualisation of the Social Public Sphere in Muslim Societies

Plural and shared public sphere arguments single out the limitations of existing liberal and republican models. They make valuable contributions to innovative thinking about the public sphere in the theoretical context of Muslim democracy. The examination of these theories in this chapter points to the need for the reconsideration of the nature and usefulness of the public–private divide. Charles Taylor and Abdullahi Ahmed An-Na'im have brought attention to 'the illegitimacy of drawing sharp ontological distinctions between "the political" and "the social"' (Cook et al., 2016: 6).

More nuanced accounts of the public sphere, to overcome the public and private dichotomy, could address the complex nature of modern societies. To this end, differentiation is needed at a theoretical plane, within the concept of the public sphere, between civil society politics and the state, to arrive at the two concepts of the 'social public sphere' and 'state public sphere'. In the previous chapter, the state public sphere was theorised under the purview of pluralist secularism. This chapter now turns to the category of 'social public sphere'.

The social public sphere is a distinct form of the public sphere where the state, voluntary organisations and individuals interact in social life. The social public sphere is institutionally differentiated to host the public roles of different normative perspectives. Thus, it is capacious and resourceful enough to accommodate the public needs and interests of people with different conceptions of a good life, based on principles of tolerance, reconciliation and respect. In this model, the state shares political space with civil society and empowers it.

The chapter on pluralist secularism conceptualised some institutional features of a political theory of Muslim democracy. Further attention to alternative institutions is provided by the social public sphere. In addition, social level change is an area of examination. I argue that the social public sphere can resolve ideological Islamic–secularist polarisation by equally including both religious and secular forces in political processes. It seeks to overcome the complex dilemma experienced by Muslim societies where

> either religion strives to colonize and subjugate worldly politics, thereby erecting itself into a public power, or else politics colonizes religious faith by expanding itself into a totalizing, quasi-religious panacea or ideology. (Dallmayr, 2011: 439)

In order to develop the conception of a social public sphere in a Muslim democracy framework, I will now turn to a closer examination of four conceptions: transformativeness, social Islam, democratic toleration and institutional pluralism.

1. Transformativeness

Transformativeness is the first concept to be discussed in the formation of the social public sphere. It moves beyond a binary relationship between religion and democracy in the call for their dialogical interaction and moral convergence. The concept of transformativeness, derived from liberal democratic theory, is articulated by thinkers such as Kymlicka, Shachar and Mookherjee as well as by Abou El Fadl and An-Naʿim. Democratic societies should reduce and eventually overcome the conflict and animosities engendered by ethnic, religious, cultural or primordial identities, within both majority and minority groups. Nancy Rosenblum describes this normative imperative as the 'liberal expectancy' that life under democratic governance will induce citizens with illiberal identities to internalise democratic norms to reach an agreement on the common good and a civic ethos (1998: 51).

Liberal thinkers such as Kymlicka and Shachar rest their multiculturalism theories on this notion of liberal expectancy. Shachar's theory on transformative accommodation consists of changes to both public policies and group practices with undemocratic propensities. Mutual interaction, through 'on-going dialogue' and 'constant interaction' between social groups and the state, increases the pressure to negotiate democratic change and transformativeness (Shachar, 2008: 146–7). Transformativeness here does not imply an interest or functionalist convergence. It is instead concerned with conceptual synergy, interconnectedness and moral convergence in the awareness that 'the internal transformation of each paradigm or discourse . . . tends toward transformation in favor of the other two' (An-Naʿim, 2005: 56). Shachar refers to 'a renovating and re-invigorating of both secular and religious traditions' (2009: 139). Convergence does not need to occur through a repudiating or loss of either Muslim or democratic normativity. On the contrary, both of these normative systems are reconstituted to achieve pluralising and inclusive ends.

First, I will revisit the concept of transformativeness within secular thought. Secularist, sovereignist state models carry the risk of an apparent lack of moral pluralism. The imposition of civil liberties in liberalism, just like in an Islamic state, under a philosophical secularist structure can turn out to be 'equivalent to the restriction of liberty' (Riley, 2012: 105). Pluralist secularism and its account of a morally minimalist state are here critical to explore the mechanisms through which the institutionalisation of moral pluralism can occur. The non-philosophical idea of a secular state based on minimal human rights can provide a context for pluralism to exist in the public sphere and function as an overarching authority in its control. Human rights is the best mechanism to curb absolutist state power. It imposes a political ideal for the sharing of power and reinforces democratic credentials amid diversity.

I will resume the discussion on how human rights can be conceptualised within the context of the Muslim democracy in the final chapter, and instead focus here on the re-invigoration of Islamic religious tradition.

Islam, conventionally understood and practised by Muslims, makes claims on their political beliefs and actions. It is often Islamic principles, not secular ethics, that inform political thought. Modernist and progressive Muslim thinkers have argued that democracy has 'to become a systematic normative goal of large numbers of Muslims' for it to succeed in Muslim countries (Abou El Fadl, 2004: 128). Islamic rationales are necessary in this process of democratic habituation. Reinterpretations of Islamic moral conceptions, nurturing respect for democratic rights and freedoms, are indispensable for a well-functioning democracy in contexts where Islam is a principal marker of social, cultural or political claims. However, commonly-held Muslim accounts of Islam are 'unrelated to modern ethical requirements' and 'irreconcilable with universal moral standards' (Abou El Fadl, 2002: 106–7). For Abou El Fadl, Islam as widely understood and practised today adheres to 'a long list of morally noncommittal legal commands', depriving it of a moral capacity to develop democratic thinking (2002: 15).

Democracy's virtues, An-Na'im urges his fellow Muslims, lie in it being a good, just and accountable governance that facilitates the active and free participation of citizens in public debate, provides channels for rectifying and correcting political mistakes, and safeguards human dignity and intellect. Moreover, democracy is not only the best political system we have today. It is also the most able to facilitate an inclusive moral environment that permits the development of a genuine moral life compatible with Islamic comprehensive visions. A moral agent, according to An-Na'im, can only genuinely seek a religiously inspired ethical life on the basis of personal reason and conviction in a free environment (2008: 3–4). Fadel makes a similar argument, that democracy, through a free, active, participatory political environment, enables Muslims and members of other faiths to 'discover those truths necessary for her salvation' (2008: 68). Justification for democracy as a moral good is developed through religious thinking to achieve normative commitments to democratic principles.

Mutual transformation also explains the concept of religious transformation. The first aspect of religious transformation is due to external factors of democratisation. Bader (2003) and Shachar (2001) argue that the introduction of democratic reform of political structures, geared to recognise the public role of religion in Muslim societies, enables more people to reconcile 'normative commitments to Islam as a comprehensive theory of the good and [their] political commitments to a liberal constitutional order' (Fadel, 2008: 9). In a state that recognises the public relevance of Islamic theories of the good, Muslims can develop a commitment to comprehensive views of Islam while endorsing a democratic order. In other words, the beliefs and practices of Muslims and liberal democracies can be reconciled.

The second aspect of religious transformation refers to an internal democratisation of Islam. According to Abou El Fadl, this aspect concerns how 'religion can legitimately play a role' in politics (2005: 202). In the concept of transformativeness a public role for religion is envisaged to endorse a tolerant path in democratic politics at the hands of individual moral agents. Religious rationales become more closely aligned with constitutionally guaranteed protections of human rights and individual freedoms, pluralism and toleration (Abou El Fadl, 2005: 202). Recognition is awarded to 'reasonable non-Islamic [as well as dissenting Islamic] ways of life [that] are nevertheless worthy of respect and constitutional protection, independent of the instrumental value of pluralism' (Fadel, 2008: 43). Thus, individuals' re-invigoration of religious understanding within a democratic social culture leads to the creation of tolerance in politics, which in turn maintains this culture with both aspects of transformation mutually reinforcing one another.

The subsequent sections, in a discussion of the various components of the social public sphere, will further articulate the notion of normative change at a religious level under the concept of social Islam. Normative change at a societal level will be identified and explored under the concept of democratic toleration. Finally, an additional layer of institutional change in building up to the debates, introduced in the category of collective rights, will be discussed with reference to the debate on institutional pluralism.

2. Social Islam

Two main political developments characterise contemporary Islam in politics. First, as Ziauddin Sardar describes, Islam was turned into a national creed, where the state defined the role and nature of religion and used it for its own interest in politics (2002: 17). In this context, Nader Hashemi argues, religious populations were not given the chance to bargain and reconcile themselves with the secular state (2009: 2). For instance, in countries like Turkey and Tunisia, secularisation was not a 'consequence of religious formation', marking 'a reversal of the European experience' (Hashemi, 2009: 70). Second, in countries where Islam had been forcefully banished from the state to the private realm, it has emerged as an ideology in political opposition aiming to capture the state. Islamic resurgence and religious politicisation in the Muslim world often took the path of Islamism or political Islam (Cesari, 2014: xv). These two developments are intertwined. The politicisation of religion has tended to be undemocratic due to the authoritarian nature of most states and the resistance to their forced modernisation programmes (Hashemi, 2009: 147). Essentially, Islam's moral capacity to cultivate the social and intellectual roots of democracy has often been marginalised.

Compatibility-based arguments, on the relationship between Islam and democracy, counter the essentialist argument that the democratic deficit in Muslim countries is attributable to Islam. However, the incorrect assumptions of the essentialist argument highlighted by compatibility-based arguments and their proposal of a compatibility between the moral precepts of Islam and democracy do not necessarily lead to a comprehensive solution for the absence of democracy. In the Islamic tradition, principles and norms can be marshalled to support democracy and human rights and to completely oppose them. The diversity of the Islamic tradition leaves considerable room for reconstruction. Therefore, the search for support or antagonism in Islam is contingent on 'the moral construction given to it' by individual Muslims (Abou El Fadl, 2002). On the basis of these insights, I have reframed the question of whether Islam is compatible with democratic values to instead ask whether, and how, Muslims can develop interpretations of the Islamic tradition that internalise the principles of democracy.

This question guides how I address the idea of social Islam as a normative alternative to political Islam and state Islam. Social Islam, a term coined by Armando Salvatore and Dale F. Eickelman, suggests that democracy will be invigorated through religious normative change organically emerging and developing in the context of social life (2004a: x–xi).[1] Salvatore and Eickelman contend that the spread of access to knowledge, due to the rise of a print culture, new technologies and social media, has had far-reaching implications for the development of people's interpretations of Islam as a form of 'social normativity', which in turn leads to new forms of political engagement (2003: 102).[2] The notion of social Islam, the emergence of modernised, civil and pluralist forms of Islam, will lead to the emergence of an independent democratic public sphere (Salvatore and Eickelman, 2004a: xi). This chapter rethinks the role of religion in the social public sphere, by articulating the necessary grounds for the development of social Islam as a category of theorisation. Social Islam, through the active and free participation and deliberation of the citizens, creates new ways of reinterpreting religious ideas and affirming religious lifestyles under democratic systems (Salvatore, 2012: 437). I will adapt social Islam as a moral imperative in my theorisation of Muslim democracy.

As I have emphasised elsewhere in this book, democratic development requires placing greater emphasis on 'learning' procedures within civil society (Held, 2007: 233). Hannah Arendt pointed out the importance of 'a healthy respect for democratic values' and civic virtues as well as 'the democratic habits of mind that can only be sustained in civil society, in initiatives (publications, civic associations, social movements, forms of disobedience) undertaken at the grassroots' (Isaac, 1994: 160, 162). Certain norms are also essential for Soroush, who argues that

> democratic regimes cannot be sustained without ethical and/or religious commitments, including respect for 'the rights of others, justice, sympathy, and mutual trust'. (as cited in Dallmayr, 2011: 445)

I reinterpret social Islam as a normative category in the reformative process of rethinking religious ideas congenial to pluralism, openness and democratic tolerance. The social public sphere allows diverse discursive communities and individual voices for deliberation and representation. It also creates avenues for interaction, coexistence and pluralism. Social mobilisation and organising go beyond hierarchical relations. More diverse forums for social communication are fostered among communities with distinct interest claims. Deliberative and contestatory mechanisms, in the social public sphere, would promote 'an effective, non-coercive encouragement of more egalitarian and reformist changes from within the [Islamic] tradition itself'

(Shachar 2016: 327). Collective reinterpretation and re-appropriation of religious discourses in this proposed normative concept of social Islam foster intra- and inter-religious pluralism. With the opening of public debate to larger numbers of people, a shift can occur from the formal bonds of the state and clergy to individuals and civil society on the basis of 'a popular trope ... [of] practices needed to live a good life as a Muslim' (Eickelman and Salvatore, 2003: 102).

In the proposed theory of Muslim democracy, the political relevance of religion is derived from social organisations and individuals who articulate their moral perspectives and civic reasoning. The relationship between the religious and the political in social Islam is redefined, making religion part of the public sphere, while dissociating rule from divine authority. Islamic principles are brought, as An-Naʻim proposes, to 'official policy and legislation through general political deliberation, but not as imperative religious doctrine' (2009: 145). Religious arguments are elaborated on and contested in the public sphere without recourse to their status of moral authority or origins. Social Islam shows how alternative public articulations of Islam, independent of the state apparatus and religious authorities, can play a positive role in democratic value change. Muslims can uphold both their comprehensive Islamic views and political democratic values. Thus, I argue, social Islam, and the processes explained in social Islam, can provide what Hirschkind calls the 'philosophical conditions for pluralist democracy' to develop in Muslim societies (2008: 66).

One of the most salient aspects of Muslim democracy is the reformative power of the social public sphere in undermining undemocratic traditional orthodoxies. The processes of social Islam can foster a rethinking of religious thought and practice, especially with regard to historical *sharīʻa* among Muslims, to develop the moral capacity for reform. Historical interpretations of *sharīʻa* often negate the fact that the *sharīʻa* is composed of diverse normative accounts. Instead, *sharīʻa* is constructed as an absolutist and penalising force hostile to human reason and dignity (Emon, 2008: 271). For Anver Emon, discriminatory rules contained in traditional interpretations of *sharīʻa*, especially intolerance and incivility against minorities, women and non-Muslim citizens, can be seen as the greatest barriers to *sharīʻa* having a public role as a part of pluralist democracy. Emon insists that contemporary reinterpretations of Islam could eliminate this discrimination. Inequality was generated by certain interpretations of the Qur'an, *ḥadīth* and an extra-textual Islamic ethos in a period of expanding conquest and identity formation rather than the eternal principles of Islam (Emon, 2008: 272).

One possible method of re-invigorating the religious tradition of Islam is suggested by An-Na'im through the theory of abrogation. The theory of abrogation, proposed by An-Na'im, prioritises the putative eternal ideals of the Meccan verses of the Qur'an while viewing Madinan ones as context-specific and time-bound implications of these ideals (1987: 334).[3] Differentiation between the ideals and the means, ruling out strict dogmatism and literalism, can aid Muslims in discovering human rights and equal rights of men and women. An-Na'im defines this process as the reformation 'under shariah that would be both Islamic and consistent with universal human rights standards' (1987: 17). The theory of abrogation, for An-Na'im, can form convictions about *sharī'a* to uphold human dignity and pluralism.

An indispensable character of successful democracies is that a significant proportion of citizens recognise pluralism. I argue that an alignment of religious commitments with the notion of pluralism can lend critical support to arriving at a broad consensus on collective democratic norms. Thus, a Muslim democracy framework aims for normative value change at the societal level, among individuals and groups with non-pluralistic sentiments, in order to reach an agreement on the normative benchmarks of the democratic society. Internal change within communities should be the result of an encounter they make with democratic structures and diverse social systems. In this process, the public sphere encourages citizens and groups 'to think in part in terms of the interests of others', understand one another and develop a civic language and espouse democratic toleration (Christiano, 2015). Religious interpretations and normative changes in favour of democracy within Muslim societies can only evolve from well-informed public debates in a free and critical political space. Value change here should emerge out of democratic processes in the public sphere and not be imposed by a moral agenda of the state or 'the wider communities' standards' (Mookherjee, 2009: 159).

Recognition of the worth of and respect for another comprehensive view does not necessarily lead to its uncritical endorsement. Democratic value change does not imply that orthodox Muslims have a presumptive moral obligation to reconcile their philosophical truth claims or endorse what they may view to be heterodox. In other words, normative change is not concerned with metaphysical, foundationalist or objective truth claims, but rather is intrinsically political. Muslims, like all other groups within a political system, have a moral duty to develop democratic toleration, civic virtues and pluralism despite their ontological distinctions and differing interests, although a scenario of mutual justifications may arise in which Muslims

> should [not] be expected to . . . endorse gay marriage . . . [or] . . . be supposed to approve heterodox traditions of Islam . . . But Islamists can be expected to justify within their own values the legitimacy of these other groups' political and civil liberties as equal to their own, for pluralistic democracy to take root. (Somer, 2011: 538)

As such, value change should support democratic toleration as the normative basis of the political community. Recognition of everyone's right to live a good life occurs within a constitutional order based on human rights. This entails commitments to equal citizenship, individual liberties, human dignity, civility, respect, and a right to a self-directed life.

By and large, social Islam conceptualises the process of normative transformation in which religious convictions and practices among Muslims are reconciled with democracy. These entail normative 'idealizations' of democracy, in Rortyian terms, such as democratic toleration, human rights, negotiation, pluralism and constitutionalism (1996: 333). As such, social Islam is a component of the moral underpinning necessary to theorise a Muslim democracy. I argue that social Islam, as a moral imperative, reinterprets Islam in a democratic direction. Islamic justifications can become a part of an enlightened, well-informed and tolerant public debate among individual citizens.

Another component of the social public sphere, democratic toleration, will now be discussed in the next section. I will illustrate the common good and overlapping consensus, constructed by the notion of normative change, as the basis of the public sphere.

3. The Establishment of Democratic Toleration

Muslim societies face the common challenges of pluralism and are divided on 'questions of the good and the path to salvation' (Galeotti, 2012: 131). Democracy embodies 'a kind of peaceful and fair compromise' among conflicting truth claims and different comprehensive and emancipatory doctrines (Christiano, 2012: 86). This compromise needs the establishment of the social virtue of toleration in public life. I conceptualise democratic toleration as the third component of the argument for the social public sphere. It is the normative foundation of the social public sphere that facilitates different moral systems, protects diverse views and serves diverse interests. Democratic toleration cultivates a shared normative commitment towards each other among citizens who can arrive at a consensus on respect, civility and human rights despite their differing views and conflicting interests. In this book, the idea of democratic toleration is derived from multiculturalism and the arguments of scholars such as Taylor and Kukathas, and enriched with the ideas of Muslim intellectuals like Talbi and An-Na'im.

Kukathas defines toleration as people's freedom to pursue 'various ends, individually or cooperatively' (1992: 108). According to Kukathas, the liberal notion of toleration is the moral foundation of democracy and the basis for the justification of cultural, moral and political pluralism (2003: 259). Similarly, Talbi advocates acceptance of religious diversity and pluralism. Talbi states that human beings can 'live together with our consciously assumed difference' through finding a 'plateau' where 'mutual respect and full acknowledgement of difference are attained' (1995a: 62; Filali-Ansari, 2009: 2). On this plateau, Talbi believes that a 'common denominator of a universal ethics', on the basis of toleration, should be the foundation of collective life (1995b: 83).

In the social public sphere, the common values for a shared life inform the idea of democratic toleration, which upholds a thin understanding of human rights. The idea of a thin notion of human rights will be further explained in the next section on constitutional provisions. I will now elaborate the role of democratic toleration in the public sphere. Democratic toleration creates an expectation that citizens will develop civility, recognise different identities and respect the rights of others in public. It acknowledges 'the legitimacy of the numerous and often contradictory options that resulted from the exercises of moral judgement' in public debate and the appeal to diverse normative systems (Fadel, 2008: 49). Individuals can be empowered to reclaim their agency 'in their choices of conscience ... to define their own life while respecting others' right to do the same' (Maclure and Taylor, 2011: 11). This amounts to accepting living in peaceful coexistence with rival doctrines and developing a firm allegiance to the political ideals of the democratic civic culture.

The social public sphere is 'the site where contests take place over the definition of the "common good"' (Eickelman and Salvatore, 2002: 94). In the social public sphere, the common good does not have to be thick to be accepted among citizens. In fact, a thin agreement 'to develop an ethics of lived experience and practice' is more effective for developing a political consensus independent from any doctrine of transcendental morality (Connolly, 2005: 116). A single vision of the common good, in democratic toleration, should not dictate the outcome of political negotiation. Rather, the social public sphere should contain a range of moral and political perspectives in public deliberation to organise the social public sphere. Believers and atheists, and people of different ethnicities, cultural identities and ways of life, can collectively agree on the shared good (Connolly, 2005: 43). In political contestation, all citizens are

> free to bring their religious views to the democratic dialogue – recognizing, of course, that to be effective in persuading others they will have to find a way to communicate their conviction in ways that resonate with people who do not share their religion [or world-views]. (Carens and Williams, 1996: 141)

These actors should reach an agreement overcoming the persistent tension of 'inter- and intra-religious domination' or ideological hegemony created within the public sphere (Bhargava, 2009: 558). Individuals with competing and different positions can consciously, responsibly, directly and equally engage in a dialogue and compromise to establish 'common public values' and 'the common good of all on a moral basis' (Maclure and Taylor, 2011: 12, 15).

A complete consensus, in which individuals and groups can reach 'the whole truth' as they see it, is not possible (Christiano, 2012: 82). However, the processes that maintain equal access to and maximum input from the citizenry to the public debate are required in a functioning democracy. Thomas Christiano clarifies that '[d]emocracy, properly understood, is the context in which individuals freely engage in a process of reasoned discussion and deliberation on an equal footing' (2012: 82). In public life, 'each citizen ought to have adequate and equal opportunities for expressing his or her preferences as to the final outcome' (Dahl, 2001: 132). While there may be disagreements on public decision-making processes, the outcome would be 'intrinsically just' because democratic toleration gives an equal public hearing and moral worth to judgements whenever they arise (Christiano, 2012: 76). Which perspective wins over others in the process of achieving the common good is decided through deliberation in various forums of civil society. In the social public sphere, the mechanisms to reach a consensus 'should be open and accessible to all citizens . . . without exposing themselves to charges of disbelief, apostasy or blasphemy' or any fear of subjugation (An-Na'im, 2009: 149). Limitations present in compatibility-based arguments, rooted in the notion of a divine sovereignty that undermines public equality and implies hierarchy, are addressed by democratic toleration.

At this point, it is important to acknowledge that a shared public perspective among individuals needs to be 'morally persuasive within their own system of moral, philosophical or religious commitments' (Fadel, 2008: 8; 2007: 4). Thus, the 'accessibility' of religious and ethical reasons is essential for the development and maintenance of the common good (Sachedina, 2009: 177). Unlike republican secularism or orthodox liberalism, the idea of Muslim democracy in this book proposes a religion-friendly account of overlapping consensus and the common good. Consequently, the social public sphere is inclusive of religious justifications in public deliberation. The moral pluralist argument is adopted here that each citizen should be involved in this ongoing democratic communication with their secular, religious or traditional comprehensive world-views to create a shared public perspective in social life. For Bhikhu Parekh, the processes of reaching

> [t]he common good and the collective will that are vital to any political society are generated not by transcending cultural and other particularities, but through their interplay in the cut and thrust of a dialogue. (2002: 341)

Mookherjee takes a similar stance, that a democratic state is obliged to protect the 'capacity for reason' for all citizens, so as to contribute to defining the common good rather than imposing its own account (2001: 79). The social public sphere rests on the conviction that citizens who have different moral ontologies, doctrines of the good or metaphysical orientations can still share a common democratic normative basis. As Taylor and Maclure have noted, 'citizens arrive at an "overlapping consensus" about the basic political principles, despite the differing conceptions they embrace regarding what a successful life is' (2011: 17). A morally thin yet inclusive notion of common good, human rights and pluralism and equality creates a normative underpinning for the social public sphere.

Closer moral alignment of individual moral judgements is promoted by the social public sphere. Inclusiveness, civility and mutual respect are the basis of social life in Muslim democracy theory. Social conditions for the cultivation of intercultural dialogue and a common language of citizens can be generated through a shared religious interest for human rights, the shared good, peace, and justice among different communities (Sachedina 2009: 176). In the discussion on democratic toleration, I have explained the role of values and processes maintaining the democratic relationship between individuals and communities in the social public sphere.

The above three conceptual components of the social public sphere can engender a political environment that paves the way for the fourth component, the institutionalisation of normative difference. The framework of Muslim democracy now continues the arguments for recognising moral difference by diversifying pluralistic institutional and jurisdictional arrangements.

4. Institutional Pluralism

Dale F. Eickelman has insightfully observed that, in Muslim majority societies,

> blurring of lines – or, intermediate, connective spaces – remind us of the impossibility of distinguishing sharply between public and private and point to more important continuities between one sphere and another. The result is to suggest new understandings of the role of religion in society. (2002: 7)

The arguments developed in favour of pluralist secularism in the previous chapter enable the consideration of the differentiation between the state and the public sphere. A clear distinction between these two domains is essential to pave the way to resolving the issue of religion in the public sphere. Two rationales justify the differentiation between state public sphere and social public sphere. First, a more sophisticated account of the political sphere is needed to address comprehensive moral doctrines. Second, states alone cannot deal with irreconcilable moral conflicts, generated by religious and non-religious reasons alike, in pluralist societies. Even a morally minimalist state cannot be innocent of bias when dealing with such real-world situations (Bader, 2003a: 4; Shachar, 2008: 575).

Shachar and Mégret have suggested that it is a mistake to think that the state can solely deliver satisfactory services to people with diverse needs generated from substantially different world-views (Mégret, 2012: 13; Shachar, 2001: 88). Unanswered questions remain about the ability of the state to respond to diverse public needs of groups and communities. The distinction within the public sphere opens up novel ways to think of institutional pluralism within democratic politics. A pluralistic alternative will be elaborated in this section, with the aim of contributing to rethinking the role of religion and politics. I will demonstrate how collective rights can be safeguarded by diversifying the provision of public services and including other social actors in the formulation of public policy.

Unlike multiculturalism's institutional pluralism, limited to minority accommodation and rights, institutional pluralism in this book seeks the expansion of religious freedoms for diverse, minority and majority alike, needs and interests. Pluralist secularism identifies the social public sphere as the space for collaboration between the state and voluntary public associations to deliver more extensive and adequate services. The social public sphere creates administrative and economic opportunities for the public functions of religion in the hands of what Paul Hirst calls 'democratically controlled voluntary associations' (1997: 13). Citizens with diverse comprehensive philosophical doctrines, in institutional pluralism, are awarded 'greater control of their affairs' in organising and funding public services and the welfare sector (Hirst, 1997: 13). Civil society actors, such as faith-based or cultural associations, can also be 'service providers' in education, healthcare, seniors' care, social work and finance (Hirst, 1997: 13). Diverse political platforms and social forums are made available to religious groups with distinct and divergent goods and interests.

Such diversity also shapes the forms in which institutional pluralism is implemented in practice. For there is no single predetermined path to institutional pluralism. The specific processes in the social public sphere determine the resulting collaboration between state and civil society. To take the example of education, we can observe different models of institutional pluralism formulated in the literature. These include Bader's model of separate faith schools and Shachar's model of 'power-dividing and sharing arrangements' (2008: 154). Bader's proposal for separate faith-based schools grants institutional autonomy to religious groups to open and run their own schools (2007a: 271). Shachar, on the other hand, advocates a common education in state schools, but, similar to in Germany and Austria, gives religious groups the right to control religious instruction and curriculum. Specificity of context in a Muslim democracy framework is important, in the provision of associational services, contingent on the political experiences and existing institutions of a particular society.

In predominantly Muslim social contexts, the characteristics of institutional pluralism can take various shapes and forms. How much power will be given to civil society actors and community-based organisations is negotiated on a continuous basis. Issues such as whether religious classes should be taught at or outside state schools, what is the appropriate age for pupils to attend religious classes, and how curricula should be organised and classes administered would be resolved differently. In some Muslim-majority contexts, separate faith schools might be the most appropriate policy, while a power-sharing education structure in other contexts may be more appropriate. Nonetheless, to resolve the state's relationship to social and religious affairs, a form of institutional pluralism seems necessary in theorising democratic accommodation.

Although the empowerment of civil society against the state is vital for institutional pluralism, it is equally important to avert the potential risk of empowering communities against individuals. Indeed, civil society is not *ipso facto* benign or tolerant in the social public sphere framework. In other words, civil society and its prevailing normative cultures should not be viewed as inexorably more pluralist than the institutional establishment of the state. Protection should be in place for the rights and freedoms of individuals. While the morally minimalist state allows a broad range of the 'governance of social affairs', higher regulatory mechanisms, governmental and non-governmental alike, should critically scrutinise service provision to ensure universal human rights standards (Hirst, 1994: 25).

The concept of state intervention, a topic broached above, can also be restrictive if the state is considered to be the only authority and the sole guarantor of rights and freedoms. Although morally minimalist, we must recognise that the state and the people who occupy political positions have their own interests. Moreover, it would be incorrect to assume that the state is consistently impartial in supervising civil society associations. Accordingly, there are benefits to having institutions, independent of the executive, legislative and jurisdictional powers, supporting the state in the task of safeguarding individual rights and freedoms. Ombudsman institutions can be formed by an amalgamation of governmental authorities, civil society actors, academics and specialists, to mediate between state institutions and civil society organisations. The ombudsman exercises an advisory role to state institutions by issuing reports that are presented to the authorities as well as to the public (Yazıcı, 2011: 148–52). These institutions can be founded to protect rights and freedoms against pressures coming from within groups themselves, and from other groups, as well as against state authority. Religious scholars can also carry out the role of ombudsmen, in fulfilment of the institution of *naṣīha* or morally corrective criticism, as a form of reasoned criticism. *Naṣīha* demonstrates how 'religion and reason, and thus, religion and critique' can come into play together in democratic politics (Enayat, 2017: 40).

The conception of institutional pluralism proposed in this book aims to give voice and agency to both civil society and individuals alongside the state. Civil society is provided with greater space to perform some of the functions of the state while simultaneously ensuring the freedom of citizens to choose among governmental and societal organisations through democratic mechanisms and constitutional safeguards. The social public sphere thus primarily aims to empower communities and give them authority by institutionalising pluralism, for several normative reasons.

First, individuals should have a right to collective goods and the ability to fully pursue what they define as the good life. By promoting religious freedoms, institutional pluralism enhances the autonomy and capacities of individuals with diverse normative systems. In addition, institutional pluralism can guarantee that all groups will have their own autonomous spheres. The freedoms enjoyed by individuals preclude any one particular school or sect of Islam from controlling or suppressing less prominent opinions in ingroups. Second, groups and ideologies excluded from political influence may pose a risk to democracy. They could become reactionary by feeding into existing forms of political extremism that aim to impose their ideology on the state. Institutional pluralist accommodation would curb these forms of reactionary activism.

Third, there ought to be a distinction between official recognition and actual presence. If religious or cultural ways of life remain officially unrecognised, this does not mean that they are non-existent. Official recognition of religious and cultural ways of life, as opposed to neglecting already existing practices, would put group interactions under scrutiny. Communal religious practices can be regulated that would otherwise remain unnoticed. Meaningful protection can be introduced, through formal state acknowledgement, of the rights of vulnerable members in religious and cultural groups. Frequent interaction between the state and these groups, within this institutionalist pluralist framework, has the potential for a more inclusive governing of a diverse citizenry. A more interactive mode of peaceful coexistence can also be engendered between the state and comprehensive moral doctrines as well as among groups with diverse normative systems.

Normative democratic changes are introduced by institutional pluralism. As mentioned earlier, the social public sphere views communicative and discursive processes as crucial for institutional change. It is in light of this insight that civil society becomes an important venue for a bottom-up democratic construction. The social public sphere empowers a form of civil society with its provision of equal share of rights and capacity in engaging public exchanges. Proponents of competing world-views are given the space to interact and communicate with their opponents on equal grounds. The democratic culture of equal participation, civic dialogue and deliberation, created by the social public sphere, would seek to improve interactions and resolve disputes in public life. In a setting of comprehensive institutional and legal protections, the interaction, frequency and familiarity of diverse ideas, practices and norms, even those which might be unorthodox or condemned, could eventually lead to toleration or gain acceptance. Visible and legal political and moral diversity can indirectly lead to the development of a tolerant civil society and the cultivation of civility and democratic toleration. Therefore, opening up the public sphere and delegating certain public powers to civil society facilitate mass-level normative change towards pluralistic political solutions.

To this end, the conception of the social public sphere endorses the idea that 'better institutional design', with public platforms that protect individual liberties and facilitate civil society, will prop up 'liberal democratic practices' and values (Volpi, 2004: 1074). Multiculturalism, associated with Western democracies, can be adapted to a Muslim-majority context through rethinking of institutionalist pluralist concepts. Conceptual resources exist in the social public sphere to organise diverse social and religious groups. Sufficient and shared normative commitments, according to this conception, are central to democratic toleration and human rights. This institutional pluralism has a Janus-faced nature. On the one hand, it aims to accommodate the demands of *sharī'a*-minded Muslims in ensuring legal and institutionalist pluralist rights for them. On the other, it necessitates moral endorsement of pluralism by these Muslims concerning human rights, freedom of speech, individual liberties, and other lifestyles. In other words, institutional pluralism involves more rights and autonomy for religious people. However, a democracy requires the collective moral endorsement of the ethos of pluralism.

V. Conclusion: The Social Public Sphere

This section has first elaborated two key notions within the public sphere derived from the typologies of Muslim political and multiculturalist political trends. The categories of plural and shared public institutions help to highlight the strengths and weaknesses in the liberal and republican public sphere models in order to revise these models. Plural and shared public institution models are here examined in a parallel, complementary fashion to conceptualise a social public sphere.

The idea of Muslim democracy asserts the need to re-orient democratic institutions in Islamic contexts and to nurture complementary normative and practical commitments in these settings. This approach has also been applied to developing a conception of the public sphere in this chapter. Four conceptual components divide the discussion on the social public sphere in the development of a political theory of Muslim democracy.

The first feature of the pluralist public sphere is transformativeness. It defines a profound ideological transformation and value change towards democratisation both structurally and socially. An epistemological bias is not implied here in the relationship between liberal democracy and Islam, in which the latter is solely expected to be compatible with liberal democratic institutions. Democratic institutions should be inclusive of religious needs and demands. Accordingly, transformativeness accounts for the change in the character of the state towards more accommodating ends. Institutions are to be founded, to give impartial access to public life, that create spaces for Islamic ways of life and their associational claims. A free and critical political space, provided by pluralist secularism, fosters reciprocal transformativeness towards collective internalisation of pluralism and democratic tolerance. Value change among Muslims reinforces the societal basis of Muslim democracy and is the best guarantor of it. The following components of social pubic sphere are elements that further demonstrate the idea of this dual transformativeness.

The second concept of the social public sphere is social Islam. Social processes are displayed in which religion can form a part of a democratic public sphere through people's self-reflexive and active understanding of Islam. This demonstrates the virtue of the grass-roots development of democratic values for the potential development of a social public sphere in Muslim societies, where religion is a primary factor in creating social, cultural and ideological identities. Theological justifications for governance by religious authorities are not relevant in the formulation of social Islam. Instead, moral weight given to individuals and their agency through social Islam can assist the process of challenging divine legitimacy in an Islamic state. Social Islam reveals how the engagement of individuals with religion in a free and critical manner can contribute to the shared good and democratic toleration.

It is not only institutional practices, regulations or rules that define democracy. Processes and norms also characterise this ideal. Democratic toleration is the third component of the argument for the social public sphere that represents the normative formation of democratic consensus and the shared good. In democratic toleration, the public accessibility of religious arguments is part of public contests over the definition of the shared good. As such, religion, articulated through social Islam, can contribute to consolidating a shared normative belief in democracy and pluralism. Essentially, democratic toleration illustrates how common will and political consensus, on the basis of civility, respect, human rights and pluralism, can serve as the normative underpinnings of the social public sphere.

The fourth component is institutional pluralism, which envisages civil society functioning in the sense of the social public sphere. An alternative sphere limits state power in the direction of a morally minimalist state. This final feature follows the institutional establishment of the earlier three features of the social public sphere. Civil society organisations, in the public sphere, share institutional powers alongside the state in delivering public services. Potential democratic development depends on contexts where moral diversity and the relationship between secularism and Islam require a pluralist approach.

Although crucial for the consolidation of a democracy, the social public sphere alone cannot lead to or maintain it. The institutional and societal face of democracy in the Middle East is 'frequently accompanied by political repression and manipulation [to constrain opposition and dissent] which sabotage the underlying principles of democracy' (Wiktorowicz, 1999: 606). Current political practices require attention at the constitutional level to protect human rights and individual freedoms and guarantee the separation of powers, judicial independence and the rule of law. Constitutional safeguards are the final area to be addressed in developing an understanding of Muslim democracy so as to ameliorate the problems democracies face. In the next chapter, constitutional provisions will be conceptualised within the political theory of Muslim democracy.

Notes

1. Eickelman and Piscatori have referred to social organisations such as salons, coffee shops, literary circles and media platforms, which are already on the ground, as factors that work in favour of an 'increasingly open discussion of issues related to democracy, gender and the common good' (1996: x). These processes were

famously called 'the objectification of Muslim consciousness' by Eickelman and Piscatori (1996: 37).
2. For instance, the Internet has created a social space where individuals can become equal citizens, carve out a level of independence from religious and political authorities, and communicate with one another in a free manner such that they are capable of developing shared democratic values (Lynch, 2011).
3. This theory of abrogation was proposed by the late Sudanese intellectual Muhammad Taha, the teacher and mentor of Abdullahi Ahmad An-Naʻim. It argues that the Meccan period of revelation exhibits the normative system of justice, freedom and equality as universal Islamic principles for all ages and contexts (An-Naʻim, 1987: 334). Yet the Madinan phase emphasising 'law, order, and obedience' evinces their application in a particular seventh-century Arabian socio-cultural context, and cannot be taken as universal (Zayd, 2006: 87). Progressives generally believe that the *sharīʻa* we have today is actually a later codification of the Madinan period, which historically concealed the importance of the eternal message of the Mecca phase. This position causes them to oppose codified *sharīʻa* in favour of viewing *sharīʻa* only as normative principles and morals envisioning personal piety and good manners. The idea that the Qur'an and *sunna* prescribe any form of political system, offer solutions to political matters or present a set of positive legal rules is rejected.

6

THE PLURALISING CONSTITUTION

I. Introduction

The functionalist perspective presents the scenario of a 'democracy without democrats'. Free and fair elections are held to be a transformative condition in which political participation can substantially contribute to democratisation. In the MENA region, we have witnessed political and civic reforms that have engendered some form of 'electoralization' (Sadiki, 1996: 401). Yet elections have often served to reinforce liberalised authoritarianism, superficially creating 'façade democracy' (Wiktorowicz, 1999: 606) or 'pseudo democracy' (Volpi, 2004: 1061). Emerging democracies in the region remain with unconsolidated transitions. One of the main reasons for this phenomenon is the fixation on electoral processes. Liberal institutions and democratic culture that ensure individual rights, constitutional liberties and the rule of law are often neglected. However, it is essential to recognise that

> [w]ithout such institutions, electoral democracies can turn into illiberal machines that sanctify the ballot box and majority rule without paying much attention to freedoms. Democracies can degenerate into populist systems in which the sovereignty of the nation and the will of the people are glorified, at the expense of individual rights. (Taşpınar, 2014: 59)

In fact, on a global scale, we have observed right-wing populist politicians coming to power through electoral processes. A strong executive's dismantling of checks and balances, undermining of opposition, restriction of freedom of speech and erosion of democratic institutions even threatens functioning democracies. The rise of jingoism, xenophobia and anti-intellectualism following political and economic crises and security threats has tested the democratic sufficiency of electoral accountability.

Escalating worldwide concerns over electoral accountability have prompted some academics to formulate alternative institutions. For instance, Alexander Guerrero advocates lotteries in the selection of congressional representatives for a more diverse and inclusive executive, earnest civic services, and significantly less nepotism and corruption (2014: 156–7). Political representatives, chosen only for one term, would refrain from temporary political calculations, have fewer connections to lobbies and donors, and be easier to monitor. In such a system, consolidation of power and political interests would not threaten democratic institutions as much as in electoral systems (Guerrero, 2014: 160–2).

While there may be other institutional alternatives, political theory tends to deal with the volatility of representative electoral democracy that surrounds the concept of the constitution. A constitution establishes a set of rules that limits the government's ability to monopolise power, protects citizens' rights and freedoms through mechanisms, shapes the state in relation to the people, defines the norms of the civil society and reflects the common good (Selçuk, 2010: 337). This institution is held to be an indispensable core of democratic politics in 'put[ting] democracy into effect' and sustaining its well-being (Holmes, 1995: 6).

My examination of constitutional provisions within the context of Muslim democracy will illustrate two key schools of thought, namely political constitutionalism and legal constitutionalism. Contemporary exponents of political constitutionalism like Tully believe that every citizen has a right to participate in the constitutional debate in a process of consensus building (1995: 26). No limit to constitutional debate should exist, and only a constitution that is a product of contestatory and participatory democratic politics can be the central institution and the guarantor of a democratic system (Bellamy, 2007: 260). On the other hand, advocates of legal constitutionalism like Tezcür argue that democracy needs a degree of constitutional protection. Imposition of limits on political authority and constraints on popular rule can protect unassailable rights. Not everything in the constitution is open to democratic politics or can be changed by electoral processes; a certain moral background as incontestable moral norms is necessary (Tezcür, 2007: 450).

Both of these constitutionalist schools will be drawn on at the end of this chapter to articulate the underlying notions of the constitutional mechanisms of the Muslim democracy idea. The conception of pluralising constitutionalism will map out how Muslim democracy can engage with human rights, the rule of law, the democratic limits of government power and jurisdictional pluralism.

II. Political Constitutionalism

Ergun Özbudun maintains that constitutions cannot be autonomous from society and insensitive to the demands of the people. He believes that it is not right to bind future generations with the provisions made by their predecessors. Each generation should have the right to revise the constitution on the basis of changing social and normative conditions and different needs and demands that arise. Thus, he asserts, the idea of permanently unassailable provisions and constitutional protection is meaningless in democratic politics (Özbudun, 2013).

James Tully's democratic constitutionalism emerges from a critique of Western constitutionalism's alleged failure to accommodate normative difference. Tully argues that a constitution is 'both the foundation of democracy and, at the same time, subject to democratic discussion and change in practice' where 'popular sovereignty is conceived as an intercultural dialogue' encompassing 'all moral and religious reasoning' (1995: 132, 190, 114). The people can fully enjoy their democratic sovereignty and freedom to participate in constitutional change in the triumph of the 'sovereignty of people' over 'sovereignty of the existing constitution' (Tully, 1995: 130). Tully's ideas on constitutions are derived from a social contract tradition. Norms and institutions in politics should be the result of free and democratic public discussions, negotiations and agreement so that people can respect the institutions, and in turn, institutions can maintain democratic governance (Tully, 1995: 191). Political constitutionalists tend to support the establishment of a more deliberative model of democracy. Crucial elements are needed such as the institutional capacity for free and equal participation of all, and open-minded discussions in the public sphere to resolve social and political problems and maintain institutions based on the common good (Mansbridge, 1990).

In contrast to Tully's criticism of the inability of liberalism and republicanism to create a democratic constitutional state, Phillip Pettit and Richard Bellamy argue that, unlike liberalism, republicanism is capable of providing a democratic solution to constitutionalism. Bellamy defines democracy 'by the fact that the people exercise control over government' through being able to 'contest the policies proposed by government and to work at getting them changed' (2007: 207). Electoral as well as contestatory politics in democracy, according to Pettit, promote the popular will and majority with the requisite institutions in place (2012: 23). In this regard, democracy is defined by the continuous involvement of citizens in law-making. A constitution is a political and public good 'depending upon and making possible mutually beneficial cooperation' (Bellamy, 2007: 66). Democratic arrangements in 'established working democracies' are considered to be more reliable and effective in the areas of individual rights, democratic debate and the rule of law than 'the counter-majoritarian' constitutional protection (Bellamy, 2007: 260, 262).

Pettit's and Bellamy's theories on political constitutionalism rest on the idea of freedom as non-domination. Impartial democratic institutions that reflect 'common, recognizable interests', political agreement, contestatory political processes and democratic channels are sufficient to protect rights (Pettit, 2000: 139). Legal constitutionalism replaces political processes, democratic self-rule and 'popular accountability', according to political constitutionalist theorists, with domination and 'arbitrary rule' by the elite (e.g. judicial review) (Bellamy, 2007: 280). For Bellamy, 'democracy is more important than constitutionalism, rights or the rule of law . . . because democracy embodies and upholds these values' (2007: 260). Brian Barry makes a similar argument that

> 'democracy' is to be understood in procedural terms . . . I reject the notion that one should build into 'democracy' any constraints on the content of

the outcomes produced . . . decision-making process is de facto affected by the preferences of the citizens but not in virtue of any constitutional rule. (1991: 3)

As opposed to only upholding constitutional rule, political constitutionalist theorists also advance other key elements. Electoral systems, executive scrutiny, competitive party politics, participatory channels and democratic law-making are necessary to maintain democracy.

I will principally engage in this chapter with political constitutionalist insights on the central role of democratic norms and processes in the framework of Muslim democracy. Greater emphasis is put on the quality of the democratic institutions by Bellamy and Pettit than on protection of liberal values. However, the expectation that the political processes will always uphold the rule of law and human rights even in established democracies is not totally realistic. The recent rise of populism, nationalism and illiberalism in the democracies of Europe and North America raises questions about their erstwhile robustness. The effectiveness of executive accountability, the electoral process and majority rule in sustaining democratic governance emerges in the foreground. Political constitutionalist arguments fall short in addressing the issue of the volatility of democracy or minority rights abuses.

A problem identified in compatibility-based arguments is the underestimation of the potential of dominant moral discourses to exert oppressive political power. Political constitutionalism provides important insights for a democratic constitution and deliberative processes. However, it cannot sufficiently address the existing majoritarian tendencies within the context of Muslim democracy. The next section will evaluate the effectiveness of legal constitutionalism in addressing the issues in compatibility-based arguments.

III. Legal Constitutionalism

Legal constitutionalism is centred on the conception of fundamental constitutional values and rights. Certain rights cannot be left unprotected from the will of the people even in societies with a comprehensive set of democratic rights endorsed by a significant number of citizens in mainstream political life. Pessimism about human nature in legal constitutionalism is in direct contrast with the optimism present in political constitutionalism (El-Affendi,

2009: 231). The idea of 'the tyranny of the majority' (Mill, 1859) influences the legal constitutionalism's protection of democracy. In addition, the existence of poorly informed and emotional citizens who can be manipulated by demagogues also anchors the legal constitutionalist position against the prospect of rule of majoritarianism.

As the elite theory of democracy concedes, democratic politics is, especially in extraordinary times, unpredictable and unstable. Volatility, for Stephen Holmes, is a general feature facing democratic systems. When there are no effective constitutional mechanisms to protect human rights, 'demagogues with paramilitary support who christen themselves "the representatives of the people"' can manipulate popular support, in times of economic and security crises, to oppress minorities and the opposition (Holmes, 1995: 9). Holmes also underlines the 'fragility of reason', society's 'inherent tendency to lapse into "group think"', and its 'debilitating passion' that 'will not conform to the dictates of reason and justice without constraint' (1995: 171, 267, 273, 274). To counterbalance this volatility, constitutional democracies possess non-voluntaristic forms of the rule of law. Non-negotiable constitutional norms are not based on popular will. Holmes is persuaded that liberal constitutions, conserving the wisdom of many generations, can 'help solve a whole range of political problems: tyranny, corruption, anarchy, immobilism, unaccountability, instability . . . the discretion of power-yielders . . . social chaos and private oppression' (1995: 6).

However, Holmes argues that legal constitutionalism is not antithetical, as political constitutionalism suggests, to the existence of a democratic public sphere and democratic political procedures. On the contrary, it requires such procedures, and here:

> Consent is meaningless without institutional guarantees of unpunished dissent. Popular sovereignty is unavailing without legally entrenched rules to organize and protect public debate. (Holmes, 1995: 171)

Constitutional mechanisms should preserve everyone's basic human rights, even though they may be at odds with certain norms and expectations of the majority. For instance, for legal constitutionalists, judicial review is 'a necessary supplement to democracy and [to] protect[ing] individual' and minority rights on a constitutional basis (Tezcür, 2007: 479). Judicial review has priority in democratic politics if and when a trade-off emerges between majoritarianism and human rights.

The constitution is the crucial sphere, noted in the above discussion, for addressing the concerns arising from compatibility-based arguments. In this matter, legal constitutionalism may be more conservative and less open to change with less citizen participation. Yet it is also more stable and robust in the wake of crises and less prone to human rights and minority abuses. This is even more applicable to developing democracies where democratic norms and institutions are unconsolidated. However, although they may be the remedy for populism, the elitist inclinations within legal constitutionalism, such as judicial review, may engender technocratic and universalising tendencies that also require critical scrutiny.

This chapter aims to contribute to the resolution of 'the tension between democracy and constitutionalism, between liberty and law, majority rule and legal limitations on power' (Wolin, 2016: 79). It will suggest an understanding of the constitution and legal framework, within the context of Muslim democracy, that holistically deals with key contested notions. The idea of a pluralist constitution will benefit from the examination of existing theories.

IV. Pluralising Constitutionalism

This chapter has so far examined contending constitutionalist theories. I will now proceed with a synthesis of these theories in formulating an idea of a constitution within the theoretical context of Muslim democracy. The current rise of far-right, nationalist populism is a reminder that, in the absence of constitutionally guaranteed rights, mob rule and authoritarianism pose a threat to actually existing democracies. To prevent this, democracy entitles the constitution to protect individual rights against the interference of political leaders and public opinion. Meanwhile, in democracies, constitutions ought to reflect the common good and shared national values as a result of the free and conscious consent of the people (Selçuk, 2010: 336).

A balance between human rights and popular will is necessary. Inalienable legal instruments, derived from legal constitutionalism and dynamic public processes, based on political constitutionalism, can coexist in a functional harmony. Members of the political community must engage to agree on the rules of their common lives. Additionally, the constitution protects the rights of everyone and guarantees that the agreed-upon shared rules do not disadvantage or discriminate against certain individuals. Pluralising constitutionalism also adopts, alongside these two dimensions, the multiculturalist critique of Western constitutionalism's universalist, difference-blind account of rights. Multiculturalists like Barzilai argue that Western constitutionalism's denial of communal needs restricts difference to the private sphere and rejects the significance of culture and religion for individuals as a source of 'constituting, articulating, and generating identities' and empowerment (2004: 24). Cultural and religious difference in societies with moral diversity is recognised by legal and institutionalist multiculturalists' advocacy of jurisdictional pluralism.

The section on pluralising constitutionalism will harmonise notions and arguments coming from legal constitutionalism and political constitutionalism as well as Muslim and multiculturalist political thought. Individual rights and freedoms, democratic law-making and jurisdictional demands of different group practices will be addressed in a democratic framework. Normative insights from the preceding chapters will be utilised in this section to conceptualise the three concepts of incontestable legal norms, democratic law-making and jurisdictional pluralism.

1. Incontestable Norms of the Constitution: The Absolute Protection of Minimal Human Rights

One of the key questions posed in this book is, how can individual freedoms and minority rights in a political theory of Muslim democracy be protected from the imposition of the comprehensive morality of the majority? The previous chapter addressed this question with reference to the ability of the reformative processes of social Islam to facilitate democratic political culture and political tolerance. It has also examined how the dynamic contestatory processes, inclusive of all segments of society, aid the internalisation of democratic norms. In addition, the chapter on pluralist secularism argued that democratic value change encompasses institutional democratisation. Such measures can include effective and open channels of participation accessible to everyone, and state guarantees for the capacity and autonomy of individuals for value formation. This chapter contends that institutions should seek to implement mechanisms safeguarding justice and equality at all times. The constitution is the most fundamental institution in democracies for the protection of liberty and conscience from discrimination or persecution. I will demonstrate that human and minority rights cannot be solely left to the outcome of public deliberation or the whims of the majority when democratic negotiations or developments are in deadlock.

Two considerations need to be clarified before proceeding further in the argument for the incontestable norms of a constitution within the Muslim democracy framework. First, 'many – not all! – Muslims' are *sharī'a*-minded and Muslim societies are more diverse, with non-Muslims, non-practising Muslims and nonconformist Muslims, than is often assumed (Berger, 2006: 335). Second, part of the Islamic moral tradition, as represented by modernist and progressive Muslim thinkers such as Abou El Fadl and al-Jabri, may be committed to the idea of human rights. However, mainstream opinion in Muslim societies, to a significant degree, does not necessarily espouse values such as freedom of expression, gender equality and moral pluralism, but favours conservative, paternalistic and stricter moral understandings. In light of the preceding considerations, the normative endorsement of democratic ideals in deeply conservative and ideologically polarised Muslim societies is quite challenging for the conceivable future. In these contexts, Tezcür provides a justification for constitutionalism:

> in Muslim majority countries, authoritative interpretations of Islam are not necessarily in liberal hands, the fear of the 'tyranny of the majority' seems to be very relevant. In the absence of constitutional and institutional limits on the legislature, Islamic democracy is most likely to decay into majority tyranny. (2007: 496)

This chapter will address the concern for the 'tyranny of the majority' within the context of Muslim democracy. I will focus on the process needed to foster democratic culture and institutional democratisation where constitutional provisions exist to guarantee the democratic benchmarks.

Constitutional democracies are grounded in non-contestable principles that maintain the rule of law and regulate democratic debates. I am interested in exploring these incontestable moral precepts in a democratic culture capable of maintaining equal participation, tolerance and pluralism. The discussion on secularism and the public sphere, in previous chapters, has affirmed that the foundations of the state should be premised on an idea of a thin morality grounded on inalienable human rights. This section will develop a minimalist understanding of universal human rights in the direction of the non-contestable normative background of constitutional provisions.

Minimalist conceptions of the state concur with Wael Hallaq's criticism of the modern state that its 'sovereignty represents an inner dialectic of self-constitution: sovereignty constitutes the state and is constituted by it' (2014: 158). Conversely, a Nozickean minimal state receives its legitimacy in enforcing law for the protection of political ideas of individual rights and liberties. This state's power is based on the authority of morality (Nozick, 1974: 52). Moral standards for assessing the legitimacy of governmental authority vary from contract to utility to traditional values (Simmons, 2001: 158, Binmore, 2000: 102). However, a discernible harmony between political democracy and conception of human rights is evident. Human rights appear to be the best possible means to limit manipulation, domination, oppression, or exploitation by state, religious and economic powers. Human rights discourses 'have become a common framework' and a foundation for democratic politics and for upholding the universal principles of justice and the rule of law (Goodhart, 2016: 5, 33). Consequently, I have illustrated a minimalist state, in contrast to an absolute state sovereignty model, that takes its moral authority from the conception of non-negotiable universal human rights in the Muslim democracy framework I am developing in this book.

I maintain that 'the basic human rights of the common moral minimalism' can constitute the departure point for Muslim democracy due to their political and non-foundationalist nature (Riley, 2012: 110). Human rights develop from political struggles for these rights in social processes. The contents of these rights, a product of political consensus, can be agreeable to members of a society. In other words, one can endorse the idea of human rights without adopting a specific value-substantive 'view about their foundations' (Beitz, 2013: 259; Langlois, 2016: 16). Political justifications for human rights can also avoid truth claims, thick moralities or instinctual values. From this position, the following conclusion arises:

> Human rights are not based upon any foundational moral spiritual facts about humans. Islamic, Christian, and secularist scholars who try to relate

human rights to foundational religious or moral systems are closer in their views to seventeenth-century natural law and natural right arguments than anything else. Such views are now largely an irrelevance. (Vincent, 2010: 223)

Despite the adoption of natural rights arguments by modernist and progressive Muslim scholars, this political notion of human rights has also found substantial support among them. Muslim thinkers have challenged the presumption of human rights being antithetical to Islam due to its perceived Judaeo-Christian foundation. Al-Jabri has argued that the universal basis of human rights transcends specific cultures (2009: 177). Abou El Fadl insists on a contextual reading of the Islamic texts that transforms the espousal of human rights into a religious duty (2003: 56). An-Na'im, on the other hand, has called for the reformation of the classical *sharī'a* in line with the universal standards of human rights (1987: 17). In essence, the existence of universal human rights as the non-contestable principles of the constitution parallels similar arguments in Muslim political thought.

Michael Ignatieff's theory of human rights is a pertinent example of how human rights can be understood in a minimalist fashion for universal applicability (2003: 54). Ignatieff has argued that there should be a universal, culturally transcendent political definition of human rights concerning negative liberties, namely the removal of obstacles. Human rights are located in a thin theory of the good by Ignatieff, for 'there are many differing visions of a good human life . . . the West's is only one of them', which should be considered in rights discourses (2003: 80). Ignatieff's conception of negative freedoms requires a state guarantee of basic human rights even against dominant philosophical and religious or cultural views. This account of human rights is more concerned with 'assumptions about the worst we can do, instead of hopeful expectations of the best' in forming inalienable legal rights (Ignatieff, 2003: 80). The minimalist human rights approach suggests that negative freedoms have a universal normative quality and should be subject to absolute constitutional guarantees. Positive liberties, on the other hand, develop within the context of political circumstances, social proccesses, and local engagement and interpretation. Collective deliberation on democratic values, associated with positive liberties, can result in commitments to toleration, pluralism and equality.

Mookherjee and Taylor reject the notion of universal reason, morality and the good. Their moral pluralist arguments suggest that people do not have to share the same conception of the good to agree on universal protection of human rights in a democracy. Taylor identifies 'a process of mutual learning' that leads to a 'fusion of horizons' through which 'the moral universe of the other becomes less strange' in democratic life (1999: 20). This can culminate in 'a [meaningful] world consensus on human rights' (Taylor, 1999: 45). Despite the intractable differences among diverse comprehensive world-views, Taylor believes a universally agreed constitutional protection of human rights is possible. If the list of human rights, in a thin theory, is kept short, they can be philosophically justified and legally enforceable on a universal basis (Taylor, 1999: 18–20).

In the framework that I propose for Muslim democracy, universal human rights does not rest on a metaphysical ontological basis. Citizens, motivated by different religious, moral, or philosophical systems, can reach a moral consensus on a political conception of human rights. A cross-cultural agreement is presented on incontestable moral norms on human dignity. These non-negotiable principles include freedom from torture, freedom from racial, gender and equivalent forms of discrimination, freedom of speech and conscience, and freedom of association and assembly. In addition, the arguments made by Taylor and Ignatieff for universal inalienable human rights allow the further theorising of the constitutional protection of human rights. Incontestable idealisations of human rights in this Muslim democracy framework also have a legal function as non-voluntaristic constitutional provisions. Non-negotiable constitutional norms of human rights would be the best mechanism to protect democracies from authoritarianism, unaccountability and oppression. I have argued here that a short list of inalienable human rights increases its potential as a legal instrument. In addition to the universal protection of human rights, I will now explore the ability of democratic law-making to critically engage with changing social and political conditions.

2. Democratic Law-making

The conception of a pluralising constitution incorporates the protection of rights from legal constitutionalism with less emphasis on its elitist tendency. Political constitutionalism can bring important insights about the improvement of democratic law-making through highlighting the problems created by an elitist conception of liberalism. Sheri Berman argues that democracy requires the simultaneous protection and upholding of both democratic procedures and liberal values. She acknowledges that without the legal protections liberalism provides democracy can easily 'slide into populism or majoritarianism' (Berman, 2017). However, Berman (2017) also critiques 'the increasingly common argument that liberalism can best be protected by constricting democracy'. Berman (2017) suggests that if ordinary people view institutions, elites and experts as inaccessible and unresponsive beyond the scope of their influence, 'the more likely they are to want to eliminate them'. Thus, she argues, 'unchecked liberalism' can easily slide into 'oligarchy or technocracy', a political condition that is no less democratically detrimental than populism (Berman, 2017). Along similar lines to Berman, Tully finds that Western constitutionalism imposed the 'imperial yoke, galling the necks of the culturally diverse citizenry' in the name of creating 'one national narrative' by 'excluding or assimilating all others' (Tully, 1995: 5, 7).

Universal moral standards of human rights and dignity, rather than elite or elitist mechanisms, in the Muslim democracy framework can mitigate the danger of unrestrained majority rule. Minimal human rights, universally agreed upon, are not considered antithetical to the idea of democratic law-making. Moreover, it is 'when human rights are modest standards [that] they leave most legal and policy matters open to democratic decision-making at the national and local levels' (Nickel, 2017). These minimal human rights provide general democratic principles while creating ample space to accommodate cultural and institutional variation in different national contexts. In other words, universally agreed-upon minimal human rights standards permit 'the different spiritual families' to have 'a voice in the determination of the rules by which they will live' in the relationship between religion and the state (Taylor, 2008: xii). This development is contingent on social contexts as they 'require different kinds of concrete realisation of agreed general [universal] principles' (Taylor, 2008: xvi–xvii).

Broad recognition of the constitution is generated by public deliberation agreeing on a political consensus, common good and national constitutional values. In democratic politics, all social actors with a viewpoint are expected to engage 'in the public dialogues and negotiations', based on principles of tolerance, reconciliation and respect, on issues that concern their lives (Tully, 2008a: 160). Tully criticises the imperial roots of the modern state and its racist discrimination against indigenous citizens (Tully, 1995: 6). This critique highlights the unitary state and the exclusive prerogatives it exercises over many functions, such as law-making. The constitution is the most important institution which requires to be democratised in Tully's arguments. Native subjects can engage in reforming the public and political space through their own identities and cultures in an increasingly democratic state (Tully, 2008a: 166).

Different models exist in the modern statist tradition. Parallels can be drawn between Tully's criticism of colonialism and political domination in the Muslim world. For instance, the invention of backward natives in hegemonic statist models is similar to the hierarchy created by imperial government. In the Muslim world, at the hands of the modernist agents of the state, rural, cultural religious social groups were often classified as backward natives in need of discipline and modernisation. The socially-engineering, homogenising and modernist tendencies of the modern state led to the formulation of a single law to the exclusion of other social actors. Democratic law-making, on the other hand, opens state institutions to citizens so they can exercise their own local agency for their reconstruction.

A constitution, drafted along the lines of political constitutionalism, reflects democratic inclusiveness and equality for all and improves the resolution of problems through a pluralistic ethos (Yazıcı, 2011: 267). The social public sphere provides mechanisms necessary for participation in a process of democratic law-making maintained by constitutional safeguards. 'Pluralising' is deliberately chosen to refer to the dynamic and progressive ability of the constitution to address social, political and economic challenges. In essence, the idea of a pluralising constitution proposes legal constraints to safeguard non-contestable constitutional rights, regardless of the views of the majority.

An account of thin morality with legal import, evidenced in instruments of democratic toleration, negative freedoms or basic human rights, contributes to the shared normative culture of a democratic system. Other matters in society with constitutional significance should be open to democratic public deliberation (Rahman, 1994: 94).

Constitutional provisions in democratic theorisations may vary from society to society. However, these provisions should be theorised to guarantee that no way of life is persecuted, political opposition is well-established, every citizen enjoys an equal share of rights and freedoms, and democratic channels are open. Constitutional guarantees in turn can maintain democratic law-making and accommodate different jurisdictional arrangements. Jurisdictional functions, the third instrument of pluralising constitution, will be conceptualised in the next section.

3. Jurisdictional Pluralism for Groups in Private Law

Secularist and paternalistic tendencies are particularly manifested by the modern state in the relationship between religion and law. Wael Hallaq attributes the exclusive exercise of power to a type of law in which

> the modern state is systemically and systematically geared towards the transformation and homogenisation of both the social order and the national citizen, features that have a direct bearing on law. (2010: 142)

However, the majority of Muslim thinkers examined in this work join Bulaç in arguing that '[f]or a Muslim, the desire to live according to the divine law [*sharī'a*] never diminishes' (1998: 177). A Pew Research Centre survey in thirty-nine countries, measuring Muslims' support for *sharī'a* law, showed that a majority in twenty-six of these countries favoured *sharī'a* as the main source of legislation and believed it should be implemented for Muslim people as official public law. When asked about the specific issue of private *sharī'a* in the domestic civil sphere, support was considerably higher in those thirty-nine countries (Lugo et al., 2013). Even in Western states, studies show that a substantial number of Muslims bring family and financial disputes to informal *sharī'a* arbitration (Turner, 2011: 320). Such data demonstrate that *sharī'a* has undeniable importance for Muslims as 'the source of a religiously sanctioned normative system' to 'organise human acts into various categories, ranging from the moral to the legal' (An-Naʿim: 1999: 29; Hallaq, 2010: 145). While all the Muslim thinkers examined in the first chapter acknowledge the importance of recognising the public role of *sharīʿa*, most emphasised the necessity for a democracy with different public institutional frameworks to fulfil this task.

However, 'there is no unified democratic theory on religious accommodation', according to Nancy L. Rosenblum, that would also address *sharīʿa*-driven demands (2000: 9). She argues that 'the difficult normative task of drawing the proper bounds of democracy and religion, and justifying accommodation' is beyond any sound resolution in political theory (Rosenblum, 2000: 4). Nonetheless, academic scholarship, most notably the multiculturalist literature, in the last two decades has expanded the scope of political theory to tackle religious accommodation. Increased attention to religiously-motivated everyday life under democratic structures by multiculturalist theorists like Shachar and Bader, discussed elsewhere in this book, has led to a rethinking of policies for religious and cultural diversity. Followers of organised faiths with distinct accounts of the good life and societal needs require different multicultural techniques of accommodation at the level of state–society relations. In this section, the treatment of the free exercise of religion and autonomy for religious groups in the context of jurisdiction contributes to this expansion in political theory.

Christiano observes that, 'while democracy has a kind of intrinsic value, citizens also attempt to realize their differing conceptions of justice within the context of a democratic society' (2012: 231). This raises the long-debated question of what citizens' rights and obligations are when the outcome of democratic decision-making conflicts with their account of the good and what justice requires in law and policy. To address this issue, I will examine which methods of accommodation could be developed to address substantial and irreconcilable comprehensive moral differences. Complex institutional mechanisms are required to move from the unitary, homogenising nation-state paradigm to a more pluralist and sophisticated paradigm.

Rowan Williams (2008), the former Archbishop of Canterbury, acknowledges the diverse nature of religious life in today's world while criticising the modern state's failure to recognise it. The liberal, secular state exclusively defined a universal account of citizenship and legitimate structure of law.

Williams (2008) suggests that democracies should recognise that people do have multiple affiliations and various forms of belonging, whether political, religious or cultural. For Muslims, argues Williams (2008), God is the ultimate source of justice, and *sharīʿa* sets certain moral obligations and limits to human action in living an ethical life. Accordingly, inhibiting Muslims' connection with *sharīʿa* would limit their autonomy for their professed version of the good life. Abou El Fadl also observed that a Muslim would 'feel torn between his duties toward the public order and God' in secular systems (2014: xlix).

Williams (2008) joins Shachar in his advocacy of enabling Muslims in democracies to abide by their comprehensive religious views in their lives. Democratic recognition of religion would require a formal inclusion of different normative and legal systems when dealing with the everyday lives of the citizenry. Religions like Islam and Judaism, with their own jurisdictional codes, would require inclusive legal methods (Shachar, 2009: 120). Western and Muslim scholars have debated whether Islamic legal norms should be accorded legal recognition by the modern state. Institutionalist and legal pluralists, as well as Muslim revivalists, argue that justice and equality in morally diverse societies require pluralist institutional mechanisms in jurisdictional matters.

Jurisdictional pluralism has been discussed at length in the chapter on multiculturalism with reference to religiously-based collective demands in a well-developed institutional structure. The topic of jurisdictional pluralism is addressed, as part of the minority rights discourse, in the context of established Western democracies. Among Muslims in the West, 'applying and enforcing sharīʿa is mostly a matter of voluntary willingness to submit to these rules', which fits with the ideals of democratic associationalism (Berger, 2013: 14). The private jurisdictional freedoms discussed by theorists of multiculturalism 'are mostly outside the scope of legislation in Western countries' (Berger, 2013: 11). Thus, the recognition of jurisdictional pluralism as part of democratic politics takes place where Muslim minorities, lacking historical claims, often do not exercise power within the state. Multiculturalist theorists suggest democratic mechanisms and norms to sustain the necessary conditions for jurisdictional pluralism based on social unity, inclusive communication and a strong commitment to human rights. Formal accommodation of religious law also works as (i) a protection of vulnerable insiders such as women in Muslim minorities by awarding official status to informal *sharīʿa* practices, and (ii) a stipulation for Muslim populations to accept democracy in return for the recognition of their jurisdictional claims (Kalanges, 2014: 280).

Within the context of Muslim democracy, certain aspects of *sharīʿa* generate challenges. These challenges are most evident in the debates about the position of *sharīʿa* in constitutions. In Muslim-majority societies, practices of *sharīʿa* gain recognition through individual and associational freedoms, and political or ideological claims about state and society. Another challenge concerns how not to favour one particular interpretation of *sharīʿa*, upheld by the dominant religious group or majority, in jurisdictional arrangements to undermine or suppress minority views (Emon, 2008: 259). Balancing religious freedoms with fundamental human rights is a task fraught with difficulties. One of the main tasks of Muslim democracy is to manage these two challenges in a balance between accepting religion in public life and staving off religious hegemony. The rest of this section will continue addressing these concerns through the further elaboration of jurisdictional pluralism.

My examination of Muslim political thought identified the problematics of instituting *sharīʿa* as a formal code of law. Modernists and progressives have explained that enforcement of law using divine authority will often be based on one school of jurisprudence or a state's own interpretation of *sharīʿa* to the exclusion of other interpretations. *Sharīʿa*, according to An-Naʿim, 'means different things to different people [in different times and contexts], even amongst practising Muslims' (1987: 334). Al-Jabri also distinguishes between *sharīʿa*, the absolute and divine truth, and its contingent and relative understanding by imperfect humans. Al-Jabri, like Abou El Fadl and An-Naʿim, perceives the world as a test of understanding religious ideals and of putting them into practice. Thus, he insists that a full application of *sharīʿa*, not expected by God, is utopian (al-Jabri 2009: 94).

Religious conviction can only be meaningful, An-Naʿim argues, when there is a free choice between belief and disbelief as well as freedom in interpretation and practice. Therefore, the constitutionalisation of *sharīʿa* would stifle human autonomy and the rational ability to understand the divine and reflect upon it spiritually and materially (An-Naʿim, 2008: 3–4). Public *sharīʿa* is 'both morally indefensible and practically impossible to maintain today' (An-Na'im, 1987: 318). An-Na'im explains that *sharī'a* cannot provide constitutional law, due to its divine nature, for both public and private as 'the legal system of each country . . . is an articulation of the political will of the state, and not [based] on the will of God' (An-Na'im, 2002a: 20).

Similar to progressive Muslim scholars, the institutionalist pluralists, belonging to the strand of multiculturalism, reject augmenting the authority of existing social elites. Bader argues against 'prescribing definitive specified institutions' that create a 'rigid' and 'inflexible' system with unaccountable power given to the leadership of religious groups (2003a: 285). Codification of *sharī'a* rules, inconsistent with its divine nature, may make it prone to exploitation by clerical and state authorities. A monopoly over *sharī'a* would then ensue. For instance, dissenting views contrary to the codified version of *sharī'a* could be labelled apostasy and criminalised. As such, the constitutionalisation of *sharī'a* risks fostering authoritarian leadership of religious or customary authorities that infringe the rights of individual group members. Ziauddin Sardar (2013) rightly observes that constitutionalising *sharī'a* would be 'a recipe for inviting dissent, inevitable disaster, and a clear attempt at suppressing diversity and plurality'.

Overall, Muslim democracy, conceptualised in this book, incorporates *sharī'a* in jurisdictional terms involving semi-public/private realms rather than its constitutionalisation. My reservations with this stance are twofold. First, codification of *sharī'a* at the hands of a formal institution, due to its divine nature, is normatively problematic. Second, attempts at constitutionalisation of *sharī'a* would create authoritarian power structures undermining Muslim democracy on institutional, societal and normative levels. I will now argue that the solution to the voluntary acceptance of Islamic comprehensive moral doctrines in a democracy should be jurisdictional pluralism instead of Islamic democracy or orthodox liberalism.

Although *sharī'a* is not intended to be positive law, it remains a source of normative ideals and 'a code of conduct for the everyday life of the Muslim' (Berger, 2006: 2; 2014: 223). Thus, unlike public *sharī'a*, the democratic accommodation of '[p]rivate sharia of family law and devotional rites', An-Na'im insists, is a personal right and freedom (1987: 318). Interpretation and social functions of private *sharī'a*, a source of comprehensive normative authority, must be left to civil society forces to prevent its enforcement by religious or state legal authorities (An-Na'im, 2008: 6–10). According to An-Na'im, the *sharī'a*'s 'proper positive and enlightening role in the lives of Muslims and Islamic societies' necessitates the institutional separation of Islam and the state (2008: 4).

According to jurisdictional pluralism, within the context of Muslim democracy, *sharī'a* is brought into play in jurisdictional terms involving semi-public/private law. Shachar broadly defines jurisdictional pluralism as a regulated, interactive and co-operative arrangement among different jurisdictional mechanisms (2008: 147). It is based on 'shared responsibility and obligations', grounded in an interaction between 'an uneasy amalgam of secular and religious traditions' (Shachar, 2009: 138). In the Muslim democracy framework, jurisdictional pluralism is a form of private conflict resolution that accommodates religious and cultural claims with distinct legal implications. Limited executive government and extended associational freedoms of the civil society demarcate the sphere of separate jurisdictional authorities. Co-ordination between the state and cultural and religious jurisdictions would permit an autonomous place for social groups in private law.

Jurisdictional pluralism within the Muslim democracy framework is not limited to *sharī'a*, but includes all normative cultural and religious systems present in a society. Social groups with cultural and religious identities can form their own civil society associations and apply to formalise their arbitration procedures. Implementation of *sharī'a* through arbitration, rather than legal pluralist arrangements of alternative courts or legislation, would provide a democratic accommodative method. The voluntary basis of arbitration permits the adherence to *sharī'a* through individual volition and conviction and prevents its imposition by a coercive force. This institution of private conflict resolution can minimise the political manipulation of religion and prevent Islamic moral doctrines from being imposed on citizens.

In arbitration, individuals opt for and agree on terms of private dispute resolution on the basis of previously set provisions and rules of jurisdictional pluralism. Religious experts and scholars, members of civil society organisations, can act as impartial third-party arbitrators on issues of private law. Civil society institutions play a part in the settlement of private law issues alongside the state courts. Litigants are not limited to a certain tribunal on the basis of their ethnic, religious or cultural belongings. They can appeal to an institution of arbitration, from among those available, motivated by the objective of obtaining the judgment that best serves their interests (Shachar, 2008: 124). The possibility exists that

> these institutions, known as *sharī'a* boards, courts, councils or tribunals, may be integrated into the formal judiciary system (as is the case in Greece) ... or may operate between formal and informal domains by means of arbitration (as in the United Kingdom and, until 2007, in Ontario, Canada). (Berger, 2013: 14)

My treatment of arbitration's general legal framework is guided by the assumption that institutional proposals are only made about the existing contexts of each society (Shachar, 2009: 133–4).[1]

Although participation in arbitration is voluntary, adhering to the procedure and outcome is binding if the two parties agree. The state, without any moral content, is an impartial mediator between opposing parties and safeguards their human rights and individual autonomy. For instance, in family law matters, '[the] couple voluntarily delegates jurisdiction over their marriage to a chosen religious institution', 'which would apply religious law' that conforms to minimal norms of universal human rights (Crane, 2005: 1253). In other words, arbitration is only subject to state intervention if fundamental human rights and freedoms are threatened. Where parties feel disadvantaged or discriminated against, the appeal to state courts exists and a court has the authority to overrule a decision of arbitration.

Measures can be introduced to safeguard the autonomy and rights of vulnerable members. Mechanisms should be provided for citizens to choose between religious and secular jurisdictions and to mitigate peer group pressure within communities to follow religious law. Shachar outlines the democratic checks and balances and state supervision in jurisdictional pluralist arrangements. Family law issues have two functions: demarcation and distribution. Religious authorities may determine the demarcating aspects, to regulate marital status, but state law supersedes religious law in issues regarding distributive aspects (Shachar, 2009: 119–21). Distinct characteristics and values of the family according to a given religion should be protected while ensuring implementation of the universal value of equality (e.g. distribution of assets and duties) (Shachar, 2009: 130).

On the other hand, Mohammad Fadel claims that some Muslims would voluntarily prefer to depart from the principle of equality to follow traditional rules of Islamic law. Fadel suggests that the willingness of women to take half of their male relatives' share, given the legal right to take the equal amount, should be treated as a matter of personal choice (2007: 4). In liberalism, he asserts, the voluntary and rational opting out from the equality principle for non-egalitarian outcomes is evaluated under personal autonomy as long as citizens are not coerced by an authority (Fadel, 2007: 3). Individuals within religious and cultural communities can therefore choose to exercise their autonomy by self-consciously opting for a life that may confine their constitutional rights and freedoms. Revisions, however, can be introduced to certain aspects of traditional constructions of *sharī'a* for the moral recognition of other, universal human rights, and a shared commitment to pluralism and diversity. The normative basis of jurisdictional pluralism should be democratic toleration. A sizeable number of citizens should internalise democratic toleration for democracy to function. Negative freedoms and basic human rights are to be protected and legally enforced in a society.

Sharī'a as '"higher law" exists, highlighted by the multiculturalism literature, both "above" and "below" state constitutions and legislation' even if it has unofficial status or remains underground (Rosenblum, 2000: 5). The notion of jurisdictional pluralism acknowledges that *sharī'a* is a collective demand for Muslim populations. Rights and freedoms divided into separate jurisdictional domains are capable of accommodating *sharī'a*-driven needs and claims in the public sphere. This framework promotes identity group interests and provides adequate and practical guarantees of basic human rights and democratic standards (Bader: 1996: 606). When the political and legal requirements of a constitutional democracy are firmly in place, protection of the rights of religious and cultural minorities is possible with a degree of judicial and institutional independence. The most effective solution for citizens who voluntarily follow *sharī'a*-inspired accounts of the good life in a democracy is jurisdictional pluralism rather than Islamic democracy or orthodox liberalism. A more normative approach, using jurisdictional pluralism, can be undertaken to conceptualise the relations between democracy and religion on the one hand and religious accommodation on the other.

V. Conclusion: Pluralising Constitutionalism

Achieving a balance between the principles of majority rule and protection of human rights is a necessary task facing Muslim societies. The urgent issue surrounding the prospect of a pluralistic democratic system in Muslim societies is located in a context where: (i) different interpretations and schools of Islam reside with un-Islamic and non-Islamic ways of life; (ii) comprehensive Islamic moral views have political and public claims; and (iii) institutions are not robust enough to maintain democratic benchmarks. In these cases, vulnerability and fragility of electoral democracies are present, and

> no matter how free and fair the elections and no matter how large the government's majority, democracy must also have a constitution that itself is democratic in that it respects fundamental liberties and offers considerable protections for minority rights. (Stephen, 2000: 39)

The potential problem of dominant moral discourses exerting oppressive political power has to be addressed at the constitutional level through a commitment to a comprehensive set of democratic principles. Constitutional guarantees of equal rights, equality of treatment before the law, mechanisms to check the executive, and separation of powers strengthen democracies. The potential problem of dominant moral discourses exerting oppressive political power has to be addressed at the constitutional level through a comprehensive set of democratic principles.

This chapter has drawn on legal constitutionalism and political constitutionalism to conceptualise the constitution within the Muslim democracy framework. Legal constitutionalism underlines the importance of legal protections and the limiting of some aspects of constitutional debate in order to protect inalienable rights for all. Political constitutionalism suggests that constitutional provisions are applied in a democracy to achieve a consensus about the common good. A pluralising constitution, conceptualised in this book, has three key principles: legally-enforced inalienable human rights, democratic law-making and jurisdictional pluralism. The conception of pluralising constitution affirms the existence of social, cultural and political particularities in a constitution. However, some non-negotiable norms for domestic protection of human rights are present in constitutional democracies. When civic relationships, democratic toleration and public negotiations erode or break down, 'human rights are important [legal] instruments for the vulnerable to protect themselves against exploitation and harm from powerful actors, particularly the state' (Chan, 2014: 197). Non-contestable norms in the conception of pluralising constitution aim to prevent the worst abuses of rights and balance this task with the needs and demands of today to aspire to the ideal application. Universal human rights serve as the incontestable moral background of a constitution. They provide safeguards against unlimited state power and arbitrary majority rule, generated by legal constitutionalism, and respect the democratic law-making and jurisdictional pluralism advocated by democratic constitutionalism and multiculturalism.

Note

1. In Muslim-majority countries like Turkey, Indonesia, Kazakhstan and Lebanon *sharī'a* is not constitutionalised, while in societies such as Pakistan, Iran and the Maldives it is a primary source of the constitution (Ahmed and Gouda, 2014: 51). The issue of jurisdictional pluralism would take an entirely different route in these two clusters of countries, as well as in each specific country, on the basis of already existing institutional designs.

GENERAL CONCLUSION TO PART THREE: THE CONCEPTUALISATION OF MUSLIM DEMOCRACY

Although there have been previous attempts to develop a conception of Muslim democracy, they fall short of offering systematic political theories. This book attempts to fill this gap by providing a cross-cultural theoretical approach to Muslim democracy. Part III has conceptualised Muslim democracy with the aim of accommodating public Islamic claims more effectively than liberal and republican models by adapting existing normative principles of democracy. I have reinterpreted 'a whole constellation of concepts relevant to democratic theorizing' such as human rights, democratic tolerance, civil society, public sphere and law (Browers, 2006: 8). An alternative perspective on the compatibility of Islam and democracy debate has been formulated through a systematic theorising of Muslim democracy without shying away from addressing the tensions present in democratic theorising. Thus, this project begins from the position that Islam and democracy are compatible rather than ending with it.

The argument for Muslim democracy in this book has addressed the tensions revolving around minority rights, personal freedoms, human rights and religious morality. Stumbling blocks towards developing normative commitments to democracy have been identified and examined. Diverse viewpoints brought into a productive dialogue to create a new framework are capable of balancing democratic principles and Islamic practices. A systematic treatment of three key areas are crucial in my theorisation of

Muslim democracy: secularism, the public sphere and the constitution. I have assessed the two most important models or theories, in each of these areas, followed by the proposal of an alternative model that integrates their respective strengths. As a result, this part of the book has reconstructed the liberal democratic notions of secularism, public sphere and constitutionalism. The roles and functions of these institutions have been redefined for the pluralistic accommodation of religion within predominantly Muslim contexts. Muslim democracy is a normative discourse that engages institutions (pluralist secularism), interactions (social public sphere) and rights (constitutional provisions).

Pluralist secularism offers a theoretical account of the institutional underpinning of Muslim democracy. It advances a new form of secularism that is applicable to Muslim societies by allowing the relationship between religion and state to reach an amicable settlement with democracy. The state's impartiality towards all normative systems can be guaranteed through its moral minimalist character. While comprehensive moral and ideological systems are separate from the state, the political implications of citizens' different accounts of morality and the good life are acknowledged. In other words, religious authority, absolutist truths and divine morality are institutionally dissociated from government while admitting references to comprehensive moral doctrines in politics.

The idea of a morally minimalist state introduces the distinction between civil society politics and the government: respectively, the social public sphere and the state public sphere. The social public sphere is a distinct form of political public sphere for the activities of civil society politics. A unique space is occupied by the social public sphere, relative to other democratic public spaces, due to its capacity to adapt to the role of religion in civil society. Awareness of the state's limitations in dealing with the communal experience also grants considerable space to the social public sphere. In the idea of Muslim democracy, religious claims arising from the freedom of conscience, rather than religious authority, are considered to be legitimate sources of public policy-making. Muslims are given accessibility in the social public sphere and autonomy to follow, through their own moral and rational motives, Islam as a comprehensive moral view. Yet no comprehensive moral doctrine can exert social or political influence on people who do not voluntarily accede to it.

The idea of balancing rights with normative differences and personal freedoms has in turn led to the designation of collective rights. Some administrative duties are to be shared between secular state institutions and non-state organisations to achieve this objective. As a form of multicultural accommodation, collective rights also include granting institutional and jurisdictional functions to religious and cultural groups. In this model, *sharī'a* belongs to the domain of the activities of civil society associations which people voluntarily join.

Systematic changes fall within the scope of pluralist secularism in democratic theorising. Yet democratic development also needs normative change and bottom-up construction that should engender a shared moral consent to democracy. This value change is discussed in Chapter 5, accompanied by attention to the transformation of forms, values and interactions towards the principles of democracy. The conceptualisation of social Islam demonstrates the processes through which Muslim communities understand their relationship with other citizens in the context of a modern pluralist society. Social Islam is a moral imperative for change from doctrinally-based non-democratic religious thought and practice towards civility, negotiation, compromise, toleration and pluralism. How political religious participation can be democratic is also conceptualised. The notion of democratic toleration further contributes to value change for the establishment of the normative foundation of the social public sphere. Although people may espouse different and even conflicting philosophical or moral truths in constitutional democracies, they can still agree on the shared good and form an overlapping consensus in politics (Fadel, 2013b: 1267).

Orientalist approaches to Islam have argued that democratic government and the public sphere cannot emerge in the Muslim world due to the totalising nature of Islam (Gellner, 1992; 1997). However, the section on the social public sphere proposed the argument that Muslims with diverse Islamic comprehensive moral doctrines can develop democratic toleration and reach an understanding of the shared good. The social public sphere is the space where people can meaningfully engage with both deeply-held religious beliefs and democratic values. The chapter on the social public sphere discussed how consensus on value change to internalise democratic norms and moral commitment to the democratic political community can be developed. In essence, social Islam demonstrates how Muslims are capable of simultaneous commitment to *sharīʿa* and pluralism and democracy

Democracy can emerge in an environment where governmental structures and collective moral understandings evolve in a more pluralist and inclusive direction. Such changes find normative support in institutions and interactions with democratic significance addressed by political theory. In addition, neither secularism nor the public sphere can fulfill the demands of pluralism without constitutional safeguards of rights, including human rights, individual rights and minority rights. In a democracy, a constitution ensures open access to opportunities for independent value formation, free public debate, and diverse public mechanisms among all citizens. The final chapter, in this part of the book, has addressed the conceptualisation of a pluralising constitution. Thick standards of the good and the reasonable are not accepted in this account of a pluralising constitution. Societies can agree on thin, universal normative benchmarks of rights and their universal protection. Despite the consensus of the majority, non-voluntaristic constitutional guarantees for justice and human rights need to be in place irrespective of religious, ethnic, cultural, political or ideological identities, or socio-economic status, gender, sexual orientation or physical abilities. In addition, as opposed to the elitism within legal constitutionalism, a pluralising constitution defends the democratic functions of law-making. Shared platforms for well-informed debates are guaranteed by a pluralising constitution for all sections of society.

However, constitutions in morally diverse societies can still be unable to reliably address the moral and political needs of the entire citizenry. Clauses on the sharing of jurisdictional power with other authorities in the form of arbitration powers may be introduced to a democratic constitution. Private *sharīʿa*, a comprehensive moral view, can here have a jurisdictional role to allow voluntary compliance among followers to pursue an ethical life. In this context, recognising the importance of *sharīʿa* to Muslim people does not mean the state is obligated to recognise or promote a single account of religious norms and values. Rather, the individual's right to collective cultural and religious practice is acknowledged and protected. The functions of *sharīʿa* are limited to certain aspects of private law at the hands of civil society associations. In the Muslim democracy framework, *sharīʿa* arbitration is one available option for the resolution social issues. It can greatly contribute to fortifying the norm of democratic toleration as well as diminishing the demands for the enactment of *sharī'a* in the form of an Islamic state.

The discussion on pluralist secularism, the social public sphere and the pluralising constitution has illustrated the necessary institutions and rights of a proposed Muslim democracy. These three formative components of the Muslim democracy mutually complement, reinforce and maintain one another. I have argued that democracy can only function when it is allied with the institutionalisation of political reforms on the level of governance. Social internalisation of democratic values at the mass level supports a democracy's endurance. Therefore, the idea of transformativeness consists of value and institutional change and a synthesis of norms. Religious interpretations, society and the state can change over time in a dynamic and multi-faceted relationship. An epistemological hierarchy implied in the binary relationship between Islam and liberal democracy is avoided in the conception of transformativeness. This hierarchy is challenged through a reversal of the argument in which liberal democracy is instead questioned about its capacity to accommodate culture and religion, namely Muslims' private and public goods, rights, needs and demands.

The idea of principled change has three facets: institutional, religious and social. The development of formal democratic institutions should also parallel bottom-up civil society activities motivated by value change. Once institutions such as the constitution are in place, they create and expand democratic channels to enable citizens to actively engage with them in civic participation and policy-making. Constant public deliberation contributes to the pluralism of institutions. Public negotiation also ensues over the roles and functions of religion in politics towards transformations of values and norms. As such, civility, equality and democratic toleration can be internalised among people in society and serve as the normative consensus of the political community.

The various accounts of pluralist secularism, social public sphere and pluralising constitutionalism contain arguments from both multiculturalism and Muslim political thought. A political theory of Muslim democracy has access to a wide range of arguments and principles from these three formative components. Pluralist secularism provides spaces for the formation of social Islam and democratic toleration. Social Islam and democratic toleration can lay down the foundations for sustaining pluralist secularism. The appearance of moral consent for democracy guarantees the institutional development and deepening of democracy. Constitutional safeguards guarantee the maintenance and success of democratic channels to include a wider body of citizens. In this model, institutional changes are supported with normative change, and constitutional safeguards protect the social conditions for these transformations to take place. I have drawn on the arguments and principles of pluralist secularism, social public sphere and pluralising constitutionalism to address the dilemmas facing the political theorising of Muslim democracy. The prospect emerges from this approach, motivated by a commitment to uphold individual rights, for the coexistence of public religiosity and the principles of democracy.

CONCLUSION

I. Theorising Muslim Democracy within the Context of Muslim and Multiculturalist Political Thought

Since the nineteenth century, Muslim discourses have debated whether and how constitutional democracy can be incorporated in their political settings without abandoning Islamic identity. The search for democracy was concerned with discovering solutions to modern political predicaments in the Muslim world through new yet Islamic approaches. Political struggles between the twentieth and twenty-first centuries have witnessed a shift in priorities in the Muslim world 'from identity to democracy' (Kassab, 2009: 145). Relativist claims of cultural and religious authenticity have decreased in significance, Elizabeth Kassab noting that

> democracy and individual liberties have become immensely vital for the very preservation and promoting of life, rather than being a question of imitation, whether one is like or not like the West, as was the prominent concern in the first half of the century. (2009: 145)

If 'the modern political consciousness favours any universal political form, it is constitutional democracy' today (Wolin, 2016: 78). Opposition to state tyranny, authoritarianism, abuse of power, modern inequalities and injustice involves 'the network of concepts that accompanied the coming of the modern state: constitutionalism, law, rights, and democracy' (El Amine, 2016: 108). Muslims across the world, following this trend, strongly desire democracy with an 'Islamic' character. However, Muslim-majority countries suffer from severe democratic deficits. The debate on 'Muslim democracy' was initially generated by studies on contemporary Turkey, which enjoyed broad recognition in the first decade of the twenty-first century. Other countries in the MENA region were to follow the ostensibly successful implementation of a Muslim democracy. However, not long after the Arab uprisings, authoritarianism has been strengthened in the region. The previously celebrated model of Muslim democracy is now considered to be at risk of falling into the categories of 'liberalised authoritarianism', 'electoral authoritarianism', 'majoritarian democracy', or 'unconsolidated democracy' (Cesari, 2014: xv; Pishchikova and Young, 2016: 44).

Doubts exist over the pragmatist and instrumentalist nature of Muslim democracy derived from the Turkish model. Democratic experimentation has demonstrated that democratisation will not come from a 'practical synthesis' of electoralisation, moderation and opportunism (Nasr, 2005: 15, 13). If there is one crucial lesson the Turkish model offers to the Muslim world, I believe it is that democratisation has to incorporate the principles of democracy; hence, it has to be derived from 'the realm of theory' not that of 'pragmatism' (Nasr, 2005: 25). The principled adoption of the values of democracy is central to the struggles waged by Muslims for democratisation. Reconceptualising democracy, through a reformulation of its normative and institutional contents, can thus make a more effective contribution to democratisation in the Muslim world. Therefore, the search for the future of democracy can be found in a political theory that addresses the cluster of concepts contained in previous chapters.

This book has argued that extant studies of Muslim democracy lack the normative rigour associated with a political theory approach. The contemporary literature does not offer systematic and well-developed theories to address entrenched social, political, normative and institutional problems in Muslim societies. Aziz al-Azmeh finds:

> Democracy as propounded in much of current Arab political discourse is generally endowed with a virtually talismanic quality, as a protean force

capable, when meaningfully put into practice, of solving all outstanding problems. (1994: 114)

As regards the discourse on Islam and democracy, Azmeh goes on to argue that it 'yields a circular notion of democracy as a self-sustaining form of historical and political miracle-making' (1994: 115). Democracy risks becoming the signifier for anything and everything, falling under the mantra of 'better governance', emptied of its normative content and significance. My line of inquiry in this book has focused on conceptualising democracy to demystify the talismanic quality it has been given. I have interpreted a range of concepts through the three interrelated frameworks of pluralist secularism, the social, plural public sphere, and pluralising constitutionalism. An epistemological pluralism has been adopted to formulate Muslim democracy.

This book began with a series of typologies examining concepts and issues relevant to democratic theory, followed by the formulation of a political theory of Muslim democracy in the final part. In the first part, I focused on Muslim political thought and multiculturalism. The first chapter engaged with a typology of Muslim political thought. I identified the relevant notions for a democratic theory and examined the tensions hindering the development of a political theory approach to Muslim democracy. In the second chapter, I examined multiculturalism's capacity to reconcile democracy with religion for the purpose of expanding the liberal democratic paradigm for more pluralistic ends. The typologies formulated in this book consisted of using heuristic devices to explore connections and overlaps between the Western political thought and Islamic political thought. I intended to contest the 'very accuracy and usefulness' of Western versus non-West binaries to view 'not only to critical points of engagement and commonality between them' but also complex differences and heterogeneity within each tradition (Euben, 2010: 260; 1997: 34). New developments and previously unexamined connections among secularism, the public sphere and law emerged as a result of these examinations. Comparisons between these two genres of political thought created the opportunity to identify categories for conceptualising a theory of Muslim democracy.

Pro-democratic thinking within Muslim discourses was examined in the third chapter. Compatibility-based arguments on Islam and democracy by

Muslim thinkers were identified. This critical exercise highlighted the theoretical reductionism present in Islamic political thought. The efforts of compatibility-based arguments to tailor democracy to fit an Islamic theological imperatives revealed considerable limitations. I arrived at the conclusion that a paradigm shift from theological to political perspectives can offer a principled perspective on the relationship between democratic governance and Islamic norms.

I understand Muslim democracy to be a dialogical mode of political theorising. In the final part, I have brought together different strands of political thought into a productive dialogue. An alternative was formulated to orthodox liberal theories and compatibility-based Islamic democracy arguments. The comparative political theory approach employed in this book enabled the incorporation of recent developments in Muslim political thought and multiculturalism. Certain notions of liberalism and constitutionalism were also adopted to develop a set of normative values and commitments within a theoretical framework. A cluster of concepts, the outcome of this line of inquiry, includes pluralist secularism, the social public sphere and pluralist constitutionalism for Muslim-majority contexts. The theory of Muslim democracy reconciles religious faith and protection of human rights through a robust commitment to pluralism in the public sphere and at constitutional level.

In Chapter 4, I developed a conception of pluralist secularism to address the institutional aspects generated by theorising Muslim democracy. I reinterpreted the scope of authority, roles and bounds of the state, the public sphere, and civil society. Pluralist secularism aims to accommodate plural and conflicting theories of the good under a morally minimalist state structure. A comprehensive theory of the good derived from religion can and does provide justifications for the social and political actions of citizens. Religious traditions, constructed in specific historical contexts, possess authority that remains persuasive to their adherents. The beliefs, practices and institutions of religious communities thus constitute an essential ground for societal life in Muslim societies. In this book, however, the conceptualisation of Muslim democracy does not situate democracy on thick transcendental and metaphysical foundations. On the basis of a thin political morality, pluralist secularism engages with metaphysical claims and demands in politics while ensuring state neutrality. To this end, private and public life are connected, on the one hand, and the state public sphere and civil society public sphere are separated on the other. I have deliberately formulated pluralist secularism against both philosophical secularism, which transgresses religious freedoms, and the notion of an Islamic state, which contravenes personal liberties. A political culture of toleration, pluralism, diversity, human rights, deliberation, contestation and moral equality can arise from such a political theory.

In the fifth chapter, the distinction between social public sphere and state public sphere aims to provide Muslims and other citizens with the resources to pursue their own conceptions of the good. Institutional differentiation creates a much-needed distance between the internal mechanisms of social groups and the coercive instruments of the state. In addition, plural public institutions are necessary to create spaces for Muslims to develop and maintain their norms without their imposition on others. I identified and elaborated in this chapter the conceptions of transformativeness, social Islam, democratic toleration and institutional pluralism. These conceptions enable Muslims and their fellow citizens to learn and develop democratic norms in a process of value change. I believe democratisation at the practical level in Muslim societies can arise through the creation of democrats. The particular conception of the social public sphere here seeks to account for novel religious values and practices with a democratic ethos. A self-critical re-appraisal of Islam can occur alongside the internalisation of norms such as democratic tolerance in the social public sphere.

Pluralising constitutionalism, in the final chapter, conceives of a new relationship between religion and democratic governance. In situations of conflicting moral interests, individual believers have a right to institutional and jurisdictional pluralism via civil society associations within which they are voluntarily members. The conception of pluralising constitutionalism proposes to improve the collective dimensions of cultural and religious life while also protecting individual agency and capacity. Legal enforcement of basic human rights and negative freedoms is a key instrument for safeguarding the rights of the individual in a collective grouping. The relationship between Islam and politics in a pluralist constitution is managed in a democratic fashion. Citizens can choose the good life, based on moral and rational grounds, in a social public sphere with rights contained in the constitution. Increased accommodation of Muslims' faith-based ways of life goes hand in hand with the recognition of ways of life motivated by other religious, cultural or secular ideals. Choices by citizens are protected at the individual, social and institutional levels in the constitution.

This book has expounded political values, attitudes and institutions, which aim to lay a viable foundation of a Muslim democracy within a theoretical framework. Theoretical reconciliation and normative synthesis have been undertaken in order to formulate a set of revised concepts and notions for interpretation. Redefining secularism, public sphere and constitutional provisions has enabled the conceptual synergies of pluralist secularism, the social, plural public sphere and pluralising constitutionalism. In my theorisation of Muslim democracy, these three formative components reinforce and maintain one another. Islamic demands and democratic politics can coexist through this proposed political theory of Muslim democracy.

II. A Comparative Political Theory as Opposed to a Theological and Jurisprudential Approach to Muslim Democracy

The general objective of this book is to fill a gap in the contemporary literature of political theory. Evident tensions between religion and politics and religious accommodation and democracy have not found any sound resolution. I was principally concerned with the accommodation of comprehensive, religious moral doctrines within the context of democracy and Muslim-majority contexts. Muslim democracy is re-conceived in a comparative political theory approach through a cluster of concepts such as human rights, tolerance, deliberation, political secularism, institutional pluralism, associational freedoms, religious representation and collective rights. The comparative political theory approach in this book departs from functionalist Islamic approaches and liberal democratic universalism. Religion and politics are studied in this comparative political theory approach to propose a form of pluralist accommodation that confounds both orthodox liberalism and compatibility-based Islamic political thought. My formulation of Muslim democracy has expanded political theory's limited engagement with religion as a source of political claims.

Muslim democracy in this book separates democracy from thick foundations, both transcendental and secular, and suggests a plurality of its meanings and institutions. By proposing a post-foundationalsit approach, I aimed to carry out this line of inquiry free from the foundationalism versus anti-foundationalism debate. Essentialist, metaphysical or objective 'foundations' should be replaced by 'idealizations', in Rortyian terms, such as pluralism, human rights or constitutionalism (1996: 333). Similar to the logic of 'idealizations', I endorse a minimalist and thin morality framework, with a non-foundationalist position. Political values and institutions of democracy were reformulated to be inclusive of diverse moral and political concerns. In this post-foundationalist epistemology, conceptual and normative rigour has been necessary to integrate values and institutions from different traditions and experiences. I articulated religion-friendly and human-rights-concordant interpretations of secularism, the public sphere and constitutionalism. Free and fair elections, separation of powers, associational autonomy, inclusive citizenship, rule of law, democratic toleration, pluralism and civil liberties appear in my political theory of Muslim democracy.

My theorising of Muslim democracy is also a contribution to the literature on Islam and democracy. The central role of religion in contemporary Muslim societies is recognised in this line of inquiry. I have sought to reinterpret the principles of democracy to accommodate the comprehensive moral doctrines of Muslims and the public claims arising from these doctrines. Democracy's relevance and responsiveness can be improved in Muslim social and cultural contexts. Moreover, I questioned the notion that democracy must 'follow a Western/liberal democratic model' (Brynen et al, 1995: 4). To this end, I proposed a comparative study of a constellation of theories, Muslim political thought, multiculturalism, secularism, the public sphere and constitutionalism. This approach towards Muslim democracy employs a mode of reasoning derived from political theory rather than theology.

Theology as a political tool implies a transcendentalist foundationalism, yet the prevalent characteristics of theology are not restricted to religions alone. In fact, traces of theology in foundationalist political thought prompted Carl Schmitt's observation that '[a]ll significant concepts of the modern theory of the state are secularized theological concepts' (1985: 36). Political theology reflects a preoccupation with singularity. Heinrich Meier defines political theology as 'a political theory, political doctrine, or a political position for which, on the self-understanding of the political theologian, divine revelation is the supreme authority and the ultimate ground' (2006: 84). Political theology is endorsed by Muslim compatibility-based arguments. Concepts and values present in compatibility-based arguments are steeped in theological imperatives based on exclusive truth-claims. Foundationalism is also evident in orthodox liberal universalism. Philosophical secularism, universalist citizenship and monistic law also betray a preoccupation with the singularity of making truth-claims and their contents. However, democracy by definition is 'a condition of freedom from ideology' (Keane, 1993: 28).

Both compatibility-based arguments on Islam and democracy and liberal universalism have essentialist dimensions that can or do undermine pluralism. What unties both of these approaches are their thick foundationalism and hegemonic narratives that restrict plurality of knowledge and being. The political theory of Muslim democracy developed in this book rejects absolutist or moralising comprehensive view, thick normative accounts and metaphysical truths in democratic theory. It is open epistemologically to different philosophical traditions and appropriates their norms, values and practices. The critique of the theological elements in compatibility-based arguments in Chapter 3 highlights the characteristics of essentialism and hegemony that also apply to orthodox liberalism and philosophical secularism and their insistence on a single version of the common good. Muslim democracy questions foundationalism and theology in the form either of political exploitation of religion or secular political marginalisation of religion.

The comparative political theory approach provided the tools for counter-hegemony in challenging against simply imposing democracy from above. My theorisation of Muslim democracy is opposed to any form of absolutism, whether religious, cultural or national. The priority of Muslim democracy is to achieve diverse and inclusive political spaces rather than establish a moral orthodoxy for society. Democracy is thus not a doctrine-based or a single narrative, but a consensus-based system of competing narratives that is inclusive enough to accommodate the different truth-based claims of citizens. This counter-hegemonic approach avoids essentialist forms of democracy. Essentialism both in religious knowledge and political theory implies a God-like comprehension of politics. I am in favour of a pluralist epistemology and dialogical form of interpreting concepts. With a non-theological study of democracy, a rethinking of the relationship between the religious and the political is made possible through a dialogue of political traditions. Muslim political and multicultural discourses participate in a common dialogue that criticises the exclusivist, top-down and paternalistic implications of modern political thought.

On the other hand, one must recognise that there is a clear correspondence between theology and politics. Many notions of good government derive from philosophical and religious discussions over how best to organise human life. Theology, as a source of political reason, can offer moral resources for normative and practical engagement with democracy at the personal and societal level. I do not reject the importance of theology in politics. However, I adopt an approach that does not resort to the politicisation of theological concepts and thus precludes the absolutism of political theology. Although Muslim democracy accepts the political validity of comprehensive religious doctrines, it rejects the proposition that a democratic system should be founded on them.

In my theorising of Muslim democracy, I engage with Muslim claims, needs and interests in different contexts. Muslims require simultaneously democratic recognition of being individual citizens and group members. Here, public accommodation of religion aims to reconcile apparent irresolvable and irreconcilable moral conflicts between individuals and groups through the institutionalisation of pluralism. As such, Muslim democracy exemplifies an alternative model of coexistence between democracy, Islam and pluralism on a non-majoritarian and non-hegemonic basis. John Locke's argument for the centrality of a just state–religion equilibrium in democratic politics (Locke, 1689: 6) has received renewed attention by Stanley Fish in his study of the problems impeding this 'just' reconciliation (Fish, 1997: 2,274). I developed a normative line of inquiry for a political theory of Muslim democracy to postulate a 'fair balance'. The arguments proposed here are not an exhaustive account of the relationship between religion and politics. It is sufficient to make a perfunctory case for a fair state–religion equilibrium, which opens more nuanced vistas in political theory.

Finally, I do not aim to articulate a universal theory of Muslim politics. Widespread disparities exist among Muslim societies, their national politics, institutional frameworks and social dynamics. I pursued a normative study of democracy that reinterpreted existing concepts and offered new categories of interpretation to Muslim contexts. A comparative political theory of Muslim democracy can be productively applied to individual societies to formulate specific models.

III. A Convergence Thesis and its Critics

This book has proposed an original framework for fostering a dialogical interaction between public claims made on Islamic grounds and democratic political values and institutions. It does not take liberal or Islamic doctrines as fixed points of reference, in two ways. First, democracy is not rooted in an Islamic theological foundation, unlike the compatibility-based arguments offered by Islamic revivalists and modernists. Instead, the political theory approach present here incorporates Islam, as represented by Muslims' viewpoints, in the journey towards democracy. Second, liberalism is not adopted as the ultimate ethical good in the study of Muslim democracy either. I have embarked on a constructive critique of liberalism to accommodate Muslim norms and practices. The examination of the weaknesses of liberal democratic norms and institutions led to a reformulation of multiculturalism to advance pluralism.

I have illustrated a convergence between the values of liberal democracy and Muslim views of democracy in this line of enquiry. This approach contributes to the debate on pluralism in both liberalism and Muslim political thought. Comparative political theorising in this book supports 'dialogical interaction over hegemonic unilateralism and monologue' (Dallmayr, 2004: 254) in more meaningful ways than existing scholarship. Convergence will not occur through a disowning or loss of either Muslim values or democratic principles. Both of these genres of norms need to be reinterpreted in a new light to pluralising and inclusive ends, as I have tried to demonstrate here.

In this book, I have reinterpreted certain moral and political concepts to provide principled justifications of Muslim democracy. I have developed an alternative to the pragmatist and structural approaches to the relationship between Islam and democracy. Islamic democracy, in these approaches, arises from an institutional restructuring that precedes value change among Muslims. My focus, however, is on a symbiotic relationship between structural and value change involved in reinforcing and strengthening one another. Social processes and norms are interdependent in societies. In the proposed theory of Muslim democracy, institutional and political developments, social interactions and value change go hand in hand and allow their complexities.

I engage with Islam within the context of political theory and other clusters of concepts developed in this book. My endorsement of certain liberal norms and institutions may meet some resistance on behalf of those who espouse a theory of Islamic democracy based on theological foundations. However, I depart from theological rationales in arguing that normative democratisation for Muslims does not need to create a democracy that is distinctly 'Islamic'. A distinct 'Islamic' theory is also unambiguous in meaning. The normative possibilities of democracy grounded in theology or jurisprudence do not seem to offer a coherent approach. The theoretical vagueness and reductionism of numerous compatibility-based discourses are likely to exacerbate problems in Muslim-majority states. Autonomous institutions, manipulation of power, the failure to protect the rights of minorities and political dissidents require a principled approach to democracy. A political theory approach provides a cluster of integrated concepts and values to arrive at a framework of Muslim democracy that addresses these problems.

Despite the wide potential of different conceptions of democracies, I have avoided relativism on the question of liberalism. My analysis of liberal institutions has sought to reconstruct democracy to better fit in Muslim-majority contexts. Eisenstadt argues:

> We cannot avoid Western concepts, but we can make them more flexible, so to speak, through differentiation and contextualization. The use of such concepts as public sphere, civil society, and collective identity is helpful as long as we do not assume that the way in which these components were put together in Europe constitutes an evaluative yardstick for other modernizing societies. (2002: 159)

The insight of the adaptation of Western social science concepts in the above passage can equally apply to the realm of political theory without deferring to a hegemonic Eurocentric perspective. This framework has simultaneously reinterpreted already-existing political concepts and created new categories of interpretation. Key liberal concepts and values such as the limited state, constitutionalism, toleration and human rights are re-appropriated to better accommodate Muslim conceptions of the good life. Although I have undertaken a critique of liberal democracy in my book, my examination of the multiculturalist literature has led to the retention of key idealisations such as pluralism and human rights. I have not articulated a radically alternative democratic theory that questions fundamental liberal democratic norms, but a more advanced theory on religious accommodation in political theory.

Two strands of critique from selected proponents of Islamic democracy and liberal thinkers are incorporated in this engagement with liberalism. Liberal democracy is criticised by some advocates of democracy for not providing an appropriate theoretical background for Muslim-majority contexts (Yenigün, 2013: 100). Other democratic theories, such as radical democracy, put forward by Chantal Mouffe and Ernesto Laclau (2001), could potentially provide normatively compelling formulations for the analysis of Muslim democracy. Radical democracy approaches may have a better potential to successfully accommodate the adherents of comprehensive moral doctrines due to their emphasis on egalitarianism, inclusiveness, political renewal, anti-hegemonic power relations, and identity and civil society politics (Little and Lloyd, 2009: 3). Liberalism's self-acclaimed philosophy of 'epistemic abstinence' in the public sphere is found wanting (Raz, 1990: 3). The advocates of radical democracy claim that liberalism has not made the shift from a 'comprehensive' and 'ontological' to a 'political' justification or application of liberal ideals (Yenigün, 2013: 104). My theorisations on democracy challenge liberalism's public sphere, defined by a comprehensive moral doctrine, in which participants leave behind their cultural or religious norms. Overall, the Muslim democracy framework proposed in this book presents a revision of existing approaches to modern democratic theory and its attendant concepts. Yet, any theorisations on democracy should recognise liberalism as an advanced source of political thought due to its evident link to democratic institutions and values such as human rights.

In addition, the conceptualisation of Muslim democracy may provoke some liberals who view with suspicion the enhanced public roles and functions of religion. An account of democracy where religion has greater institutional and political power, even at the hands of civil society forces, may cause scepticism or resentment within liberal circles. In this line of thought, dangers to liberal democracy emerge, in a form fuelling conflicts or animosities, when religion operates beyond the private sphere. However, orthodox liberal solutions will not help democratic consolidation in contexts where the role of religion is substantially different from the original context in which liberalism created democratic regimes. Moreover, the secularist state paradigm will increase the isolation of and discrimination against religious groups, and can engender fundamentalist struggles for power. My arrival at the convergence thesis provides theoretical tools with which to reconcile and enrich liberal democratic norms and institutions with Muslim political articulations. The political theory of Muslim democracy considers institutions, actors, norms and interactions at a more normative level than accounts of Islamic democracy and orthodox liberal democracy.

Muslim democracy aims to achieve a level of maturation by expanding the boundaries of interpretations through employing a comparative political theory. Certain tensions or even paradoxes may emerge from the dialogical approach employed in this book. I seek to reach a fair balance between majority rule and minority rights, public deliberation and constitutional guarantees, common good and individual freedoms, civic unity and accommodation, and religion and politics. The talismanic allure of democracy is misleading. Proclamations about democracy's inevitability promise more than they can deliver. I have adopted the position in this book that democracy is and always will be a work in progress or a continuous struggle for justice, equality and freedom. The liberal democracies of the West are suffering from the manipulation of electoral processes, the rise of the far right and the violations of minority rights. Authoritarianism and electoralism continue to hold sway in the Muslim world. Thus, the struggle goes on globally.

Democratic theory and practice have created shared norms of justice, freedom and good governance. However, there are no settled means to a universal model of democratic practice. Current efforts to formulate models are subject to differing interpretations and contexts. For '[n]ot even democracy itself can pretend to be democratic if it continues to be imagined as "fixed"' (Sadiki, 2004: 47). Within the context of Muslim democracy, Islamicity or Muslimness and democratic theory, which both harbour the potential for diverse interpretations, are continually questioned and renewed in ever pluralising forms. Considerable room exists for syncretic and dialogical reconstructions of democracy. The political theory of Muslim democracy formulated here is one representation of the many possibilities for democracy in different cultural and religious contexts.

Reinhold Niebuhr found democracy to be 'a method of finding proximate solutions to insoluble problems' (2011: 118). *A Political Theory of Muslim Democracy* makes the case for the institutional accommodation of religious pluralism in Muslim-majority societies. I have sought to find a fair balance in the public sphere between irreconcilable normative differences deriving from comprehensive moral doctrines. Strong epistemic claims by a single foundationalist discourse have been rejected in favour of an open dialogue between Muslim political thought and multiculturalism. Political theory has been deployed to develop a syncretic understanding of Muslim democracy to reconcile religious commitment with liberty.

BIBLIOGRAPHY

Abootalebi, A. R. (1999). 'Islam, Islamists, and Democracy'. *Middle East Review of International Affairs*, 3(1), 14–24.

Abou El Fadl, K. (1996). 'Muslim Minorities and Self-Restraint in Liberal Democracies'. *The Loyola of Los Angeles Law Review*, 29(4), 1,525–42.

Abou El Fadl, K. (1998). 'Muslims and Accessible Jurisprudence in Liberal Democracies: A Response to Edward B. Foley's Jurisprudence and Theology'. *Fordham Law Review*, 66, 1,227–31.

Abou El Fadl, K. (2001). *Speaking in God's Name: Islamic Law, Authority and Women*. Oxford: Oneworld.

Abou El Fadl, K. (2002). *The Place of Tolerance in Islam*. Boston: Beacon Press.

Abou El Fadl, K. (2003). 'The Ugly Modern and the Modern Ugly: Reclaiming the Beautiful in Islam'. In O. Safi (ed.) *Progressive Muslims: On Justice, Gender, and Pluralism*. London: Oneworld.

Abou El Fadl, K. (2004). 'Islam and the Challenge of Democracy: A Boston Review Book'. In J. Cohen and D. Chasman (eds) *An Argument for Liberal Democracy from within the Framework of Islamic Values*. Princeton, NJ: Princeton University Press.

Abou El Fadl, K. (2005). *The Great Theft: Wrestling Islam from the Extremists*. New York: Harper San Francisco.

Abou El Fadl, K. (2009). 'God Does Not Have an Equal Partner: Interview with Khaled Abou el-Fadl. Interviewed by M. Jung-Mounib for Qantara'. http://en.qantara.de/God-Does-Not-Have-an-Equal Partner/9506c9605i1p657/ (last accessed 19 September 2014).

Abou El Fadl, K. (2014). *Reasoning with God: Reclaiming Sharī'ah in the Modern Age.* Maryland: Rowman & Littlefield.

Adams, C. J. (1983). 'Mawdūdī and the Islamic State'. In J. Esposito (ed.) *Voices of Resurgent Islam.* New York: Oxford University Press, pp. 99–134.

Adonis (2012). 'Adonis: A Life in Writing'. *The Guardian.* https://www.theguardian.com/culture/2012/jan/27/adonis-syrian-poet-life-in-writing (last accessed 10 February 2016).

Afsaruddin, A. (2006). 'The "Islamic State": Genealogy, Facts, and Myths'. *Journal of Church and State,* 48(1), 153–73.

Afsaruddin, A. (2008). 'Absolutism vs. Pluralism in Islam Today'. *The Review of Faith and International Affairs,* 6(4), 23–7.

Afsaruddin, A. (2011). 'Theologizing about Democracy: A Critical Appraisal of Mawdūdī's Thought'. In A. Afsaruddin (ed.) *Islam, the State, and Political Authority: Medieval Issues and Modern Concerns.* Basingstoke: Palgrave Macmillan, pp. 131–54.

Ahmad, M. (2002). 'Islam and Democracy: The Emerging Consensus'. *Milli Gazette,* 2(94). http://www.milligazette.com/Archives/01022002/0102200259.htm (last accessed 2 April 2014).

Ahmed, D. I. and Gouda, M. (2014). 'Measuring Constitutional Islamization: The Islamic Constitutions Index'. *Hastings International and Comparative Law Review,* 38(1), 1–74.

Ahmad, I. (2006). 'The State in Islamist Thought'. *The International Institute for the Study of Islam in the Modern World Review,* 1(18), 12–13.

Ahmad, I. (2009). 'Genealogy of the Islamic State: Reflections on Maududi's Political Thought and Islamism'. *Journal of the Royal Anthropological Institute* (N.S.), 15 (30), 145–62.

Ahmad, I. (2015) 'In Conversation with John Keane: Gods, Power, Democracy'. *Journal of Religious and Political Practice.* 1(1), 73–91.

Akkoyunlu, K. (2017). 'Contending with Authoritarian Turkey: A Measured Realist Perspective'. *Open Democracy,* 29 May. https://www.opendemocracy.net/karabekir-akkoyunlu/contending-with-authoritarian-turkey-measured-realist-perspective (last accessed 23 September 2017).

Alam, L. A. (2007). 'Keeping the State Out: The Separation of Law and State in Classical Islamic Law'. *Michigan Law Review,* 105(6), 1,255–64.

Al-Azmeh, A. (1994). 'Populism Contra Democracy: Recent Democratist Discourse in the Arab World'. In G. Salamé (ed.). *Democracy without Democrats? The Renewal of Politics in the Muslim World.* London: I. B. Tauris, pp. 112–30.

Al-Dakkak, K. (2011). 'Religious Dialogue, Pluralism, and Historical Interpretation: The Works of Mohamed Talbi'. Ph.D. thesis, Oxford University.

Al-Ghannushi, R. (1994). 'Tunisia's Islamists are Different from Those in Algeria, Interview with Rached Ghannouchi'. *Cornell*. https://www.library.cornell.edu/colldev/mideast/ghanush.htm (last accessed 12 October 2015).

Al-Ghannushi, R. (2011a). 'Interview Transcript: Rachid Ghannouchi'. *Financial Times*. http://www.ft.com/intl/cms/s/0/24d710a6-22ee-11e0-ad0b-00144feab49a (last accessed 2 March 2013).

Al-Ghannushi, R. (2011b). 'Ghannushi: Public Made Revolution, Our Model, Is Turkey'. *World Bulletin*, 25 January. http://www.worldbulletin.net/haber/68984/ghannushi-public-made-revolution-our-model-is-turkey (last accessed 22 May 2014).

Al-Ghannushi, R. (2012). 'Secularism and Relation between Religion and the State from the Perspective of the Nahdha Party'. *Center for the Study of Islam and Democracy (CSID)*. http://archive.constantcontact.com/fs093/1102084408196/archive/1109480512119.html (last accessed 2 March 2013).

Al-Jabri, M. A. (1996). *Al-Din wa al-dawla wa tatbiq al-shari'a* (Religion, the State and the Application of Islamic Law). Beirut: Center for Arab Unity Studies.

Al-Jabri, M. A. (2009). *Democracy, Human Rights and Law in Islamic Thought*. London: I. B. Tauris.

Al-Qaradawi, Y. (2002). 'How Islam Views Secularism'. *Islam Online*. http://www.islamonline.net/servlet/Satellite?pagename=IslamOnlineEnglish-Ask_Scholar/FatwaE/FatwaE&cid=1119503545396 (last accessed 2 May 2014).

Al-Raziq, A. A. (1982). 'The Caliphate and the Bases of Power'. In J. Donohue and J. Esposito (eds) *Islam in Transition: Muslim Perspectives*, pp. 29–37. Oxford: Oxford University Press.

Al-Sayyid, R. (2009). 'Pluralism and Liberalism in Contemporary Islamic Thought'. In A. Filali-Ansary and S. K. Ahmed (eds) *The Challenge of Pluralism: Paradigms from Muslim Contexts*. Edinburgh: Edinburgh University Press in association with the Aga Khan University, Institute for the Study of Muslim Civilisations.

Altan, O. (2007). 'Turkey: Sanctifying a Secular State'. In E. Abdella Doumato and G. Starrett (eds) *Teaching Islam: Textbooks and Religion in the Middle East*. Colorado: Lynne Rienner.

Anderson, J. N. D. (1954). 'The Sharia and Civil Law'. *The Islamic Quarterly*, 1, 29–46.

Anderson, J. N. D. (1960). 'The Significance of Islamic Law in the World Today'. *American Journal of Comparative Law*, 19(2), 187–98.

Anderson, J. N. D. (1971). 'Modern Trends in Islam: Legal Reforms and Modernisation in the Middle East'. *International and Comparative Law Quarterly*, (20)1, 1–21.

Anderson, J. N. D. (1976). *Law Reform in the Muslim World*. London: Athlone Press.

An-Na'im, A. A. (1987). 'Religious Minorities Under Islamic Law and the Limits of Cultural Relativism'. *Human Rights Quarterly*, 9(1), 1–18.

An-Na'im, A. A. (1995). 'Toward an Islamic Hermeneutics for Human Rights'. In A. A. An-Na'im, J. D. Gort and H. Jansen (eds) *Human Rights and Religious Values: An Uneasy Relationship?* Amsterdam: William B. Eerdmans.

An-Na'im, A. A. (1998). 'Shari'a and Positive Legislation: Is an Islamic State Possible or Viable'. *Yearbook of Islamic and Middle Eastern Law*, 5, 29–37.

An-Na'im, A. A. (2000a). 'Islam, State and Politics: Separate but Interactive'. *Brookings*. Available at https://www.brookings.edu/wp-content/uploads/2012/04/2007 islamforum_an-naim.pdf (last accessed 1 February 2014).

An-Na'im, A. A. (2000b). 'Shari'a and Positive Legislation: Is an Islamic State Possible or Viable?'. *The Hague: Kluwer Law International*, 5, 29–42.

An-Na'im, A. A. (2002a). *Islamic Family Law in a Changing World: A Global Resource Book*. London: Zed Books.

An-Na'im, A. A. (2002b). 'Muslims Must Realize that There is Nothing Magical about the Concept of Human Rights, Interview with Asghar Ali Engineer'. In F. A. Noor (ed.) *New Voices of Islam*. Leiden: ISIM.

An-Na'im, A. A. (2002c). 'The Islamic Counter Reformation'. *New Perspectives Quarterly*, 19(1), 29–35.

An-Na'im, A. A. (2003). 'The Synergy and Interdependence of Human Rights, Religion and Secularism'. In J. Runzo, M. N. Martin and A. Sharma (eds), *Human Rights and Responsibilities in the World Religions*. Oxford: Oneworld, pp. 27–50.

An-Na'im, A. A. (2004). 'The Best of Times and The Worst of Times: Human Agency and Human Rights in Islamic Societies'. *Muslim World Journal of Human Rights*, 1(1), 1–11.

An-Na'im, A. A. (2005). 'The Independence of Religion, Secularism, and Human Rights: Prospects for Islamic Societies'. *Common Knowledge*, 11(1), 56–80.

An-Na'im, A. A. (2008). *Islam and the Secular State: Negotiating the Future of Shari'a*. Cambridge, MA: Harvard University Press.

An-Naʻim, A. A. (2009). 'A Theory of Islam, State and Society'. In K. Vogt, L. Larsen and C. Moe (eds) *New Directions in Islamic Thought: Exploring Reform and Muslim Tradition*. London: I. B. Tauris.

An-Naʻim, A. A. (2010). 'Best of 2010: Islam, Apostasy and Freedom of Belief'. *ABC*. http://www.abc.net.au/religion/articles/2010/09/24/3021228.htm (last accessed 19 March 2014).

An-Naʻim, A. A. (2014). 'Epilogue: The Normative Relevance of Sharia in the Modern Context'. In P. Bearman (ed.) *The Ashgate Research Companion to Islamic Law*. New York: Ashgate, pp. 307–21.

Anwar, Z. (2005). 'Law-making in the Name of Islam: Implications for Democratic Governance'. In K. S. Nathan and M. H. Kamali (eds) *Islam in Southeast Asia: Political, Social and Strategic Challenges for the 21st Century*. Singapore: Institute of South Asian Studies, pp. 121–34.

Arat, Y. (2012). *Rethinking Islam and Liberal Democracy: Islamist Women in Turkish Politics*. New York: SUNY Press.

Asad, M. (1961). *The Principles of State and Government in Islam*. Berkeley: University of California Press.

Asad, T. (1992). 'Religion and Politics: An Introduction'. *Social Research*, 3–16.

Asad, T. (1993) *Genealogies of Religion: Discipline and Reasons of Power in Christianity and Islam*. Baltimore and London: Johns Hopkins University Press.

Asad, T. (2003). *Formations of the Secular: Christianity, Islam, Modernity*. Stanford, CA: University Press.

Atasoy, S. (2011). 'The Turkish Example: A Model for Change in the Middle East?'. *Middle East Policy*, 18(3), 86–100.

Aykol, M. (2015). 'Turkey's Authoritarian Drift'. *New York Times*, 10 November. https://www.nytimes.com/2015/11/11/opinion/turkeys-authoritarian-drift-election-erdogan.html (last accessed 11 April 2016).

Ayubi, N. N. (1992). 'State Islam and Communal Plurality'. *American Academy of Political and Social Science*, 524(1), 79–91.

Ayubi, N. N., Nader, H. and Emran, Q. (2012). 'Islamic State'. *Oxford Islamic Studies Online*. http://www.oxfordislamicstudies.com/article/opr/t236/e0394 (last accessed 12 May 2014).

Bader, V. (1999). 'Religious Pluralism: Secularism or Priority for Democracy?'. *Political Theory*, 27, 597–633.

Bader, V. (2001). 'Associative Democracy and the Incorporation of Ethnic and National Minorities'. In P. Hirst and V. M. Bader (eds) *Associative Democracy: The Real Third Way*. London: Frank Cass, pp. 187–202.

Bader, V. (2003a). 'Religious Diversity and Democratic Institutional Pluralism'. *Citizenship Studies*, 31(2), 265–94.

Bader, V. (2003b). 'Democratic Institutional Pluralism and Cultural Diversity'. In C. Harzig and D. Juteau (eds) *The Social Construction of Diversity: Recasting the Master Narrative of Industrial Nations*. New York: Berghahn, pp. 131–67.

Bader, V. (2003c). 'Taking Pluralism Seriously: Arguing for an Institutional Turn'. *Ethical Theory and Moral Practice*, 6(1), 3–22.

Bader, V. (2005). 'Dilemmas of Multiculturalism'. *Canadian Diversity/Diversité Canadienne*, 4(1), 83–9.

Bader, V. (2007a). *Secularism or Democracy? Associational Governance of Religious Diversity*. Amsterdam: Amsterdam University Press.

Bader, V. (2007b). 'The Governance of Islam in Europe: The Perils of Modelling'. *Journal of Ethnic and Migration Studies*, 33(6), 871–86.

Bader, V. (2009a) Legal Pluralism and Differentiated Morality: Shari'a in Ontario? In R. Grillo et al. (eds) *Legal Practice and Cultural Diversity*. Farnham: Ashgate, pp. 49–72.

Bader, V. (2009b). 'Review Symposium: Reply'. *Ethnicities*, 9(4), 566–70.

Bader, V. (2010). 'Constitutionalizing Secularism, Alternative Secularisms or Liberal-Democratic Constitutionalism: A Critical Reading of Some Turkish, ECtHR and Indian Supreme Court Cases on Secularism'. *Utrecht Law Review*, 6(3), 8–35.

Bahlul, R. (2000). 'People vs God: The Logic of "Divine Sovereignty" in Islamic Democratic Discourse'. *Islam and Christian–Muslim Relations*, 11(3), 287–97.

Bahlul, R. (2003). 'Toward an Islamic Conception of Democracy: Islam and the Notion of Public Reason'. *Critical Middle Eastern Studies*, 12(1), 43–60.

Bahlul, R. (2004). 'Democracy without Secularism?'. In J. Bunzi (ed.) *Islam, Judaism, and the Political Role of Religions in the Middle East*. Gainesville: University Press of Florida.

Bakht, N. (2006). 'Were Muslim Barbarians Really Knocking on the Gates of Ontario?: The Religious Arbitration Controversy Another Perspective'. *Ottowa Law Review*, 40, 67–82.

Bâli, A. Ü. (2011). 'A Turkish Model for the Arab Spring?'. *Middle East Law and Governance*, 3(1–2), 24–42.

Bâli, A. Ü. (2016a). 'Shifting into Reverse: Turkish Constitutionalism under the AKP'. *Theory & Event*, 19(1).

Bâli, A. Ü. (2016b). 'Turkish Constitutionalism: A Model for Reform in Arab Countries'. In R. Grote and T. J. Röder (eds) *Constitutionalism, Human*

Rights, and Islam After the Arab Spring. New York: Oxford University Press.

Banchoff, T. (2007). *Democracy and the New Religious Pluralism.* New York: Oxford University Press.

Baker, R. W. (2015). *One Islam, Many Muslim Worlds: Spirituality, Identity, and Resistance across Islamic Lands.* Religion and Global Politics. New York: Oxford University Press.

Barkey, K. (2005). 'Islam and Toleration: Studying the Ottoman Imperial Model'. *International Journal of Politics Culture and Society,* 19(5), 1–19.

Barkey, K. (2012). 'Rethinking Ottoman Management of Diversity: What Can We Learn for Modern Turkey?'. In A. T. Kuru and A. Stepan (ed.) *Democracy, Islam, and Secularism in Turkey.* New York: Columbia University Press.

Barry, B. (1991). 'Is Democracy Special?'. *Democracy and Power,* 24–60.

Barzilai, G. (2003). *Communities and Law: Politics and Cultures of Legal Identities.* Ann Arbor: University of Michigan Press.

Barzilai, G. (2004). 'Legal Categorizations and Religion: On Politics of Modernity, Practices, Faith, and Power'. In S. Austin (ed.) *The Blackwell Companion to Law and Society.* Malden: Blackwell.

Barzilai, G. (2008). 'Beyond Relativism: Where is Political Power in Legal Pluralism?'. *Theoretical Inquiries in Law,* 9, 395–416.

Bayat, A. (2007). *Making Islam Democratic: Social Movements and the Post-Islamist Turn.* Stanford, CA: Stanford University Press.

Bearman, P. and Rudolph, P. (2014). *The Ashgate Research Companion to Islamic Law.* Farnham: Ashgate.

Beitz, C. R. (2013). 'Human Dignity in the Theory of Human Rights: Nothing but a Phrase?'. *Philosophy & Public Affairs,* 41(3), 259–90.

Bekaroğlu, E. A. (2016). 'The Ambiguity of Turkish Secularism'. *The Critical Muslim,* 16(3), 32.

Bellamy, R. (2007). *Political Constitutionalism: A Republican Defence of the Constitutionality of Democracy.* Cambridge: Cambridge University Press.

Benhabib, S. (1996). *Democracy and Difference: Contesting the Boundaries of the Political.* Princeton, NJ: Princeton University Press.

Benhabib, S. (2004). *The Rights of Other: Aliens, Residents and Citizens.* Cambridge: Cambridge University Press.

Benhabib, S. (2011) 'The Arab Spring: Religion, Revolution and the Public Sphere'. *Eurozine,* 10 May. http://www.eurozine.com/the-arab-spring-religion-revolution-and-the-public-sphere/?pdf (last accessed 10 June 2017).

Benhabib, S. (2013) 'Turkey's Authoritarian Turn'. *New York Times*, 3 June. http://www.nytimes.com/2013/06/04/opinion/turkeys-authoritarian-turn.html (last accessed 10 June 2017).

Bennett, D. (1998). *Multicultural States: Rethinking Difference and Identity*. London: Routledge.

Berger, M. (2006). 'Sharia – A Flexible Notion'. *Nederlands Tijdschrift voor Rechtsfilosofie en Rechtstheorie*, 35(3), 215–21.

Berger, M. S. (2010). *Religion and Islam in Contemporary International Relations*. The Hague: Netherlands Institute of International Relations Clingendael.

Berger M. S. (2013) (ed.). *Applying Shari'a in the West*. Leiden: Leiden University Press.

Berger, M. (2014). 'Sharia and the Nation State'. In P. Bearman and R. Peters (eds) *The Ashgate Research Companion to Islamic Law*. Farnham: Ashgate.

Berlinerblau, J. (2017). 'Political Secularims'. In Zuckerman, P. (ed.). *The Oxford Handbook of Secularism*. New York: Oxford University Press.

Berman, H. (1974). *The Interaction of Law and Religion*. London: Student Christian Movement Press.

Berman, S. (2017). 'Some Argue that the West Should Limit Democracy to Save Liberalism. Here's Why They're Wrong'. *Washington Post*, 18 July. https://www.washingtonpost.com/news/monkey-cage/wp/2017/07/18/some-argue-that-the-west-should-limit-democracy-to-save-liberalism-heres-why-theyre-wrong/?utm_term=.3c8decef690c (last accessed 1 September 2017).

Bhargava, R. (1999). *Secularism And Its Critics*. Delhi; New York: Oxford University Press.

Bhargava, R. (2009). 'Review symposium: Why not seular democracy?' *Ethnicities*, 9(4), 553–60.

Bhargava, R. (2011). 'States, Religious Diversity, and the Crisis of Secularism'. *Open Democracy*. https://www.opendemocracy.net/rajeev-bhargava/states-religious-diversity-and-crisis-of-secularism-0 (last accessed 8 June 2015).

Bhargava, R. (2014). 'Should Europe Learn from Indian Secularism?'. In B. Black, G. Hyman and G. M. Smith (eds) *Confronting Secularism in Europe and India: Legitimacy and Disenchantment in Contemporary Times*. London: Bloomsbury.

Binder, L. (1998). *Islamic Liberalism: A Critique of Development Ideologies*. Chicago: University of Chicago Press.

Binmore, K. (2000). 'A Utilitarian Theory of Legitimacy'. In A. Ben-Ner and L. G. Putterman (eds) *Economics, Values, and Organization*. Cambridge: Cambridge University Press, pp. 101–32.

Black, B. (2014). 'Confronting Secularism in Europe and India: An Introduction'. In B. Black, G. Hyman and G. M. Smith (eds) *Confronting Secularism in Europe and India: Legitimacy and Disenchantment in Contemporary Times*. London: Bloomsbury.

Blond, P. and Adrian, P. (2008). 'Integrating Islam into the West'. *New York Times*, 8 November. http://www.nytimes.com/2008/02/14/opinion/14iht-edpabst.1.10050495.html?pagewanted=2 (last accessed 11 January 2013).

Bohman, J. (1995). 'Public Reason and Cultural Pluralism: Political Liberalism and the Problem of Moral Conflict'. *Political Theory*, 23(2), 253–79.

Bohman, J. (2000). *Public Deliberation: Pluralism, Complexity, and Democracy*. New Baskerville: MIT Press.

Boix, C. and Stokes, S. C. (2007). *The Oxford Handbook of Comparative Politics, Vol. 4*. New York: Oxford Handbooks of Political Science.

Bokhari, K. and Senzai, F. (2013). *Political Islam in the Age of Democratization*. New York: Palgrave Macmillan.

Bouchard, G. and Taylor, C. (2014). 'Building the Future. A Time for Reconciliation'. *In Report of the Consultation Commission on Accommodation Practices Related to Cultural Differences*. Quebec City: Movement of Quebec.

Boyes, R. (2017). 'Erdogan Threatens a Summer of Chaos for the EU'. *The Times*. https://www.thetimes.co.uk/article/erdogan-threatens-a-summer-of-chaos-for-the-eu-sf7mpzd8l (last accessed 8 September 2017).

Bozeman, A. B. (1971). *The Future of Law in a Multicultural World*. Princeton, NJ: Princeton University Press.

Bradney, A. (1993). *Religions, Rights and Laws*. Leicester: Leicester University Press.

Browers, M. L. (2006). *Democracy and Civil Society in Arab Political Thought: Transcultural Possibilities*. NY: Syracuse University Press.

Browers, M. L. (2009). *Political ideology in the Arab World*. Cambridge: Cambridge University Press.

Brown, J. A. C. (2014) *Misquoting Muhammad: The Challenge and Choices of Interpreting the Prophet's Legacy*. Oxford: Oneworld.

Brubaker, R. (2015). *Grounds for Difference*. Cambridge, MA: Harvard University Press.

Brynen, R., Korany, B. and Noble P. (eds) (1995). *Political Liberalization and Democratization in the Arab World. Vol. 1*. Boulder, CO: Lynne Rienner.

Bulaç, A. (1992). 'Medine Vesikası Hakkında Genel Bilgiler' [General information on the Charter of Madina]. *Birikim Dergisi*, 38–9.

Bulaç, A. (1993). 'Medine Vesikası Uzerine Tartışmalar' [General debates on the Constitution of Madina]. *Birikim Dergisi*, 47.

Bulaç, A. (1995). 'Asr-ı Saadette bir arada yasama projesi: Medine Vesikası' [A project of living together: The Charter of Madina]. In V. Vecdi Akyüz (ed.) *Bütün Yönleriyle Asr-ı Saadet İçinde*. İstanbul: Beyan Yayinlari, pp. 186–95.

Bulaç, A. (1998). 'The Medina Document'. In C. Kurzman (ed.) *Liberal Islam: A Source Book*. New York: Oxford University Press, pp. 169–78.

Bulaç, A. (2006). 'Asr-ı Saadette Bir Arada Yaşama Projesi: Medine Vesikası' [The Charter of Madina as a project of coexistence during the time of the prophet]. In V. Akyüz (ed.) *Bütün Yönleriyle Asr-ı Saadette İslam* (vol. 2). İstanbul: Beyan Yayınları, pp. 169–95.

Bulaç, A. (2011b). 'Postkemalist laiklik' [Post-Kemalist secularism].

Bulaç, A. (2012f). 'Pluralism within Islam'.

Bulaç, A. (2012b). 'Demokrasinin Islam'la sinavi!'. (2) [Democracy's test with Islam! (2)].

Bulaç, A. (2012e). 'İslâm ve Modern Zamanlarda Din-devlet Ilişkisi' [Islam and the relationship of religion–state in modern times]. http://yazivekitap.blogspot.co.uk/2012/04/ali-Bulaç-islam-ve-modern-zamanlarda.html (last accessed 24 April 2013).

Bulaç, A. (2013). 'Hakim Değil, Hakem' [Not a judge, but a referee].

Bulliet, R. W. (ed.). (1994). 'Under Siege: Islam and Democracy'. Proceedings of a Conference Held at Columbia University, 18–19 June 1993, Vol. 1. New York: Middle East Institute, Columbia University.

Butler, J., Habermas, J., Taylor, C. and West, C. (2011). *The Power of Religion in the Public Sphere*. Columbia: Columbia University Press.

Calvert, J. (2010) *Sayyid Qutb and the Origins of Radical Islamism*. London: Hurst.

Çakır, R. (2017) 'Bir büyük iflas olarak Türkiye İslamcılığı' [Turkish Islamism as a great failure]. *Medyascope*, 12 January. http://medyascope.tv/2017/01/12/bir-buyuk-iflas-olarak-turkiye-islamciligi/ (last accessed 29 August 2017).

Candaş Bilgen, A. (2008). 'Is "Muslim" Democracy Synonymous with "Constitutional" Democracy?'. *ResetDOC*, 30 October. http://www.resetdoc.org/story/is-muslim-democracy-synonymous-with-constitutional-democracy/ (last accessed 22 May 2017).

Casanova, J. (1994). *Public Religions in the Modern World*. Chicago: University of Chicago Press.

Casanova, J. (2001). 'Civil Society and Religion: Retrospective Reflections on Catholicism and Prospective Reflections on Islam'. *Social Research*, 68(4),1,041–80.

Casanova, J. (2006) 'The Long Difficult and Tortuous Journey of Turkey into Europe and the Dilemmas of European Civilization'. *Constellations*, 13(2), pp. 234–47.

Casanova, J. (2011). *Public Religions in the Modern World*. Chicago: University of Chicago Press.

Castles, S. (2005). Multiculturalism. In M. J. Gibney and R. Hansen (eds), *Immigration and Asylum: From 1900 to the Present*. Santa Barbara: ABC Clio.

Cesari, J. (2014). *When Islam and Democracy Meet: Muslims in Europe and in the United States*. New York: Palgrave Macmillan.

Chan, J. (2013). *Confucian Perfectionism: A Political Philosophy for Modern Times*. Princeton, NJ: Princeton University Press.

Chiba, M. (1984). 'Cultural Universality and Particularity of Jurisprudence'. In M. L. Marasinghe and W. E. Conklin (eds) *Third World Perspectives in Jurisprudence*. Singapore: Malayan Law Journal, pp. 302–26.

Christiano, T. (2012). 'Democracy'. In McKinnon, C. (ed.). *Issues in Political Theory*. Oxford: Oxford University Press.

Christiano, T. (2015). 'Democracy'. In E. N. Zalta (ed.) *The Stanford Encyclopedia of Philosophy*, Spring 2015 edition. https://plato.stanford.edu/archives/spr2015/entries/democracy/ (last accessed 2 May 2016).

CNN. (2009). 'Obama says U.S., Turkey Can Be Model for World'. *CNN*, 6 April. http://www.cnn.com/2009/POLITICS/04/06/obama.turkey/index.html (last accessed 12 June 2017).

CNS News (2011). 'Clinton Eyes Turkey as Model for Arab Reform'. *Cnsnews*, 16 July. http://www.cnsnews.com/news/article/clinton-eyes-turkey-model-arab-reform (last accessed 12 June 2017).

Commins, D. (2012). 'Modernism'. In J. L. Esposito (ed.) *The Oxford Encyclopedia of the Modern Islamic World*. http://www.oxfordislamicstudies.com/article/opr/t236MIW/e0539 (last accessed 11 June 2013).

Connolly, W. E. (1995). *The Ethos of Pluralization*. Minneapolis, MN: University of Minnesota Press.

Connolly, W. E. (1999). *Why I Am Not a Secularist*. Minneapolis, MN: University of Minnesota Press.

Connolly, W. E. (2005). *Pluralism*. Durham, NC: Duke University Press.

Cook, J., Long, N. J. and Moore, H. L. (2016). *The State We're In: Reflecting on Democracy's Troubles*. New York: Berghahn.

Cook, S. A (2017). 'No, Erdogan Was Not an Authoritarian All Along'. *The Washington Post*. https://www.washingtonpost.com/posteverything/wp/2017/04/20/no-erdogan-was-not-an-authoritarian-all-along/?utm_term=.401e06986d76 (last accessed 29 July 2017).

Cook, S. A. (2019). 'Turkish Democracy Can't Die, Because It Never Lived'. https://foreignpolicy.com/2019/05/13/turkish-democracy-cant-die-because-it-never-lived/?fbclid=IwAR3P4hIBdaDylXbAKjyMZiGqudSWBiAPltJNzJbElExh8rHtj0VKebIzEMM (last accessed 20 June 2020).

Cunningham, F. (2002). *Theories of Democracy: A Critical Introduction*. Routledge.

Crane, D. A. (2005). 'A Judeo-Christian Argument for Privatizing Marriage'. *Cardozo Law Review*, 27 (3), 1,221–59.

Dabashi, H. (2016). 'The Future of Democracy in the Muslim World'. *Al Jazeera*, 26 October. http://www.aljazeera.com/indepth/opinion/2016/10/future-democracy-muslim-world-161026073928966.html (last accessed 29 August 2017).

Dağı, I. (2012). 'Islamcilarin Demokrasiyle Sinavi' [Islamists' challenge with democracy].

Dahl, R. A. (1956). *A Preface to Democratic Theory*. Chicago: University of Chicago Press.

Dahl, R. A. (1976). *Politics, Economics, and Welfare*. New Brunswick: Transaction.

Dahl, R. A. (1982). *Dilemmas of Pluralist Democracy: Autonomy vs. Control*. New Haven: Yale University Press.

Dahl, R. A. (1989). *Democracy and Its Critics*. New Haven: Yale University Press.

Dahl, R. A. (1998). *On Democracy*. New Haven and London: Yale University Press.

Dahl, R. A. (2001). 'Pluralist Demoracy'. In T. C. Conte (ed.) *Theories of Democracy: A Reader*. Lanham: Rowman & Littlefield.

Dallmayr, F. (1997). 'Introduction: Toward a Comparative Political Theory'. *The Review of Politics*, 59(3), 421–8.

Dallmayr, F. (2004). 'Beyond Monologue: For a Comparative Political Theory'. *Perspectives on Politics*, 2 (2): 249–53.

Dallmayr, F. (2008). 'Introductory Note by the Editor'. *The Review of Politics*, 70, 1–4.

Dahl, R. A. (2005). 'What Political Institutions Does Large-Scale Democracy Require?'. *Political Science Quarterly*, 120(2), 187–97.

Dallmayr, F. (2010). *Comparative Political Theory: An Introduction*. New York: Palgrave Macmillan.

Dallmayr, F. (2011). 'Whither Democracy? Religion, Politics and Islam'. *Philosophy & Social Criticism*, 37(4), 437–48.

Darwich, M. (2017). 'International Politics of Authoritarian Resilience and Breakdown in the Middle East'. *Mediterranean Politics*, 1–9.

Demir, H. (2013). 'İslâm'da Ozel Hayat ve Ozel Hayatın Gizliliği' [Private life and the confidentiality of private life in Islam]. *Sosyal ve Kültürel Araştırmalar Merkezi*. http://tasav.org/htmldocs/index/calisma_detay/55/index.html (last accessed 13 May 2015).

Denli, O. (2006). 'An Islamic Quest for a Pluralistic Model: A Turkish Perspective'. In M. Khan (ed.) *Islamic Democratic Discourse: Theory, Debates, and Philosophical Perspectives*. Lanham: Lexington Books.

DePoy, E. and Gilson, S. F. (2010). *Studying Disability: Multiple Theories and Responses*. Thousand Oaks, CA: Sage.

Derrida, J. (1992). *The Other Heading: Reflections on Today's Europe*. Bloomington: Indiana University Press.

Derrida, J. (2007). *Acts of Religion*. New York: Routledge.

Deveaux, M. (2000). *Cultural Pluralism and Dilemmas of Justice*. London: Cornell University Press.

Deveaux, M. (2006). *Gender and Justice in Multicultural Liberal States*. Oxford: Oxford University Press.

Diamond, L. (2005). 'Facing Up to the Democratic Recession'. *Journal of Democracy*, 26(1), 141–55.

Dimova-Cookson, M. and Stirk, P. M. R. (eds). (2010). *Multiculturalism and Moral Conflict*. Milton Park, Abingdon: Oxon.: Routledge.

Duran, B. and Yılmaz, N. (2011). 'Whose Model? Which Turkey?'. *Foreign Policy*, 8, 1–2.

Eickelman, D. F. and Piscatori, J. (1996). *Muslim Travelers: Pilgrimage, Migration and the Religious Imagination*. London: Routledge.

Eickelman, D. F. and Anderson, J. W. (1997). 'Print, Islam, and the Prospects for Civic Pluralism: New Religious Writings and Their Audiences'. *Journal of Islamic Studies*, 8(1), 43–62.

Eickelman, D. F. (2002). 'Foreword: The Religious Public Sphere in Early Muslim Societies'. In M. Hoexter, S. N. Eisenstadt and N. Levtzion (eds) *The Public Sphere in Muslim Societies*. SUNY Press.

Eickelman, D. F. and Salvatore, A. (2002). 'The Public Sphere and Muslim Identities'. *European Journal of Sociology*, 43(1), 92–115.

Eickelman, D. F. and Piscatori, J. (2004). *Muslim Politics*. Princeton, NJ: Princeton University Press.

Eickelman, D. F. and Salvatore, A. (2004a). 'Muslim Publics: Public Islam and the Common Good'. *Brill*, 95, 3–27.

Eickelman, D. F. (2010). Justice, Morality, and Modernity: What Makes the Risale-i Nur modern?. In I. Abu Rabi' (ed.) *Theodicy and Justice in Modern Islamic Thought: The Case of Said Nursi*. Farnham: Ashgate, pp. 135–46.

Eisenstadt, S. N. (2000). 'Multiple Modernities'. *Daedalus*, 129(1).

Eisenstadt, S. N. (2002). 'Concluding Remarks: Public Sphere, Civil Society, and Political Dynamics in Islamic Societies'. In M. Hoexter, S. N. Eisenstadt and N. Levtzion (eds) *The Public Sphere in Muslim Societies*. Albany, NY: SUNY Press.

Ekinci, T. Z. (1999). *Demokrasi, Çok Kültürlülük ve Bir Yargısal Serüven* [Democracy, multiculturalism, and a judicial journey]. Çemberlitaş, İstanbul: Küyerel Yayınları.

El-Affendi, A. (2004) 'On the State, Democracy and Pluralism'. In S. Taji-Farouki (ed.) *Islamic Thought in the Twentieth Century*. London: I. B. Tauris, pp. 172–94.

El-Affendi, A. (2006). Democracy and Its (Muslim) Criics: An Islamic Alternative to Democracy? In M. A. Muqtedar Khan (ed.) *Islamic Democratic Discourse: Theory, Debates, and Philosophical Perspectives*. Lanham: Lexington Books.

El-Affendi, A. (2008). *Who Needs an Islamic State?* (2nd edn). London: Malaysia Think Tank London.

El-Affendi, A. (2009). 'Islamic Revivalism and the Elusive Ethical State: Revisiting the "Damascus Model"'. In W. Krause (ed.) *Citizenship, Security and Democracy: Muslim Engagement with the West*. London: Association of Muslim Social Scientists, pp. 201–38.

El Amine, L. (2016). 'Beyond East and West: Reorienting Political Theory through the Prism of Modernity'. *Perspectives on Politics*, 14(1), 102.

El-Awa, M. S. (1980). *On the Political System of the Islamic State*. Trans. Ahmad Naji al-Imam. Indianapolis: American Trust Publications.

El-Din S. E. (2012). 'Salafiyah'. *The Oxford Encyclopedia of the Islamic World, The Oxford Islamic Studies Online*. http://www.oxfordislamicstudies.com/article/opr/t236/e0700 (last accessed 19 November 2012).

Ekim, S. and Kirişci, K. (2017). 'The Turkish Constitutional Referendum, Explained'. *Brookings*, 13 April. https://www.brookings.edu/blog/order-from-chaos/2017/04/13/the-turkish-constitutional-referendum-explained/ (last accessed 15 July 2017).

Enayat, H. (2017). *Islam and Secularism in Post-Colonial Thought: A Cartography of Asadian Genealogies*. Berlin: Springer.

Emon, A. M. (2006). 'Conceiving Islamic Law in a Pluralist Society: History, Politics and Multicultural Jurisprudence'. *Singapore Journal of Legal Studies*, 20(2), 331–5.

Emon, A, M. (2008). 'The Limits of Constitutionalism in the Muslim World: History and Identity in Islamic Law'. *Islamic Law and Law of the Muslim World Paper*, 8–9, 258–86.

Emon, A. M. (2012). 'On Sovereignties in Islamic Legal History'. *Middle East Law and Governance*, 4, 265–305.

Emre, A. (2011). 'Bir Aydın Sınavı Olarak Laiklik' [Secularism as a test for the enlightened]. *Yenisafak*, 20 September. http://www.yenisafak.com/yazarlar/akifemre/bir-ayd%C4%B1n-s%C4%B1nav%C4%B1-olarak-laiklik-29035 (last accessed 19 November 2016).

Engineer, A. A. (1985). *Theory and Practise of the Islamic State*. Lahore: Vanguard.

Engineer, A. A. (2002). 'The Compatibility of Islam, Secularism and Modernity: Interview with Asghar Ali Engineer'. In F. A. Noor (ed.) *New Voices of Islam*. Leiden: ISIM.

Engineer, A. A. (2003). 'Religion, Pluralism and Modern Society'. *Institute of Islamic Studies (IIS)*. http://www.csss-isla.com/iis-archive76.htm (last accessed 19 January 2013).

Engineer, A. A. (2006a). 'Islam and Secularism'. In I. M. Abu-Rabi' (ed.) *The Blackwell Companion to Contemporary Islamic Thought*. Malden: Blackwell.

Engineer, A. A. (2006b). 'Economic Justice as a Religious Mission'. Qantara.de. https://en.qantara.de/content/asghar-ali-engineer-economic-justice-as-a-religious-mission (last accessed 9 November 2016).

Esack, F. (2003). 'In Search of Progressive Islam Beyond 9/11'. In O. Safi (ed.) *Progressive Muslims: On Justice, Gender and Pluralism*. Oxford: Oneworld, pp. 78–97.

Esposito, J. L. and Piscatori, J. P. (1991). 'Democratization and Islam'. *Middle East Journal*, 45(3), 427–40.

Esposito, J. L. (1992). *The Islamic Threat: Myth or Reality?* Oxford: Oxford University Press.

Esposito, J. L. and Voll, O. J. (1994). 'Islam's Democratic Essence'. *Middle East Quarterly*, 1(3), 3–11.

Esposito, J. L. and Voll, J. O. (1996). *Islam and Democracy*. New York: Oxford University Press.

Esposito, J. L. and Mogahed, D. (2008). 'Islam and the West: Clash or Coexistence?'. *Gallup*. http://www.gallup.com/press/178991/islam-west-clash-coexistence.aspx (last accessed 10 June 2015).

Esposito, J. L. (2011). *Rethinking Islam and Secularism*. State College: Association of Religion Data Archives, Pennsylvania State University.

Esposito, J. L. (2012). 'Faith. What Everyone Needs to Know About Islam'. *The Oxford Islamic Studies Online*. http://www.oxfordislamicstudies.com/article/book/acprof-9780199794133/acprof-9780199794133-div1-39 (last accessed 19 November 2012).

Esposito, J. L. (2016). 'Democracy'. *The Oxford Dictionary of Islam*, Oxford Islamic Studies Online. http://www.oxfordislamicstudies.com/article/opr/t125/e518 (last accessed 2 November 2016).

Esposito, J. L. (n.d.). 'Pluralism (Religious)'. *The Oxford Encyclopedia of the Islamic World*, Oxford Islamic Studies Online. http://www.oxfordislamicstudies.com/article/opr/t236/e1223 (last accessed 12 April 2013).

Euben, R. L. (1997). 'Comparative Political Theory: An Islamic Fundamentalist Critique of Rationalism'. *The Journal of Politics*, 59(1), 28–58.

Euben, R. L. (1999). *Enemy in the Mirror: Islamic Fundamentalism and the Limits of Modern Rationalism: A Work of Comparative Political Theory*. New York: Princeton University Press.

Euben, R. L. (2010). 'Comparative Political Theory'. Encyclopedia of Political Theory. In M. Bevir (ed.) *Encyclopedia of Political Theory*. Thousand Oaks: Sage, 260–1.

Fadel, M. (2004). 'Too Far from Tradition'. In K. Abou El Fadl et al. (ed.) *Islam and the Challenge of Democracy*. Princeton, NJ: Princeton University Press, pp. 81–6.

Fadel, M. (2007). 'Public Reasons as a Strategy for Principled Reconciliation: The Case of Islamic Law and International Human Rights Law'. *Chicago Journal of International Law*, 8(1), 1–20.

Fadel, M. (2008). 'The True, the Good and the Reasonable: The Theological and Ethical Roots of Public Reason in Islamic Law'. *The Canadian Journal of Law and Jurisprudence*, 21(1), 5–69.

Fadel, M. (2009a). 'Back to the Future: The Paradoxical Revival of Aspirations for an Islamic State'. *Review of Constitutional Studies*, 14(1), 105–23.

Fadel, M. (2009b). 'Islamic Politics and Secular Politics: Can They Co-Exist?'. *Journal of Law and Religion*, 25(1), 187–204.

Fadel, M. (2012a). 'Islamic Law and American Law: Between Concordance and Dissonance'. *The New York Law School Law Review*, 57, 231–42.

Fadel, M. (2012b). 'Muslim Reformists, Female Citizenship, and the Public Accommodation of Islam in Liberal Democracy'. *Politics and Religion*, 5(1), 2–35.

Fadel, M. (2013a). 'Judicial Institutions, the Legitimacy of Islamic State Law and Democratic Transition in Egypt: Can a Shift Toward a Common Law Model of Adjudication Improve the Prospects of a Successful Democratic Transition?'. *Int J Const Law*, 11(3), 646–65.

Fadel, M. (2013b). 'Seeking an Islamic Reflective Equilibrium: A Response to Abdullahi A. An-Na'im's Complementary, Not Competing, Claims of Law and Religion: An Islamic Perspective'. *Pepperdine Law Review*, 39(5), 11.

Fadel, M. (2014). 'State and Sharia'. In P. Bearman and R. Peters (eds) *The Ashgate Research Companion to Islamic Law*. Farnham: Ashgate.

Farrow, D. (2004). *Recognizing Religion in a Secular Society: Essays in Pluralism, Religion, and Public Policy*. Montreal: McGill-Queen's University Press.

Feldman, N. (2012). *The Fall and Rise of the Islamic State*. Princeton, NJ: Princeton University Press.

Feroz, A. (1991). 'Politics and Islam in Modern Turkey'. *Middle Eastern Studies*, 27(1), 3–21.

Ferrari, S. (2003). 'The Legal Dimension'. In B. Mare´chal, S. Allievi, F. Dassetto and J. Nielsen (eds) *Muslims in the Enlarged Europe: Religion and Society*. Boston: Brill.

Filali-Ansary, A. (2009). 'Introduction: Theoretical Approaches to Cultural Diversity'. In A. Filali-Ansary and S. K. Ahmed (eds) *The Challenge of Pluralism: Paradigms from Muslim Contexts*. Edinburgh: Edinburgh University Press in association with the Aga Khan University, Institute for the Study of Muslim Civilisations.

Filali-Ansary, A. (2010). ''Alī 'Abd al-Rāziq'. In G. Krämer, D. Matringe, J. Nawas and E. Rowson (eds) *Encyclopaedia of Islam*. http://www.brillonline.nl.ezproxy.aus.edu/subscriber/entry?entry=ei3_SIM-22594 (last accessed 19 July 2012).

Fish, S. (1997). 'Mission Impossible: Settling the Just Bounds Between Church and State'. *Colum. L. Rev.*, 97, 2255.

Fitzmaurice, D. (1993). 'Autonomy as a Good: Liberalism, Autonomy and Toleration'. *Journal of Political Philosophy*, 1(1), 1–16.

Freedman, J. (2007). 'Women, Islam and Rights in Europe: Beyond a Universalistic/Culturalist Dichotomy'. *Review International Studies*, 33, 29–44.

Freedom House (2007). 'Freedom of the Press: Turkey'. *Freedom House*. https://freedomhouse.org/report/freedom-press/2007/turkey (last accessed 10 May 2017).

Freedom House (2008). 'Freedom of the Press: Turkey'. *Freedom House*. https://freedomhouse.org/report/freedom-press/2008/turkey (last accessed 10 May 2017).

Freedom House (2009). 'Freedom of the Press: Turkey'. *Freedom House*. https://free

domhouse.org/report/freedom-press/2009/turkey (last accessed 10 May 2017).
Freedom House (2010). 'Freedom of the Press: Turkey'. *Freedom House.* https://free domhouse.org/report/freedom-press/2010/turkey (last accessed 10 May 2017).
Fuller, G. E. (2004). 'Turkey's Strategic Model: Myths and Realities'. *The Washington Quarterly,* 27 (3), 51–64.
Galanter, M. (1981). 'Justice in Many Rooms: Courts, Private Ordering and Indigenous Law'. *Journal of Legal Pluralism,* 19, 1–47.
Gellner, E. (1994) 'From the Ruins of the Great Contest: Civil Society, Nationalism and Islam'. In *Encounters with Nationalism.* Oxford: Blackwell, pp. 170–81.
Gill, G. (2017). *The Nature and Development of the Modern State.* Palgrave. https://www.macmillanihe.com/resources/sample-chapters/9780333804506_sample.pdf (last accessed 12 May 2018).
Ghobadzadeh, N. (2013). 'Religious Secularity'. In *Muslim Secular Democracy.* New York: Palgrave Macmillan, pp. 31–52.
Ghobadzadeh, N. (2014). *Religious Secularity: A Theological Challenge to the Islamic State.* Oxford: Oxford University Press.
Goodhart, M. E. (Ed.). (2016). *Human Rights: Politics and Practice.* Oxford: Oxford University Press.
Gökarıksel, B. and Secor, A. (2015). 'Post-Secular Geographies and the Problem of Pluralism: Religion and Everyday Life in Istanbul, Turkey'. *Political Geography,* 46, 21–30.
Göle, N. (2011). *Islam in Europe: The Lure of Fundamentalism and the Allure of Cosmopolitanism.* Princeton, NJ: Markus Wiener.
Göle, N. (2015) *Islam and Secularity: The Future of Europe's Public Sphere.* Durham, NC: Duke University Press.
Greenberg, U. and Steinmetz-Jenkins, D. (2016). Is Religious Freedom a Bad Idea?. *The Nation.* https://www.thenation.com/article/archive/is-religious-freedom-a-bad-idea/ (last accessed 2 March 2018).
Gregg, B. (2003). *Thick Moralities, Thin Politics: Social Integration across Communities of Belief.* Durham, NC: Duke University Press.
Gregg, B. (2012). 'Comparative Perspectives on Social Integration in Pluralistic Societies: Thick Norms versus Thin'. *Comparative Sociology,* 11(5), 629–48.
Griffiths, J. (1985). Four Laws of Interaction in Circumstances of Legal Pluralism: First Steps Toward an Explanatory Theory. In A. Allott and G. R. Woodman (eds) *People's Law and State Law: The Bellagio Papers.* Dordrecht: Foris.
Griffiths, J. (1986). 'What is Legal Pluralism?'. *Journal of Legal Pluralism and Unofficial Law,* 24, 1–56.

Grillo, R. D. (1998). *Pluralism and the Politics of Difference*. Oxford: Clarendon Press.
Guerrero, A. A. (2014). 'Against Elections: The Lottocratic Alternative'. *Philosophy & Public Affairs*, 42(2), 135–78.
Guida, M. (2010). 'The New Islamists' Understanding of Democracy in Turkey: The Examples of Ali Bulac and Hayrettin Karaman'. *Turkish Studies*, 11(3), 347–70.
Gürses, M. (2014). 'Islamists, Democracy and Turkey: A Test of the Inclusion-Moderation Hypothesis'. *Party Politics*, 20(4), 646–53.
Gürsel, K. (2011). 'Who Really Wants a Muslim Democracy?'. *Turkish Policy Quarterly*, 10(1), 96.
Habermas, J. (1989). *The Structural Transformation of the Public Sphere: An Inquiry into a Category of Bourgeois Society*. Cambridge: Polity Press.
Habermas, J. (1992). *Postmetaphysical Thinking: Philosophical Essays*. Trans. William Mark Hohengarten. Cambridge, MA and London: MIT Press.
Habermas, J. (2006). 'Religion in the Public Sphere'. *European Journal of Philosophy*, 14, 1–25.
Haddad, Y. Y. (1983). Sayyid Qutb: Ideologue of the Islamic Revival. In J. Esposito (ed.) *Voices of Resurgent Islam*. New York: Oxford University Press.
Haddad, Y. Y. (1995). *Islamists and the Challenge of Pluralism*. Washington: Center for Contemporary Arab Studies and Center for Muslim–Christian Understanding, Georgetown University.
Hale, W. and Özbudun, E. (2009). *Islamism, Democracy and Liberalism in Turkey: The Case of the AKP*. London: Routledge.
Haleem, M. A. (Ed.). (2005). *The Qur'an*. Oxford: Oxford University Press.
Hallaq, W. B. (2004). Can the Shari'a Be Restored?. In Y. Y. Haddad and B. Freyer Strowasser (eds) *Islamic Law and the Challenges of Modernity*. Walnut Creek: Altamira Press.
Hallaq, W. B. (2010). 'Islamic Law: History and Transformation'. *The New Cambridge History of Islam*, 4, 142–83.
Hallaq, W. (2012). *The Impossible State: Islam, Politics, and Modernity's Moral Predicament*. New York: Columbia University Press
Harvey, B., Viscusi, G. and Darhally, M. (2011). 'Arabs Battling Repression See Erdogan's Muslim Democracy as Model'. *Bloomberg News*. http://www.bloomberg.com/news/2011-02-04/arabs-battling-regimes-see-erdogan-smuslim-democracy-in-turkey-as-model.htm (last accessed 25 March 2017).
Harzig, C. (2003). *The Social Construction of Diversity: Recasting the Master Narrative of Industrial Nations*. New York: Berghahn.

Hashemi, N. (2009). *Islam, Secularism, and Liberal Democracy: Toward a Democratic Theory for Muslim Societies*. New York: Oxford University Press.

Hashemi, N. (2011). 'The Arab Revolution of 2011: Reflections on Religion and Politics'. *Insight Turkey*, 13(2), 15–21.

Hefner, R. W. (2001). 'Public Islam and the Problem of Democratization'. *Sociology of Religion*, 62(4), 491–514.

Hefner, R. W. (2005). *Remaking Muslim Politics: Pluralism, Contestation, Democratization*. Princeton, NJ: Princeton University Press.

Held, D. (1995). *Democracy and the Global Order: From the Modern State to Cosmopolitan Governance*. Stanford, CA: Stanford University Press.

Held, D. (2006). *Models of Democracy*. Cambridge: Polity Press.

Heydemann, S. and Reinoud, L. (2011). 'Authoritarian Learning and Authoritarian Resilience: Regime Responses to the "Arab Awakening"'. *Globalizations*, 8(5), 647–53.

Hirschkind, C. (2008). 'Religious Difference and Democratic Pluralism: Some Recent Debates and Frameworks'. *Temenos*, 44(1), 67–82.

Hirschl, R. (2009). 'Juristocracy vs. Theocracy: Constitutional Courts and the Containment of Sacred Law'. *Middle East Law and Governance*, 1(2), 129–65.

Hirschl, R. (2011). *Constitutional Theocracy*. Boston: Harvard University Press.

Hirst, P. (1994). *Associative Democracy: New Forms of Economic and Social Governance*. Cambridge: Polity Press.

Hirst, P. (1997). *From Statism to Pluralism: Democracy. Civil Society and Global Politics*. London: University College London Press.

Hofmann, M. (1993). *Islam: The Alternative*. Reading: Garnet.

Holmes, S. (1995). *Passions and Constraints: On the Theory of Liberal Democracy*. Chicago: University of Chicago Press.

Hooker, M. B. (1975). *Legal Pluralism: An Introduction to Colonial and Neo-colonial Laws*. Oxford: Clarendon Press.

Houghton, D. P. (2007). 'Reinvigorating the Study of Foreign Policy Decision Making: Toward a Constructivist Approach'. *Foreign Policy Analysis*, 3(1), 24–45.

Houston, C. (2013a). 'Militant Laicists, Muslim Democrats, and Liberal Secularists'. In L. Z. Rahim (ed.) *Muslim Secular Democracy*. New York: Palgrave Macmillan, pp. 253–69.

Houston, C. (2013b). 'Thwarted Agency and the Strange Afterlife of Islamism in Militant Laicism in Turkey'. *Contemporary Islam*, 7(3), 333–51.

Ibrahim, A. (2005). 'From Islamism to Muslim Democracy: The Challenges of Political Inclusion in Muslim Countries'. Wilson Center. https://www.wilsoncenter.org/event/islamism-to-muslim-democracy-the-challenges-political-inclusion-muslim-countries (last accessed 18 March 2015).

Ibrahim, A. (2006). 'Universal Values and Muslim Democracy'. *Journal of Democracy*, 17(3), 5-12.

Ibrahim, S. E. (2006). 'From Islamism to Muslim Democracy: The Challenges of Political Inclusion in Muslim Countries'. Wilson Center. https://www.wilsoncenter.org/event/islamism-to-muslim-democracy-the-challenges-political-inclusion-muslim-countries (last accessed 18 March 2015).

Ignatieff, M. (2003). *Human Rights as Politics and Idolatry*. Princeton, NJ: Princeton University Press.

Isaac, J. C. (1994). 'Oases in the Desert: Hannah Arendt on Democratic Politics'. *American Political Science Review*, 88(1), 156–68.

Jaggar, A. M. (1999). 'Multicultural Democracy'. *Journal of Political Philosophy*, 7(3), 308–29.

Jakobsen, J. R. and Pellegrini, A. (2008). *Secularisms*. Durham, NC: Duke University Press.

Jennings, J. (2000). 'Citizenship, Republicanism and Multiculturalism in Contemporary France'. *B.J.Pol.S.*, 30, 575–98.

Jessop, B. (1990). *State Theory: Putting Capitalist States in Their Place*. University Park: Penn State Press.

John, K. (1993). 'Power-sharing Islam?'. In A. Tamimi (ed.) *Power-sharing Islam?* London: Liberty for Muslim World Publications.

Jones, P. (2006). 'Toleration, Recognition, and Identity'. *Journal of Political Philosophy*, 14(2), 123–43.

Jones, P. (2008). 'Group Rights'. *The Stanford Encyclopaedia of Philosophy* http://plato.stanford.edu/entries/rights-group/ (last accessed 1 March 2014).

Kabbani, S. M. H. (n.d.). 'Understanding Islamic Law'. http://www.islamicsupremecouncil.org/understanding-islam/legal-rulings/52-understanding-islamic-law.html (last accessed 19 March 2015).

Kadivar, M. (2011). 'Human Rights and Intellectual Islam'. In K. Vogt, L. Larsen and C. Moe (eds) *New Directions in Islamic Thought: Exploring Reform and Muslim Tradition*. New York: I. B. Tauris.

Kalanges, K. (2014). 'Sharia and Modernity'. In P. Bearman and R. Peters (eds) *The Ashgate Research Companion to Islamic Law*. Farnham: Ashgate.

Kalyvas, S, N. (2012). 'The "Turkish Model" in the Matrix of Political Catholicism'.

In A. Stepan (ed.) *Democracy, Islam, and Secularism in Turkey*. New York: Columbia University Press.

Kamrava, M. (2006). *The New Voices of Islam: Rethinking Politics and Modernity: A Reader*. Berkeley: University of California Press.

Karagiannis, E. (2018). *The New Political Islam: Human Rights, Democracy, and Justice*. Philadelphia: University of Pennsylvania Press.

Karaman, H. (2002). *Laik Düzende Dini Yaşamak* [Living religion in a secular system], Vol. 2. Istanbul: Iz Yayıncılık.

Karaman, H. (2003). *Hayatımızdaki İslam* [Islam in our life]. Istanbul: İz Yayıncılık.

Karaman, H. (2004). *İslam'da İnsan haklari: Din, Vicdan ve Düsünce Hürriyeti* [Human rights: freedom of religion, conscience and thought]. Istanbul: Ensar Nesriyat.

Karaman, H. (2005). 'Federasyon ve Hilafet' [Federation and caliphate]. http://www.hayrettinkaraman.net/yazi/laikduzen/4/0149.htm (last accessed 19 February 2015).

Karaman, H. (2008). 'İngiltere'de Seriat Mahkemeleri' [The *sharī'a* courts in England]. *Yeni Şafak*. http://yenisafak.com.tr/yazarlar/HayrettinKaraman/ingilterede-seriat-mahkemeleri/12868 (last accessed 19 February 2015).

Karaman, H. (2009). 'İslâmî Düzen' [Islamic order]. *Yeni Şafak*. http://yenisafak.com.tr/yazarlar/HayrettinKaraman/isl%C3%A2m%C3%AE-duzen/20221 (last accessed 12 December 2013).

Karaman, H. (2010). 'Çok Hukukluluk' [Legal pluralism]. *Yeni Şafak*. http://yenisafak.com.tr/yazarlar/HayrettinKaraman/cok-hukukluluk/20229 (last accessed 12 December 2013).

Karaman, H. (2012a). 'Demokrasiyi Kutsallaştırma' [Sanctifying democracy]. *Yeni Şafak*. http://yenisafak.com.tr/yazarlar/HayrettinKaraman/demokrasiyi-kutsallastirma/31118 (last accessed 17 February 2014).

Karaman, H. (2012b). 'Demokrasi bir Araçtır' [Democracy is a tool]. *Yeni Şafak*. http://yenisafak.com.tr/yazarlar/?t=20.04.2012&y=HayrettinKaraman (last accessed 20 April 2014).

Karaman, H. (2012c). 'Gannûşî'yi Doğru Anlamak' [Understanding Ghannushi correctly]. *Yeni Şafak*. http://yenisafak.com.tr/yazarlar/?t=29.07.2012&y=HayrettinKaraman (last accessed 29 July 2013).

Karaman, H. (2014a). 'İslam, Demokrasi ve Medine Vesikası' [Islam, democracy, and the Constitution of Madina]. *Yeni Şafak*. http://yenisafak.com.tr/yazarlar/HayrettinKaraman/islam-demokrasi-ve-medine-vesikasi/53922 (last accessed 20 May 2015).

Karaman, H. (2014b). 'İslam'a Davet ve Din Hürriyeti' [The call for Islam and religious freedoms]. *Yeni Şafak*. http://www.yenisafak.com.tr/yazarlar/Hayrettin Karaman/islama-davet-ve-din-hurriyeti/56103 (last accessed 20 April 2015).

Karaman, H. (2014c). 'Semi-structured Interview with Hayrettin Karaman, by Ravza Altuntas-Cakir', Yalova, Turkey, 24 August.

Karaman, H. (2014d). 'Siyasal İslam ve Ak Parti' [JDP and the Political Islam]. *Yeni Şafak*. http://yenisafak.com.tr/yazarlar/HayrettinKaraman/siyasal-islam-ve-ak-parti/50170 (last accessed 26 April 2014).

Karen, B. (2012). 'The Turkish Model in the Matrix of Political Catholicism'. In A. Kuru and A. Stepan (eds) *Democracy, Islam, & Secularism in Turkey*. New York: Columbia University Press.

Kassab, E. S. (2010). *Contemporary Arab Thought: Cultural Critique in Comparative Perspective*. Columbia University Press.

Kaufman, J. (1999). 'Three Views of Associationalism in 19th-century America: An Empirical Examination'. *American Journal of Sociology*, 104(5), 1,296–345.

Kaviraj, S. (2001). 'In Search of Civil Society'. In S. Kaviraj and S. Khilnani (eds) *Civil Society: History and Possibilities*. Cambridge: Cambridge University Press.

Kaviraj, S. (2005). 'An Outline of a Revisionist Theory of Modernity'. *European Journal of Sociology*, 46(3), 497–526.

Keane, J. (1993) 'Power-Sharing Islam?'. In A. Tamimi (ed.) *Power Sharing Islam?*. London: Liberty for Muslim World Publications.

Khan, M. A. (2003). 'Prospects for Muslim Democracy: The Role of US Policy'. *Middle East Policy*, 10(3), 79–89.

Khan, M. A. (2004). 'The Primacy of Political Philosophy'. In J. Cohen and D. Chasman (eds) *Islam and the Challenge of Democracy*. New York: Cornell University.

Khatab, S. (2006). *The Power of Sovereignty: The Political and Ideological Philosophy of Sayyid Qutb*. New York: Routledge.

Klausen, J. (2005). *The Islamic Challenge: Politics and Religion in Western Europe*. Oxford: Oxford University Press.

Kleinhans, M. M. and Macdonald, R. A. (1997). 'What Is a Critical Legal Pluralism?'. *Canadian Journal of Law & Society/La Revue Canadienne Droit et Société*, 12(2), 25–46.

Kösebalaban, H. (2014a). 'Bulaç, Ali'. *The Oxford Encyclopedia of the Islamic World*, Oxford Islamic Studies Online. http://www.oxfordislamicstudies.com/article/opr/t236/e0884 (last accessed 7 April 2014).

Kösebalaban, H. (2014b). 'Medina Charter'. *The Oxford Encyclopedia of the Islamic*

World, Oxford Islamic Studies Online. http://www.oxfordislamicstudies.com/article/opr/t236/e0964 (last accessed 7 April 2014).
Krämer, G. (1993). 'Islamist Notions of Democracy'. *Middle East Research and Information Project (MERIP)*, 23(183), 2–8.
Krämer, G. (1995). 'Islam and Pluralism'. In R. Brynen, B. Korany and P. Noble (eds) *Political Liberalization and Democratization in the Arab World, Vol. 1*: 113–28.
Krämer, G., Syed, Z. and Saleha, M. A. (2014). 'Minorities'. In J. L. Esposito (ed.) *The Oxford Encyclopedia of the Modern Islamic World*, Oxford Islamic Studies Online. http://www.oxfordislamicstudies.com/article/opr/t236MIW/e0536 (last accessed 12 April 2014).
Krause, W. E. (2012). *Citizenship, Security and Democracy: Muslim Engagement with the West*. Richmond: Association of Muslim Social Scientists.
Kukathas, C. (1992). 'Are There Any Cultural Rights?'. *Political Theory*, 20(1), 105–39.
Kukathas, C. (1998). 'Liberalism and Multiculturalism: The Politics of Indifference'. *Political Theory*, 26(5), 686–99.
Kukathas, C. (2001). 'Distinguished Lecture in Public Affairs: Is Feminism Bad for Multiculturalism?'. *Public Affairs Quarterly*, 83–98.
Kukathas, D. C. (2003). *The Liberal Archipelago: A Theory of Diversity and Freedom*. Oxford: Oxford University Press.
Kuru, A. T. (2007). 'Passive and Assertive Secularism: Historical Conditions, Ideological Struggles, and State Policies Toward Religion'. *World Politics*, 59(4), 568–94.
Kuru, A. T. (2008). 'Secularism, State Policies, and Muslims in Europe: Analyzing French Exceptionalism'. *Comparative Politics*, 41(1), 1–19.
Kuru, A. T. and Stepan, A. (2012). *Democracy, Islam, & Secularism in Turkey*. New York: Columbia University Press.
Kuru, A. T., Stephan, A., Tatoğlu, H. and Tüzün, C. (2013). *Türkiye'de Demokrasi, Islam ve Laiklik* [Democracy, Islam, and secularism in Turkey]. Istanbul: İstanbul Bilgi Üniveristesi Yayınları.
Kurzman, C. and Naqvi, I. (2010). 'The Islamists Are Not Coming'. *Foreign Policy*, 177, 34.
Kymlicka, W. (1989). *Liberalism, Community and Culture*. Oxford: Clarendon Press.
Kymlicka, W. (1992). 'Two Models of Pluralism and Tolerance'. *Analyse & Kritik*, 14(1), 33–56.

Kymlicka, W. (1992b). 'The Rights of Minority Cultures: Reply to Kukathas'. *Political Theory*, 20(1), 140–6.

Kymlicka, W. (1995). *Multicultural Citizenship: A Liberal Theory of Minority Rights*. Oxford: Clarendon Press.

Kymlicka, W. (1997). 'Do We Need a Liberal Theory of Minority Rights? Reply to Carens, Young, Parekh and Forst'. *Constellations*, 4(1), 72–87.

Kymlicka, W. (2007). *Multicultural Odysseys: Navigating the New International Politics of Diversity*. Oxford: Oxford University Press.

Kymlicka, W. (2008). 'Review Symposium: Historical Settlements and New Challenges'. In V. Bader (ed.) *Secularism or Democracy? Associative Governance of Religious Diversity*. Amsterdam: Amsterdam University Press.

Kymlicka, W. (2010). *The Politics of Reconciliation in Multicultural Societies*. Oxford: Oxford University Press.

Kymlicka, W. (2011). 'Liberal Multicutlraism and Human Rights'. In F. R. Coll and M. C. Badia (eds) *Political Liberalism and Plurinational Democracies*. London: Routledge.

Kymlicka, W. (2012). *Multiculturalism: Success, Failure, and the Future*. Washington, DC: Migration Policy Institute.

Kymlicka, W. and Norman, W. (2000). *Citizenship in Diverse Societies*. Oxford: Oxford University Press.

Laborde, C. (2002). 'On Republican Toleration'. *Constellations*, 9(2), 167–83.

Laborde, C. (2006). 'Female Autonomy, Education and the Hijab'. *Critical Review of International Social and Political Philosophy*, 9(3), 351–77.

Laborde, C. (2008). *Critical Republicanism: The Hijab Controversy and Political Philosophy*. Oxford: Oxford University Press.

Laborde, C. (2010). Secularism and Fair Treatment for Muslims. In M. Dimova-Cookson and P. M. R. Stirk (eds) *Multiculturalism and Moral Conflict*. London: Routledge.

Laborde, C. (2018a). Toleration and Laïcité. In C. McKinnon and D. Castiglione (eds) *The Culture of Toleration in Diverse Societies: Reasonable Tolerance*. Manchester: Manchester University Press.

Laborde, C. (2018b). *Liberalism's Religion*. Cambridge, MA: Harvard University Press.

Laclau, E. and Mouffe, C. (2001). *Hegemony and Socialist Strategy: Towards a Radical Socialist Politics*. London: Verso.

Langlois, A. J. (2016). Normative and Theoretical Foundations of Human Rights.

In M. E. Goodhart (ed.) *Human Rights: Politics and Practice*. Oxford: Oxford University Press.

Lambert, G. (2016). *Return Statements: The Return of Religion in Contemporary Philosophy*. Edinburgh: Edinburgh University Press.

Lapidus, I. M. (1975). 'The Separation of State and Religion in the Development of Early Islamic Society'. *International Journal of Middle East Studies*, 6(4), 363–85.

Levey, G. B. and Modood, T. (2009). *Secularism, Religion, and Multicultural Citizenship*. Cambridge, UK: Cambridge: University Press.

Levinson, M. (Jul., 1997). 'Liberalism versus Democracy? Schooling Private Citizens in the Public Square'. *British Journal of Political Science*, Vol. 27, No. 3, pp. 333–60. Cambridge University Press. http://www.jstor.org/stable/194121 (last accessed 5 November 2010).

Levine, M. (2011). 'Is Turkey the Best Model for Arab Democracy?'. *Al Jazeera*. www.aljazeera.com/indepth/opinion/2011/09/201191684356995 273.html (last accessed 13 May 2016).

Lewis, B. (1993a). 'Islam and Liberal Democracy'. *Atlantic Boston*, 271(2), 89–98.

Lewis, B. (1993b). *Islam and the West*. Oxford: Oxford University Press.

Lewis, B. (1994). 'Why Turkey is the Only Muslim Democracy'. *Middle East Quarterly*, 1(1), 41–9.

Lilla, M. (2007). *The Stillborn God*. New York: Alfred Knopf.

Linz, J. J. and Stepan, A. C. (1996). 'Toward Consolidated Democracies'. *Journal of Democracy*, 7(2), 14–33.

Little, A. and Lloyd, M. (eds) (2009). *The Politics of Radical Democracy*. Edinburgh: Edinburgh University Press.

Locke, J. (1689). *Treatise of Civil Government and A Letter Concerning Toleration*. Ontario: Broadview Press.

Locke, J. (1955). *A Letter Concerning Toleration*. New York: Bobbs-Merrill.

Lugo, L., Cooperman, A., Bell, J., O'Connell, E. and Stencel, S. (2013). *The World's Muslims: Religion, Politics and Society*. Washington DC: Pew Research Center.

Lynch, M. (2011). 'After Egypt: The Limits and Promise of Online Challenges to the Authoritarian Arab State'. *Perspectives on Politics*, 9(2): 301–10.

Maclure, J. and Taylor, C. (2011). *Secularism and Freedom of Conscience*. Cambridge, MA: Harvard University Press.

Mahçupyan, E. (1998). *Turkiyede Merkeziyetci Zihniyet, Devlet ve Din* [The centralist mentality, state and religion in Turkey]. Istanbul: Yol Yayinlari.

Mahmood, S. (2004). Is Liberalism Islam's Only Answer. Islam and the Challenge of Democracy'. In J. Cohen and D. Chasman (eds) *An Argument for Liberal Democracy from within the Framework of Islamic Values*. Princeton, NJ: Princeton University Press.

Mahmood, S. and Danchin, P. (2014). 'Contested Genealogies of Religious Freedom'. *South Atlantic Quarterly*, 113(1), 1–8.

Mandaville, P. (2014). *Islam and Politics*. London: Routledge.

Mangini, M. (2016). 'From Transcultural Rights to Transcultural Virtues: Between Western and Islamic Ethics'. *European Journal of Legal Studies*, 9, 250–300.

Mansbridge, J. J. (Ed.). (1990). *Beyond Self-interest*. University of Chicago Press.

March, A. F. (2009). 'What is Comparative Political Theory?'. *The Review of Politics*, 7(4), 531–65.

March, A. F. (2011). *Islam and Liberal Citizenship: The Search for an Overlapping Consensus*. New York: Oxford University Press.

March, A. F. (2013). 'Genealogies of Sovereignty in Islamic Political Theology'. *Social Research*, 80(1): 293–320.

March, A. F. (2014). Constitutional Authority. In P. Bearman and R. Peters (eds) *The Ashgate Research Companion to Islamic Law*. Farnham: Ashgate.

March, A. F. (2015). 'The Problem of Sovereignty in Modern Islamic Thought'. https://cuptw.files.wordpress.com/2015/09/march_the-problem-of-sovereignty-in-modern-islamic-thought-columbia-pt-workshop.pdf (last accessed 19 May 2016).

March, A. F. (2019). *The Caliphate of Man: Popular Sovereignty in Modern Islamic Thought*. Cambridge, MA: Harvard University Press.

Mardin, Ş. (1973). 'Center–Periphery Relations: A Key to Turkish Politics?'. *Daedalus*, 169–90.

Margaret R. S. (2008). *Genealogies of Citizenship: Markets, Statelessness and the Right to Have Rights*. Cambridge: Cambridge University Press.

Marri, A. R. (2003). 'Multicultural Democracy: Toward a Better Democracy'. *Intercultural Education*, 14(3), 263–77.

Martin, F. (2011). 'Turkey Can Model Democracy for the Arab World'. *CNN*. http://edition.cnn.com/2011/OPINION/02/16/martin.egypt.turkey/ (last accessed 18 January 2017).

Masud, M. K., Salvatore, A. and Van Bruinessen, M. (2009). *Islam and Modernity: Key Issues and Debates*. Edinburgh: Edinburgh University Press.

Mawdūdī, S. A. A. (1978). *Islamic Law and Constitution*. Lahore: Islamic Publications.

Mawdūdī, S. A. A. (1960a). *Islamic Law and Constitution*. Trans. Khurshid Ahmed. Lahore: Islamic Publications.

Mawdūdī, S. A. A. (1960b). *First Principles of the Islamic State*. Trans. and ed. Khurshid Ahmed. Lahore: Islamic Publications.

Mawdūdī, S. A. A. (1960c). *Political Theory of Islam*. Trans. and ed. Khurshid Ahmed. Lahore: Islamic Publications.

Mawdūdī, S. A. A. (1999). 'Political Theory of Islam'. In B. Gupta and J. N. Mohanty, J. N. (eds) *Philosophical Questions: East and West*. Lanham: Rowman & Littlefield.

May, S. (2002). 'Multiculturalism'. Blackwell Reference Online. http://www.blackwellreference.com/subscriber/tocnode?id=g9780631206163_chunk_g978063120616316 (last accessed 19 June 2012).

McConnell, M. (1992). 'Accommodation of Religion'. *George Washington Law Review*, 60(3), 685–742.

McConnell, M. (2000). 'Believers as Equal Citizens'. In N. Rosenblum (ed.) *Obligations of Citizenship and Demands of Faith*. Princeton, NJ: Princeton University Press, pp. 90–110.

McClure, J. A. (1997). 'Post-secular Culture: The Return of Religion in Contemporary Theory and Literature'. *CrossCurrents*, 332–47.

Meier, H. (2006). *Leo Strauss and the Theologico-Political Problem*. Cambridge: Cambridge University Press.

Mégret, F. (2012). 'Is There Ever a "Right to One's Own Law"? An Exploration of Possible Rights Foundations for Legal Pluralism'. *Israel Law Review*, 45(1), 3–34.

Mégret F. (2013) 'International Human Rights and Global Legal Pluralism: A Research Agenda'. In R. Provost and C. Sheppard (eds) *Dialogues on Human Rights and Legal Pluralism*. Dordrecht: Springer.

Melissaris, E. (2009). *Ubiquitous Law: Legal Theory and the Space for Legal Pluralism*. Burlington: Ashgate.

Merry, S. E. (1988). 'Legal Pluralism'. *Law & Society Review*, 22, 869–96.

Meyrowitz, J. (1986). *No Sense of Place: The Impact of Electronic Media on Social Behaviour*. New York: Oxford University Press.

Milde, M. (1998). 'Critical Notice of James Tully's "Strange Multiplicity"'. *Canadian Journal of Philosophy*, 28(1), 119–43.

Mitchell, T. (1991). 'The Limits of the State: Beyond Statist Approaches and their Critics'. *American Political Science Review*, 85(1), 77–96.

Modood, T. (2007). *Multiculturalism: A Civic Idea*. London: Polity Press.

Modood, T. (2010a). 'Moderate Secularism, Religion as Identity and Respect for Religion'. *The Political Quarterly*, 81(1), 4–14.

Modood, T. (2010b). 'Muslims, Religious Equality and Secularism'. In M. Dimova-Cookson and P. M. R Stirk (eds) *Multiculturalism and Moral Conflict*. London: Routledge.

Modood, T. and Ahmad, F. (2007). 'British Muslim Perspectives on Multiculturalism'. *Theory, Culture & Society*, 24(2), 187–213.

Modood, T. (2010). 'Moderate Secularism, Religion as Identity and Respect for Religion'. *The Political Quarterly*, 81(1), 4–14.

Modood, T. (2015). 'State–Religion Connections and Multicultural Citizenship'. In J. Cohen and C. Laborde (eds) *Religion, Secularism, and Constitutional Democracy*. New York: Columbia University Press, 182–203.

Mookherjee, M (2001). 'Justice as Provisionality: An Account of Contrastive Hard Cases'. *Critical Review of International Social and Political Philosophy*, 4(3), 67–100.

Mookherjee, M. (2005). 'Affective Citizenship: Feminism, Postcolonialism and the Politics of Recognition'. *Critical Review of International Social and Political Philosophy*, 8(1), 31–50.

Mookherjee, M. (2009). *Women's Rights as Multicultural Claims: Reconfiguring Gender and Diversity in Political Philosophy*. Edinburgh: Edinburgh University Press.

Mookherjee, M. (2012). 'Multiculturalism'. In C. McKinnon (ed.) *Issues in Political Theory*. Oxford: Oxford University Press, pp. 190–212.

Moore, S. F. (1986). *Social Fact and Fabrications: Customary Law and Kilimanjaro, 1880–1980*. Cambridge: Cambridge University Press.

Moors, A. and Salih, R. (2009). 'Muslim Women in Europe: Secular Normativities, Bodily Performances and Multiple Publics'. *Social Anthropology*, 17(4), 375–78.

Moussa, M. (2014). 'The Neo-Modernity of Soroush'. *Critical Muslim* 12(2), 101–14.

Moussalli, A. S. (1999). *Moderate and Radical Islamic Fundamentalism: The Quest for Modernity, Legitimacy, and the Islamic State*. Gainesville: University Press of Florida.

Moussalli, A. S. (2001). *The Islamic Quest for Democracy, Pluralism, and Human Rights*. Gainesville: University Press of Florida.

Mufti, M. (1999). 'Elite Bargains and the Onset of Political Liberalization in Jordan'. *Comparative Political Studies*, 32(1), 100–29.

Müftüler-Baç, M. and Keyman, E. F. (2015). 'Turkey's Unconsolidated Democracy:

The Nexus between Democratisation and Majoritarianism in Turkey'. In S.Aydın-Düzgit, D. Huber, M. Müftüler-Baç, E. F. Keyman, M.Schwarz and N. Tocci (eds) *Global Turkey in Europe III: Democracy, Trade, and the Kurdish Question in Turkey–EU Relations*, 19(1), 1–16.

Nasr, S. V. R. (2005). 'The Rise of Muslim Democracy'. *Journal of Democracy*, 16(2), 13–27.

Nasr, S. V. R. (2006). 'From Islamism to Muslim Democracy: The Challenges of Political Inclusion in Muslim Countries'. Wilson Center. https://www.wilsoncenter.org/event/islamism-to-muslim-democracy-the-challenges-political-inclusion-muslim-countries (last accessed 25 May 2015).

Navaro-Yashin, Y. (2002). *Faces of the State: Secularism and Public Life in Turkey*. Princeton, NJ: Princeton University Press.

Nettler, R. L. (2000). 'Islam, Politics and Democracy: Mohamed Talbi and Islamic Modernism'. *The Political Quart*erly, 71(1), 50–9.

Nettler, R. L. (n.d.). 'Dhimmi'. *The Oxford Encyclopedia of the Islamic World*, Oxford Islamic Studies Online. http://www.oxfordislamicstudies.com/article/opr/t236/e0194 (last accessed 11 June 2014).

Nickel, J. (2017). 'Human Rights'. In E. N. Zalta (ed.) *The Stanford Encyclopedia of Philosophy*. https://plato.stanford.edu/archives/spr2017/entries/rights-human/ (last accessed 10 January 2017).

Niebuhr, R. (2011). *The Children of Light and the Children of Darkness: A Vindication of Democracy and a Critique of Its Traditional Defense*. Chicago: University of Chicago Press.

Nieuwenhuis, A. J. (2012). 'State and Religion, a Multidimensional Relationship: Some Comparative Law Remarks'. *International Journal of Constitutional Law*, 10(1), 153–74.

Nizam al-Mulk, A. (2001). *The Book of Government or Rules for Kings (Siyasat-nama)*. Trans. H. Darke. London: Curzon Press.

Novak, D. (2004). 'Revealed Law and Democracy'. In K. Abou El Fadl (ed.) *Islam and the Challenge of Democracy*. Princeton, NJ: Princeton University Press, pp. 87–92.

Nozick, R. (2001). *Anarchy, State and Utopia*. Malden: Blackwell.

Okin, S. M. (1999). *Is Multiculturalism Bad for Women?* Princeton, NJ: Princeton University Press.

Okyar, O. (1984). 'Ataturk's Quest for Modernism'. In J. M. Landau (eds) *Atatürk and the Modernization of Turkey*. Boulder, CO: Westview Press, pp. 49–52.

Otto, J. M. (2011). 'Sharia and Law in a Bird's-Eye View: Reform, Moderation and Ambiguity'. In J. M. Otto and H. Mason (eds) *Delicate Debates on Islam: Policymakers and Academics Speaking with Each Other*. Leiden: Leiden University Press.

Özbudun, E. (2012). 'The Turkish Constitutional Court and Political Crisis'. In A. Kuru, A. and A. Stepan (eds) *Democracy, Islam, & Secularism in Turkey*. New York: Columbia University Press.

Özbudun, E. (2013). 'Özbudun: Anayasa Imrali'da yazilmiyor' [Özbudun: The constitution is not written in Imrali]. Interview by Hulya Okur. http://www.haberx.com/Özbudun_anayasa_imralida_yazilmiyor(17,n,11266620,613).aspx (last accessed 12 January 2016).

Özbudun, E. (2016). 'İlk Uc Madde Kalirsa Yeni bir Anayasa Yapmis Olmazsiniz' [You cannot make a new constitution with the first three provisions intact]. Interview by Hülya Okur. http://politik-acilar.blogspot.com.tr/2016/11/ilk-uc-madde-kalirsa-yeni-bir-anayasa.html (last accessed 1 September 2017).

Öniş, Z. (2015). 'Monopolising the Centre: The AKP and the Uncertain Path of Turkish Democracy'. *The International Spectator*, 50(2), 22–41.

Öniş, Z. and Kutlay, M. (2017). 'Global Shifts and the Limits of the EU's Transformative Power in the European Periphery: Comparative Perspectives from Hungary and Turkey'. *Government and Opposition*, 1–28.

Paley, J. (2002). 'Toward an Anthropology of Democracy'. *Annual Review of Anthropology*, 31(1), 469–96.

Parekh, B. (2000). *The Future of Multi-ethnic Britain*. London: Profile Books.

Park, B. (2014). 'Turkey Has Elections, But Not Democracy'. *Open Democracy*. https://www.opendemocracy.net/bill-park/turkey-has-elections-but-not-democracy (last accessed 12 January 2017).

Parla, T. and Davison, A. (2004). *Corporatist Ideology in Kemalist Turkey: Progress or Order?*. Syracuse: Syracuse University Press.

Pew Global. (2012). 'Most Muslims Want Democracy, Personal Freedoms, and Islam in Political Life'. *Pew Global*. http://www.pewglobal.org/2012/07/10/most-muslims-want-democracy-personal-freedoms-and-islam-in-political-life/# (last accessed 9 December 2016).

Philpott, D. (2016). 'Sovereignty'. In E. N. Zalta (ed.) *The Stanford Encyclopedia of Philosophy*. http://plato.stanford.edu/archives/sum2016/entries/sovereignty/ (last accessed 19 October 2016).

Piscatori, J. (1986). *Islam in a World of Nation-States*. Cambridge: Cambridge University Press.

Piscatori, J. and Saikal, A. (2019). *Islam Beyond Borders: The Umma in World Politics*. Cambridge University Press.

Pishchikova, K. and Young, R. (2016). 'Divergent and Partial Transitions'. In M. M. Mohamedou and T. D. Sisk (eds) *Democratisation in the 21st Century: Reviving Transitology*. New York: Taylor & Francis.

Plattner, M. F. (2015). 'Is Democracy in Decline?'. *Journal of Democracy*, 26(1), 5–10.

Price, D. E. (1999). *Islamic Political Culture, Democracy, and Human Rights: A Comparative Study*. Westport, CT: Greenwood.

Provost, R. and Sheppard, C. (2013). *Dialogues on Human Rights and Legal Pluralism*. Dordrecht: Springer.

Qutb, S. (1964). *Milestones*. Cedar Rapids: Unity.

Qutb, S. (1986). *Ma'alim fi al-Tariq* [Milestones]. Istanbul: Risale.

Qutb, S. (2001). *In the Shade of the Qur'ān: Sūrahs 1–2. Al-Fātiḥah, Vol. 5*. Leicester: Islamic Foundation.

Rahman, F. (1965). *Islamic Methodology in History*. Karachi: Central Institute of Islamic Research.

Rahman, F. (1966). *Islam*. London: Weidenfeld & Nicolson.

Rahman, F. (1967). 'Implementing of the Islamic Concept of State in the Pakistani Milieu'. *Islamic Studies*, 6(3), 205–23.

Rahman, F. (1979). *Islam*. Chicago: University of Chicago Press.

Rahman, F. (1980). 'A Survey of Modernization of Muslim Family Law'. *International Journal of Middle East Studies*, 11(4), 451–65.

Rahman, F. (1981). 'A Recent Controversy over the Interpretation of Shura'. *History of Religions*, 20(4), 291–301.

Rahman, F. (1982). *Islam and Modernity: Transformation of an Intellectual Tradition*. Chicago: University of Chicago Press.

Rahman, F. (1984). 'The Principle of "Shura" and the Role of the Umma in Islam'. *American Journal of Islamic Social Sciences*. http://i-epistemology.net/politics-a-government/330-the-principle-of-shuraand-the-role-of-the-umma-in-islam.htm (last accessed 23 August 2015).

Rahman, F. (1986). 'Non-Muslim Minorities in an Islamic State'. *Journal Institute of Muslim Minority Affairs*, 7(1), 13–24.

Rahman, F. (1994). *Islamic Methodology in History*. New Delhi: Adam.

Rahman, F. (2009). *Major Themes of the Qur'an*. Chicago: University of Chicago Press.

Ramadan, T. (2011). 'Democratic Turkey is the Template for Egypt's Muslim

Brotherhood'. *Huffington Post.* http://www.huffingtonpost.com/tariqramadan/post_1690_b_820366.html (last accessed 23 August 2015).

Rand, A. (1963). 'The Nature of Government. Objectivist Newsletter'. https://fee.org/articles/the-nature-of-government-by-ayn-rand/ (last accessed 20 June 2015).

Rane, H. (2013). 'The Relevance of a Maqasid Approach for Political Islam Post Arab Revolutions'. *Journal of Law and Religion*, 28(2), 489–520.

Rawls, J. and Nussbaum, M. (2005). *Political Liberalism.* Columbia Classics in Philosophy. New York: Columbia University Press.

Rawls, J. (2005). *Political Liberalism.* Columbia University Press.

Raz, J. (1990). 'Facing Diversity: The Case of Epistemic Abstinence'. *Philosophy & Public Affairs*, 19(1), 3–46.

Riley, J. (2012). Liberty. In McKinnon, C. (ed.). *Issues in Political Theory.* Oxford: Oxford University Press.

Rorty, R. (1996). 'Idealizations, Foundations, and Social Practices'. In S. Benhabib (ed.) *Democracy and Difference: Contesting the Boundaries of the Political.* New York: Princeton University Press, pp. 333–5.

Rosati, J. A. (1995). 'A Cognitive Approach to the Study of Foreign Policy'. In L. Neack, J. A. K. Hey and P. J. Haney (eds) *Foreign Policy Analysis: Continuity and Change in Its Second Generation.* Cambridge, MA: Prentice-Hall, pp. 49–70.

Rosenblum, N. L. (1998.). *Membership and Morals: The Personal Uses of Pluralism in America.* New York: Princeton University Press.

Rosenblum, N. L. (2000). 'Introduction: Pluralism, Integralism, and Political Theories of Religious Accommodation'. In N. L. Rosenblum (ed.) *Obligations of Citizenship and Demands of Faith.* Princeton, NJ: Princeton University Press, pp. 3–31.

Rosenthal, E. I. J. (1965). *Islam in the Modern National State.* London: Cambridge.

Rutherford, B. K. (2006). 'What Do Egypt's Islamists Want? Moderate Islam and the Rise of Islamic Constitutionalism'. *Middle East Journal*, 60(4), 707–31.

Rustow, D. A. (1970). 'Transitions to Democracy: Toward a Dynamic Model'. *Comparative politics*, 2(3), 337–63.

Sachedina, A. (2006). 'The Role of Islam in the Public Square: Guidance or Governance?'. In M. A. Khan (ed.) *Islamic Democratic Discourse: Theory, Debates, and Philosophical Perspectives.* Lanham: Lexington Books.

Sadiki, L. (1996). 'The Palestinian Uprising, Bread Riots and Arab Democratisation'. *Australian Journal of Political Science*, 31(3), 401–20.

Sadiki, L. (2004). *The Search for Arab Democracy: Discourses and Counter-Discourses.* New York: Columbia University Press.

Sadowski, Y. (1993). 'The New Orientalism and the Democracy Debate'. *Middle East Report*, 183, 14–40.

Saeed, A. (2007). 'Rethinking Citizenship Rights of Non-Muslims in an Islamic State: Rashid al-Ghannushi's Contribution to the Evolving Debate'. *Islam and Christian–Muslim relations*, 10(3), 307–23.

Safi, O. (2003). 'What Is Progressive Islam?'. *ISIM Newsletter*, 13(2), 48–9.

Sajjad, F. and Javaid, U. (2016). 'The Civilizational Rift and the Idea of the Turkish Model: A Case Study (2002–2014)'. *Journal of Political Studies*, 23(1), 133–56.

Sajoo, A. B. (2004). *Civil Society in the Muslim World: Contemporary Perspectives*. London: I. B. Tauris.

Salamé, G. (ed.) (1994). *Democracy without Democrats? The Renewal of Politics in the Muslim World*. London: I. B. Tauris.

Salvatore, A. and Eickelman, D. F. (2004b). *Public Islam and the Common Good*. Leiden: Brill.

Salvatore, A. and Eickelman, D. F. (2003b). 'The Public Sphere and Public Islam'. *ISIM Newsletter*, 13, 1.

Salvatore, A. and LeVine, M. (2005). 'Introduction: Reconstructing the Public Sphere in Muslim Majority Societies'. In A. Salvatore and M. LeVine (eds) *Religion, Social Practice, and Contested Hegemonies*. New York: Palgrave Macmillan.

Salvatore, A. (2006). 'Power and Authority within European Secularity: From the Enlightenment Critique of Religion to the Contemporary Presence of Islam'. *The Muslim World*, 96(4), 543–61.

Salvatore, A. (2007). 'The Exit from a Westphalian Framing of Political Space and the Emergence of a Transnational Islamic Public'. *Theory, Culture & Society*, 24(4), 45–52.

Salvatore, A. (2012). 'Public Sphere'. In G. Böwering, P. Crone, W. Kadi, D. Stewart and M. Q. Zaman (eds) *The Princeton Encyclopedia of Islamic Political Thought*. Princeton, NJ: Princeton University Press, pp. 436–8.

Salvatore, A. (2014). 'A Public Sphere Revolution? Social Media versus Authoritarian Regimes'. In L. Sadiki (ed.) *Routledge Handbook of the Arab Spring: Rethinking Democratization*. New York: Routledge.

Sardar, Z. (1991). 'Islam and the Future'. *Futures*, 23(3), 223–30.

Sardar, Z. (2002). 'Rethinking Islam'. *Journal of Futures Studies*, 6(4), 117–24.

Sartori, G. (1987). *The Theory of Democracy Revisited*. Chatham, NJ: Chatham House.

Schacht, J. (1960). 'Problems of Modern Islamic Legislation'. *Studia Islamica*, 12, 99–129.

Schacht, J. (1986). *An Introduction to Islamic Law*. New York: Oxford University Press.
Schwedler, J. (2011). 'Can Islamists Become Moderates? Rethinking the Inclusion-Moderation Hypothesis'. *World Politics*, 63(2), pp. 347–76.
Selçuk, S. (1999). *Demokrasiye Doğru* [Longing for democracy]. Ankara: Yeni Türkiye Yayınları.
Selçuk, S. (2010). *Demokratik Yönetim Ozgür Birey* [Democratic governance, free individual]. Istanbul: İmge Kitabevi.
Selznick, P. (1999). 'Communitarian Jurisprudence'. In D. E. Carney (ed.) *To Promote the General Welfare: A Communitarian Legal Reader*. Boston: Lexington Books.
Sen, A. K. (1999). 'Democracy as a Universal Value'. *Journal of Democracy*, 10(3), 3–17.
Sezgin, Y. (2013). *Human Rights under State-Enforced Religious Family Laws in Israel, Egypt, and India*. Cambridge: Cambridge University Press.
Sezgin, Y. (2014). 'Why Is Tunisian Democracy Succeeding While the Turkish Model Is Failing?'. *Washington Post*, 8 November. https://www.washingtonpost.com/news/monkey-cage/wp/2014/11/08/why-is-tunisian-democracy-succeeding-while-the-turkish-model-is-failing/?utm_term=.ef50cad572a9 (last accessed 13 November 2015).
Shachar, A. (1998a). 'Group Identity and Women's Rights in Family Law: The Perils of Multicultural Accommodation'. *Journal of Political Philosophy*, 6(3), 285–305.
Shachar, A. (1998b). 'Reshaping the Multicultural Model: Group Accommodation in Individual Rights'. *Journal of Political Philosophy*, 8, 83–112.
Shachar, A. (2000). 'On Citizenship and Multicultural Vulnerability'. *Political Theory*, 28(1), 64–89.
Shachar, A. (2001). *Multicultural Jurisdictions: Cultural Differences and Women's Rights*. Cambridge: Cambridge University Press.
Shachar, A. (2008). 'Privatizing Diversity: A Cautionary Tale from Religious Arbitration in Family Law'. *Theoretical Inquiries in Law*, 9, 573–587.
Shachar, A. (2009). 'Entangled: State, Religion, and the Family'. *Harvard International Law Journal*, 49, 135142.
Shachar, A. (2016). 'Faith in Law: Diffusing Tensions between Diversity and Equality'. In S. Benhabib and K. Volker (eds) *Toward New Democratic Imaginaries–İstanbul Seminars on Islam, Culture and Politics*, 2. Wiesbaden: Springer.
Shadid, W. A. R. and van Koningsveld, P. S. (1999). *Political Participation and Identities of Muslims in Non-Muslim States*. Kampen: Kok Pharos.

Shahar, I. (2008). 'Legal Pluralism and the Study of Shari'a Courts'. *Islamic Law and Society*, 15, 112–41.
Shavit, U. (2010). 'Is S͟hūrā a Muslim Form of Democracy? Roots and Systemization of a Polemic'. *Middle Eastern Studies*, 46(3), 349–74.
Shils, E. (1997). *The Virtue of Civility: Selected Essays on Liberalism, Tradition, and Civil Society*. Indianapolis: Liberty Fund.
Sinanovic, E. (2004). 'The Majority Principle in Islamic Legal and Political Thought'. *Islam and Christian–Muslim Relations*, 15(2), 237–56.
Simmons, A. J. (2001). *Justification and Legitimacy: Essays on Rights and Obligations*. Cambridge: Cambridge University Press.
Schmitt, C. (1985). *Political Theology: Four Chapters on the Concept of Sovereignty*. Chicago: University of Chicago Press.
Somer, M. (2004). 'Muslim Democrats in the Making? Explaining Turkey's AKP'. Paper prepared from a presentation at the Annual Convention of the International Studies Association, Montreal, 17–20 March.
Somer, M. (2011). 'Does It Take democrats to Democratize? Lessons from Islamic and Secular Elite Values in Turkey'. *Comparative Political Studies*, 44(5), 511–45.
Somer, M. (2014). 'Moderation of Religious and Secular Politics: A Country's "Centre" and Democratization'. *Democratization*, 21(2), 244–67.
Song, S. (2007). *Justice, Gender and the Politics of Multiculturalism*. Cambridge: Cambridge University Press.
Song, S. (2014). 'Multiculturalism'. In E. N. Zalta (ed.) *The Stanford Encyclopedia of Philosophy, Spring Edition*. http://plato.stanford.edu/archives/spr2014/entries/multiculturalism/ (last accessed 11 January 2013).
Sonn, T. A. (n.d.). 'Rahman, Fazlur'. In *The Oxford Encyclopedia of the Islamic World*, Oxford Islamic Studies Online. http://www.oxfordislamicstudies.com/article/opr/t236/e0666 (last accessed 19 November 2012).
Soroush, A. (2007). 'Militant Secularism', http://www.drsoroush.com/English/On_DrSoroush/E-CMO-2007-Militant%20Secularism.html (last accessed 19 July 2015).
Soroush, A. (2000). *Reason, Freedom, and Democracy in Islam: Essential Writings of Abdolkarim Soroush*. Oxford: Oxford University Press.
Sözen, S. (2013). 'New Public Administration in Turkey'. In C. Rodriguez, A. Avalos, H. Yılmaz and A. I. Planet (eds) *Turkey's Democratization Process*. New York: Routledge.
Stepan, A. C. (2000). 'Religion, Democracy, and the Twin Tolerations'. *Journal of Democracy*, 11(4), 37–57.

Stepan, A. C. and Robertson, G. B. (2003). 'An "Arab" More than a "Muslim" Democracy Gap'. *Journal of Democracy*, 14(3), 30–44.

Steven, S. and Schmidtz, D. (2002). 'State, Civil and Classical Liberalism'. In N. L. Rosenblum and R. C. Post (eds) *Civil Society and Government*. Princeton, NJ: Princeton University Press.

Stone, J. (1966). *Social Dimensions of Law and Justice*. Stanford, CA: Stanford University Press.

Stuvland, A. (2012). 'Religion and the Prospects for "Thin" Politics'. *Comparative Sociology*, 11(5), 710–32.

Swaine, L. A. (2003). 'Institutions of Conscience: Politics and Principle in a World of Religious Pluralism'. *Ethical Theory and Moral Practice*, 6, 93–118.

Tāghūt. (2013). *Encyclopaedia of Islam* (2nd edn). A B. Brill Online. http://referenceworks.brillonline.com/entries/encyclopaedia-of-islam-2-Glossary-and-Index-of-Terms/taghut-SIM_gi_04636 (last accessed 6 June 2013).

Talbi, M. (1992). *Iyāl Allāh*. Tunis: Ceres Editions.

Talbi, M. (1995a). 'Is Cultural and Religious Co-Existence Possible?'. *Encounters: Journal of Inter-Cultural Perspectives*, 1(2), 74–84.

Talbi, M. (1995b). 'Unavoidable Dialogue in a Pluralist World: A Personal Account'. *Encounters: Journal of Inter-Cultural Perspectives*, 1(1), 56–69.

Talbi, M. (2000). 'Arabs and Democracy: A Record of Failure'. *Journal of Democracy*, 11(3), 58–68.

Talbi, M. (2005). *Réflexion d'un Musulman Contemporain*. Casablanca: Éditions le Fennec.

Talbi, M. (n.d.). 'Religious Liberty'. *The Oxford Islamic Studies Online*. http://www.oxfordislamicstudies.com/article/book/islam-9780195116212/islam-9780195116212-chapter-18 (last accessed 12 April 2013).

Tamale, S. (2007). 'The Right to Culture and the Culture of Rights: A Critical Perspective on Women's Sexual Rights in Africa'. *Fahamu*. http://fahamu.org/mbbc/wp-content/uploads/2011/09/Tamale-2007- Right toCulture.pdf (last accessed 1 June 2012).

Tamanaha, B. Z. (2008). 'Understanding Legal Pluralism: Past to Present, Local to Global'. *Sydney Law Review*, 30(3), 375–411.

Taşkın, Y. (2013). 'Hegemonizing Conservative Democracy and the Problems of Democratization in Turkey: Conservatism Without Democrats?'. *Turkish Studies*, 14(2), 292–310.

Taşpınar, O. (2014). 'The End of the Turkish Model'. *Survival*, 56(2), 49–64.

Tatari, E. (2009). 'Theories of the State Accommodation of Islamic Religious Practices in Western Europe'. *Journal of Ethnic and Migration Studies*, 35(2), 271–88.
Taylor, C. (1985). 'Atomism'. *Philosophical Papers*, 2, 187–210.
Taylor, C. (1994 [1992]). 'The Politics of Recognition'. In A. Gutmann (ed.) *Multiculturalism: Examining the Politics of Recognition*. Princeton, NJ: Princeton University Press, pp. 25–73.
Taylor, C. (1999). 'Conditions of an Unforced Consensus on Human Rights'. In O. Savic (ed.) *The Politics of Human Rights*. London: Verso, pp. 101–19.
Taylor, C. (1998). 'Modes of Secularism'. *Secularism and Its Critics*, 33.
Taylor, C. and Gutmann, A. (1997). 'The Politics of Recognition'. *New Contexts of Canadian Criticism*, 98, 25–73.
Taylor, C. (2007). *A Secular Age*. Cambridge, MA: Harvard University Press.
Taylor, C. (2008). 'Foreword'. In G. Brahm (ed.) *Secularism, Religion and Multicultural Citizenship*. Cambridge: Cambridge University Press.
Tezcür, G. M. (2007). 'Constitutionalism, Judiciary, and Democracy in Islamic Societies'. *Polity*, 39(4), 479–501.
Tezcür, G. M. (2010a). *Muslim Reformers in Iran and Turkey: The Paradox of Moderation*. Austin: University of Texas Press.
Tezcür, G. M. (2010b). 'The Moderation Theory Revisited: The Case of Islamic Political Actors'. *Party Politics*, 16(1), 69–88.
Tibi, B. (2008). 'Islamist Parties and Democracy: Why They Can't Be Democratic'. *Journal of Democracy*, 19(3), 43–8.
Tom, J. (2019). 'Contextualizing the Rise of Comparative Political Theory'. *JHIBlog*. https://jhiblog.org/2019/05/15/contextualizing-the-rise-of-compara tive-political-theory/ (last accessed 1 June 2012).
Tully, J. (1995). *Strange Multiplicity: Constitutionalism in an Age of Diversity*. Cambridge: Cambridge University Press.
Tully, J. (2008a). *Public Philosophy in a New Key*. Cambridge: Cambridge University Press.
Tully, J. (2016). 'Deparochializing Political Theory and Beyond: A Dialogue Approach to Comparative Political Thought'. *Journal of World Philosophies*, 1(1).
Turner, B. S. (2007). 'Managing Religions: State Responses to Religious Diversity'. *Contemporary Islam*, 1(2), 123–37.
Turner, B. S. (2011). 'Legal Pluralism, State Sovereignty, and Citizenship'. *Democracy and Security*, 7, 317–37.
Valadez, J. (2001). *Deliberative Democracy, Political Legitimacy, and Self determination in Multicultural Societies*. Boulder, CT: Westview.

Vallentyne, P. and van der Vossen, B. (2014). 'Libertarianism'. In E. N. Zalta (ed.) *The Stanford Encyclopedia of Philosophy*. https://plato.stanford.edu/archives/fall2014/entries/libertarianism/ (last accessed 15 July 2017).

Van der Zweerde, E. (2014). 'Confronting the Confrontation: Europe beyond Secularism?'. In B. Black, G. Hyman and G. M. Smith (eds) *Confronting Secularism in Europe and India: Legitimacy and Disenchantment in Contemporary Times*. London: Bloomsbury.

Vincent, A. (2010). *The Politics of Human Rights*. Oxford: Oxford University Press.

Volpi, F. (2004). 'Pseudo-democracy in the Muslim World'. *Third World Quarterly*, 25(6), 1,061–78.

Volpi, F. (2011). 'Framing Civility in the Middle East: Alternative Perspectives on the State and Civil Society'. *Third World Quarterly*, 32(5), 827–43.

Walker, G. (2000). 'Illusory Pluralism, Inexorable Establishment'. In W. M. McConnell (ed.) *Obligations of Citizenship and Demands of Faith: Religious Accommodation in Pluralist Democracies*. Princeton, NJ: Princeton University Press, pp. 111–26.

Waterbury, J. (1994). 'Democracy Without Democrats? The Potential for Political Liberalization in the Middle East'. In G. Salame (ed.). *Democracy without Democrats? The Renewal of Politics in the Muslim World*. London: I. B. Tauris, pp. 23–47.

Wiktorowicz, Q. (1999). 'The Limits of Democracy in the Middle East: The Case of Jordan'. *The Middle East Journal*, 53(4), 606–20.

Williams, R. (2008). 'Civil and Religious Law in England: A Religious Perspective'. Lecture by the Archbishop of Canterbury Dr Rowan Williams at the Royal Courts of Justice, 7 February. *The Guardian*. http://www.guardian.co.uk/uk/2008/feb/07/religion.world3 (last accessed 24 May 2013).

Williams, M. S. and Warren, M. E. (2014). 'A Democratic Case for Comparative Political Theory'. *Political Theory*, 42(1), 26–57.

Wolff, R. P. (1990). *The Conflict Between Authority and Autonomy*. Oxford: Basil Blackwell.

Wolin, S. S. (2016). *Fugitive Democracy: And Other Essays*. Princeton, NJ: Princeton University Press.

Woodman, G. R. (1996). 'Legal Pluralism and the Search for Justice'. *Journal of African Law*, 40(2), 152–67.

Woodman, G. R. (1999). 'The Idea of Legal Pluralism'. In B. Dupret (ed.) *Legal Pluralism in the Arab World*. The Hague: Kluwer International Law, pp. 3–19.

Wright, R. (1996). 'Islam and Liberal Democracy: Two Visions of Reformation'. *Journal of Democracy*, 7(2), 64–75.

Yavuz, M. H. (2003). *Islamic Political Identity in Turkey*. New York: Oxford University Press.

Yavuz M. H. (2007). 'Islam, Sovereignty, and Democracy: A Turkish View'. *The Middle East Journal*, 61(3), 477–93.

Yavuz, M. H. (2009). *Secularism and Muslim Democracy in Turkey*. New York: Cambridge University Press.

Yazıcı, S. (2011). *Yeni bir Anayasa Hazırlığı ve Türkiye: Seçkincilikten Toplu Sözleşmesine* [A new constitutional preparation and Turkey: From elitism to social contract]. Istanbul: İstanbul Bilgi Üniversitesi Yayınları.

Yenigün, H. I. (2013). 'The Political Ontology of Islamic Democracy: An Ontological Narrative of Contemporary Muslim Political Thought'. Ph.D. thesis, University of Virginia.

Tezcür, H. (2007). 'Islam, Sovereignty, and Democracy: A Turkish View'. *The Middle East Journal*, 61(3), 477–93.

Yılmaz, I. (2005). *Muslim Laws Politics and Society in Modern Nation States: Dynamic Legal Pluralism in England Turkey and Pakistan*. Burlington: Ashgate.

Young, I. M. (1990). *Justice and the Politics of Difference*. Princeton, NJ: Princeton University Press.

Young, I. M. (2002.). *Inclusion and Democracy*. New York: Oxford University Press.

Yousif, A. (2000). 'Islam, Minorities and Religious Freedom: A Challenge to Modern Theory of Pluralism'. *Journal of Muslim Minority Affairs*, 20(1), 29–41.

Zaman, M. Q. (2015). 'The Sovereignty of God in Modern Islamic Thought'. *Journal of the Royal Asiatic Society*, 25(3), 389–418.

Zubaida, S. (2011). 'Turkey as a Model of Democracy and Islam'. *Open Democracy*, 30 May. https://www.opendemocracy.net/north-africa-west-asia/sami-zubaida/turkey-as-model-of-democracy-and-islam (last accessed 6 March 2016).

INDEX

Abou El Fadl, Khaled
  on compatibility of democracy and Islam, 46, 139, 198, 200
  on human rights, 61
  on pluralism, 60
  on the Qur'an, 45
  on *sharī'a*, 43, 44
  on sovereignty, 129, 141
  on tradition, 143, 144
absolutism, 147, 254–5
  religious absolutism, 21, 34, 49, 56, 202
  secular absolutism, 97, 104, 113
accommodation
  consensual accommodation, 100
  contingent accommodation, 101
  federal-style accommodation, 100
  multicultural, 81–2, 100, 115, 243
  religious, 90, 95, 100, 169, 232, 238, 252, 258
  temporal accommodation, 100
  transformative accommodation, 101–5
accountability, 2, 5, 128, 138, 218, 220, 221
Al-Dakkak, Kelly, 48, 50
Al-Jabri, Muhammad, 44–6, 61–2, 163, 234
Al-Ghannūshī, Rāshid al-
  on democracy, 40, 162
  on pluralism, 55–8, 171
  on state, 38, 39, 128
  on *umma*, 127
An-Na'im, Abdullahi Ahmed
  on democracy, 50, 198
  on human rights, 63–4
  on pluralism, 203, 207
  on secularism, 66, 166–7, 174, 178, 181
  on *sharī'a*, 48–9, 227, 234–5
anti-foundationalism, 20, 148, 252
Armando, Salvatore, 173, 189, 200–2, 206
associational life, 107, 129, 210, 214
authoritarianism, 6, 12, 70, 71, 161–3, 235, 248
autonomy, 24, 78–81, 85, 141, 184, 194, 234, 238; *see also* jurisdictional autonomy, 24, 77, 90, 101, 110, 224
Azmeh, Aziz al-, 5, 248

Bader, Veit, 97–117, 164–70, 182–5, 194–5, 209–10
Bâli, Aslı, 8–9
Barzilai, Gad, 90–4, 184, 193
Bellamy, Richard, 220–1
Bulaç, Ali, 40–1, 57–9, 162, 171, 193–4

caliphate, 45, 48
Casanova, José, 8, 183
Cesari, Jocelyn, 161, 164
choice options
  education, 100, 105, 107–8
  family law, 100, 102, 238, 231, 235, 237
civil society, 8, 9, 11, 105, 113–15, 128, 180–3, 195–6, 209–14, 236, 242–5

civility, 204, 205, 208, 213, 243, 245
citizenship, 5, 24, 53, 55, 60, 64, 71, 185, 194, 204, 253–4
   cultural and religious legitimacy for, 87, 100, 113–14
citizenship rights
   differentiated rights, 80–2
   and multiculturalism, 81, 82, 87, 102, 137
   and secular absolutist model, 24, 27, 33
civic reason, 134, 202
collective rights 183–6, 194, 209, 243
compatibility-based arguments 118, 123–7, 132, 139, 147–50
Connolly, William Eugene, 169, 206
Constitution of Medina (Charter or Medina), 57–8, 69, 149
constitutionalism
   and constitutional guarantees, 163, 227, 231, 239
   legal constitutionalism, 221–3
   pluralising constitutionalism 223–9
   political constitutionalism, 219–21
   and *sharīʿa*, 234–5
   Western, 84, 87, 91
contestation, 138–9, 172, 218, 220
convergence, 13–14, 197–8, 256
culture
   accommodation of, 18, 74, 84, 87, 90, 95, 192, 245
   dialogue across, 20, 84
   vs religion, 74, 82–3, 97, 108
   significance of, 18, 79–80, 86, 110, 111, 176, 224

Dahl, Robert, 5, 171
Dallmayr, Fred, 14–15, 157, 198, 256
ḍarūra (necessity), 40
decentralisation, 90, 94, 100, 105, 182
deliberation, 87, 98, 135–9, 145–8, 191–2, 201–2, 207
democracy
   associative democracy, 105–6
   consolidation of, 7, 11, 134, 215, 254
   liberal democracy, 18–19, 50–2, 86, 113, 256–8
   radical democracy, 258
   struggles for 17, 247, 259–60
   volatility of 129, 218, 221–2
democratisation 3, 6, 7, 9, 10, 13, 27, 51, 103, 107–8, 199, 248
*dhimmī*s, 53–4, 59

   orthodox liberal response to, 66, 81, 113, 224
   recognition of, 113, 115, 184
dialogical approach, 15, 27, 157, 196, 250, 254, 256, 259
dialogue
   between citizens, 191–2, 197, 206, 208, 230
   intercultural, 20, 64, 65, 89, 177, 260
difference
   blindness, 184, 224
dīn wa dawla (religion and state), 48
discrimination
   against (Muslim and other) minorities, 6, 103, 105, 193, 230, 259
   against non-Muslims 60, 63
diversity
   accommodation of, 99, 104, 162, 183, 194
   protection of, 17, 24, 78, 80, 83, 89
divine law
   constitutionalisation of, 34, 43
   divine law vs fallible human interpretations, 44, 127, 133, 141
   instrumentalisation of, 40, 141
divine sovereignty, 35–6, 43, 68, 127–34
divorce, 77, 99, 112
Dworkin, Ronald, 24, 76

education
   institutional pluralism, 59, 100, 102, 105–8, 161, 171, 184–5, 209–10
Eickelman, Dale, 173, 189, 200–8
Eisenstadt, Shmuel Noah, 1, 28
El-Affendi, Abdelwahab, 160
electoralism, 217, 248, 259
   electoral accountability, 217–18
elite, 7, 229, 235
Emon, Anver, 203
Emre, Akif, 13
Engineer, Asghar Ali, 47–8, 64–5
equality
   a concept of 61, 63, 237–8
   vs justice 59
   Muslim accommodation, 91
   politics of recognition 78, 84, 86, 164
essentialism, 149, 200, 252, 257
Eurocentric, 15, 257
exit, 80, 106–8, 164

Fadel, Mohammed, 66, 177, 198, 238
fatwa, 143

foundationalism, 20, 148, 204, 252, 253, 254, 260
Freedom House, 6
freedom of expression, 5, 39, 137, 150, 156
freedom of religion, 21, 39, 56, 63, 162, 182
fuqahā, 49, 63, 136

Gallup, 1–2
Gellner, Ernest, 243
gender equality, 6, 59, 73, 81, 88, 150, 215, 225, 228, 244
ghettoisation, 115
Ghobadzadeh, Naser, 134, 172–3
good government, 255, 259
good life, 15, 77, 79, 156, 169, 177, 179, 185, 186, 196, 202, 204, 212, 232, 238, 242, 257
group members, 80, 88, 100, 103, 106, 178, 185, 194–5, 235, 255

ḥākimiyya
  concept of, 35, 124, 127
  ḥākimiyya Allah (God's political dominion), 32, 37
Hallaq, Wael, 140, 142, 151, 226, 231–2
Hashemi, Nader, 160, 161, 166, 200
hegemonic, 6, 7, 11, 17–18, 114, 230, 254, 256, 257
hermeneutic, 52, 62
Hirst, Paul 105, 107, 182–3, 209–11
Holmes, Stephan, 222
homogenising, 6–8, 11, 16, 89, 98, 113, 230–2
human rights
  and citizenship, 20, 23, 64, 71
  and Islam, 40, 46, 61, 64, 203
  for local application, 80, 94
  minimal human rights, 174–5, 197–8, 205, 208, 222–3, 226–8, 237–8, 39–40
  protection of, 81, 106, 194, 199, 211, 219, 224–8
  question of universality of, 61, 64, 229

identity
  collective, 83, 110, 257
  cultural, 76, 172
  ethnic, 172
  hybrid and multiple, 97, 100, 104, 181, 233

majority and minority, 20, 109, 179, 183, 186, 190, 197, 209, 259
  religious, 58, 69, 117, 172, 182, 247
ideology
  Islamist 12, 36, 143, 178, 200
  Secularist 12–13, 97–8
Ignatieff, Michael, 227–8
ijma (consensus), 7, 39, 139
ijtihād (independent judgment), 23, 32, 42, 143
inclusion-moderation hypothesis, 10, 12, 248
individual rights, 78, 81–2, 156, 174, 190, 211, 217, 233, 226, 244
institutionalist pluralists, 96–110
integration, 88, 110
intervention
  of state, 41, 79, 82, 88, 93, 100, 144, 211, 237
  postcolonial innovation, 41, 47, 51
  totalitarian state as model for, 53, 132, 173
Islamic democracy
  crisis of idea of, 20–1, 134, 147, 156, 167, 225, 256
  definition of, 40, 128, 146, 162, 257
Islamic law
  codification of, 45, 51, 69, 235
  and *ijtihād*, 44, 143
  implementation of, 44, 4, 58, 118
  modernisation of, 62, 63, 143, 167
  as a private law, 185, 236, 244
  see also sharīʿa
Islamic modernism, 42–7, 52, 62, 67, 70–1, 124–5, 130–1, 138, 142, 163, 230
Islamic revivalism, 32, 38–42, 51, 56, 57, 59, 69, 71, 124–5, 127–8, 137–8
Islamic state
  enforcement of *sharīʿa* by, 32–8, 51, 53, 56, 143
Islamisation, 35, 186
Islamism, 12, 36, 143, 178, 200
Islamist
  doctrinate 23, 179
  moderate 23, 35, 38, 71, 125
  post-Islamism 10, 12
  vs secularists, 11, 13

joint governance, 97, 99–101, 194
jurisdiction
  allocation of, 93, 101–2, 109, 194, 244
  conflicts over, 97, 99, 157

jurisdictional autonomy, 77, 90, 100–1, 110, 118
jurisdictional pluralism, 104, 106, 113, 184, 186, 190, 224, 233–8
jurisprudence (*fiqh*), 44, 52, 94, 108, 123, 132, 139, 148, 257

Karaman, Hayrettin, 38–41, 56, 58, 69, 71, 126, 128, 137
Kaviraj, Sudipta, 15
Keane, John, 21, 147, 149, 181, 254
Kukathas, Chandran, 79–82, 110, 170–1, 184, 205
Kymlicka, Will, 78–82, 92, 100, 112, 176, 177, 184, 196–7

Laborde, Cecile, 111, 113, 159
law
　family law, 100, 102, 238, 231, 235, 237
　private law, 231, 236, 244
　public and private areas of, 77, 102, 112, 194, 235–6
　see also Islamic law
legal monism, 77, 94, 112
legal pluralism, 58–9, 90, 93–5, 244
legal pluralists, 90–6, 112–13
legitimacy, 7, 38, 40, 47, 104, 117, 127–135, 161, 177, 226
Lewis, Bernard, 3
liberal pluralists, 76, 78–9, 83
liberalism
　critique of orthodox liberalism, 78–80, 83–5, 91, 184, 254
　individualism, 76, 79, 91, 176, 184

Maclure, Jocelyn, 85, 86, 111, 160, 167, 206
Mahmood, Saba, 18, 65, 162
March, Andrew, 15, 36, 124, 127, 131, 134, 148, 149, 150
Mawdūdī, Abu'l-A'lā
　interpretation of *sharī'a*, 34–5
　on Islamic state, 35–7, 70
　on pluralism, 53–4
　theo-democracy of, 136
Mégret, Frédéric, 92, 5, 113, 209
minimalist state, 115, 170–4, 176, 181–2, 211, 226, 242
minority
　cultural, 74, 75, 76, 80, 82, 197
　religious, 74, 75, 95, 95, 97, 195, 197

minority rights, 4, 6, 13, 60, 71, 78, 82, 132, 147, 185, 225, 259
modernisation
　of minorities, 89, 230
　top-down, 9, 70, 200
modernist Muslim political though, 42–5, 131, 138–9
Modood, Tariq 83, 111, 118
Mookherjee, Monica, 85, 87–9, 114–16, 191–2
moral pluralists, 83–6, 87–9, 109–13, 207
morality
　comprehensive, 36, 66, 90, 110, 111, 133, 139, 145, 147, 166, 181, 183, 232, 242, 258
　deontological, 175
　divine, 129, 131, 133, 141, 142, 156, 242
　non-transcendental, 174
　thick vs thin, 178, 226
　transcendental, 206
multiculturalism, 18, 74–7, 90, 97, 108, 110–14, 118, 249, 256–7
Muqtedar Khan, 144, 170

Nasr, Vali, 3, 10, 14, 248
nation-state, 77, 90, 94, 100, 113, 140, 187
　reform, 7, 13, 113, 129, 187, 214
neutrality, 9, 66, 86–7, 89, 98, 159, 164, 174, 176–9, 181–2
non-constitutional pluralism, 105–8, 194
non-intervention, 79, 86; *see also* intervention
Nozick, Robert, 174, 226

oppression, 12, 93, 132, 161, 222, 226, 228
overlapping consensus, 116, 176, 191, 195, 207, 243
Özbudun, Ergun, 7, 8, 219

people
　exercising authority, 82, 88, 130, 147
　sovereignty of, 31, 40, 127, 148–9, 161, 219, 221
　will of, 40, 84, 128–9, 137, 217
People of the Book, 54, 63
Pettit, Philip, 220–1
Piscatori, James, 128, 215–16
pluralism, 17–18, 26–7, 55–6, 58–60, 64–5, 85, 132, 162, 171, 201, 203, 205, 256; *see also* jurisdictional pluralism, institutional pluralism

pluralist secularism, 168–86, 209, 214, 224, 243, 245–6
political culture, 7, 24, 48, 66, 84, 109, 172
political expediency, 12
political Islam, 200
political learning, 10
popular sovereignty
　as protection against tyranny, 134, 144, 149
　as sole source of legitimacy, 219
　versus divine sovereignty, 24, 69, 70, 72, 126, 127, 129, 130, 133, 150
political theory, 17–18, 21, 6, 140, 148, 232, 248–60
　comparative political theory, 14–15, 252–4
political theology, 150, 253, 255
popular will, 41, 127, 132, 135, 220, 222
post-foundationalism, 20, 253
power
　absolute, 9, 197
　coercive, 49, 130–1
　-holder authority, 102
　legitimisation of, 9
　moralising, 7
　restraining, 19, 26, 215
　rivalry for, 11, 259
　-sharing system, 11, 77, 102–3, 105, 109, 197, 210, 244
pragmatism, 3, 13, 23, 126, 248, 256
progressive Muslim political though, 25, 43, 47–51, 62–65, 134, 148
public good, 26, 98, 181, 245
public Islam, 2, 27, 241
public opinion, 136, 223
public reason, 71, 84, 88, 90, 98, 116, 131, 138, 191
public sphere, 11, 66, 97, 104, 109, 115, 176, 180–1, 189, 190–5, 222, 242–3, 250–1
　differentiated public spheres, 181, 196
　public–private divide, 195
　social public sphere, 26, 182–3, 195–6, 201–2, 205–6, 208–9
　state public sphere, 26, 182–3, 212–15

Qaraḍāwī, Yūsuf al , 38–41, 545–57, 160, 162
Qur'an
　on apostasy and unbelief, 59, 62
　on consultation in public affairs, 39, 50, 135

reform process in meaning and implementation of, 32, 43, 63
Quṭb, Sayyid
　on concept of *ḥākimiyya*, 35–7
　on rule of *sharīʿa*, 34, 127, 130, 140

Rahman, Fazlur, 42–3, 46, 59–60, 62, 129, 126, 141–4
rationality, 77, 83, 84, 91, 98, 163, 173
Rawls, John, 24, 74, 76–8, 92, 98, 176
recognition, 3, 18, 24, 74, 78, 84, 86, 95, 101, 106, 111, 113, 164, 184, 199, 212, 238
religion
　Christianity, 56, 64, 85, 93
　instrumental use of, 7, 9, 11, 142, 196, 236
　Judaism, 56, 64, 85, 93, 94, 95, 233
　and political theory, 91, 94, 232, 252, 255
　Protestantism, 165
　renewed importance of, 1, 111, 161, 164, 166
　Shi'a Islam, 17
　as a source of meaning, 18, 20, 51, 155, 160, 184, 214
　and state, 4, 8, 9, 23, 38, 71, 113, 117–18, 162, 176–9, 200
　Sunni Islam, 7, 8, 16, 45
representation, 2, 39, 55, 98, 105, 108, 138, 171, 184, 191, 201, 252, 259
revivalist Muslim political though, 32, 38–46, 55–9, 69, 125, 127–8
Rorty, Richard, 3, 204, 252
Rosenblum, Nancy, 197, 232, 238
Rustow, Dankwart, 2

Salamé, Ghassan, 6, 8, 12
Sardar, Ziaouddin, 199, 235
Sartori, Giovanni, 1
secularisation, 85–6, 91, 161, 165–6, 168, 200
secularism
　authoritarian secularism, 8, 9, 160–3, 166, 179
　definitions of, 86, 111, 155, 159–60, 165, 167, 177, 242
　Muslim challenge to, 70
　philosophical understanding of, 71, 85, 97–9, 112, 116, 181, 186, 193
　political, 47, 48, 66, 89, 168
　see also pluralist secularism, 168–86, 209, 214, 224, 243, 245–6

separation of powers, 4, 21, 71, 98, 162, 211, 215, 239
Shachar, Ayelet, 97–105, 115, 177, 185, 194, 197, 209, 210, 233, 236–7
Shahar, Ido, 91–3, 180
sharī'a
  as all-embracing social order, 34–5
  centrality/primacy of, 2, 142, 231
  coercive enforcement of, 35, 127, 135, 235
  as divine perfection, 44, 63, 69
  historical development of, 45, 62–3, 202
  and human agency, 44, 49, 234
  implementation of, 44, 58, 118
  interpretations of, 31–3, 48, 63, 69, 142, 234
  maqāsid, 32, 50, 55, 59, 60, 65, 69
  normative supremacy of, 43, 49, 67, 70, 216, 233, 238
  principles of, as source of public policy and legislation, 38–9, 42–3
  and *ulama*; 129, 143, 144
  voluntary observation of, 145, 213, 234, 235–6, 243
  see also Islamic law
shūrā (Islamic process of consultation), 39, 50, 68, 135–9
social contract, 13, 58, 87, 89, 174, 219
social Islam, 199–204, 243
Soroush, Abdolkarim, 13, 113–14, 201
sovereignty
  concept of, 127, 131, 148–9, 161, 226
  divine versus popular, 24, 32, 35, 69, 118, 126, 128–30, 132–4, 146
  dualism of, 40, 46, 147
  of the *sharī'a*, 34, 43
  of the state, 113–14, 140
state
  morally minimalist, 170, 174–5, 182, 211
  neutrality of, 9, 66, 86–7, 89, 98, 159, 164, 174, 176–9, 181–2
  politics distinguished from, 178, 181, 187
  separation of Islam from, 9, 47, 71, 91, 138–9, 143, 160, 162, 168, 181–2, 185–6, 236

statist Muslim political though, 34–40, 43–7, 51–5
Stepan, Alfred, 1, 11, 178, 182

Talbi, Mohammad, 48, 50–1, 65, 139, 205
Taşkın, Yüksel, 12–13
tawhīd, (oneness of God), 31, 51
Taylor, Charles, 83–7, 111–13, 159–60, 167–8, 189–90, 205–8, 228
Tezcür, Murat G., 8, 10, 131, 147, 219, 225
theocracy, 2, 21, 36, 135
toleration, 65, 74, 80–1, 110, 175, 184, 199
  democratic toleration, 201, 203–8, 213–15
transformative accommodation, 101–4, 108, 110
transformativeness, 196–8, 214, 245
Tully, James, 84, 87–9, 112, 115–16, 191–2, 219–20, 230
Turner, Bryan 162, 231
Turkey
  authoritarian secularism in, 9, 11
  constitutions of, 8, 11
  Justice and Development Party (JDP) in, 3–4, 9–13
  Kemalism, 6, 8
  reforms in, 3, 4, 9, 11, 13
  Turkish model, 3–12

ulama (Islamic scholars), 126, 129, 135–6, 143–4
umma
  authority of, 40, 135
  as political community, 127
'universal ugliness', 56, 71, 138
universalism, 43, 84–5, 114, 164–5, 223, 252, 254
unsecular democracy, 163–5, 171

vicegerency, 43, 127, 135, 141
Volpi, Frédéric, 11, 213, 217

Williams, Rowan Douglas, 232–3

Yavuz, Hakan M., 3, 9, 144–5, 161–2, 179, 183

Zubaida, Sami, 6, 9, 12, 173

EU representative:
Easy Access System Europe
Mustamäe tee 50, 10621 Tallinn, Estonia
Gpsr.requests@easproject.com